THAT ALL MAY FLOURISH

THAT ALL MAY FLOURISH

Comparative Religious Environmental Ethics

Edited by Laura M. Hartman

OXFORD
UNIVERSITY PRESS

OXFORD
UNIVERSITY PRESS

Oxford University Press is a department of the University of Oxford. It furthers
the University's objective of excellence in research, scholarship, and education
by publishing worldwide. Oxford is a registered trade mark of Oxford University
Press in the UK and certain other countries.

Published in the United States of America by Oxford University Press
198 Madison Avenue, New York, NY 10016, United States of America.

Library of Congress Cataloging-in-Publication Data
Names: Hartman, Laura M., editor.
Title: That all may flourish : comparative religious environmental ethics /
edited by Laura M. Hartman.
Description: New York, NY : Oxford University Press, 2018. |
Includes bibliographical references and index.
Identifiers: LCCN 2017057389 (print) | LCCN 2018016178 (ebook) |
ISBN 9780190456047 (updf) | ISBN 9780190456054 (online component) |
ISBN 9780190882693 (epub) | ISBN 9780190456023 (hardcover : alk. paper) |
ISBN 9780190456030 (pbk. : alk. paper)
Subjects: LCSH: Human ecology—Religious aspects. | Environmental ethics. |
Human beings—Effect of environment on. | Nature—Effect of human beings on.
Classification: LCC BL65.E36 (ebook) | LCC BL65.E36 T478 2018 (print) |
DDC 205/.691—dc23
LC record available at https://lccn.loc.gov/2017057389

9 8 7 6 5 4 3 2 1

Paperback printed by Webcom, Inc., Canada
Hardback printed by Bridgeport National Bindery, Inc., United States of America

CONTENTS

ACKNOWLEDGMENTS

The idea for this book was born in a "secret office" in Sorensen Hall at Augustana College in Rock Island, Illinois. Thanks to Mary Koski for setting up an extra room for my research work at a time when I needed the space and solitude. Thanks are also due to my excellent colleagues in the religion department at Augustana College. The work of Jason Mahn, Cyrus Ali Zargar, Richard Priggie, Sarah Skrainka, and Eric Stewart gave me the courage to believe that interfaith dialogue can be taken in both practical and scholarly directions. I am also grateful for Dan Lee's mentorship in academic life and professional development, which came at just the right time to move this book forward.

While this book was in process, I switched jobs, shifting my academic home from the study of religion to environmental studies, from Augustana College to the University of Wisconsin Oshkosh. I owe a major debt of gratitude to those at UW Oshkosh who gave me the opportunity to start a new chapter in my career: Jim Feldman, Misty McPhee, Elizabeth Barron, Colin Long, Paul Van Auken, and others. The career shift necessarily meant delays in the progress of this chapter; I thank the contributors for their patience as this book simmered on my back burner during the transition. At UW Oshkosh I have received support from the Faculty Development Fund for expenses related to this project. I also received helpful, insightful critique from Michael Baltutis on this project and certain chapters in it, for which I am very grateful. And I thank Kim Bullington for the excellent administrative support.

I credit Kevin O'Brien with helping to midwife this book into existence: he read early proposal drafts, offered valuable feedback, and essentially gave me the idea for the dialogue chapters. Other early supporters include Aaron Stalnaker and Elizabeth Bucar, who read early proposal drafts and helped to shape my understanding of the field of comparative religious ethics. Thanks are also due to Jim Childress, Peter Ochs, Charles Mathewes, Emily Filler, Daniel Weiss, Jacob Goodson, and others from the University of Virginia who helped establish my grounding in comparative ethics and Scriptural Reasoning.

I thank all the book's contributors for their hard work, insightful research, clear writing, and patience with my edits and badgering. I am especially grateful that they were willing to engage in a dialogue process that was new to them. Those scholars who were part of the volume but had to drop out (you know who you are!): I also honor your good work and am grateful for it. Special thanks to Dianna Bell and Amanda J. Baugh for playing the role of late additions to the project.

One contributor, in fact, died before she was able to compose her chapter: Julia Finomo Awajiusuk. I had been looking forward to her chapter about indigenous religions in the oil-rich Niger Delta. Her colleague at the University of Port Harcourt, Rev. Dr. Amadi Enochahiamadu, wrote these words about her:

> Julia Finomo Awajiusuk died on the 1st of August 2015. She was a member of the academic staff of the Department of Religious and Cultural Studies of the Humanities Faculty of the University of Port Harcourt. Dr. Julia was fully accepted and spent most of her daily life contributing to the up building, success and achievements of her immediate academic community. Although a burgeoning ethicist Julia was not yet fully formed as an academic in that field but had the promise of becoming one of the most formidable scholars in the field of environmental ethics before her sudden demise. She had been sick, hospitalized for several weeks, but later discharged, and in the process of recuperating before the cold hands of death snatched her unexpectedly. May her gentle soul rest in peace.[1]

I am delighted to cite some of Julia's work in the introduction to this book, as a way to honor her contributions to the field of religious environmental ethics.

Thanks also to those at Oxford University Press: with gratitude for patience and advice from the incomparable Cynthia Read; and in appreciation for extremely competent help from Aiesha Krause-Lee, excellent editing from Leslie Safford and skilled coordination work from Rajesh Kathamuthu.

Finally, the biggest thanks are due to my family. Many thanks to my parents and sisters, who taught me to value scholarship and ideas, and to seek points of understanding and dialogue. And infinite gratitude is due to my dearest Anne Dickey, whose very presence nourishes my own flourishing every single day; and to our beloved son, Theo Hartman, who is both my best student and best teacher. I thank God for all of the above blessings, and I thank you, dear reader, for taking the time to read this book. It no longer lurks in a secret office: may this book now live a flourishing and public life of its own.

---

1. Personal correspondence, June 6, 2017.

CONTRIBUTORS

Amanda J. Baugh is Associate Professor in Religious Studies at California State University, Northridge, where she is also Director of the Program in Civic and Community Engagement. Her research examines issues related to race, ethnicity, and class in American religious environmental movements. Baugh is the author of *God and the Green Divide: Religious Environmentalism in Black and White* (2017).

Dianna Bell is Mellon Assistant Professor of Religious Studies and Anthropology at Vanderbilt University. She studies the history and ethnography of religion in West Africa. Her current research employs biographical research to understand how people in southern Mali have used ritual to understand and manage their environment in the postcolonial era.

David E. Cooper is Professor of Philosophy Emeritus at Durham University, United Kingdom. He has been a visiting professor in many countries, including the United States, Canada, and Sri Lanka, and has been the chair or president of several learned societies, including the Aristotelian Society and the Friedrich Nietzsche Society. His many books include *World Philosophies: An Historical Introduction* (2nd edition, 2002); *The Measure of Things: Humanism, Humility and Mystery* (2002), *A Philosophy of Gardens* (2006), and *Convergence with Nature: A Daoist Perspective* (2012).

Cheryl Cottine is Assistant Professor at Oberlin College in the Religion Department. She earned her PhD from Indiana University (Bloomington). She works in the area of comparative religious ethics with an emphasis on early Confucianism. She is particularly interested in thinking about how certain concepts in early Confucian texts can be retrieved and used as lenses for thinking critically about various issues in contemporary society. Her recent research has worked to develop a role ethic that attends to contemporary philosophical currents while also drawing on insights from early Confucian texts. In the area of practical ethics, her primary interests are in medical and environmental ethics.

Rebecca J. Epstein-Levi is the Friedman Postdoctoral Fellow in Jewish Studies at Washington University in St. Louis. She received her PhD from the University of Virginia in 2017 and her BA from Oberlin College in 2008. She is interested in ethical issues of gender, sexuality, science, and ecology in Judaism. Her current project examines the moral and hermeneutical implications of treating sex as a species of social intercourse rather than as a sui generis category.

Michael Hannis is Senior Lecturer in Environmental Humanities at Bath Spa University, United Kingdom. His recent book *Freedom and Environment: Autonomy, Human Flourishing, and the Political Philosophy of Sustainability* (2015) uses ideas of flourishing and ecological virtue to explore complementarities and apparent conflicts between the two political objectives of achieving ecological sustainability and protecting human freedom(s).

Chris Klassen teaches in Religion and Culture at Wilfrid Laurier University, in Ontario, Canada. She is the author of *Storied Selves: Shaping Identity in Feminist Witchcraft* (2008) and *Religion and Popular Culture: A Cultural Studies Approach* (2014). She has had articles published in *Journal for the Study of Religion, Nature, and Culture; Environmental Ethics; Cultural Studies Review;* and *Journal of Contemporary Religion*, among others.

Christopher Patrick Miller is an assistant professor of Religious Studies at Loyola Marymount University in Los Angeles, California. His research focuses on modern yoga as well as the religious traditions of India in light of the natural world. He has a BS in Accounting as well as an MA in Comparative Theology from Loyola Marymount University, and a PhD in Religious Studies from UC Davis; he is also a certified public accountant in the states of Hawaii and California. Christopher was the past recipient of the Mellon Research Initiative in Reimagining Indian Ocean Worlds Research Grant; the UC Davis Provost's Fellowship in the Arts, Humanities, and Social Sciences; and the Doshi Bridgebuilder Grant for his research and work with Tamil Nadu's surfing communities.

Jennifer Phillips is an independent scholar and principal of JLP Strategy, a strategy and ethics consultancy. Previously, she was chief strategy officer at the Avalon Consulting Group, a fundraising consulting agency for progressive, environmental and arts nonprofits. She earned her PhD from the University of Virginia's department of Religious Studies, with doctoral research on Catholic social thought and microeconomics. Current research interests include racial justice in organizational strategy and theologies of nonviolence.

Nelson Reveley is a PhD candidate in the Religious Studies Department at the University of Virginia. He is in the Theology, Ethics, and Culture program, with an emphasis on theological ethics as they relate respectively to economics, the environment, food, consumerism, virtue, and flourishing. Although his focus is primarily on the Christian tradition and Augustinian conceptions of ordered loves, he has interests as well in Buddhist beliefs and practices regarding joy, suffering, and the formation of desire. An ordained minister in the Presbyterian Church (United States), Reveley also holds an MDiv from Union Presbyterian Seminary and works on justice issues regarding public transportation, food access, and poverty alleviation in his hometown of Richmond, Virginia.

Sarah E. Robinson-Bertoni is a critical-constructive scholar of religion, ecology, and social justice at Santa Clara University. She earned the MA History degree from the Graduate Theological Union in 2005 and the PhD Religion degree from Claremont Graduate University in 2015. She employs comparative, feminist, and qualitative research methods to study eco-food, sustainable agriculture, and climate concerns in religious contexts (her dissertation is titled "Refreshing Religions with Edible Ethics: Local Agriculture and Sustainable Food in Muslim, Christian, and Buddhist Projects in the U.S."). She actively engages with religious, political, and ethnic pluralism, identifying food-oriented cultural forms that concentrate meaning and religious identity for diverse, local communities in the United States.

Colette Sciberras was awarded a PhD in Buddhist Philosophy and the Ideals of Environmentalism from Durham University in 2011, and since then has been teaching philosophy, including courses in environmental ethics and in Buddhism, in Malta. In her research, she enjoys exploring the intersections between diverse academic areas and disciplines—including science, psychology, mythology, and religion—as well as those between Eastern and Western worldviews. Furthermore, she attempts to incorporate into her academic work insights from her informal training in philosophy and meditation within the Nyingma and Kagyu schools of Tibetan Buddhism. Past publications have focused on the value attributed to nature in various Buddhist texts and traditions, and the question of whether these display speciesist tendencies. Currently, she is focusing on the philosophy of mind, especially with regard to Darwinian evolution.

Sian Sullivan is Professor of Environment and Culture at Bath Spa University, United Kingdom. She has conducted ethnographic research in northwest Namibia since 1992, focusing on cultural relationships beyond the human, and has also published on political ecology, biodiversity offsetting, and the financialization of nature.

INTRODUCTION

Laura M. Hartman

The Problem of Flourishing

The industrialized, developed world seems to "flourish" at great expense. As philosopher Breena Holland puts it, "What many people in the developed world understand as basic to a good or flourishing human life is only sustainable if much of the underdeveloped world remains impoverished."[1] When we look at the size of the human population and the resources required to live a "comfortable" life, the math simply doesn't compute: there is not enough to go around. Indian novelist Amitav Ghosh analyzes the situation in terms of modernity: "the patterns of life that modernity engenders can only be practiced by a small minority of the world's population." He adds, "Every family in the world cannot have two cars, a washing machine, and a refrigerator."[2] The operative limits here are not technological or economic, but physical: earth simply does not have the resources to facilitate such an expansion of what most would consider a "good life." As the Ecological Footprint literature has it, if everyone on the planet lived like North Americans, we'd need four earths' worth of resources and services.[3] Ghosh acknowledges that it seems only fair that people of the developing world should have a turn at the relatively luxurious

1. Breena Holland, "Environment as Meta-capability: Why a Dignified Human Life Requires a Stable Climate System," in *Ethical Adaptation to Climate Change: Human Virtues of the Future,* Allen Thompson and Jeremy Bendik-Keymer, eds. (Cambridge, MA: MIT Press, 2012), 146.

2. Amitav Ghosh, *The Great Derangement: Climate Change and the Unthinkable* (Chicago: University of Chicago Press, 2016), 92.

3. See, for example, Charlotte McDonald, "How Many Earths Do We Need?" *BBC News,* June 16, 2015, http://www.bbc.com/news/magazine-33133712. For more on the Ecological Footprint concept, see William Rees and Mathis Wackernagel, *Our Ecological Footprint: Reducing Human Impact on the Earth* (Gabriola Island, BC: New Society Publishers, 1998).

thriving that is available to industrialized humans. But to do so, he writes, is to pursue "our self-annihilation" because of the ecological effects that would ensue; he names this tragic, doomed scenario "the Great Derangement."[4]

Furthermore, this version of human flourishing—unequal across global difference as it is—already exacts a significant toll on nonhuman flourishing. For example, the excesses of an industrialized economic system place stresses on threatened and endangered species around the globe. Philosopher Kathleen Dean Moore wonders, "Can the human species thrive in a world where the other species are disappearing, even as we watch?"[5] She answers in the negative, asserting, rather, that "all flourishing is mutual"—and thus that when (some) humans' flourishing comes at the expense of others, be they impoverished humans or threatened nonhumans, it should not truly be considered as flourishing.[6] Our current model of so-called flourishing human life in the developed world is really an elaborate form of suicide, since we are attacking the very basis for our survival. Whether the developing world achieves affluence or not, as a species we are still headed for Ghosh's "self-annihilation."

While many creatures cause some small-scale harm in order to survive (life frequently feeds on life, after all), industrialized humans have intensified this existential tension to the breaking point. Those of us in the industrialized world now live with this paradox: my well-being also entails harm to other humans and to various ecosystems. For example, driving a car is integral to my well-being. Arguably, it is essential to my flourishing: without it, I would be hard pressed to get to work, to get groceries, to visit loved ones, and so forth. Driving my car requires fossil fuels, which come from many places around the globe, but let us focus on oil from Nigeria, which supplies 9% of US oil and is a major exporter to many other countries in the industrialized world.[7] The oil-producing Niger Delta is home to several groups of indigenous people (many of whom are exploited by their own government), as well as the world's largest mangrove forest and much unique wildlife.[8] Because of oil exploration and production in this region, "an average of one oil spill occurs every week"; "when it rains, people run inside because

4. Ghosh, *Great Derangement*, 111.

5. Kathleen Dean Moore, *Great Tide Rising: Towards Clarity and Moral Courage in a Time of Planetary Change* (Berkeley, CA: Counterpoint, 2016), 7.

6. Ibid., 24.

7. U.S. Energy Information Administration, "Nigeria, the Largest Crude Oil Producer in Africa, Is a Major Source of U.S. Imports," September 13, 2011, https://www.eia.gov/todayinenergy/detail.php?id=3050.

8. Finomo Julia Awajiusuk, "Aquatic Pollution and Women's Health: Waves from the Niger Delta, Nigeria," *Canadian Woman Studies* 20, nos. 2–3 (Summer–Fall 2013): 41.

rain water (brackish in color from acid and chemicals and gas flaring) irritates the skin."[9] Farming is severely affected by these phenomena, and fishing yields a kerosene-flavored catch; effects on human health include asthma, cancer, premature deaths, and high infant mortality.[10] The human and nonhuman inhabitants of the Niger Delta bear, to a significant extent, the cost of my and my community's flourishing.

Religion plays an interesting role in the social and political landscape of Nigeria. Rather unusually, Nigeria's population is composed of about 50% Muslims and 50% Christians. Both religions teach care for God's creation, and indeed, sociologist Muazu Usman Shehu found that although both groups adhere to a dominion-over-nature theology, they both interpret this belief to include responsibility for the earth. According to Shehu, Christians and Muslims in Nigeria evince approximately equal care and concern for environmental issues, though they differ somewhat in their motivation, whether based in concern for ecosystems, human well-being, or God's will.[11] In a country where so much harm has occurred because of strife between Christians and Muslims, it is remarkable that environmental issues and care for creation constitute a potential point of connection. This connection might prove a fruitful place for the work of interfaith dialogue, or comparative religious ethics, or both.

In Nigeria, oil companies should adhere to better regulations, and the Nigerian government should hold them to high standards. Instead, each entity ends up blaming the other for the human and environmental costs of oil production.[12] According to Shehu, it would seem that religious groups care about these issues but lack the coordination and economic or educational resources to act.[13] Unfortunately, this situation and others like it are not uncommon. An industrialized way of life necessitates the existence of "sacrifice zones": "places that, to their extractors, somehow don't count and therefore can be poisoned, drained, or otherwise destroyed, for the supposed greater good of economic

---

9. Finomo Julia Awajiusuk and Lomo-David Ewuuk, "Deployment of the Four Way Test in the Discourse of Oil Exploitation in the Niger Delta of Nigeria," in *Fourth Annual General Business Conference*, vol. 3 Sam Houston State University, College of Business Administration, Huntsville, TX, 13–14 April 2012, Steve Nenninger, ed., 95–96.

10. Ibid.

11. Muazu Usman Shehu, *Religion and the Environment in Northeast Nigeria: Dominion, Stewardship, Fatalism and Agency* (PhD diss., University of Sheffield, 2015), 177–180.

12. Rob Nixon, *Slow Violence and the Environmentalism of the Poor* (Cambridge, MA: Harvard University Press, 2011), 107.

13. Shehu, *Religion and the Environment*, 122–123.

progress."[14] Connected to the idea of sacrifice zones are the related ideas of imperialism (taking what is good from far-flung colonies to serve the seat of power) and racism (one of the most potent ways to justify the "sacrifice people" whose well-being is threatened by those sacrifice zones).[15] Governments, religious organizations, and other civil society actors fight this phenomenon as they are able, but in the face of such an economic juggernaut, progress is halting at best. Flourishing, if it means resource use on the model of industrialized countries, is grounded in cruel yet intractable practices.

Problems like the destruction of the people and ecosystems of the Niger Delta require a re-examination of the idea of flourishing. Is mutual flourishing, flourishing that does not come at the expense of people or ecosystems, possible? Or is some conflict inevitable? What may be done to expand the scope of flourishing in a world in which the well-being of so many people and ecosystems is thwarted?

About Flourishing

The language of flourishing derives from philosophical virtue ethics in the tradition of Aristotle. Flourishing is one translation of Aristotle's central concept, *eudaimonea*, which he takes to be the goal of all human lives, the necessary effect of a life of virtue. As Nelson Reveley points out in this volume, *eudaimonea* is "at root a term more directly religious than botanical in origin and valence, given that it means literally 'good spirit.'"[16] Reveley's point is well taken: true *eudaimonea* has a spiritual grounding, hence, the project's focus on religious ethics. Nevertheless, the botanical metaphor—the flower within the term "flourish"—serves as a useful image for the work this book attempts to accomplish. Rather than focus on environmental devastation only, this book seeks out understandings of human and earth thriving that lead to beauty, wholeness, and a sense of holistic naturalness captured by the term flourishing.

Flourishing has been the subject of much philosophizing since Aristotle. Elizabeth Anscombe's influential 1958 essay, "Modern Moral Philosophy," called for a revival of virtue ethics but acknowledged that a clear description of the "flourishing" concept would be required in order to make sense of it.[17] Philosophers from Philippa Foot to Nancy E. Snow have explored the meaning and parameters

---

14. Naomi Klein, *This Changes Everything: Capitalism vs. the Climate* (New York: Simon and Schuster, 2014), 169.

15. Ibid., 169–170.

16. See p. 55, this volume.

17. G.E.M. Anscombe, "Modern Moral Philosophy," *Philosophy* 33, no. 124 (1958): 15–16.

of human flourishing.[18] Most conclude that flourishing is a debated concept, with roots in both objective welfare and subjective well-being.[19] Flourishing's related concepts include health, wholeness, growth, happiness, virtue, peace, self-cultivation, development, holistic well-being, excellence, fruitfulness, liberation, self-realization, thriving, and interconnectedness. A case like the Niger Delta—in which the flourishing of both humans and ecosystems is clearly threatened—would be fruitfully addressed with this language, as a way to clearly articulate what is lost when resource extraction creates such sacrifice zones.

Ecofeminist philosopher Chris Cuomo, in *Feminism and Ecological Communities: An Ethic of Flourishing*, demonstrates how to take Aristotle's flourishing concept as an invitation to a broader environmental conversation.[20] Cuomo rejects Aristotle's emphasis on rationality and restriction but appreciates his relatively holistic and communal vision of good human living.[21] This vision affords space to extend the good of human flourishing to include the good of nonhuman flourishing, since humans live in deep connection with, and utter dependence upon, the nonhuman world.[22] Cuomo explores synergies between human and nonhuman flourishing, rather than viewing it as a zero-sum game in which any flourishing necessarily comes at others' expense.[23] Such synergies are referred to by Michael Hannis and Sian Sullivan (this volume) as "symbiosis"; they write, "(Re)building this capacity for symbiosis is perhaps the most urgent challenge facing humanity."[24] Herein lies a glimmer of hope for the people of the Niger Delta and other sacrifice zones around the world: in some cases symbiosis, or what Amanda J. Baugh (this volume) calls "mutual flourishing," is possible.[25]

A vision of a world in which all flourishing is mutual and symbiotic sounds very good. It is reminiscent of the same ideal future envisioned by the biblical

---

18. See Philippa Foot, *Natural Goodness* (Oxford: Oxford University Press, 2001), and Nancy E. Snow, "Virtue and Flourishing," *Journal of Social Philosophy* 39, no. 2 (Summer 2008): 225–245.

19. Snow, "Virtue and Flourishing," 229–230.

20. Christine Cuomo, *Feminism and Ecological Communities: An Ethic of Flourishing* (New York: Taylor and Francis, 1998), 68.

21. Ibid., 69.

22. See Michael Hannis, "The Virtues of Acknowledged Ecological Dependence: Sustainability, Autonomy, and Human Flourishing," *Environmental Values* 24. no. 2 (April 2015), 145–164.

23. Ibid., 64–65.

24. See p. 293, this volume.

25. See p. 250, this volume.

author of Isaiah: "The wolf shall live with the lamb, the leopard shall lie down with the kid, the calf and the lion and the fatling together, and a little child shall lead them."[26] Isaiah even describes the lion eating "straw like the ox," an image that raises difficult questions about predation and perhaps brings the appealing vision back to the constraints of reality. There are certain harms embedded in the natural order, and it is simply true that one individual's flourishing does sometimes come at the expense of another. In fact, "the flourishing of every being without exception requires the death of many others," according to Colette Sciberras (this volume).[27] Overcoming this type of tragedy may be (and perhaps should be) beyond human capacity. The biblical author seems, rather, to find solace in the practice of envisioning the peace of what should be, and he seems to recognize that such a deep transformation, from nature red in tooth and claw to nature as a peaceable kingdom, comes from a transcendent force, not from human action alone.

The transition from philosophy to religion brings more tools for examining the concept of flourishing. We now have visions and revelations; nonhuman agency to call upon; myth, ritual, and other cultural elements to play with. Perhaps the reader can recognize why a deep and tangled problem like human and nonhuman flourishing benefits from the tools of religious thought. To expand this example, I now briefly examine the discourse on flourishing from some Christian and Buddhist perspectives.

Christian theological ethicist Jonathan Warner describes flourishing as *shalom*, a deep sort of peace that reflects the world as it should be, in right relation with God and in vibrant life and relationality.[28] Other Christian thinkers add the well-being of the natural world to this comprehensive vision of *shalom*. David Warner (a biologist) and Larry Borst (a Reformed theologian) write, "God's desire for humans to flourish (materially or otherwise) should not preempt the ability of the broader creation to flourish; instead, in shalom such blessing will be realized by all."[29] Shalom, in Christian thought, is a future state

---

26. Isaiah 11:6 (New Revised Standard Version).

27. See p. 37, this volume.

28. Jonathan Warner, "Rights, Capabilities, and Human Flourishing," in *Christianity and Human Rights: Christians and the Struggle for Global Justice,* Frederick Shepherd, ed. (Lanham, MD: Lexington Books, 2009), 163–166. Cristina L.H. Traina, in her *Feminist Ethics and Natural Law* (Washington, DC: Georgetown University Press, 1999), makes similar arguments about Thomistic visions of universal, communal flourishing as eschatological fulfillment (see especially chapter 9). Neither Warner nor Traina extends flourishing beyond humans, however.

29. David Warners and Larry Borst, "The Good of a Flourishing Creation: Seeking God in a Culture of Affluence," *Perspectives on Science and Christian Faith* 57, no. 1 (March 2005): 30.

to be worked toward and prayed for; ultimately, its realization is in God's hands. Christian feminist theologian Grace Jantzen describes flourishing as "abundance, overflowing with vigor and energy and productiveness, prosperity, success, and good health. . . . [O]ne who flourishes is going from strength to strength."[30] She prefers flourishing to salvation as the core metaphor of Christian life, an image that would have implications for Christians' view of nature.[31] In Jantzen's view, flourishing is inherently social, rather than individualistic, and thus it also raises important political questions: who suffers in order for me to flourish?[32] Thus, this religious perspective need not be quietistic about the tragedies of flourishing at another's expense, but it offers a transcendent context in which to address the injustices and tragedies of life.

From a Buddhist perspective, philosopher Simon P. James wrestles with the concept of self-realization, as articulated in deep ecology,[33] as he attempts to find parallels with Zen Buddhism. Self-realization, and its Zen equivalents, approximate human and earth flourishing for James. Though Zen hardly teaches a belief in a "self" at all—the cycles of samsara (death and rebirth) and the need to escape them by attaining enlightenment are the only "true" reality—James does note that for both Zen and deep ecology, "the key virtues bearing upon our relations with the natural environment are . . . the selflessness and empathy which allow one to identify with other beings."[34] True human goodness, then, involves both a certain type of knowledge—seeing the other as deeply related to one's own self—and also certain feelings or dispositions—compassion, empathy, self-emptying. Understanding interconnections and being virtuous amount to individual human flourishing, but these virtues also permit earth flourishing. Pragati Sahni agrees: she writes that individual spiritual flourishing, the supreme goal of Buddhist teaching and practice, includes "environmentally virtuous behavior." [35] In this view, then, human flourishing entails a type of personal excellence that

30. Grace Jantzen, "Feminism and Flourishing: Gender and Metaphor in Feminist Theology," *Feminist Theology* 4, no. 81 (1995), 85.

31. Ibid., 89.

32. Ibid., 91–93.

33. Deep ecology is a philosophy of human identification with the natural world, articulated by Arne Naess and colleagues. See Naess, *The Ecology of Wisdom: Writings by Arne Naess* (Alan Drengson and Bill Devall, eds.) (Berkeley, CA: Counterpoint, 2008) or Devall and Sessions, *Deep Ecology: Living as if Nature Mattered* (Layton, UT: Gibbs Smith, 1985).

34. Simon P. James, *Zen Buddhism and Environmental Ethics* (Aldershot, UK: Ashgate, 2004), 79.

35. Pragati Sahni, *Environmental Ethics in Buddhism: A Virtues Approach* (New York: Routledge, 2008), 143.

includes attending to the flourishing of nonhuman life on earth. When conflicts arise, a context of samsara helps make sense of the tragedies: doctrines of rebirth and the workings of karma create something like otherworldly justice in this world of suffering.

These very basic Christian and Buddhist sketches show fascinating points of overlap and variety. At a minimum, both perspectives agree that human flourishing is important and ideally should include flourishing for the nonhuman natural world, but they recognize that points of conflict do arise. James and Sahni both bring religious ideas and vocabulary to bear, to help make sense of conflicts that are both mundane and tragic. But in certain details—the existence of God, of a self, and the general trajectory of history—they are deeply divergent. James and Sahni embrace a rather individualistic, virtue-based perspective aiming at a personal pursuit of nirvana, whereas the Christian theologians emphasize a social, communal vision of shalom, a collective felicity. Clearly, this contrast may not be generalizable: some Buddhist thinkers would be more collective and some Christian thinkers would be more individualistic, so these observations do not characterize entire traditions. Rather, we are getting glimpses into this particular perspective on Buddhism and that particular subset of Christianity, and the glimmers of convergence and divergence are tantalizing and inspiring.

Ultimately, I hope such insights can help us, as scholars and as citizens, to fully conceive the differences between the world we have and the world as it ought to be. Starting with concepts like flourishing, perhaps, would be a way to unite conversation partners in places like the Niger Delta, where the divides between religious groups and various stakeholders have caused generations of tragedy and degradation.

Comparative Religious Ethics

For however one sees the fundamental project, CRE [comparative religious ethics] seems always to involve a profoundly aspirational kind of attention and listening—the kind that rejects a passive/active dichotomy and embraces the responsibility or onus for understanding the "other" by proactively studying and learning another language, culture, or mode of reasoning—and all this done so as not to keep one's enemies closer, but in the commitment to making a stranger into a friend.[36]

In order to create this book, a group of strangers—scholars of various religions—did precisely what Mathewes, Puffer, and Storslee describe above. They read

---

36. Charles Mathewes, Matthew Puffer, and Mark Storslee, *Comparative Religious Ethics: Critical Concepts in Religious Studies*, vol. 1 (London: Routledge, 2016), 30.

one another's work, paid attention, listened, and learned from one another. The result is the remarkable volume before you now. This book contains twelve chapters written by a variety of scholars—some established, some emerging— and six shorter essays created as a result of a process of learning and dialogue. The chapters exhibit what Mathewes et al. would call a "methodological bonanza" characteristic of comparative religious ethics: approaches that range from the philosophical and textual to the anthropological and historical.[37] The dialogic essays give readers a taste of the "adventure" of comparative religious ethics and invite further comparison.[38]

Comparative religious ethics (CRE) is a relatively small field, but it is growing with each successive generation of scholars. Elizabeth Bucar and Aaron Stalnaker, comparative ethicists working with Islam and Confucianism, respectively, describe CRE as an important and growing field because of our increasingly diverse and globalized world. "To study ethics today," they write, "we would suggest that everyone must be a comparativist."[39] Just as no religion exists in a vacuum, so no religious ethics exists in a vacuum: there is always a conversation with other lifeways and traditions (and with secular forces in society as well). Taken as a whole, this volume reflects that comparativist spirit by incorporating a diversity of religious viewpoints, communities, and cultures.

The best comparative religious ethics, writes Sumner B. Twiss, will recognize and comprehend the "diverse cultural and historical context[s]" of various religions, while also seeking out the "similar sorts of tasks and . . . similarities of thought amid differences sufficient to ground dialogue across cultural boundaries."[40] It's a balancing act, between seeking what is particular and seeking what is universal. Historically, CRE has emphasized the universal, but Bucar and Stalnaker observe that "third wave" CRE is moving toward the particular and concrete, and away from the universal and theoretical.[41] This book fits that trend to some degree: most contributors have emphasized the particular practices, texts, and worldviews of the religions they study, and the dialogues that result aim not at broad generalizations but at further understanding of the particulars.

---

37. Ibid., 1.

38. Ibid., 2.

39. Elizabeth Bucar and Aaron Stalnaker, "On Comparative Religious Ethics as a Field of Study," *Journal of Religious Ethics* 42, no. 2 (June 2014): 378.

40. Sumner B. Twiss, "Four Paradigms in Teaching Comparative Religious Ethics," in *Explorations in Global Ethics: Comparative Religious Ethics and Interreligious Dialogue*, Sumner B. Twiss and Bruce Grelle, eds. (Boulder, CO: Westview, 1998), 25.

41. Elizabeth M. Bucar and Aaron Stalnaker, eds., *Religious Ethics in a Time of Globalism: Shaping a Third Wave of Comparative Analysis* (New York: Palgrave MacMillan, 2012), 4.

Nevertheless, any comparative enterprise must find concepts that might act as "bridges" (Stalnaker's word) between traditions.[42] To take concepts from one religious tradition and apply them to another might be inappropriate, even imperialist. As Mathewes et al. put it, "any project of comparative *anything*, at least in religious studies, must acknowledge from the beginning the profound skepticism about and multiple critiques of the sort of project it attempts to be."[43] And yet, "if we are not allowed to use any alien categories at all, it is unclear how comparisons outside of a single context are possible, or how traditions themselves could adapt to new circumstances."[44] The comparative ethicist, it seems, must carefully choose concepts that bridge between traditions, allowing space for those concepts to be critiqued or re-thought as they are adapted, transformed, or rejected by thinkers working with another tradition. Interestingly, Bucar and Stalnaker refer to "flourishing" as a relatively universal concept, noting that CRE might concern itself with flourishing by assessing social structures and institutions that foster or impede it; or indeed, CRE might also "rethink what it means 'to be human' and 'to flourish' in the first place."[45] This book may be taken as one response to this apt suggestion.

This book seeks common ground between the scholarly enterprise of CRE and the lay practice of interreligious dialogue. One disadvantage of scholarly CRE is the apparent requirement that one must be an expert in more than one tradition in order to work across traditions. This requirement necessarily limits the number of people who are qualified to contribute to the field. Interreligious dialogue, a common non-scholarly practice in which adherents of different religions engage in forms of discussion and mutual learning, does not require such expertise. One must simply be able and willing to listen receptively and to reflect critically on one's own tradition: participants offer compassionate attention and engage in active listening, all in pursuit of mutual understanding. Some movements, such as Scriptural Reasoning and Receptive Ecumenism, bridge interreligious dialogue on the part of religious adherents with the work of scholars. These movements describe the importance of intellectual "hospitality" in encounters between practitioners of varying religions.[46] And they focus on the pragmatic task of

---

42. See Aaron Stalnaker, *Overcoming Our Evil: Human Nature and Spiritual Exercises in Xunzi and Augustine* (Washington, DC: Georgetown University Press, 2006).

43. Mathewes et al., *Comparative Religious Ethics*, 6.

44. Bucar and Stalnaker, "On Comparative Religious Ethics," 373.

45. Ibid., 370 n12.

46. David F. Ford, "An Interfaith Wisdom: Scriptural Reasoning between Jews, Christians, and Muslims," *Modern Theology* 22, no. 3 (July 2006): 349. For a similar description of the importance of hospitality in interreligious relationships, see James L. Fredericks, "Interreligious

exploring difference and learning from it, rather than seeking carefully worded platitudes of agreement or boiled-down common essentials.[47] The goal is to learn from one another in order to live together and to solve problems together.

The book as a whole, then, can be taken as a delightfully cacophonous chorus of contributions to a multivocal discussion of the topic. When the voices work in harmony or in marked contrast, this approach can be a source of learning, interest, hope for cooperation, self-reflection, and so forth. This book is a bit of an experiment, since no other volumes have used quite this same methodology. I would argue that it is a successful experiment, insofar as the reader can use the chapters and dialogue essays as points of reflection and inspiration, to join in and further the conversation about human and nonhuman flourishing in a world that is both fragile and resilient.

Religious Environmental Ethics

This book is not simply an exercise in CRE: it has a specific topic within environmental ethics. Surprisingly little work has been done in comparative religious environmental ethics, so this book fills a genuine need in the field.[48] As Wesley J. Wildman writes, "comparison inevitably is a socially and politically contextualized act of interpretation."[49] As with all environmental ethics, these authors share a particular agenda: inquiry into, and advocacy for, the well-being of the nonhuman natural world (usually as it relates to the well-being of humans). Environmental ethics, as a field of relatively recent development, is driven by crisis and advocacy. The problems are urgent, and scholars in this field devote their skills to finding solutions under the specter of impending catastrophe.

Friendship: A New Theological Virtue," *Journal of Ecumenical Studies* 35, no. 2 (Spring 1998): 166.

47. Nicholas Adams, "Long-Term Disagreement: Philosophical Models in Scriptural Reasoning and Receptive Ecumenism," *Modern Theology* 29, no. 4 (October 2013): 164.

48. A few recent works of note: David Landis Barnhill and Roger S. Gottlieb, eds., *Deep Ecology and World Religions: New Essays on Sacred Ground* (Albany, NY: State University of New York Press, 2001); J. Baird Callicott, *Earth's Insights: A Multicultural Survey of Ecological Ethics from the Mediterranean Basin to the Australian Outback* (Berkeley, CA: University of California Press, 1994); Donald K. Swearer and Susan Lloyd McGarry, *Ecologies of Human Flourishing* (Cambridge, MA: Harvard University Press, 2011), an edited collection based on a series of lectures given at the Harvard Center for the Study of World Religions; and Robin Globus Veldman, Andrew Szaz, and Randolph Haluza-DeLay, *How the World's Religions Are Responding to Climate Change: Social Scientific Investigations* (New York: Routledge, 2014).

49. Wesley J. Wildman, "Comparing Religious Ideas: There's Method in the Mob's Madness," in *Comparing Religions: Possibilities and Perils?* Tohmas Athanasius Idinopulos, Brian C. Wilson, and James Constantine Hanges, eds. (Leiden, The Netherlands: Brill, 2006), 87.

The comparative method of this book, then, is at least partly motivated by the desire to find workable solutions to looming crises. If, say, Muslims and Hindus can agree on the importance of clean water, or if Daoists and Confucianists can agree about respect for animals, or if Christians and Muslims in Nigeria can agree on the need to drastically clean up and repair the biotic community in the Niger Delta—then this consensus offers hope for overcoming the political delays that seem to stymie environmental reforms on every continent. Given the extreme urgency and dire conditions of environmental crises, surely every tool available to humanity should be deployed toward solutions, including the tools of comparative religious ethics. Obviously, the impact of this book alone is scant, but if it leads to further exploration and constructive dialogue, it may have a significant impact.

Some readers may be surprised that religious ethics would be relevant to environmental issues, perhaps having absorbed the message from an earlier generation of environmentalists that religions are "part of the problem" and too anthropocentric to be relevant to environmental concerns.[50] Such readers will, I hope, be pleasantly surprised to find in these pages a rebuttal to that view. The book contains a wide array of religious voices expressing concern about environmental issues—from more or less anthropocentric viewpoints—to the extent that such a distinction is even helpful (see Cheryl Cottine's chapter for an insightful discussion of this array). According to the Pew Research Center's Forum on Religion and Public Life, 84% of people worldwide adhere to a religion of some kind, with Christianity, Islam, and Hinduism holding the largest populations of adherents.[51] Given the prevalence of religious people on this planet, any attempts to address environmental issues should work with, rather than against or in ignorance of, religions.

Why do religious environmental ethics in comparative mode? Just as the various features of the natural world—the skies, the waters, the trees, the land—do not adhere to any one religion, so do the environmental issues that plague the natural world transcend religious boundaries. Fruitfully addressing environmental problems means working in the spaces of overlap, friction, and encounter between religious worldviews. The deep divides that have led to environmental and humanitarian disaster in Nigeria are, among other factors, cultural and religious. If

---

50. Anthropocentrism is a perspective that places humans at the center. Environmental thinkers, from Lynn White ("The Historical Roots of our Ecologic Crisis," *Science* 155: 3767, March 10, 1967, 1203–1207) onward, have blamed this perspective—and the religions (particularly Western ones) that seem to promote it—for various environmental ills.

51. Pew Forum, "The Global Religious Landscape," Washington, DC, December 18, 2012, http://www.pewforum.org/2012/12/18/global-religious-landscape-exec.

Muslims and Christians can leverage the points of agreement they already possess with regard to environmental stewardship, and (an even bigger challenge) rally a defense of the small minority of non-Abrahamic indigenous Nigerians who are most affected by the degradation of the Niger Delta, they could marshal adequate power to change things in this region. But effective work across religious and cultural difference is required here: the tendency to see denizens of the sacrifice zone as religious and cultural "others" compounds the difficulty in Nigeria. Such patterns exist in other areas as well (see, for example, the Dakota Access Pipeline and the "others" who are most affected): the work of comparative religion and interreligious dialogue is vital to bridging the cultural gaps that are used to justify such sacrifices.

About This Book

One of the challenges of editing a collection like this one is getting a good mix of contributors, topics, and approaches. Although this is a work of comparative religious ethics, for the most part I did not seek out scholars with expertise in more than one religion. I did deliberately seek as wide a range of religions as possible—hence, inclusion of less populous religions like Neopaganism, Daoism, and ‖Khao-a Dama. Only Christianity and Islam are featured in more than one chapter—and given that these are the two most populous religions in the world, it may be justified. In my selection I chose a mix of established and emerging scholars. Though I did not purposely seek them out, I was gratified to find so many female contributors in a field that remains fairly male dominated. This book also encompasses contributors from a variety of methodologies within the study of religion: philosophical, theological, historical, textual, anthropological, and so forth. Such variety, I hope, indicates the generativity and plurality that comparative religious ethics, and environmental ethics, inspire.

As delighted as I am with the diversity represented in these pages, I am disappointed in one dimension of our group: race. I tried to get a mix of race and ethnicity among the contributors but largely failed: in the process of creating this collection, I lost three scholars of color but was unable to replace them with other scholars of color. I add my failed attempt as further evidence, if it isn't already obvious, that the study of religion and environmental ethics needs more scholars of color in its ranks.[52] This book exhibits diversity of subject matter,

---

52. According to the *AAR [American Academy of Religion] Career Guide for Racial and Ethnic Minorities in the Profession*, scholars of color represented 13% of the full members in the organization. Kwok Pui-Lan and Rosetta Ross, "Chapter 1," *AAR Career Guide for Racial and Ethnic Minorities in the Profession*, 2006, https://www.aarweb.org/node/283.

and of geographic coverage around the globe, more than diversity of authors, unfortunately.

I created guidelines for the dialogues, which asked the participants to begin by using the phone or video calling to create as much personal connection as possible in spite of often large distances between parties. I encouraged them to constructively critique one another's chapters; to look for points of confluence and divergence in their chapters; to discuss the flourishing concept; and if possible to imagine an environmental problem that could be addressed by adherents of the two (or more) religions in dialogue. I then asked participants to compose either one cohesive essay with two or three voices, or to write out the dialogue in a script style, for inclusion in the book. I offer my reflection on the outcome of the dialogue process in the conclusion; suffice it to say that all of them surprised me. I invite readers, as you go along, to imagine participating in these dialogues yourselves. What insights and questions would you bring? What ideas and points of convergence or divergence interest you the most? The possibilities abound.

The book, then, is organized according to pairs (and one trio) of dialogue partners. Each section contains two chapters and one dialogue. Below I introduce each pair so that readers get a sense of the overall scope of the volume.

In "Flourishing and Its Costs," this pair introduces important concepts behind the idea of flourishing as it is encountered by environmental and religious thought. The conversation begins with Buddhism, as Colette Sciberras explores Buddhist ideas of purpose and value in nature as they relate to Aristotle and Darwin. She sketches a fundamental duty of respect for the flourishing of all organisms, even as she recognizes that "the flourishing of every being without exception requires the death of many others."[53] Sciberras's conversation partner, Nelson Reveley, also wrestles with the inevitability of death in what is sometimes a zero-sum game: "Life being necessarily rooted in death, with its attendant suffering, seems a rampant scandal for a 'good' creation," he writes.[54] Using concepts from Christian ethics, Reveley seeks glimpses of goodness in eating and farming, which may guide human conduct in a less than perfect world. In their dialogue Sciberra and Reveley discuss whether the world may be seen as good, and this topic brings them to a discussion of what counts as good, and where value lies.

In "Animals and Care," this pair explores the role of the human with respect to the nonhuman world, with an emphasis on care and relationality. David E. Cooper begins with a discussion of Daoist virtues that lead to human

---

53. See p. 37, this volume.
54. See p. 47, this volume.

flourishing. Qualities such as *ziran* (spontaneity or naturalness) lead to a relationship with animals characterized by care and nurture. According to Cooper, Daoists are more likely to be "responsible gardeners, farmers, and foresters" than "eco-warriors."[55] Sarah E. Robinson-Bertoni describes a similar emphasis on responsibility in her chapter about animals and Islam. With a theme of care and viceregency, Robinson-Bertoni builds a case that Muslims may avoid factory farms and pursues eco-halal meat as an expression of their religious duties to foster flourishing in God's creation. In their dialogue, Cooper and Robinson-Bertoni light on the concept of stewardship as a useful, helpfully paradoxical concept: it effectively places human beings both within nature and in a role of "special responsibility" for nonhuman nature.[56]

In "Climate and Culture," this pair examines climate change in two different regions of the globe: India and Mali. Christopher Miller analyzes the confluence of environmental politics with the cultural role of Yoga in India. He notices Yoga rhetoric used to support a neoliberal economic boom, which fuels climate change, while Yoga may also be deployed to resist the massive hydroelectric projects that threaten India's aquatic environments. Dianna Bell's Muslim subjects in Mali also encounter climate change and respond to it with a fascinating and creative blend of religious and political ideas. In dialogue, Miller and Bell uncover deep themes of economic power, environmental epistemology, and power politics that emerge from the intersection of their chapters. The power to flourish depends on politics as much as religion, it seems. They end with provocative and practical suggestions to "incorporate localized ways of knowing into environmental protection and management programs."[57]

In "Texts and Traditions," this pair explores the text-heavy traditions of Judaism and Roman Catholicism, applying both innovative method and insightful content to the question of human and environmental flourishing. Rebecca J. Epstein-Levi examines genetic engineering through analogy with the Torah: if Judaism permits rabbis, in some very specific circumstances, to alter the text of the sacred Torah, might it not also permit alteration of the "sacred text" of a plant's genome? Epstein-Levi carefully plots these specific circumstances and their plant-based analogs to argue for respectful "dialogical engagement" to promote human and nonhuman flourishing.[58] Jennifer Phillips's chapter models such dialogical engagement with the tradition of Roman Catholic Social Teaching,

55. See p. 88, this volume.

56. See p. 120, this volume.

57. See p. 176, this volume.

58. See p. 195, this volume.

particularly Pope Francis's environmental encyclical, *Laudato Si'*. Phillips insightfully underscores the profound connections between poverty and environmental concerns for the Roman Catholic tradition, and provocatively pushes the tradition to more fully consider animals and gender. In their dialogue, Epstein-Levi and Phillips fruitfully prompt each other to consider the economic and feminist implications of their respective chapters; this dialogue strikingly shows the potential for innovation and challenge in comparative religious ethical dialogue.

In "Communities and Human Agency," this pair explores particular religious communities, asking what effects human work has on environmental questions. Both chapters use interviewing and participant observation as methodological lenses on environmental beliefs and behavior. Chris Klassen writes about contemporary Canadian Pagans, examining their beliefs about the nature of nature and the "naturalness" of technology. She evaluates these beliefs and practices with reference to a standard of "ecosocial flourishing," a concept rooted in synergy between the human and the ecological.[59] Amanda Baugh explores two communities—a Unitarian women's urban garden and a green mosque—to examine motivations and effects of both "mainstream" and "alternative" environmental practices. She calls readers to acknowledge "the extreme diversity in the category of 'human' that must be acknowledged when we consider the flourishing of humans and the rest of the earth."[60] In their dialogue, Klassen and Baugh fruitfully explore the complexities and nuances of their subjects' relationship to technology. They also discuss the very real impediments to interfaith dialogue and collaborative work between monotheist and polytheist groups.

In "Respect and Relationality," the final pair asks which human qualities or virtues might engender the elusive goal: mutual flourishing for humans and for the rest of nature. Cheryl Cottine creates the framework for a Mengzian environmental ethic by reference to respect and restraint, relying primarily on ancient Confucian texts. These qualities underpin a "tempered anthropocentrism" because, she writes, "flourishing . . . includes both role-based virtue cultivation *and* attention to larger ecological cycles."[61] Michael Hannis and Sian Sullivan, by contrast, use ethnography rather than textual analysis, and they examine the ||Khao-a Dama people of west Namibia. According to Hannis and Sullivan, a ||Khao-a Dama perspective requires a type of "relational environmental ethics"

---

59. Thomas Crowley, "From 'Natural' to 'Ecosocial Flourishing': Evaluating Evaluative Frameworks," *Ethics and the Environment* 15, no. 1 (2010).

60. See p. 252, this volume.

61. See p. 276, this volume.

characterized by respect and reciprocity.[62] They connect this worldview with contemporary environmental virtue ethics, arguing for an "ecological eudaimonism" in "pluralistic perspective and dialogue," as a fitting response to this complex world of "wicked" environmental problems.[63] In their dialogue, these two extremely different approaches find common ground in their perspectives that foreground human flourishing—in all its relational interconnection with the rest of nature—as the central concern of environmental ethics.

Taken together, this book represents a significant contribution to the fields of comparative religious ethics, environmental ethics, and dialogue across religious, methodological, and other difference. The contributors and I are proud to offer this book, in the hopes of sparking further research, conversation, dialogue, and action.

---

62. See p. 284, this volume.
63. See p. 292, this volume.

FLOURISHING AND ITS COSTS

1

BUDDHA, ARISTOTLE, AND SCIENCE

REDISCOVERING PURPOSE AND THE VALUE OF FLOURISHING IN NATURE

Colette Sciberras

The founders of modern science—including Bacon and Descartes—planted the seeds of our modern understanding of what is real and what is "just in our minds," and today we extol their achievements at having overcome the dogmatism of religion and of medieval philosophy. Yet our exclusive reliance on the scientific approach, in a word, *scientism*, has resulted in a very partial understanding of reality, and one that is impossible to reconcile with our pre-theoretical way of conceiving and interacting with the world. Scientism, in its concern to remove unverifiable and anthropomorphic postulates, has left us without a way to differentiate between better or worse lives, and the sense of *purpose*, which is foundational for ethics, has no place in its worldview. We might be able to explain how we got here, but we cannot say anything about why we are here, or what we are supposed to do.

Western religions and philosophies have traditionally postulated purpose in life through some form of "eternalist" doctrine—such as the immortal Soul, eternal God, or inalienable dignity of Human Nature. When such postulates are abandoned, as in the philosophy of Nietzsche, the tendency is to totter close to nihilism. Without faith in something eternal and good, the recognition of universal and somewhat random change throughout the universe leaves us in the dark as to why we live.

Buddhist philosophy[1] includes a deep awareness of the pervasiveness of change,[2] and steers a Middle Path between the two

---

1. In this chapter, I refer to ancient foundational languages and texts of Buddhism and of Greek philosophy by using the following abbreviations: *Anguttara Nikāya* (A); *Cullavagga* (Cv); *Dīgha Nikāya* (D); *De Anima* (DA); Greek (G); *Majjhima Nikāya* (M); *Mūlamadhyamakakārikā* (MMK); *Metaphysics* (Met); *Nicomachean Ethics* (NE); Pali (P); *Physics* (Ph); *Republic* (Rep.); *Samyutta Nikāya* (S); Sanskrit (Sk); *Sutta Nipata* (SN); English (E).

2. P. *anicca*; Sk. *anitya*

extremes of eternalism[3] and nihilism[4] described above. This path can offer a way out of the impasse between the objective facts of science and subjective values of religion and faith, and it can accommodate the intuition that we live in order to flourish. In fact, some parts of Buddhist philosophy can be reconciled with contemporary science, although it demands that we lift the arbitrary and historical constraints that limit the scope of science to material phenomena.

Purpose, Value, and Science

From ancient times, it has been believed that the universe was created by a Deity, for the sake of a future ultimate Good.[5] This view of history as the unfolding of a grand plan, conceived by a God who wills others to share in his Goodness, is known as external teleology, in which *telos*—the ancient Greek word for the completion, end, or purpose of a thing[6]—is bestowed upon that thing by an external agency. In the Christian account, God created the world so that humans could enjoy His Presence, and the Creator and created are usually understood to be completely independent substances.[7] Yet, the purpose of the universe, and of human life, is inseparable from God's will.

Human artifacts too have an external *telos*; all our tools, buildings, weapons, and electronic devices perform their proper functions[8] and are useful because we designed them with some purpose in mind.[9] In the same way, it is thought by

---

3. P. *sassatavāda*; Sk. *śāśvatavāda*

4. P., Sk. *ucchedavāda*

5. This historical account of creation mainly belongs to the Judeo-Christian tradition; however, the modern European understanding also finds its roots in ancient Greek philosophy (especially in Plato's *Timaeus* 90a–d, and *Theaetetus* 176a–177a) as well as in the Bible (e.g., Revelation 21–22, and Ephesians 1:5–10). This progressive and linear view of change lies in contrast with indigenous and Eastern views of an eternal cycle between creation and destruction (Mircea Eliade, *The Sacred and the Profane: The Nature of Religion* [Orlando, FL: Harcourt, 1959], 72–80).

6. Francis E. Peters, *Greek Philosophical Terms: A Historical Lexicon* (New York: New York University Press, 1967), 191.

7. I use "substance" here in its philosophical sense to mean that which can exist by itself or that which bears properties, some of which are essential to it (Simon Blackburn, *Oxford Dictionary of Philosophy* [Oxford: Oxford University Press, 1996], 366).

8. G. *ergon*. Peters defines this term as something done or made, the activity proper to a thing, or the product of that activity (*Greek Philosophical Terms*, 61).

9. What of the possibility, depicted in movies like *The Matrix*, that future artificially intelligent machines will have purposes and objectives of their own? As I hope will become apparent

those who believe in a purely external teleology that the world and our lives have no purpose or value in and of themselves, but only insofar as they participate in the Divine Plan.

The *locus classicus* for the discussion of *telos* is Aristotle's *Physics* and *Metaphysics;* yet, these presentations—which were held as dogma for centuries of medieval scholasticism—differ greatly from the Christian account. Aristotle, unlike his teacher Plato, allowed for an *internal* teleology; he saw in nature a purpose that is not bestowed by an external agency but that arises from what a thing is.[10] It is that goal, easily recognizable in a general sense as its own flourishing,[11] toward which a living being moves of its own accord.[12]

The distinction between the natural and artificial might be obscured by the fact that Aristotle used the word *organon*, which means "tool," to describe living creatures and their parts.[13] He claims that technology imitates nature[14] and this concept highlights the fact that all "tools," whether natural or artifact, can be described as being *for* something. The parts of a living organism, its organs, clearly serve a purpose; they enable the organism to survive and can be replaced with mechanical substitutes. Organs, then, are readily seen as tools. More controversially

---

throughout the chapter, there are probably no grounds to negate life of these machines if they satisfy the criterion of *autopoiesis* (see n12), or can be described as performing some of the functions of life, or soul (G. *psychē*—E. psyche) as Aristotle would put it.

10. G. *physis*. The nature of a thing is its matter (G. *hylē*) and form (G. *morphē*) and it can be defined (Ph. 200a34). Thus, like Socrates and Plato before him, Aristotle too was an essentialist, although he did not postulate independently existing ideal essences, as Plato did (Ph. 198b10–200a34).

11. G. *euzen* (lit. "living well') and G. *eudaimonia* (lit. "good spirits') are attained through engaging in one's functions (G. *ergon*) and activities (G. *energeia*) in an excellent way (G. *aretē*—"virtue"). Although the human-specific *eudaimonia* is often translated as "happiness," this meaning is not to be understood as a fleeting pleasure or feeling of satisfaction that disappears when circumstances change (NE 1097b9–1098a16).

12. Aristotle distinguishes nature from man-made things through the fact that only living beings contain, within themselves, a source of movement and of rest (Ph. 192b8). Unintelligent artifacts have no inner tendency to change, except to perish. Natural beings, on the other hand, grow, move, or remain at rest of their own accord. Aristotle is generally credited with having been the first to study the living world systematically and, in so doing, he anticipated the contemporary understanding of life as *autopoiesis* (Colin Dougall, "Autopoiesis and Aristotle: Rethinking Organisation as Form," *Kybernetes* 28, nos. 6–7 [1999]: 777–791) in his definition of natural "tools" as those which contain, by virtue of what they are, the source of their own production (Ph. 192b10–35).

13. E.g., DA 412a. The Greek word *organon* is, in fact, the source of our current words "organ," "organism," and "organic."

14. E.g., Ph. 194a21

with respect to the modern scientific view, Aristotle held that organisms too have a *telos* and that this purpose, unlike that of tools and organs, belongs to their very nature.[15]

What is the purpose of an animal or a plant? Aristotle recognized various types of activity that are typical of organisms; they obtain nutrition, grow, move about, and sense their environment; some perceive the world around them. They reproduce, some engage in social relations, and some animals are able to reason.[16] To the extent that an organism successfully fulfils the functions and activities typical of its kind,[17] it can be said to be flourishing. On the other hand, a living creature that is undernourished, say, cannot be said to be living the best kind of life it might have. It must be emphasized here that, for Aristotle, *telos* has no suggestion of necessity and he recognized that many, perhaps most beings, failed altogether to fulfil their purposes.[18] Most seeds simply land on unfertile ground.

This account of *telos* is tied up with Aristotle's list of "four causes," which are intended as an exhaustive set of questions that might be asked about anything at all. Besides inquiring into what a thing is made of, the material cause, we want to know how this matter is structured, or what the essence of this thing is, the formal cause. No amount of detail in such a description can provide a complete picture, however, unless we also explain why the thing is there.

One obvious way to is to refer to the past, and this third cause—the efficient cause—is the one emphasized by science. For this reason, perhaps, it is also what most people mean by the word "cause" today. It captures the general intuition that, on the material plane at least, a present effect can be explained only by past events and not future ones.

---

15. Although, when describing nonhuman purposes, Aristotle more frequently uses the word *ergon* than *telos* (e.g., NE 1176a8; see nn8 and 11), in Met 1050a he is explicit about the identity between these concepts (see also Peters, *Greek Philosophical Terms*, 61).

16. DA 413a–413b.

17. See n8.

18. NE 1099a15–1100a9. An interesting question is whether such failure to flourish can be construed as a moral failing. Alasdair MacIntyre provides a genealogical reply: "if we begin by asking for an account of goodness which is compatible with the good man suffering any degree of torture and injustice" as Plato and as Christianity needed to do, "the whole perspective of our ethics will be different from that of an ethic which begins from asking in what form of life doing well and faring well may be found together." (Alasdair MacIntyre, *A Short History of Ethics* [London: Routledge and Kegan Paul, 1998], 40). The modern two senses of "a good life"—the moral sense, and the biological sense of flourishing—are already suggested in Plato's argument that it is better to suffer injustice, as Socrates did, rather than to commit it (Rep. 1.354a). Aristotle, however, does not assume a split between duty and inclination, and inasmuch as living well is an art with specific purposes, a person of *eudaimonia* does not merely know the Good, but also brings it about successfully as flourishing (NE 1098b –1099b1; 1140a1–23).

Yet, to complete our explanation of what a thing is, we often need to refer to some value, some good that may be achieved in the future. There is no way we could explain what a hammer is, without saying what it is for. Similarly, it is seriously lacking to describe a tooth, for instance, without explaining that it is there to cut, tear, or grind food, so that, ultimately, an animal can eat and flourish. Biology is peppered with teleological assumptions; it would be impossible to understand the circulatory, respiratory, nervous, or digestive systems, without the notions that these served the good of their owners.[19]

Tools and organs have functions and typical activities and through these, they derive their purposes. For Aristotle, organisms too have typical functions, activities, and purposes, although unlike organs and tools, which promote the good of something else, the *telos* of a living being is internal, since it functions and acts to promote its own good. Everything that animals, plants, and humans do, they do ultimately, for that most elusive and abstract good—flourishing. Despite his notion of a general Final Good, Aristotle was aware that flourishing was relative to species and not something absolute. His break with Plato came through his realizing that form and purpose are not independent from matter and the laws of nature. This fourth kind of cause—the final cause[20]—is Aristotle's understanding of *telos*.[21]

A common complaint against this kind of discourse is that, if we abandon faith in a Creator, there are no grounds to attribute purpose to anything in nature. Teeth do not come up in order that I might chew, since teeth do not make plans, and neither did nature "design" them consciously for this purpose. Organs may indeed be described as though they served the good of the organism; yet, scientific consensus is that this purpose is merely metaphorical. It may seem as though happiness was the purpose of human life, just as it may seem that the function of bees is to pollinate flowers, but this explanation is no more appropriate than saying that the function of rain is to irrigate farms. Indeed, since the scientific revolution we have learned to regard such language and explanations as illegitimate anthropomorphisms.

---

19. Strictly speaking, not all adaptations serve the good of individual organisms. For example, most types of altruistic behavior increase biological fitness in the sense that an individual's genes are successfully passed onto the next generation, and yet such behavior may result in the death of that individual. As will become clear, the recognition of a general sense of a good of the organism does not suggest or require that all its biological processes aim at this result.

20. This understanding of cause, although it will be unintuitive to the modern reader, retains its sense in expressions like "for a good cause" or "to fight for a cause."

21. Ph. 194b15–195b5

In the late 16th century, Francis Bacon[22] rejected Aristotle's finalism, which Bacon saw as the result of a "pernicious and inveterate habit of dwelling on abstractions" and "of scarcely any avail to real and active knowledge."[23] He emphasized that science would advance through understanding the laws of nature, and not through contemplating final causes. To understand these laws, he maintained, the scientist has to *dissect* nature rather than abstract it; he should "consider matter, its conformation, and the changes of that conformation, its own action, and the law of this action or motion."[24] In short, in emphasizing the practical utility of science, Bacon restricted the scope of its inquiry to causes whose effects could be observed and used directly; i.e., he emphasized efficient causes rather than final ones, proximate causes rather than remote ones, and material ones rather than ideal, abstract notions.[25] To say that flourishing is the purpose of life makes no useful addition to knowledge, he would argue.

The overwhelming successes of this "mechanistic" approach at improving the human condition have persuaded us of its validity. Although it is hard to ignore the intuition that teeth grow for the sake of an animal's well-being, teleological thinking is regarded with suspicion in science, and trainees must learn to leave their values and religious beliefs outside the laboratory. Biology, in general, still follows the program outlined by Bacon.

Indeed, Darwin's great contribution, which changed the theory of evolution from speculative philosophy into science, lay in uncovering one of the

---

22. Often referred to as a founding father of science, Bacon published his *Novum Organum* in 1620, intended as a replacement for Aristotle's canonical text, the *Organon*.

23. John Devey, ed., *Bacon's Novum Organum* (New York: Collier, 1905), 109–111. Though Bacon denied that studying final causes could be useful for science, this denial does not mean he disbelieved entirely in their existence. See Étienne Gilson, *From Aristotle to Darwin and Back Again: A Journey in Final Causality, Species and Evolution* (San Francisco: Ignatius Press, 2009), 27–30.

24. Gilson, *From Aristotle to Darwin*, 27.

25. A similar agenda was put forward by Descartes (1596–1650), also considered one of the founders of science. Descartes's reasons were different from Bacon's; he believed we could never know final causes because we can never know the mind of God (John Cottingham, trans., *Descartes's Meditations on First Philosophy: With Selections from the Objections and Replies* [Cambridge: Cambridge University Press, 2003], 38–39). At the same time, he subscribed to Bacon's project in that he too saw it as the business of science "to render ourselves masters and possessors of nature" (Donald A. Cress, trans., *Descartes's Discourse on Method and Meditations on First Philosophy*, 4th ed. [Indianapolis, IN: Hackett, 1998], 35). Descartes denied inner *telos* outright of all nonhuman nature. He viewed plants and animals as mechanical "automata" (Cress, *Descartes's Discourse*, 31), mere matter reacting to the laws of physics. This is one, extreme extent to which the scientific revolution emptied nature of an inner purpose, and of soul and life, or psyche.

mechanisms—natural selection—by which evolution proceeds. Even though Darwin never denied final causes outright, his theory includes only efficient and material ones; thus, it is perfectly consistent with Bacon's method.[26] Darwin explained how the immense diversity of nature had arisen, without needing to refer to a Creator or anything like a *telos*, and by uncovering the "how" of evolution, he persuaded the world that there might not be an ultimate "why."

The Debate Goes On

Today, many of us are familiar with the view that the universe, our planet, and our individual existence all result from a series of fortuitous events. Still, the question of purpose has continued to arise since Darwin's times.[27] Although the scientific consensus is that teleological thinking is an "obstacle" to understanding natural selection,[28] biologists mostly admit that adaptations seem *as if* they were designed for the functions they serve. Even adamant non-teleologists, such as Richard Dawkins or Ernst Mayr, make extensive use of the metaphors of design, games, and computer programs,[29] in order to explain life. These concepts all point to something fundamentally *goal oriented*, demonstrating

---

26. This position does not mean that final causation was immediately abandoned in scientific circles. Some of Darwin's contemporaries interpreted his theory as a "deathblow to teleology," while others took it to confirm teleology (Michael Ruse, *Darwin and Design: Does Evolution Have a Purpose?* [Cambridge, MA: Harvard University Press, 2003], 138–149; Gilson, *From Aristotle to Darwin*, 99–101).

27. See Ruse, *Darwin and Design,* and Gilson, *From Aristotle to Darwin.*

28. Leonardo González Galli, Leonardo Martin, and Elsa N. Meinardi, "The Role of Teleological Thinking in Learning the Darwinian Model of Evolution," *Evolution: Education and Outreach* 4 (2011): 145–152.

29. Richard Dawkins criticizes the design metaphor in so far as it is used to support belief in an intelligent Designer. He emphazes instead that the "designer" is blind, and more like a tinkerer than an architect. Nature makes small but cumulative modifications, without any long-term goal in mind (*The Blind Watchmaker: Why the Evidence of Evolution Reveals a Universe without Design* [New York: Norton, 1996], 50; see also François Jacob, "Evolution and Tinkering," *Science* 196 [1977]: 1161–1166, 1163–1164). Stephen Hawking uses the metaphor of design, though he mainly considers the subject from physics, not biology (Stephen Hawking and Leonard Mlodinow, *The Grand Design: New Answers to the Ultimate Questions of Life* [London: Bantam, 2010]). Hawking (Hawking and Mlodinow, *Grand Design*., 172–178), Dawkins (*The Blind Watchmaker*, 43–74), and Ernst Mayr (*Toward a New Philosophy of Biology: Observations of an Evolutionist* [Cambridge, MA: Belknap (of Harvard University Press, 1988], 44–51) all resort to explaining natural selection in terms of a computer program or game. The emphasis in each case is that there is no target held consciously, although Dawkins admits that the goal could be understood as "anything that would improve survival chances" (72). Ruse (*Darwin and Design*, 273–289) makes an excellent case for why the metaphor of design should be retained in biology.

Aristotle's point once again that teleological language is unavoidable, when we talk about life. The best scientific minds cannot seem to help attributing purpose to nature.

This is not to say, however, that all the multiple meanings of "teleological" are apt descriptions of life. Insofar as *telos* is supposed to imply the existence of a plan in some being's consciousness, we have no evidence that this plan exists. When nature "selects" she does so unconsciously, and this so-called selection can be described in purely mechanistic terms.

The fact that natural selection works on past events without conscious purposes is emphasized by Ernst Mayr, a leading evolutionary biologist. In his words, "if teleological means anything it means goal-directed. Yet natural selection," he goes on "is strictly a posteriori which rewards current success but never sets up future goals."[30]

Most processes in nature—the growth of teeth, tusks, and most organs, mating calls and rituals, seed dispersal, nest building, gathering food, escaping from predators, and almost everything living creatures do, in fact—seem inescapably goal directed. Mayr explains the difference between these processes and nonliving ones like erosion, through the former "ow[ing] their goal-directedness to a program."[31] The program is "coded or prearranged information that controls a process (or behaviour) leading it towards a given end."[32] The reason such programs are not "teleological" as Aristotle understood them to be is that the end is the maintenance of the status quo—health and life in an organism—and not a future goal.[33] The program, which is stored in DNA, is material, and it exists before the processes it brings about. Life, then, can be explained in mechanistic terms, and the appropriate word to use for its seeming goal directedness, according to Mayr, is teleonomic and not teleological. [34]

Be that as it may, the main complaint against teleology from the scientific community is that it implies the existence of a conscious designer, of which there is no evidence. Even if one thinks of the Creator as the laws of Nature, rather than a personal god, to say that these laws have a goal, or that teeth and the like have

---

30. Mayr, *Toward a New Philosophy of Biology*, 43.

31. Ibid., 45.

32. Ibid., 49.

33. Ibid., 53. Mayr's focus seems to be on adaptations and homeostasis and not so much on the cyclic processes of reproduction. That the goal is not always the status quo can readily be seen in the development of seeds, embryos, and all the processes of re-production, as distinct from "self-production."

34. There are problems with both parts of Mayr's claim, namely, that the program is material, and that it exists prior to the processes it causes. First, DNA is material, to be sure, but the

purposes, implies a naive pan-animistic and anthropomorphic view that good science rejects. In short, it posits mind and consciousness, desires and intentions, to things that can conclusively be shown not to have them.

The second problem is that of backward causation.[35] How can a goal that lies in the future have an effect on the present, unless it is anticipated by someone and motivates an action? How can the biological fitness that teeth contribute have caused the evolution of teeth in the first place? The future, being open and indeterminate, cannot possibly have an effect upon the present.

A third criticism of teleology questions the progressive tone that some believers adopt.[36] Inbuilt into the discourse about purposes and function is talk about value, and many of the processes of nature can be described as aiming for the same good, flourishing. It is not a great leap of the imagination, then, to assume that there is some Universal Final Good that all things aim for. Teleologists sometimes claim that humans were somehow destined to arrive, or that we are the peak of the evolutionary tree. This "anthropic principle" often reappears in science and is sometimes accompanied by a new faith in (Post-)Humanism.

It is relatively easy to demolish this faith by pointing out that every organism's final end is not perfection, but death, and that most species that ever existed are now extinct.[37] It is quite likely that all forms of life, including *homo sapiens*, will disappear from the earth someday. What then of our great civilizations, cultures, and technological advancement? Nature does not aim at perfection, but could humans attain it, perhaps through a symbiosis with machines? Whether or not

---

program—that is, information—does not seem to be the same thing as its complex structure of nucleic acids. If we use the computer program analogy, the information contained in a set of instructions for a game of chess, say, does not seem to be reducible to silicon and its configuration. Second, the program, in computers and in DNA, exists before any particular instance of it. In computer programming, it exists in the programmer's mind. In any particular strand of DNA, similar programs would seem to exist already in its parents' DNA. Although Mayr is right that "this history is completely irrelevant for the functional analysis of a given teleonomic process" (ibid., 45) this assertion does not erase that history, and we must be allowed to wonder how, and why, the programs came about in the first place.

35. Mayr, *New Philosophy of Biology*, 40. Ruse, following Kant, explains that some natural things seem to be both cause and effect of themselves. The biological fitness that teeth give rise to appears to be the cause of their evolution and development. Ruse compares these to rain clouds, which can also be said to be their own causes, since rain is a cyclical phenomenon. However, we do not say that rain is for replenishing rivers or that the sea's purpose is to produce clouds. Thus, what distinguishes a truly teleological process from a nonteleological one is that the end is something that is *valued* (Ruse, *Darwin and Design*, 258–264).

36. Mayr describes this attitude as a belief in "unidirectional evolutionary sequences" (*New Philosophy of Biology*, 42).

37. Mayr takes this route (ibid., 105–106).

we believe we might, science demands we avoid anthropomorphism and anthropocentrism. Evolution is more akin to an aimless wandering around than a journey with a fixed destination.

What Buddhism Can Add

Buddhism has been presented, from its very introduction to the West, as being more compatible with the scientific outlook than Christianity is.[38] Among the reasons for this view are, first, that it does not affirm the existence of a Creator God[39] and second, that it suggests a precursory notion of evolution.[40] The Buddhist Middle Way approach can also guide us out of the quandaries between the two apparently mutually exclusive alternatives presented above. From the discussion so far, it seems to have two options: we must believe that a conscious Being, separate from ourselves, has made a Divine Plan to bring about our ultimate Good, or else we can believe science and give up looking for purpose in the natural world, which we know came about through chance and mechanistic laws. My claim is that the Buddhist Middle Way between these two extremes, together with a healthy dose of Aristotelian finalism, can restore that prescientific intuition that nature is "for" life; that flourishing is good. We can understand the facts of how we got to be here, how life came to be so marvelously complex; we can

38. David L. McMahan, "Modernity and the Early Discourse of Scientific Buddhism," *Journal of the American Academy of Religion* 72, no. 4 (2004): 897–933.

39. Although there are myriads of god-realms within Buddhist cosmology, rebirth as a god or goddess is impermanent. The gods are like humans, but with extremely long and pleasant lives. One of these gods, the Great Brahma, because he was born first became deluded into thinking that he is the Creator of the Universe (D i 18–19), and he misleads others into believing he is omniscient (D i 222).

When Buddha explicitly rejects the notion of a Creator God, his reasons seem to be based on pragmatic considerations. To believe in a God who created all species and individuals, one must give up the spiritual path, since there is no room left for self-development. (A i 174). Interestingly, Buddha would have concurred with Bacon that it is useless to ask questions about the ultimate origin of the universe, and for the same reason that it does not lead to the improvement of the human condition (e.g., A ii 80). See Thera Nyanaponika, "Buddhism and the God-Idea" (*Access to Insight [Legacy Edition]* 2013, http://www.accesstoinsight.org/lib/authors/nyanaponika/godidea.html), and Asanga Tilakaratne, "Buddhist Non-Theism: Theory and Application" (in *Approaching the Dhamma: Buddhist Texts and Practices in South and South-East Asia,* Anne M. Blackburn and Jeffrey Samuels, eds. [Onalaska, WA: BPS Pariyatti Editions, 2003], 125–149) on how Buddhism reconciles philosophical atheism with the psychological need for a Creator, and on the relation between deep meditative states and godliness.

40. See McMahan, "Modernity and the Early Discourse," for a historical explanation of why these two features are emphasized in contemporary Buddhism.

allow chance its important role, without losing the sense that there is value in nature and a purpose to life, that there is also, in short, a "why" we are here.

The Middle Way

The Buddha's Middle Way[41] is well known as an ethical theory and has obvious comparisons with Aristotle's;[42] less known are the philosophical implications of this teaching. In *Kaccāyanagotta Sutta*, the Buddha explains that there are two extreme philosophical positions, and that these can be reduced to the views that "it is . . ." and that "it is not. . . ." Regarding anything at all, any proposition will take one of these forms, and both are ultimately incorrect.[43] So that, for our examples, both the statements that "there is a Creator God" and that "there isn't a Creator God" are mistaken; similarly, to say that "there is . . ." or that "there isn't purpose in nature" is extreme.

How does this philosophy fit with what was said above? How can the Buddha be atheist if he does not claim that "there isn't a God" and how can he find purpose in life if he does not affirm the existence of something like *telos*? In general, Mahayana Buddhism distinguishes between two levels of reality; on the one hand, there is conventional truth,[44] which includes all possible true statements about the existence of this or that, and indeed any truth we could ever hope to express conceptually. On the other hand, there is ultimate truth,[45] which is beyond all words and definition, but which can yet be known.[46] The recognition of two

---

41. Buddhism is a vast and far from homogenous phenomenon, and to talk of it as a single thing, as I attempt to do here, is misleading. My discussion is mostly rooted in the Indian Mādhyamika and Yogācāra schools of Mahayana Buddhism, which trace their roots to the Pali canon, and especially the *Kaccāyanagotta Sutta*.

42. Besides both being teleological (although in different ways), Aristotelian and Buddhist Ethics broadly coincide in placing virtue in between two extremes. See Nicholas F. Gier, *The Virtue of Nonviolence: From Gautama to Gandhi* (Albany: State University of New York Press, 2004), 73–76; Peter Harvey, *An Introduction to Buddhist Ethics* (Cambridge: Cambridge University Press, 2000), 50.

43. S ii 17.

44. P. *sammuti sacca*; Sk. *saṃvṛti satya*.

45. P. *pāramārtha sacca*; Sk. *pāramārtha satya*.

46. This is the standard Mahayana interpretation, as found in the Mādhyamika and Yogācāra schools. The Pali canon and early exegeses merely distinguish between those sayings of the Buddha that require interpretation, and those that were definitive; thus, early Buddhism did not rule out the possibility of communicating truth directly (David J. Kalupahana, *Mūlamadhyamakakārikā of Nāgārjuna: The Philosophy of the Middle Way* [Delhi: Motilal Banarsidass, 2004], 16–17; see K.N. Jayatilleke, *Early Buddhist Theory of Knowledge* [Delhi: Motilal Banarsidass, 1998], 361–368 for further discussion).

truths is fundamental to the Middle Way, and to experience ultimate truth an important step on the journey to nirvana.[47]

When the Buddha describes the Middle Way as the avoidance of affirmation and negation, what he is claiming is that nothing can be said that is ultimately true. If we apply this assertion to teleological thinking, the propositions that affirm the existence of a Creator or of purpose in nature, as well as those that negate their existence, can be only conventionally true, if true at all. That there is a Creator God is neither ultimately nor conventionally true, according to Buddhism. That there is purpose in nature can be maintained conventionally, together with all the other true propositions we might make, including those of science, mathematics, and philosophy. Still, of all these claims, none are ultimately true. The Middle Way reveals nothing that is eternal, independent, or unchanging, or whose essence can be captured once and for all by a definition. The first extreme avoided by the Middle Way is the belief in substances that exist independently with fixed essential properties. We see this extreme in the belief in God, and the soul, but also sometimes in the idea of a self, such as in Descartes's thinking substance, as well as in atomistic ideas about matter.

The Antidote to Eternalism

The Buddhist reply to eternalist philosophy—which asserts an eternal God, soul, or universal—is to analyze this alleged substance into its various parts, all of which are found to be impermanent, stressful, and subject to change.[48] In Mahayana Buddhism, all things are said to be "empty" or "without inherent existence,"[49] although this belief is recognized as only an approximation to ultimate truth. In the canonical texts, the most common starting point is the self, [50] also known as

---

Famously, though, the Buddha refused to answer several questions; he would not affirm that the universe was created, or that it was eternal, and he refused to comment on whether an enlightened being survives death (e.g., M i 483-489). The reasons for this refusal appear to be merely pragmatic; such speculation does not help solve the problem of suffering, stress, and dissatisfaction, in general dis-ease (P. *dukkha*; Sk. *duḥkha*. E.g., D i 191–192), which is the Buddha's primary concern (see n84).

The *Kaccāyanagotta* eventually became the basis for the Mahayana approach that distinguishes two levels of truth, and the eventual conclusion in the *Vimalakīrti Sutra* (*c.* 100 C.E.) or Nāgārjuna's *Mūlamadhyamakakārikā* (*c.* 150–250 C.E.), that the truth about these matters is inexpressible (see Kalupahana, *Mūlamadhyamakakārikā of Nāgārjuna*, 5–8).

47. MMK 14:9–10

48. S iii 67–68.

49. S. *śūnya; niḥsvabhāva*. See the *Prajñāpāramitā* sutras.

50. P. *atta*; Sk. *Ātman*.

the "mind or soul," or as Descartes referred to it, the thinking substance.[51] The discussions center on whether this concept is the same, or different from, one's body, one's thoughts, perceptions, feelings, and so on.

In more recent times, the view that Buddhism challenges has been described as the "pearl view of self," the belief in an essential "me-ness," underlying the various incidental aspects of who we are.[52] The Buddha taught that when we analyze our being into its parts—the traditionally listed "five aggregates":[53] material "atoms,"[54] and momentary feelings, impulses, thoughts and so forth[55]—we find nothing substantial that remains unchanged throughout the physiological and psychological processes of our life. In fact, whatever we analyze, whether nature, humans, or gods, everything we find turns out to be transient and unsubstantial. Material atoms and moments of consciousness arise, exist for a while, and then perish.[56] There is nothing that can be grasped as the self, or that can be pointed to as the "thing-in-itself" and our prying away at the various skins which cloak our impressions of the world reveals no ultimate reality.

I do not rehearse the Buddhist arguments against a Creator here, since scientism seems to have rendered this task superfluous.[57] Instead, I explore how such an analysis can reveal the inadequacies of an eternalist interpretation of "purpose

---

51. In the Latin text, Descartes refers to this thinking substance, the "I," as "mens, sive animus, sive intellectus, sive ratio"—the mind, or soul, or intellect, or reason. (*Meditations* II:6; Cottingham, *Descartes's Meditations*, 18).

52. Julian Baggini, *The Ego Trick* (London: Granta, 2011), 7.

53. P. *khanda;* Sk. *skhanda*. These are (1) "form" or corporeality (P., Sk. *rūpa*); (2) sensation or feeling (pleasant, unpleasant, or neutral) (P., Sk. *vedanā*); (3) perception, apperception, and cognition (P. *saññā*; Sk. *saṃjñā*); (4) "mental formations," including instincts, impulses, and volition (P. *saṅkhāra;* Sk. *saṃskāra*); and (5) (states of) consciousness (P. *viññāṇa*; Sk. *vijñāna*). Consciousness can be understood as a type of sixth sense to which mental events appear, or else as a sort of base for the other mental aggregates, and responsible for the ego's sense of continuity. This list need not be taken as definitive, and the point being made here is simply that the experience of selfhood can be analyzed into a multitude of highly diverse phenomena.

54. P., Sk. *kalapa*. These are atoms of fire, water, earth, or air, whose essential properties are heat, fluidity, solidity, and movement, respectively.

55. The project of analyzing the aggregates further into different types of phenomena was taken up by the Abhidharma School of early Buddhism, which enumerates the different types of feelings, perceptions, and so on.

56. Early-20th-century physicists already knew that particles are not solid and do not behave in predictable ways. Today physicists speak of "virtual particles" that "pop in and out of existence" and combine with other types of particles. See Gordon Kane, "Ask the Experts: Do Virtual Particles Really Exist?," *Scientific American* 296, no. 3 (2007): 104.

57. But see n39.

in nature." From the earliest conception of such a notion, philosophers have been acutely aware of how difficult it is to define goodness in a way that captures its every sense. What do a good person, a good tree, and a good pizza have in common? How can the good of humans and that of the HIV virus be reconciled in one Universal Final Good? When we look for the essence of goodness, when we try to capture what it means to flourish, in a way that includes the flourishing of all beings, we find such an abstract notion that, as Bacon rightly pointed out, it may not be very helpful in practical terms.

Darwinism shows that at the most general level, natural goodness involves biological and reproductive *fitness;* however, what this means, other than the circular definition of doing well, is hard to define. If we try to be specific about fitness, we find such resourcefulness in life, and so many different strategies for flourishing that its various forms adopt, that very little can be said that will be true for all kinds.[58] Furthermore, reproductive fitness has its limits as a defining good, since population limitations relative to an ecosystem's carrying capacity also come into play. Teeth probably evolved originally to aid feeding, yet they can also be used to warn off potential aggressors, to bite oneself in frustration, to impress a potential mate, or to open a bottle. Some form of proto-tooth was used for

---

58. Stricter Darwinists define fitness as the ability of a genotype or phenotype to contribute to the gene pool; however, mathematically, absolute fitness is defined in relation to a constant population. This relation recognizes the intuition that mere reproductive success is not absolutely good; a growing population that "eats itself out of house and home" and "fouls its own nest" will not flourish for very long.

This concept has led some evolutionary theorists to look for value at higher levels: the flourishing of a population, a species, an ecosystem, or the ecosphere. Just as the self cannot be found in Buddhism, all of these natural aggregates cannot be fixed by a scientific definition. Given that all species evolved from a single source through an unbroken line of reproduction, Mayr's scientific definition through reproductive isolation cannot capture any true essence of species-hood, as it cannot distinguish between species over time. Ecosystems are also known to be fluctuating, somewhat unpredictable, open systems, and the planet, it is now known, has changed drastically since life began on it.

If we start from a more general concept of fitness or flourishing as the good, then we can attribute negative value to relative lack and absolute disappearance of fitness, and whatever causes these. The death and extinction of individuals, species, and ecosystems are not evil in this absolute sense, if new lives and new forms of life can yet arise. Thus, if an updated more scientific version of Aristotle's Final Good were to be proposed, this might be something like "evolvability." The relativity of this good must be emphasized; evolvability is not necessarily good for the members of a species, yet, it does not exist without individuals. A Buddhist would emphasize that evolvability is empty, too, or rather that it is not nonempty. See Colette Sciberras, "Buddhist Philosophy and the Ideals of Environmentalism" (PhD diss., Durham University, UK, 2010) https://www.dur.ac.uk/resources/philosophy/doctoraltheses/colette_BuddhistPhilosophyandtheIdealsofEnvironmentalism.pdf. (Unfamiliar with the scientific term, I referred to evolvability as the Buddhist-inspired "pliancy" in this dissertation.)

different purposes as it evolved into a canine or a tusk. Purpose in nature, then, cannot be defined once and for all except in very general terms as flourishing.

It is nonsense, however, to conclude from this supposition that there is no biological fitness at all or that for a human, for instance, having a well-formed set of teeth is not better than having none at all. Simply because we cannot capture universal goodness with a definition does not mean we cannot recognize what is relatively good. A Buddhist might argue that in the same way as we can distinguish ourselves from others, even though we cannot define the "self," we can distinguish biologically better or worse lives, though we may not be able to define the essence of goodness. Just like the multitude of impressions through which we recognize "selves" and "others," the purposes and functions that give us our idea of "goodness" in nature are transient.

The Middle Way avoids claiming that gods, selves, purposes, and goodness do not exist at all.[59] They do not exist in the way that eternalists believe, as immutable essences, or independent and self-sufficient substances, but they do exist, conventionally. Is the purpose we see in nature just "in our minds," then, an illusory experience of something that ultimately does not exist, in the same way that our mind tricks us into thinking that we have a self, and, very often, even a soul?[60] Buddhism would suggest so.

Yet, final causation is not the only cause under question: in the 2nd century C.E., the Indian Madhyamaka philosopher Nāgārjuna argued that efficient causation is empty, too, and cannot be explained on the eternalist view. We cannot nonarbitrarily draw a line between what exists now, the effect, and the past cause that no longer exists. We either end up destroying the relation—for if a seed and a flower are separate substances, one could never give rise to the other—or else we lose the distinction—for if they are the same in substance, then nothing new has come about.[61]

In the 18th century, David Hume was also concerned about causation, and that although we are able to observe a regular conjunction between certain events, we cannot explain the connection between them. The mind, Hume says, is "carried by habit" to superimpose an idea of cause and effect.[62] Immanuel Kant could improve this solution only by arguing that causation, like space and time, is one of

---

59. See *Water-Snake Sutta*, M I 130–142.

60. Baggini, *The Ego Trick*. See also Malcolm Owen Slavin and Daniel Kriegman, *The Adaptive Design of the Human Psyche: Psychoanalysis, Evolutionary Biology, and the Therapeutic Process* (New York: Guildford, 1992) for an adaptationist account of the construction of self.

61. MMK I.

62. David Hume, *Enquiries Concerning Human Understanding*, Tom L. Beauchamp, ed. (Oxford: Oxford University Press, 2006 [1748]), 59.

the innate categories that humans use to make sense of the world, an a priori mental precondition of all possible experience. Happily this process restores the sense of necessity that we feel must belong to cause and effect relations.[63] The implication, though, is still that causation is "in the mind" and not necessarily "out there," in the world we observe. [64]

Despite these well-known difficulties, scientists and lay people accept efficient causation universally and make very successful use of the notion. There should be no surprise, then, that final causation is a bit mysterious, too, and seemingly "all in the mind." The difference between our experiences of efficient and of final causality seems to rest on the fact that because we have memories and records of past events, but only anticipations of possible future ones, the future strikes us as less real. It is hard to see how final causes, which do not exist yet, could affect anything, say, how the future well-being of an animal could have caused the first teeth to evolve. On the other hand, when we plant seeds in the spring and see flowers the following summer, we feel more secure in the knowledge that the seed caused the flower.

Given time, flowers turn back into seeds. This is the very meaning of reproduction, a fundamental function of life. In biology, then, as naturalists since Aristotle have pointed out, we do observe final causation at work, and we experience the chain of causation in its entirety. We see future "goals" and final causes, such as flowers, in their present "effects," the seeds, which we watch reproducing flowers, over and over. To the extent that we observe cyclic processes in nature,[65]

---

63. Immanuel Kant, *Prolegomena to Any Future Metaphysics and the Letter to Marcus Herz*, 2nd ed., James W. Ellington, trans. (Indianapolis, IN: Hackett, 1977 [1772]), 49–51.

64. In fact, evolutionary and cognitive scientists have identified an " agency detection device," which is often hypersensitive, and explains the propensity of humans to attribute the presence of an agent where there is none. This type of behavior would have been selected for in our ancestors because those who erred on the side of caution could survive to contribute to the gene pool. The device explains only a small subset of our beliefs about causation; thus, the epistemological implications of this finding are hardly as vast as the claims of Hume or Kant. The "device" has been put forward as an explanation for religious belief (Justin L. Barrett, *Why Would Anyone Believe in God?* [Lanham, MD: Alta Mira, 2004]), 31, and all supernatural belief (Bertolotti Tommaso and Lorenzo Magnini, "The Role of Agency Detection in the Invention of Supernatural Beings: An Abductive Approach," in *Model-Based Reasoning in Science and Technology: Abduction, Logic and Computational Discovery*, Lorenzo Magnini, Walter Carnielli and Claudio Pizzi, eds. [Berlin: Springer-Verlag, 2010]), 238, and for the experience of a felt presence during sleep paralysis (J. Allan Cheyne and Todd A. Girard, "The Natures and Varieties of Felt-Presence Experience: A Reply to Nielson," *Consciousness and Cognition* 16 [2007]: 984–991). Scientism emphasizes the negation involved in this psychological fact—that these things are all in the mind and do not really exist. The Buddhist, as explained below, can more or less concur with this position, while recognizing the relative value of perceiving agency as though it existed independently of us.

65. Paradoxically, perhaps the reluctance of scientism to accept final causation springs from a remnant of Christian belief, in that it presumes a linear view of time (see n5).

our knowledge of final causes seems as secure as that of efficient causation. If we recognize adaptations that today increase fitness, we can see the *telos* of past instances of natural selection. Just as with efficient causation, we cannot explain this except through consistent association and experience. Even if the first tooth-like structure just "happened to" increase fitness; we cannot help experiencing teeth as though they had evolved for that very reason. We say, in fact, that they were "selected" for that reason.

It is not necessary to know how causation works, whether from the past or from the future, if we want to limit ourselves to practical purposes. Bacon was right to question the utility of speculating about ultimate causes, yet he was wrong to throw out all final ones as a result. To insist that matter makes up the whole of our reality is woefully partial, and to accept the truth of propositions about efficient causes, but not final ones, when it is so difficult to explain how causation works at all, is biased.

In recap, Buddhism seems to be saying that there is no God, no self or soul, and nothing specific that is good in and of itself. Everything is empty of inherent existence, and all our experiences of cause and effect are in the mind. Although controversial, it has often been claimed that contemporary science resonates with these Buddhist doctrines.[66] The position that all purpose and goodness is just in our minds might seem rather depressing, and an immediate question that arises is why do Buddhists spend so many years in meditation, and why do they make a virtue of generosity, say, if they believe in no God, and no eternal soul? Absent a belief in final causes, both Buddhism and scientism are vulnerable to the charge of nihilism.

The Problem of Nihilism

If we subtract the benevolent Creator from our universe, forget about finding an Ultimate Good, and understand that the flourishing of every being without exception requires the death of many others, it seems there is little left to say about how the world should be, except for how we want it to be. If the human species arose due to chance and mechanistic laws, and if there is only death and extinction at the end, then it seems we are free to do with the

---

66. E.g., Vic Mansfield, *Tibetan Buddhism and Modern Physics: Towards a Unity of Love and Knowledge* (West Conshohocken, PA: Templeton Foundation Press, 2008); B. Alan Wallace, *Hidden Dimensions: The Unification of Physics and Consciousness* (New York: Columbia University Press, 2010). The latest "theory of everything," which includes string theory, suggests that our reality is a "hologram" or "just one big projection" (Ron Cowen, "Simulations Back Up Theory That Universe Is a Hologram," *Nature News* [2013] http://www.nature.com/news/simulations-back-up-theory-that-universe-is-a-hologram-1.14328#/b1).

other inhabitants of this planet exactly what we please. Protection of nature and of life—and ethics in general—begin to appear somewhat misguided unless undertaken specifically for the good of the individual, community, or species, whether we pursue economic, psychological, social, ecological or other goods.

Richard Dawkins suggests that the only purpose in the universe that we know of results from our own human intention, and, like Bacon, he emphasizes the potential of science to further improve human lives.[67] However, the value of human life and purposes may also be questioned, and the less optimistic will emphasize that humanity will most likely end in extinction. A position that finds no value anywhere at all is typically called nihilism and is condemned as too negative and arbitrary to hold traction with everyday people, who generally prefer to seek meaning and purpose in their lives and in the universe.

A nihilist might argue that this preference is nothing but wishful thinking and will conclude that there is nothing worth valuing and no purpose to nature, save that, perhaps, of serving human interests.[68] What other good could one rationally desire?

The Antidote to Nihilism

Rather than arguing against nihilism philosophically, Buddhism points to evidence against it. This evidence must be perceived for oneself, as it is an inner experience. The cure for this extreme way of thinking is found in the realization of the Middle Way; the perception of emptiness[69] that leads eventually to the "Deathless."[70]

The purpose of Buddhist practice, that is to say, is to see for ourselves that what we took to be ultimate truth is actually conventional truth. The very *experience* of this insubstantiality, described as "consciousness without feature, without end, luminous all around,"[71] is itself what guards against the conclusions that nihilists draw from the fact of insubstantiality. Overcoming nihilism

---

67. In *The God Delusion*, he compares science's quest to widening the slit on the "burka" of human ignorance ([London: Transworld, 2006] 362–374). Please note the anti-religious rhetoric in this choice of metaphor.

68. Strictly speaking, a nihilist does not value human life, either. Here I use "nihilist" in a loose sense to refer to someone who tends to deny value and purpose, and not in the strict sense of someone who believes there is absolutely none.

69. Sk. *Śūnyatā*.

70. *Sañña Sutta*. A iv 46–53. Bhikku Thanissaro, trans., *Access to Insight*.

71. *Kevaddha Sutta*. D i 223, Thanissaro, trans., *Access to Insight*.

requires more than a conceptual grasp of emptiness; *seeing* emptiness, that is, perceiving the conventionality of what we took to be real, is what provides motivation for the Buddhist. Rather than reaching depressing, dead-end conclusions from thinking about the emptiness of life, once he or she has entered the "path of seeing,"[72] a Buddhist makes perception of emptiness, a glimpse of nirvana, his or her purpose in life.

Despite the teachings on nirvana, Buddhism was interpreted as nihilistic even during the Buddha's own times and, centuries later, the Yogācāra School had to emphasize once more the experiential aspect of emptiness. The antidote to nihilism is notoriously hard to present philosophically, since it does not employ analyses and reductions, like the Mādhyamika, but makes a claim about an inner experience, and in fact, the schools associated with this approach focus on meditation and the mind.[73] The method to overcome nihilism is a scientific one—observation—yet this observation is of an event within one's mind. The issues of whether or not it can be confirmed by others, and how much specialized training is required in order to be able to witness the "facts" of meditation, are clearly comparable to the same questions posed of science.

Throughout the ages, contemplatives have told us about their experiences of time in meditation. As Augustine of Hippo wrote, the past moment, though we remember it, does not exist anymore and the next one we anticipate does not exist yet.[74] This fact is what makes even efficient causation so hard to explain. Yet, meditators report that when one looks directly at the mind, one has a sense of an "eternal moment" or being "out of time,"[75] when the distinction between past, present, and future fades.

Similarly, the duality between subject and object falls away.[76] Our ordinary experience is usually subjective and the object-in-itself forever elusive. To study an object scientifically we must suppress our subjective impressions. In meditation, the duality—subject and object as separate things—is not found; yet this

---

72. *Darśanamārga*.

73. The various names of these schools are: *cittamātra* (lit. "The Totality of Mind" or "Mind-Only"), *vijñānavāda* (lit. "Consciousness Doctrine"), and *yogācāra* (lit. "The Practise of Yoga"). It must be noted that the ancient meaning of "yoga" comprises all forms of meditation, and not just physical asanas.

74. Augustine, *Confessions,* Henry Chadwick, trans. (Oxford: Oxford University Press, 1992 [*c.* 400]), 231, §XI.

75. Daniel Goleman, "Meditation as Meta-therapy: Hypotheses towards a Proposed Fifth State of Consciousness," *Journal of Transpersonal Psychology* 3, no. 1 (1971): 16.

76. Zoran Josipovic, "Duality and Nonduality in Meditation Research," *Consciousness and Cognition* 19 (2010): 1120.

experience is often described as finding the "True Self," or "God."[77] In fact, the eternalist tone of the antidote to nihilism can be seen in the *Nibbana Sutta,* in which the Buddha affirms that

> [t]here is, monks, an unborn, unbecome, unmade, unfabricated. If there were not that unborn, unbecome, unmade, unfabricated, there would not be the case that escape from [samsara] is discerned.[78]

How are we to understand unconditioned nirvana and its relation to the samsaric world of cause and effect? For Buddhists, nirvana plays a similar role to that of *telos* in Aristotle. Yet the Middle Path avoids describing this Final Good, emphasizing instead the pervasiveness of change and thus avoiding the problems of eternalism, with its emphasis on an unchanging, immortal Good. Although the passage above seems to assert an eternal truth, such instances are rare in the Buddhist canon, and indeed the vast majority of texts are dedicated to explaining impermanence, no-self, suffering, and emptiness.

We have seen how this approach answers some of the complaints scientists make against teleology. Although Buddhist philosophy recognizes something like *telos*, this is an internal purpose that does not imply the existence of a Creator. Moreover, there is no suggestion that the goal of nirvana is in any way preordained; rather, there is recognition of suffering and ever-present change. We saw that Buddhist and Western philosophy both have difficulty accounting for causation in general, whether from the past or from the future, and that there seems to be no valid reason for accepting efficient causes but not final ones. One problem remains, however: that of pan-psychism, the idea that nature itself is conscious.

We might accept final causes as well as efficient ones, on the grounds that both stem from the mind. Efficient causes are often material: they can be measured and seem more real. Final ones seem more mental, in the sense that we know them primarily from our own purposes and intentions, and recognize something similar in nature. This concept might suggest to some that nature is conscious. If the purpose of bees is to pollinate flowers (among other things), and that of seeds to produce flowers, do bees and seeds thus know of their purposes? Does nature know that she selects and designs? Do beings have to be conscious of the fact, for us to say that flourishing is their purpose?

Clearly not, and in fact, Yogācāra philosophy does not suggest that the entirety of nature is conscious, as the Stoics did in their development of Aristotle. This question

77. In Buddhism, this is the "abode of Brahma" (P., Sk. *Brahma-vihāra*).

78. Ud 80., Thanissaro, trans., insert added, *Access to Insight.*

of consciousness arose in the Chinese and Japanese debate about whether blades of grass and particles of dust could attain enlightenment, too.[79] In meditation, the grass or dust is not found as something separate from one's experience of them. The not-finding is a step toward the goal of the Middle Way, since in the dissolution of subject-object duality, one experiences oneself as a timeless and expansive being, that resembles the God or soul of eternalism. One identifies with the totality of existence, and there is no enlightenment that does not include grass and dust.

To have such an experience is part of the Buddhist *telos*; however, practitioners are constantly reminded to avoid eternalism, with the emphasis always remaining upon change.[80] Thus, one avoids fixating on the experience as a revelation of something ultimate. The meditator, the blades of grass, and the particles of dust do not "attain nirvana," but neither do they "not attain it."[81] Conventionally we can assert the existence of ephemeral experiences that feel like a universal and timeless presence, and in which grass and dust are included. We cannot assert, however, that grass and dust have mind and experiences like ours. We can accept that conscious experience is unlikely without some kind of nervous system and brain.

We can also acknowledge—and here the ethical implications for our treatment of other animals are enormous—that any being with a physiological makeup similar to ours probably has similar experiences. Contra Descartes, who suggested that all forms of nonhuman life were merely mechanical,[82] if an elephant bleeds, we can be reasonably sure it feels pain. If she appears to lament the loss of a calf, it is probably because she feels emotion. Mahayana Buddhism emphasizes the inseparability of emptiness and compassion.[83] Through experiencing the

---

79. See William LaFleur, "Saigyō and the Buddhist Value of Nature Part I," *History of Religions* 13, no. 2 (1973): 93–128.

80. E.g., M i 350–353.

81. Buddhist logic can be both liberating and frustrating. Westerners familiar with Aristotle's Laws of the Excluded Middle and Non-Contradiction will find it impossible to accept both these negations; necessarily, grass either does or does not attain enlightenment, it would seem. Indian commentaries generally distinguish between two forms of negation; the negation that implies the "contrary" (Sk. *paryudāsa*) and "non-affirming negation" (Sk. *prasajya*) Sometimes, when I negate a property of a thing, e.g., "the tea isn't hot," I imply the contrary, e.g., "the tea is lukewarm or cold." A classic example of a non-affirming negation is "the present King of France is not bald." Here, what is negated is the very existence of a present King of France who could have any property at all. In a similar way, the negations of the Buddhist tetralemma (*catuṣkoṭi*) have generally been read as illocutionary negations; they do not deny the content but the eternalist presuppositions of a statement (Jan Westerhoff, *Nāgārjuna's Madhyamaka. A Philosophical Introduction* [Oxford: Oxford University Press, 2009]).

82. See n25.

83. In the Pali canon, love (P. *mettā*; Sk. *maitrī*) and compassion (P., Sk. *karuṇā*) are important virtues, cultivated on the path to wisdom (P. *paññā*; Sk. *prajñā*) and nirvana (e.g., M i

insubstantiality of the self and world, a natural feeling of compassion arises for all beings. As Aristotle and Buddha both knew, most creatures, sadly, do not fulfill their purposes, and many suffer greatly during their lives. The Buddha's teachings, in fact, are aimed at fixing this problem.[84] Understanding of emptiness leads not to nihilism, then, but to compassionate action.

Buddhism and Environmental Ethics

It seems we have taken a rather long way round to establish the obvious—that flourishing is good. Making this point must be attempted in a volume like this because unless we want to reduce environmental ethics to mere egoism or anthropocentrism,[85] we will need a description of natural goodness, of some value that is independent of human interests and purposes. If we can be reasonably certain that flourishing in general is good, and that the flourishing of organisms is *their* good, we can begin to ask whether other natural things, say, organs or ecosystems, can be said to be healthy or flourishing. What do we do when interests conflict? Is there any reason to give more weight to human flourishing?

351–353). The Mahayana differs in identifying compassion with wisdom, in the *bodhisattva* ideal (Christmas Humphreys, *The Wisdom of Buddhism* [London: Curzon, 1990], 107, 162).

84. The most fundamental of Buddhist teachings are the "Four Noble Truths;" in brief, there is *dukkha*, dis-ease; there is a cause for this dis-ease; a way out of it; and an end to all suffering, stress, and unsatisfactoriness in nirvana. The Buddha often professes to have taught only this and likens himself to a doctor with a cure for *dukkha* (Bhikkhu Thanissaro, "The Four Noble Truths: A Study Guide," *Access to Insight* [1999], http://www.accesstoinsight.org/lib/study/truths.html).

Can nirvana be likened to biological flourishing? There are several passages in the Pali canon that indicate otherwise (e.g., M i 501–510; S iv 207; SN 758); yet, the Buddhist *telos* is not altogether divorced from natural flourishing. This closeness emerges from the story of the Buddha's fifty years of life after enlightenment, during which he continued to teach and to thrive. The Pali canon distinguishes between nirvana "in life" (P. *sa-upādisesa-nibbāna*; Sk. *sopadhiśeṣa-nirvāṇa*. lit. "nirvana with remainder") and the Buddha's final "parinirvana" (P. *an-upādisesa-nibbāna*; Sk. *nir-upadhiśeṣa-nirvāṇa*, lit. "nirvana without remainder").

In short, nirvana can be approached in life through the virtues, and for lay people, at least, these bring benefits that are analogous with those of Aristotle's *eudaimonia* (D ii 85–86; D i 60–73).

85. Environmental philosophers have generally tried to establish that nature is valuable for its own sake and not just for the services it renders us (e.g., Richard Routley, "Is There a Need for a New, Environmental Ethic?" *Proceedings of the XVth World Congress of Philosophy*, vol. 1 [Varna, Bulgaria: Sophia Press, 1973], 205–210), but perhaps we could accomplish our environmental purposes if we only recognized our dependence upon the planet, and we do not need to value it morally or spiritually. Katie McShane ("Anthropocentrism vs. Nonanthropocentrism: Why Should We Care?" *Environmental Values* 16, no. 2 [2007]: 169–186) argues, on the contrary, that we need a non-anthropocentric approach in order to account for the *felt* aspect of ethical human-nature relations.

Aristotle recognized goodness in nature, yet his anthropocentric concept of a *scala naturae*,[86] which Christianity adopted, led followers to think of all nonhuman creatures as tools at the service of humankind. One of the positive outcomes of science and of Darwinism in particular is that humans have been definitively knocked off this self-exalted state. We are only now, perhaps, beginning to recognize our affinity with the other products of natural selection.

Buddhism has a less anthropocentric world view[87] and is explicit about the flourishing of nonhumans. The *Cullavagga,* part of the *Vinaya* rules included within the earliest canon, recommends the following attitude:

> For those without feet, I have love.
> I have love for all with two feet.
> For those with four feet, I have love.
> I have love for all with many feet.[88]

Love, *mettā,* is defined in an eponymous sutta as the wish that

> In gladness and in safety,
> May all beings be at ease.
> Whatever living beings there may be;
> Weak or strong, omitting none,
> The great, the mighty, medium, short or small,
> The seen and the unseen,
> Those living near and far away,
> Those born and to-be-born—
> May all beings be at ease![89]

The last phrase, usually, "may all beings be happy" is a common Buddhist refrain, and the term *sukha* (happy) has analogies with Aristotle's sense of performing

---

86. Lit. the "ladder of nature," also translated as the "Great Chain of Being," the concept posits a value hierarchy over natural beings in terms of their complexity, so that the lower rungs contain inanimate objects, above which lie, progressively, fungi, grass, and vegetation, fish, birds, mammals, humans, and gods at the very top. This model of nature conveys a belief that among the purposes of lower forms of life was the contribution they made, e.g., as food, toward those of the higher beings.

87. For further discussion of this claim, see Colette Sciberras, "Animals in Buddhism: In Defence of Hierarchical Evaluation," in *Being for the Other: Issues in Ethics and Animal Rights,* Manish Vyas, ed. (Delhi: Daya, 2011), 223–236.

88. Cv 5.6. Andrew Olendzki, trans., *Access to Insight.*

89. SN 143–152. Amravati Sangha, trans., *Access to Insight.*

one's typical activities well.[90] Buddhism, then, seeks to promote flourishing universally, and its ecological credentials have been widely discussed.[91] As well as sharing Aristotle's sense of purpose and value, it shares in science's project to remove unverified metaphysical postulates,[92] although it appeals to a wider notion of what is observable.

What would a Buddhist attitude toward nonhuman nature be? Knowing that our own teeth and organs do us good, we can infer the same of other animals. If we recognize the inner purposes of elephants, poaching for tusks becomes inexcusable, as does all human abuse of other organisms for food and other products. This belief is especially true if we can recognize their suffering. If all organisms have an internal purpose, respect for their flourishing is a fundamental duty.

Buddhism appreciates diversity. The above distinction based on number of feet can include all of life, if "those with none" is construed to include plants, fungi, and simpler organisms. All of these various forms of life have their own purposes, yet in general, we can say that seeds give rise to new life. Perhaps even higher-order natural systems—grasslands or forests, human and nonhuman communities, right up to the planet itself—might be construed as having inbuilt purposes and the potential to flourish. Disrupting these natural processes and replacing them with our multifarious methods of artificial insemination becomes an offense, in this light. A Buddhist could applaud Bolivia and Ecuador's recent establishing of the "Rights of Nature."[93]

A Buddhist might appreciate the value of seeing the earth as alive,[94] without fixating on the truth of the claim. Clearly the earth does not perform all the functions recognizable in life.[95] Yet the precise set of these which we choose to

90. A ii 69; A iv 281.

91. For an introduction to the issues, see Leslie E. Sponsel and Puranee Natadecha-Sponsel, "Environment and Nature in Buddhism," in *Encyclopaedia of the History of Science, Technology, and Medicine in Non-Western Cultures,* Helain Selin, ed. (Dordrecht: Springer, 2014), 1–15.

92. A i 188–189.

93. Ecuador included the Rights of Nature in its new constitution in 2008, which claims that nature has the right to exist, to persist, and to maintain its vital cycles, its structure, its functions, and its processes in evolution, and that all citizens can demand these rights. Bolivia followed suit in 2009. See Global Alliance for the Rights of Nature, http://therightsofnature.org/.

94. James Lovelock has argued that the planet can be understood as being "alive" in the limited sense of being homeostasic, i.e., that "it is a self-organizing system characterised by an actively sustained low entropy" (James Lovelock, *The Ages of Gaia: A Biography of Our Living Earth,* new ed. [Reading, UK: Oxford University Press, 1995], 27).

95. There is no universally accepted definition of life, save for, perhaps, the definition in terms of functions that biology students learn. According to Mackean and Hayward, life is characterized by possession of all or some of the following processes: growth, motion,

call "life"[96] is hardly as interesting as the very fact that there is function and purpose in life, remarked upon by the very first thinkers. Nature's parts seem to fit one another like clockwork, if we use an old metaphor, and clocks, as we know, have a purpose.

A Buddhist ethic based upon scientific knowledge could preserve for "Nature" and for "Mind" that sense of awe, respect, and moral obligation that, in the West, has traditionally been reserved for the Clockmaker God. Since the Enlightenment, we have transferred such sentiments onto the human species and person. Now that we know more about how the universe, planet, and life came about, perhaps we might recognize a value independent of ourselves in that which truly "created" us, a nature that, billions of years before we arrived, had "life," "mind," and "soul," in the classical sense.

---

reproduction, sensitivity, respiration, nutrition, and excretion (D.G. Mackean and Dave Hayward, *IGCSE Biology*, 3rd ed. [London: Hodder Education, 2014], 1). The earth is clearly not alive in this sense.

96. Not all of the functions listed in n93 are performed by each form of life. Viruses, for example, are a borderline case, and therefore it is often claimed that reproduction, variation, and evolution constitute the minimal definition of life (E. N. Trifonov, "Vocabulary of Definitions of Life Suggests a Definition," *Journal of Biomolecular Structural Dynamics* 29, no. 2 [Oct. 2011]: 259). Still, this definition then does not exclude computer programs from being considered alive (David Moreira and Purificatión López-Garcia, "Ten Reasons to Exclude Viruses from the Tree of Life," *Nature Reviews Microbiology* 7 [April 2009]: 306).

2 EATING

GLIMPSING GOD'S INFINITE GOODNESS

Nelson Reveley

"There's something about this healing space we've created," she says of her field. This is what the farm life is all about. "Life is valued . . . and made to thrive—humans and plants and insects."

She pauses.

"Well, except for the bugs that eat the vegetables."[1]

Introduction

From a Christian perspective, existence is good because God formed and declared it as such. This created goodness is manifest utmost in the flourishing of life, teeming across the land, sea, and sky, and in the intricate number of ways that living beings mutually benefit one another. Yet, despite the vibrant mutuality among many creatures, life on earth also depends inextricably and intimately upon death. In order to thrive, plants need the fertilizing remains of dead organisms, and animate creatures need the nourishing flesh of other living beings, be they similarly animate or vegetative. Furthermore, although creatures gain life through ingesting the nutrients of other beings—and not through the death or pain of the devoured—being hunted, eaten, pinned in, bereaved, and wounded entails untold suffering that pervades ecologies across the globe. Life being necessarily rooted in death, with its attendant suffering, seems a rampant scandal for a "good" creation.

Christians have dealt with this raw wound of existence in a variety of ways. Some have claimed the horrors of sentient eater-and-eaten reflect the fallen state of creation at present, and so are not part of the

---

1. Gail Taylor, head of Three Part Harmony Farm in Washington, DC, quoted in Lavanya Ramanathan, "That Empty Patch of Grass? That Could Be the District's Next Farm," *Washington Post*, September 4, 2015.

goodness of creation. Alternatively, some have maintained that humans, particularly our souls, are the sole beings worthy of concern because they alone bear God's image. Others have simply embraced predation as part of a cruciform, sacrificial structure that God gave to creation. These respective views all harbor significant shortcomings. For instance, given the deep scientific consensus that life on earth enormously predates humanity, it is unclear how human sin could have caused predation. And given the scriptural affirmations that God made the world "very good" and is in the business of bodily resurrection, it is unclear what warrant there is for caring only about people's souls apart from both their bodies and the rest of creation. Finally, if one considers being eaten alive a horrifying prospect (something to be avoided for oneself and loved ones, at least), it is also not clear how predation could be considered unequivocally good or justified by the cross. From our vantage point in this life, there is ultimately something unanswerable about the suffering and death that attend eating. That suffering is unsettling, and as will be discussed, that fact can and should train us to be ethically attuned to the lives on which we feed and depend in order to flourish.

This chapter seeks to provide a way of perceiving goodness in eating while appreciating the death it entails. It builds upon the work of philosophical theologian Robert Adams and his understanding of goodness. Adams draws creatively upon Platonic and Christian views that good things in creation resemble and image God's infinite goodness. From this perspective, finite good things offer glimpses of infinite goodness, and this chapter explores the glimpses of God that eating affords us. It ultimately argues that the nourishment that eating entails images God's *grace* and *transcendence*, while the human activities cultivating, preparing, sharing, and tasting food image divine *creativity, care, generosity*, and *compassion*.

The chapter's argument unfolds as follows. The first section examines how flourishing life is rooted in death. The second lays out the idea that finite goods provide glimpses of God's infinite goodness. The third argues that a world in which life comes through eating richly images God's grace and transcendence. The final section uplifts cultural activities around eating that image God and how we can develop them to be attentive to minimizing and mitigating the deaths on which our lives depend.

Flourishing Death

"Flourishing" is a commonly referenced aim in contemporary religious and environmental ethics, and it is the central bridge concept for this collection of essays. It is important to highlight, however, that discussion of human and nonhuman flourishing enlists "flourishing" as a metaphor, rooted in the imagery of a flowering plant. This visual conveys a sense not only of beauty, vitality, and fruitfulness, but also of preciousness, rarity, and fragility. Flourishing is something that is at once internally powerful, with beings growing strongly into their full potential, and yet highly conditional, with beings depending utterly upon a huge number of ecological prerequisites. Focusing on flourishing also entails an implicit valuing of living beings and that which makes life possible over and above that which either is inanimate or undermines life. A key accompanying question also arises regarding which particular beings or species one values and wants to see flourish.

The reality that there is inclusion and exclusion in flourishing can be easily overlooked, because flourishing, like any metaphor, obscures even as it illuminates. While "flourishing" brings to mind life, growth, beauty, and fruitfulness, it tends to hide from view the death attending and nourishing such thriving. While it is common to think of death as a necessary part of something like predation, death is needed for life in general as we know it. Carnivores, herbivores, and omnivores alike eat living things that do not survive ingestion. Death undergirds plants' thriving as well, with their roots absorbing nutrients from soil fertilized by compost (deceased plant life devoured and broken down into essential absorbable minerals by microbes, fungi, and worms in the soil) and manure (predominately the unabsorbed and deposited remains of organisms that have been eaten).

The flowering plant imagery of flourishing also tends to obscure the foraging, hunting, and killing that occur for many animate organisms to thrive. Although we might consider a cheetah to be flourishing when it is gliding impressively and majestically across the plain to tackle a gazelle, we do not tend to adorn the ensuing bloody kill or disemboweled dinner with language of flourishing, and yet absent that feast, there is no cheetah to offer finite reflections of infinite goodness in its stride.

Whether via digestive tracts or sprawling roots, flourishing lives depend upon nourishingly bringing remains of the dead into themselves as themselves, and this absorption is not simply instrumental to flourishing but intimately constitutive of it. In other words, although we often colloquially talk of "fueling" our bodies, there is a significant difference between a person eating and a machine being fueled. While a car consumes gasoline, it is essentially left unaltered by its fuel. Yet, when an organism takes in nutrients, those nutrients quite directly become part of that organism's cellular structure. Along this line, while a car would simply not function absent gas, a person would wither and perish absent regular and formative absorption of food. Furthermore, unlike a vehicle, people have habits—dispositions of desire, perception, and action—that are formed directly by what and how that person regularly eats.[2]

Eating, the intake and absorption of nutrients, is neither incidental nor instrumental but rather an integral part of life. In his text *Food and Faith: A Theology of Eating* Norman Wirzba examines this reality with his overarching question, "Why did God create a world in which every living creature must eat?"[3] Wirzba points out, "Life as we know it depends on death, needs death, which means that death is not simply the cessation of life but its precondition."[4] This reality is embedded as the heartbeat of creation, pumping life forward day after day, generation after generation, and while it includes some beings that simply take in the already deceased—for instance, scavengers or plants—it also consists of creatures that kill, directly seizing the life of another, in order to be nourished.[5]

Predation, one sentient being feasting upon another, either after killing it to that end or digging in while the other is still alive, is what can seem particularly like the handiwork of an at best indifferent, at worst sadistic deity. It seems as if the God proclaimed in the Old and New Testaments, who created life abundant, was harboring a twisted secret, because everything that grows, breathes, and has its being in the Living God is on the menu for some fellow creature of God. Wirzba captures this existential setup poignantly as follows: "Every time we eat, we are called to recognize the profound mystery that God created a world that, from the beginning (even in something like a pre-fallen state), lives through the eating of its members."[6] This particular orchestration of life might be of limited

---

2. See Leon Cass, *Hungry Soul: Eating and the Perfecting of Our Nature* (New York: Maxwell Macmillan, 1994).

3. Norman Wirzba, *Food and Faith: A Theology of Eating* (New York: Cambridge University Press, 2011),1.

4. Ibid., 134.

5. Broader theological questions about mortality lie outside the parameters of this chapter, which focuses on the related but under-investigated area of life's dependence upon eating and the death that accompanies it.

6. Wirzba, *Food and Faith*, 134. Some eating is more destructive than others. Harvesting certain fruits and seeds does not necessarily destroy the plant from which they came, though does of course destroy the fruit that was a living part of the plant. Seeds often make it unharmed and ready for generating new life when deposited out the other end of the digestive tract. Milk also on its face is less destructive, though the milk was only generated by the mother devouring other living things, whether plant or animal. Honey is perhaps the least destructive both in its production and consumption within bee species. Careful beekeepers also minimize harm to life when sustainably harvesting honeycomb. The fact that not all foods are equally destructive also seems to be an insight appreciated in the Bible, given that the idealized land of promise in Exodus is one flowing with milk and honey. See Laura Hartman, e-mail message to author, October 15, 2015.

effect on microbial and vegetative beings, lacking what we commonly take to be the capacity to suffer via a nervous system,[7] but animate beings suffer to varying physical and psychological degrees in being eaten, whether it happens swiftly or stretched parasitically over time.

The seeming incompatibility between a good God and this reality, with its attendant suffering, is mitigated substantially if one interprets Genesis 1–3 as historical record, because notably all animate creatures were vegans in the Garden of Eden, eating "every green plant for food" while Adam and Eve tended the garden, eating of its abundant fruit. If this narrative encapsulates our historical origin, then the devouring of sentient beings does not appear to be what God laid out in the beginning but rather is a sharp declension from it. While eating still stands as an integral aspect of creation in this picture, not an incidental but intentional and constitutive element of what it is to be alive as a finite creature of God, there is no predation. Interpreting Genesis 1–3 in this manner often comes with an accompanying attribution of predation to human sin, as a sad collateral consequence thereof. On this view, when Adam and Eve sinned, somehow they severely upended the created order—only later after the flood did God permit humans to eat meat absent its life blood. From this perspective, predation is presumably something to lament, something from which we can only wait to be delivered by God.[8]

Yet, when these passages from Genesis are paired with scientific perspectives, such as those of chemistry, astronomy, paleontology, and biology, they take on more of a poetic cast,[9] and life on earth appears to have had a far lengthier, more winding past, intimately interwoven with forms of predation that vastly predate

---

7. These life forms, though, do generally stretch toward life and away from irritants and death to whatever extent possible. Certain plants also appear capable of sending and responding to biochemical distress signals. See Michael Marder, "If Peas Can Talk, Should We Eat Them?" *New York Times*, April 28, 2012.

8. Certain scripture passages seem to indicate meat eating is an aberration from God's intent for creation. For instance, Isaiah's prophetic vision of a time when the lion will eat straw like the ox and the leopard will lie down with the goat (See Isaiah 11:1–9; 65:25) recalls descriptions of Eden, where plants supply the nourishment needed by all moving creatures so that no bloodletting is necessary for sustenance (See Genesis 1:29–31; 2:4–17). These images lie in tension, though, with passages like Psalm 104, which celebrates "lions [that] roar for their prey, seeking their food from God" (see also Job 38:39–41; 39:26–30).

9. Reading those chapters more poetically entails seeing them not as a record of something that happened in a single historical moment, but rather as stories highlighting aspects of existence that happen again and again throughout time, such as creation flowing perennially from God or humans' disastrously prevalent dispositions to give into wayward impulses, hide behind self-justifying excuses, and avoid taking responsibility for their actions.

humanity and a creation-upending sin.[10] Furthermore, when evolution is included in this picture, the eating of sentient beings seems to have not only been present pre-humans, but also critical to the development of complex forms of life that exist today, including humans. In this vein, some argue that the vast array of incredibly elaborate capacities across life forms today might not have even arisen absent the particular pressures that predation placed upon creatures, culling the offspring of predator and prey alike in ways that increasingly heightened abilities to eat and avoid being eaten, to capture and evade, to attack and defend. These capacities were undoubtedly also formed by and enlisted for more welcoming activities such as play and care, but philosophers and environmental ethicists like Holmes Rolston III contend they were shaped indelibly and crucially by assault and evasion. Rolston maintains, "The cougar's fangs have carved the limbs of the fleet-footed deer, and vice versa."[11] From this perspective, the eating of animate creatures appears to be far more constitutive to the formation of life on earth than a reading of Genesis 1–3, as historical record might suggest.

If predation is not the result of a sin but a part of God's creation, though, one might wonder whether it remains something that we should lament or even that demands our repentance. The appropriate human response to predation could still simply be a sorrowful cry of "how long, O Lord?" Or it could entail asking forgiveness for killing other sentient creatures for food and refraining from such killing and eating to whatever extent possible. Ultimately, even if killing to live is built into creation from the start, the question remains, in what respects could this world of eat and be eaten be good?

Resembling God

Before sketching ways we can glimpse goodness in this world of eat and be eaten, it is key to lay out what is meant by "good" here. Although great debate rages

---

10. To explore arguments regarding theodicy, cosmodicy, and predation, see Christopher Southgate, *The Groaning of Creation: God, Evolution, and the Problem of Evil* (Louisville, KY: Westminster John Knox Press, 2008); Ronald Osborn, *Death before the Fall: Biblical Literalism and the Problem of Animal Suffering* (Downers Grove, IL: InterVarsity Press, 2014); Trent Dougherty, *The Problem of Animal Pain: A Theodicy for All Creatures Great and Small* (New York: Palgrave Macmillan, 2014); Nicola Hoggard Creegan, *Animal Suffering and the Problem of Evil* (Oxford: Oxford University Press, 2013); Michael Murray, *Nature Red in Tooth and Claw: Theism and the Problem of Animal Suffering* (Oxford: Oxford University Press, 2008); and Elizabeth Johnson, *Ask the Beasts: Darwin and the God of Love* (London: Bloomsbury, 2015).

11. Holmes Rolston III, *Science and Religion: A Critical Survey* (Philadelphia: Temple University Press, 1987), 134. See Ned Hettinger, "Bambi Lovers versus Tree Huggers," *Environmental Ethics* 16, no. 1 (1994): 3–20.

about whether "goodness" has any existence beyond human desires or evaluation, this chapter draws upon Robert Adams's description of goodness in *Finite and Infinite Goods*.[12] While good and goodness can mean a variety of things colloquially, Adams seeks to mark out territory for intrinsic goodness (the Good) as an objective reality that exists beyond human desires and values. According to Adams, although our longings and values of course connect with it, goodness is not reducible to them and it would exist even if we did not. This objectively real good is also intrinsically valuable, meaning its worth does not stem from something else, such as its instrumental usefulness in attaining some other goal, but it is innately valuable and worthy of admiration in itself—regardless of whether, for instance, even we humans are around to do the admiring.

Adams also maintains that goodness has an infinite divine form, the living God who came incarnate as Christ,[13] and that encountering goodness with enough perception and awareness (it is possible to overlook, whether via lack of attention or training) elicits feeling of awe, admiration, and joy. For Adams, those encounters come foremost through finite goods, which he believes resemble God to varying degrees and in different respects. Adams writes that finite goods provide "fragmentary glimpses . . . of a transcendently wonderful object," and when we experience them, "we are dimly aware of something too wonderful to be contained or carried either by our experience or by the physical or conceptual objects we are perceiving."[14]

This inarticulate sense of transcendence also conveys another point about goodness: it is ultimately something we cannot define with sharp precision. Although we can tie it to objective reality, intrinsic value, and God, and we can associate finite objects and activities with it, goodness is ultimately something mysterious that lies beyond our capacity to understand and define adequately. In this view of goodness, Adams is drawing upon Platonic traditions, and he notes that "[m]uch of the intuitive appeal of broadly Platonic theories of value lies in the thought that experienced beauty or excellence points beyond itself to an ideal or transcendent Good of which it is only an imperfect suggestion or imitation." Adams muses with a sentiment borne in this chapter as well, "We may also be

12. Robert Adams, *Finite and Infinite Goods: A Framework for Ethics* (Oxford: Oxford University Press, 1999).

13. Although Adams's project is not an explicit, confessional work of Christian theology but rather of broader philosophical theology, it is influenced and rooted deeply in a Christian conception of God as a personal and gracious lover of the Good and the array of finite goods in creation.

14. Ibid., 13, 51.

tempted to dismiss this feeling as a romantic illusion; but I am inviting the reader to make, in good Platonic company, the experiment of regarding it as veridical."[15]

According to Adams, goodness is a nature that is genuinely being tracked both by our evaluative language and by our experiences of love and wonder. Consequently, goodness is a lodestar for Adams. When we pursue it, we "reach out toward an objective standard that is actually glimpsed ... [even if] never fully or infallibly," and as we perceive and describe good things, we engage in a process, however faltering, of recognizing this objective reality.[16] Adams contends, "I think we cannot always or even usually be totally mistaken about goodness. . . . [I]f we do not place some trust in our own recognition of the good, we will lose our grip on the concept of the good, and our cognitive contact with the Good itself."[17]

Stating that he lacks a better word for it, Adams labels this kind of intrinsic goodness "excellence" and distinguishes it from both instrumental goodness, geared to some other end, and well-being goodness, oriented toward what is "good for" a given creature or group. According to Adams, although enjoyment of "excellence" is critical to any creature's well-being, excellence extends infinitely beyond the well-being of any and all creatures. Similarly, although we commonly associate the word "excellence" with highly developed skills or dispositions, Adams has in mind a wider range of finite goods, one that includes not only such heightened capacities, but also a lot from everyday life, like healthily functioning bodies, catching up with a close friend, dawn's rosy fingers, or the taste of a sun-warmed tomato ripe off the vine.[18]

These finite intrinsic goods arise in fields as diverse as aesthetics, simple pleasures, academics, athletics, music, morality, and friendship, among others. Adams does not try to provide a comprehensive list of excellences, because he thinks that excellences, in imaging infinite goodness, will always outstrip human understanding or attempts at categorization. Some have criticized Adams for vagueness on this point, with philosopher Susan Wolf arguing that this conception of goodness offers "little epistemological help in discovering what is good."

---

15. Ibid., 29, 51.

16. Ibid., 50, 81–82. "God is the standard of goodness, to which other good things must in some measure conform, but never perfectly conform." Ibid., 29. For instance, in the field of excellence that is morality, Adams contends that although people often disagree vociferously, "[T]here is enough overlap among the different received evaluative beliefs and practices for us to be talking about the same thing." Adams holds that despite our incapacity to fully perceive or comprehend God, "[w]e must have been able, very often, to recognize the good and the right." Ibid., 364.

17. Ibid., 20.

18. See Robert Adams, *A Theory of Virtue: Excellence in Being for the Good* (Oxford: Oxford University Press, 2006), 25. Also see Adams, *Finite and Infinite Goods*, 83, 147.

Wolf critiques, "[T]he idea that what is good is good because it resembles or images God is totally baffling if we are to understand the idea of resemblance or imaging literally. In what sense can a good meal, a good basketball game, a good performance of the Brandenburg Concerti, a field of wildflowers, the *Critique of Pure Reason* and my next door neighbor all resemble or image the same thing? How, in any event, can a good meal be said to image God?"[19]

Adams readily agrees it is often difficult to see the kinship between various forms of excellence, but also highlights that if their kinship is ultimately rooted in "an excellence so transcendent that it largely escapes our understanding, we should perhaps not be surprised if it is hard to understand that more momentous resemblance."[20] Overall, Adams is not claiming to have pinned down the criteria for discerning and delineating excellent things. He is simply positing their objective and transcendent existence, based in large part on the sense we often have that there is something amazing going on here, even if we do not know what it is—something that reaches far beyond simply us, our feeling of wonder, and whatever finite thing has elicited that wonder.[21]

We regularly associate many forms of excellence that Adams roots in God with the idea of human flourishing. In *A Theory of Virtue*, Adams writes that recent ethical and academic interest in "flourishing," often as a translation for *eudaimonia* from Aristotle's works, bears with it a hope that perhaps there is a way of living and thriving that is as innate and natural to humans as flowering is to a healthy plant. Adams points out, though, that *eudaimonia*, which is notoriously difficult to translate, is at root a term more directly religious than botanical in origin and valence, given that it means literally "good spirit."[22] Although flourishing does convey the largely Aristotelian idea that every being has an innate biological *telos*, no one has yet been able to pin down a compellingly comprehensive articulation of this *telos* for humans that is rooted foremost in our physical and psychological makeup. The analogy of thriving people to blossoming plants is enticing, but it does not seem to take into account the heightened complexity of people compared to plants.[23]

19. Susan Wolf, "A World of Goods," *Philosophy and Phenomenological Research* 64, no. 2 (March 2002): 472. Also see David Decosimo, "Intrinsic Goodness and Contingency, Resemblance and Particularity: Two Criticisms of Robert Adam's Finite and Infinite Goods," *Studies in Christian Ethics* 25, no. 4 (November 2012): 418–441.

20. Robert Adams, "Responses," *Philosophy and Phenomenological Research* 64, no. 2 (March 2002): 476.

21. Adams, *Finite and Infinite Goods*, 13, 51.

22. See Adams, *A Theory of Virtue*, 49–52.

23. Ibid.

We could envision "flourishing" as being more closely tied to experiencing and enjoying glimpses of God, both now and evermore fully in the resurrection to come, than with reaching an innate biological potential that is circumscribed simply within this finite world. Given the Platonic overtones in this conception of goodness, it is critical at this juncture to note that it is not being suggested that these glimpses provide a foretaste, if we mix metaphors, of leaving the body or creaturely existence behind. Glimpsing God does not entail here an effort, aspiration, or expectation of escaping the material world. Rather, recognizing finite resemblances of God's infinite goodness consists of appreciating the finite and infinite interwoven intimately together.

From this perspective, the finite is not a disposable ladder to the infinite as it is in many Platonic lines of thought. For instance, in considering the glimpse of God one might catch in something as simple as sunlight on leaves, Adams notes, "It is our love, our liking, our admiration and enjoyment of the light on the leaves that suggest to us the greater good [of God]. If we did not care for the light on the leaves, for its own sake, the divine glory will not be visible to us in this experience. So if this is an experience of loving God in the mode of admiring (or adoring) and enjoying God, it would seem to be a case in which love for a finite good is an integral part of love for God."[24] According to Adams, the intrinsic love for a finite good and the more reflective appreciation of it as a glimpse of infinite goodness are not in competition with each other but tightly interconnected, and this chapter argues that eating—the nourishment of life through death along with the way humans creatively and culturally play upon this need—harbors many of these twofold experiences of loving a finite good in concert with God.

Glimpsing God in the Nourishment of Life

What glimpses of infinite goodness could this world of eat and be eaten offer? To begin, the nourishment that eating affords images divine *grace* and *transcendence*. In Christian circles, the word "grace" usually refers to salvation and being considered righteous by God even though one is unrighteous, but at a more basic level, grace is simply a gift. Offering grace is giving something unmerited, something that the recipient either does not deserve or could not attain on his or her own. In reverse, experiencing grace is getting what one has not earned (and in some cases, could never earn) through exercising one's abilities.

---

24. Adams, *Finite and Infinite Goods*, 194. Also see p. 152, in which Adams calls the conclusion that particular goods serve only as ladders to infinite good an "outrageous" "misunderstanding and undervaluing" of finite goods, persons in particular.

In this vein and in regard to eating, anything living creatures eat is ultimately an unmerited gift from God. Even though creatures put forth intense effort seeking food—and people in particular mix in their distinct forms of labor in cultivating, processing, cooking, and sharing food—the existence of food is not something that lies within any creature or creatures' self-sufficient capacity to generate.[25] Created beings have important but extremely circumscribed influence over their sustenance, and so much lies beyond creaturely control that it is unclear how human claims to have earned or deserve our food are warranted. Although we commonly deem ourselves worthy of a given yield based on things like hard work, skills, or property ownership, the basic conditions that make any such bounty even conceivably possible lie completely beyond our capacity to secure.[26] Diligently tending, nurturing, and preparing animals or vegetation for food would not only be ineffectual, but also simply impossible absent aspects of creation like the sun, the atmosphere, gravity, photosynthesis, fresh water, and nutrient-rich soil, among others. From a theological perspective, the fact that those conditions are laid out morning by morning, that creation does not simply dissolve into nothingness, offers a daily glimpse of divine grace, God's intentional ongoing action to create life.[27]

Yet, while the sheer possibility of having food to eat expresses divine grace, the ways nourishment takes place, particularly via predation, still appear to throw the goodness of food off kilter. There is something chilling in the slaughter of sentient beings for sustenance, not to mention predators digging in while the prey is still kicking. Even though the suffering of prey peaks in the chase and the kill, as most sentient creatures seem to lack a foreboding sense of mortality, this kind of "integration" of life has a ring of horror about it, as one can easily imagine the lamb preferring just as well not to be integrated into the wolf. That horror becomes particularly poignant when one hears stories about humans being eaten. For instance, in the summer of 2016, headlines in the United States flashed about a two-year-old boy who was attacked by an alligator in Disneyland. The child was simply making sandcastles at dusk with other children by a lakeside and had waded into the lake to fill a bucket with water. As he bent over, an alligator splashed up and

25. Wirzba makes a distinction between earning food and being able to make a claim upon food on the basis of the efforts one has put into tending and cultivating its growth. The point being made here is simply that even if at some degree one can lay claim to a yield, there is a vastly more fundamental gift at play. See Wirzba, *Food and Faith*, 121.

26. Talk of self-sufficiency is predominately an issue of human interactions, as even the most rugged individual would not last long in the middle of a desert, an ocean, or, more pointedly, the cold emptiness of outer space.

27. See Wirzba, *Food and Faith*, 121, 134, 184.

snatched the boy with a crushing blow upon his neck and head. Frantic attempts from the boy's father to save his son from the alligator's jaws failed, as the ancient predator dragged the child away. Although alligators very rarely hunt humans, experts concluded that in this particular incidence the alligator had acted in ways that indicate it perceived the little boy to be prey.[28] This story and others like it, and nearly every monster tale we have, reinforce a certain sympathy we have with prey and fear of being the one integrated into another being.

Some Christian thinkers have sought to address the issue of predation by framing it in terms of Christ's sacrifice. They see resonance between the life-giving sacrificial death of Christ and the life-giving death of the devoured. Holmes Rolston III has pressed this theological point most directly, arguing that creation is "cruciform" in that life forms of lower capacities are nourishingly "transformed" into creatures of more complex abilities, both in an immediate sense of sustaining the predator and in a broader sense of driving the evolutionary generation of diverse creatures and capacities. Rolston speaks of this devouring as redemptive, holding that "destruction of the old, lower life is not really destruction but renovation, the creation of newer, higher levels of life."[29] The suffering and demise of the eaten is not utter annihilation but rather transformation, and Rolston further argues that this sacrificial transformation echoes the life of Christ. He contends that being eaten exhibits the "abundant life that Jesus exemplifies and offers to his disciples [which] is that of a sacrificial suffering." Rolston maintains, "There is something divine about the power to suffer through to something higher. . . . The cruciform creation is, in the end, deiform, godly, just because of this element of struggle, not in spite of it."[30]

Wirzba similarly discusses a "sacrificial logic of life through death to new life" that stretches back to the "foundation of the world,"[31] and Wendell Berry poignantly invokes this kind of perspective in the closing lines of his classic essay, "The Gift of Good Land":

28. Steve Visser, "Florida Disney Alligator Saw Boy as Prey, Report Says," CNN, August 23, 2016, http://www.cnn.com/2016/08/22/us/orlando-disney-gator-attack.

29. Holmes Rolston III, "Does Nature Need to Be Redeemed?" *Zygon* 29, no. 2 (June 1994): 211. Holding that predation in particular has been necessary to provide the kind of environmental pressure that cultivated and created beings with the kind of enhanced capacities we see on earth today, Rolston also writes, "[A]n Earth with only herbivores and no omnivores or carnivores would be impoverished—the animal skills demanded would be only a fraction of those that have resulted in actual zoology—no horns, no fleet-footed predators or prey, no fine-tuned eyesight or hearing, no quick neural capacity, no advanced brains." Ibid., 213.

30. Ibid., 220.

31. Wirzba, *Food and Faith*, 125, 135.

[I do not] suggest that we can live harmlessly, or strictly at our own expense; we depend upon other creatures and survive by their deaths. To live, we must daily break the body and shed the blood of Creation. When we do this knowingly, lovingly, skillfully, reverently, it is a sacrament. When we do it ignorantly, greedily, clumsily, destructively, it is a desecration. In such desecration we condemn ourselves to spiritual and moral loneliness, and others to want.[32]

Framing eating, and predation in particular, in terms of sacrifice and redemption does correctly highlight that creaturely existence inescapably costs the lives of fellow beings. As such, life is precious (costly) not only in terms of its innate value, but also in terms of the lethal payments we must make to keep living. Furthermore, in the sense of "life coming through death," eat and be eaten resonates powerfully and evocatively with the saving death of Christ. The sheer fact that we could look down at the dinner table and appreciatively recognize that everything on it was once alive but now is dead so that we might live does provide a compelling metaphor for salvation in Christ.[33]

Even so, it is a step too far to claim that this good creation bears a cruciform or sacrificial logic, because Christ's crucifixion differs from predation and eating in critical ways. To begin, the purpose of Roman crucifixion was to subjugate conquered peoples with one of the most calculatingly vicious forms of torture that people have been perverse enough to invent and inflict upon one another. By contrast, the drive of predators killing to eat is nourishment, not the suffering of either the eaten or any who might grieve the eaten. The murderous cross also does not give or nourish life in itself. It is something from which life has to be redeemed and raised in Christ. By contrast, predatory eating does give life in itself, regenerating the very flesh of the one eating. Finally, Christ gave himself over to death and crucifixion willingly, but prey do not generally appear willing to submit to being eaten, given their routine flight from it.[34]

Reconsideration of Berry's quotation above also brings into sharp relief the difference between Christ's crucifixion and killing to eat. As Berry describes, killing to eat can be done with knowing reverence of the cost of the life taken and

---

32. Wendell Berry, "The Gift of Good Land," in *The Art of the Commonplace: The Agrarian Essays of Wendell Berry* (Berkeley: Counterpoint, 2002), 304.

33. Eating and drinking, of course, are also the prime ritual celebration of Christ's death and resurrection.

34. While resistance to death is comparable between predation and crucifixion in its general form, the comparison Rolston makes is between predation and Christ's saving death in particular.

a loving skill that nurtures the to-be-eaten during life and minimizes any pain in death. Yet, we would not similarly claim a crucifixion, if simply done knowingly, reverently, lovingly, and skillfully, could be a sacrament. There are glimpses of God on the cross in the compassion, forgiveness, generosity, and self-control that drove Christ to proclaim reconciling justice and peace even to the point of death on the imperial cross, and there are glimpses of eternal life in Christ being raised from the dead, but there is no good to be glimpsed in the intentions and implementation of the cross itself.

One could appeal at this point to a Job-esque mystery, and maintain that we simply do not know why God would make creation cruciform. The book of Job does not answer why God allows the righteous to suffer, and one could argue that, similarly, we do not know why God made it so that life comes through eating, with the suffering and death that attend it. Like Job before the whirlwind, perhaps all we can do is stand in awe at the fact that we are part of a leviathan-like "eat and be eaten" world.[35] It is important to note, however, that a cruciform explanation of creation actually ends up explaining away the mystery of suffering to which Job attests. For instance, Rolston ultimately gives two direct explanations for why God made a world in which life comes through death and predation: the regeneration of the eater, and the evolutionary spur to ever more complex and creative beings, hunter and hunted.

By contrast, the book of Job leaves the suffering of the righteous—and by extension, the suffering of the eaten—far more open ended. According to Job, no clear explanation is given for that suffering. Instead, the point is simply made that life in creation transcends far beyond the well-being (and the suffering) of any given creature. When we consider eating and the nourishment through death it entails, we can similarly appreciate the glimpse of divine *transcendence* it affords us. As part of creation, we are part of something far larger than any of us can comprehend, something that is rooted and centered ultimately on God. Furthermore, emphasizing that eating images God's transcendence rather than Christ's crucifixion is important because it protects against the danger of instrumentalizing, and thereby underappreciating, the countless lives lost to digestive tracts.

Eating gives us glimpses of both the *transcendence* of life (divine, as well as created) beyond any individual creature and the *grace* of sheer existence. When we are attentive to these aspects of eating, we can cultivate due humility, respect, and gratitude for the innumerable lives we consume. We cannot repay or merit the lives we eat, or simply claim that their deaths lead to something greater, such as ourselves. We cannot understand why God made the world this way. We can,

---

35. See Rolston, "Does Nature Need to Be Redeemed?": 210–211; Job 38–42.

though, live in reverence by killing and eating in ways that are responsible rather than careless, wasteful, and exhaustingly destructive of life on earth. As we turn in the final section to consider the goodness of food and eating in the realms of human culture, the terrain will feel much less lethally fraught, but it is critical to remember again (and again) that the nourishing things on our plates were once alive but now are dead so that we might live.

Glimpsing God in Human Cultures of Eating

With regard to human culture and eating, the glimpses of God's goodness arise in four primary activities: cultivating, preparing, sharing, and tasting food. Each of these areas harbors incredible moments in which God can be glimpsed, even amidst the long hours and often repetitious work some of them require. Such moments are the stuff of human flourishing. Sharing a meal with family and friends in which one becomes mutually immersed in the delight of conversation and shared appreciation for delicious food is perhaps the most regular experience of excellence around eating. Celebrations and holidays revolve, often quite piously, around such companionship over food, with participants accumulating traditions and richly savored memories around these moments and specific foods prepared and enjoyed with one another. Gathering around shared meals is not simply an incidental occasion for relationship, but constitutes the *care* and *abiding connection* people have with one another and images divine care for and connection to creation.

Adams notes that he is not precisely sure which aspect of God's goodness is glimpsed in the taste of something deliciously prepared but rests assured of the resemblance, given the widely experienced relish of a first bite, and the psalmist's view that enough of a resemblance exists to declare, "O taste and see that the Lord is Good!"[36] While taste is deeply shaped and variated according to cultural upbringing, it taps into something transcendently wonderful, as does the preparation of food itself. Glimpses of infinite *creativity* are daily displayed in the dishes envisioned and crafted by chefs and amateurs alike.[37] This creativity and accompanying attentiveness arises not only in the food itself, but also in the details of table settings, flower arrangements, garnishes, plating, and other such aesthetics.

Sharing food with those who lack it additionally bears images of divine *generosity* and *compassion*. This kind of goodness is often what people think of first

---

36. Psalm 34:8.

37. See Adams, *Finite and Infinite Goods*, 30.

when they consider food in light of theological ethics, but it is important to recognize that a single-minded focus on the moral call to meet physical needs overlooks other aspects of eating that image God's goodness. It can feel as though nothing else mattered in the face of malnutrition, but the flourishing of any person, hungry or otherwise, extends far beyond nutrition alone.[38] If nutritious calorie count becomes the sole criterion of goodness in food and eating, things like fellowship, taste, and culinary craft noted are easily missed. In the words of the psalmist, God causes plants to grow so that humans can not only make bread for food, but also craft wine to gladden the human heart and oil to make the face shine.[39]

Appreciating that food is about more than merely staying alive can be seen in a homelessness shelter program in Richmond, Virginia, called CARITAS, in which congregations around the metropolitan area offer places to stay as well as meals on a rotating weekly basis. If nourishment were the sole focus with regard to providing food as part of this ministry, the participants could simply be handed packets of enriched peanut butter or nutrient-dense meal-replacement beverages. Yet, concerns for compassion and care drive congregations to consider more than nutrition alone, such as serving meals that actually taste delicious and coming out from behind the kitchen counter to join in fellowship around the meal, showing the kind of personal respect and welcome one would to guests in one's own home. Nutritious food is necessary but not sufficient to sharing the goodness of eating with others.

The cultivation of food itself is another area of cultural excellence in relation to eating, one that images divine *creativity* and *care*. Yet farming can easily become romanticized, particularly when viewed from a distance, as a place of pure harmony, of deathless flourishing where vegetative and animate species thrive seamlessly side by side.[40] It is crucial to recognize our tendency to romanticize death away from our food, especially those of us in urban areas, where global populations are becoming increasingly concentrated at a far distance from the agricultural origins of our food. This disposition to romanticism may be particularly prevalent among city dwellers because it offers such a verdant contrast to horizons of pavement and parking lots.

---

38. Adams even reads fixation on people's physical needs as a form of idolatry that precludes "caring about other instances or types of good." Ibid., 181, 200.

39. See Psalm 104.

40. In the epigraph of this chapter, the head of Three Part Harmony, an urban farm in Washington, DC, slips into this rosy picture of all life being made to thrive before catching herself to note that insects that eat the vegetables are not harmoniously welcome to flourish, on the farm at least.

Romanticizing farming undermines not only appreciation of the costly processes that bear food but also awareness of the way current agricultural practices exact a heavier toll of suffering and death than is needed for humans to thrive. Detachment from food's roots comes via the decentralized maze of market exchanges that currently take food from field to fork. As Wendell Berry notes, it can seem at the grocery-store checkout counter as if getting food were an economic act rather than an "agricultural act," that food comes from money and trade rather than sun, seed, soil, and rain.[41] A key problem with that misperception is that markets, while having many merits, also tend to hide the death in which we must deal in order to live, and if we do not realize the death inherent to our lives, we are vastly more prone to slip into excess, killing or harming objectively good beings more than is necessary and in ways that undermine the long-term ecological capacities of soil and species to replenish.

Participation in growing food-bearing plants offers one avenue for people's desires, viewpoints, and actions to be more fully trained toward gratitude, wonder, and responsibility regarding the roots of our sustenance and the costs therein. As Wirzba writes about gardens, "[E]very garden *by necessity* presupposes a massive amount of plant and animal death. . . . The sight and aroma of death are simply unavoidable. . . . Soil, we could say, is the ever-open receptacle for death. Deep in the bowels of the earth countless bacteria, microorganisms, fungi, and insects are engaged in a feeding frenzy that absorbs life into death and death back into the conditions for life."[42]

This kind of education occurs regularly at Shalom Farms, a nonprofit located on a ten-acre farm in Midlothian, Virginia, that is focused on (1) growing healthy organic produce for underserved communities in Metro Richmond, (2) providing learning experiences to all ages on growing food as well as cooking and eating nutritionally, and (3) helping foster individual and community self-sufficiency. Established in 2009, the farm now generates over 100,000 pounds of produce annually, grown with the diligent help of about 4,400 volunteers, many of whom drive thirty to forty minutes from the city to the farm to be of assistance and get their hands in the soil. The food is produced organically without synthetic fertilizer, pesticides, or herbicides, and made available at reduced or no financial cost to local communities that do not have easy access to nutritious food because of a lack of nearby grocery stores.

41. Wendell Berry, "The Pleasures of Eating," in *What Are People For? Essays* (Berkeley: Counterpoint, 1990), 145–146.

42. Wirzba, *Food and Faith*, 53.

Shalom Farms' mission is to generate food that is "good for our bodies, good for our environment, and good for our communities." While the term "good" here is used in a way focused on physical and relational well-being, Shalom's ministry extends into each of the areas of excellence discussed above, cultivating, preparing, tasting, and sharing. Executive director Dominic Barrett unpacks Shalom's mission as seeking affirmatives not only to questions like "can we all afford it? can we all access it?" but also "is it food that we like? can we share that food?"[43] Growing lots of affordable fresh produce is a key component of Shalom's call, but that aim flows with efforts to generate educated relationships around healthy eating, sustainable agriculture, and awareness of food's origin in the soil.

When considering this work, head farmer Steve Miles explains, "To me it's an art form. It's a way of expressing myself creatively, and it's a way to not only do something I love, which is working outside with my hands, but also benefit a lot of people at the same time. And people love coming out here. It's a great environment. I feel like it's always sort of a learning lab. For me I'm always learning patience and frugality. I'm learning humility."[44] Participating in the farm provides ground from which people can engage not only the death-enriched roots of food, but also the culinary arts, table fellowship, and hospitality, as those receiving or purchasing the food also have opportunities to get recipes and instruction in cooking the produce so that they can not only enjoy its tastes themselves but also share it around a table with family and friends.

The four primary activities around food that reflect God's goodness (cultivating, preparing, sharing, and tasting food) are accessible via the work of Shalom Farms. Shalom Farms offers glimpses into the goodness of life's nourishment as well. With a flock of about thirty chickens, the farm engages in some animal husbandry. These chickens lay eggs and work diligently each day, fertilizing, weeding, and mowing the soil on a rotating basis around the farm. They also provide opportunities for teaching and talking about predation with volunteers and student groups, given that the chickens peck up insects, spiders, and worms while residing unquestionably in the sights and at times grip of neighboring opossums, foxes, and coyotes. More so than even the crops, these creatures offer ambulatory instruction that life preciously depends on death. Farms like Shalom provide people with spaces and times to appreciate the images of divine grace and transcendence present in our food system.

---

43. Dominic Barrett, "Shalom Farms," Doug Callahan, Tisha McCuiston, and Daryl McCuiston, producers (Richmond, VA: Ross Media Services, 2012), https://www.youtube.com/watch?v=JufM0cKbHIc.

44. Steven Miles, "Shalom Farms."

Conclusion

This chapter highlights the need to take seriously the fact that eating inextricably entails death. It costs lives. Though we cannot answer here and now why God made the world in such a way that life depends on death, particularly when it entails predation, this chapter argues that we can still see glimpses of divine goodness in eating. In the nourishment that eating entails we can see images of God's grace and transcendence, and in the human practices of cultivating, preparing, tasting, and sharing food we can see divine creativity, care, generosity, and compassion. Appreciating such glimpses of God are key components of human flourishing, especially to the extent that they train us to care for one another, delight in God's creation, and deal carefully with the deaths in which our lives are rooted. In recognizing the goodness revealed in eating, we can live into Wendell Berry's core charge to take life only as needed, and to do so "knowingly, lovingly, skillfully, reverently," minimizing suffering and death.

3 DIALOGUE

Colette Sciberras and Nelson Reveley

REVELEY: From the Buddhist perspectives you've studied, how is material flourishing (doing well bodily and emotionally as part of this world) related to spiritual flourishing (meditation or glimpsing God)?

SCIBERRAS: In early Buddhist texts, material and spiritual flourishing are occasionally contrasted,[1] and in fact, the final goal of nirvana is sometimes described as being beyond ordinary happiness and unhappiness.[2] At the same time, rebirth as a rich and powerful being in the "happy realms" results from a subset of the spiritual practices that lead to nirvana.[3]

In early Buddhism, mundane goods—food, wealth, partners, children—are generally seen as a distraction from the spiritual path, and are given up by monks and nuns. Later Mahayana schools draw a closer link between worldly and spiritual flourishing. The monk is no longer the only spiritual role model; there are more references to lay practitioners, such as *bodhisattvas*, who can partake in the enjoyment of worldly goods and yet be enlightened.

REVELEY: It seems that the kind of contrast you noted in early Buddhist texts between material and spiritual flourishing has echoes in Christian writings as well. Some Christians have viewed this life and world as something to be endured prior to the spiritual

---

1. E.g., M i 501–513, Sn 758. (In this dialogue, I use the following abbreviations for citations from ancient Buddhist texts: *Dīgha Nikāya* (D); *Majjhima Nikāya* (M); *Sutta Nipata* (Sn); *Samyutta Nikāya* (S).)

2. E.g., S iv 235.

3. E.g., in D 11, the protagonist, Kevatta, is able to travel through the heavens to ask the gods how to attain nirvana. The gods and Kevatta are able to experience the heavens because of their virtue and skill at concentration. However, none of the gods can answer his question, and Kevatta ends up returning to the Buddha for a reply.

rest of death, which precedes the ultimate bodily resurrection.[4] For instance, worried about the trap of idolizing material well-being and losing sight of God's kingdom to come, Protestant reformer John Calvin wrote, "When it comes to comparison with the life to come, the present life can not only be safely neglected but, compared to the former, must be utterly despised and loathed."[5] He did also affirm, though, that this life remained a blessing, in spite of its difficulties, and that good things of the world are simply to be used for the purpose God gave them as revealed in scripture. For instance, food was not just for "necessity, but also for delight and good cheer," clothing likewise not just for bodily warmth but "comeliness and decency," and plants not just for their usefulness but their beauty and pleasant smells.[6]

But some Christians, particularly in the first few centuries after Jesus's death, stressed spiritual union with God to such an extent that they have veered toward "gnosticism." Gnostics believed that this world of suffering and physical limitations—a world that could at best provide only transient material flourishing—is something innately negative to be escaped through spiritual disciplines and wisdom. While many gnostics saw themselves as followers of Jesus, others saw them as waywardly denying the goodness of creation, not to mention other affirmations like Christ's incarnation and bodily resurrection. Are there other spots within Buddhist traditions where you have seen this tension between the spiritual and material resolved nicely?

SCIBERRAS: For me, it is resolved most satisfactorily in the Pure Land traditions. Practitioners of this tradition, which is rooted in Indian Mahayana but survives mostly in Japan and Tibet, aspire to renounce this world and be reborn in Sukhavati—which literally translates as "the world of bliss"—a world where there is no suffering whatsoever and from where one can easily proceed to nirvana. In these traditions, "worldly" physical and emotional flourishing is seen as a necessary step on the way to nirvana, and only attainable in the Pure Land. At the same time, practitioners know that Buddha Amitabha, whom they petition, is none other than their own mind, and Sukhavati, his Pure Land, is this very world.[7] There is no place other than earth where a human

4. From a different—albeit less biblically supported—perspective, many Christians understand the afterlife not in terms of an ultimate day of resurrection, but rather in terms of heaven as an ever-present, cloud-filled relief from this life. In this vein, people tend to reference and imagine heaven as a place one's soul goes after death, rather than a place for (or with) resurrected bodies.

5. John Calvin, *The Institutes of the Christian Religion,* Ford Lewis Battles, trans. (Louisville, KY: Westminster John Knox Press, 1960), III.IX.4.

6. Ibid., III.X.2.

7. See, e.g., Hakuin Ekaku, *Song of Zazen,* in *Selections from the Embossed Tea Kettle,* R.D.M. Shaw, trans. (London: George Allen and Unwin, 1963), 182–183.

could reach nirvana, and yet one prays to be reborn in Sukhavati. Perhaps it seems quite contradictory, but there are probably similar issues of reconciling a view of perfection with this less-than-perfect earth in every major faith. Your chapter reveals a significant way in which these can be reconciled with regard to the problem of eating God's creatures. Could you say something about how the tensions between material and spiritual flourishing play out in other aspects of our lives?

REVELEY: Well, along this line, it seems that beneath the question of how material and spiritual flourishing relate lies a deeper consideration: whether this world is at root good? If so, it seems its aspects—food, wealth, partners, children—are worthy of concern and focus, but if not, they would ultimately just be distractions from true flourishing (i.e., a spiritual flourishing detached from this material world). I personally believe the material world is good and seek the ways in which it images or expresses God's goodness. In this vein, I think spiritual flourishing occurs when we accurately perceive and engage material goods as glimpses of God, or prime points of contact with God. And that kind of spiritual flourishing can still occur even when those material goods are lost, as they inevitably will be, whether because of decay, accident, or sin. Does it seem that kind of view could have some overlap with Pure Land traditions?

SCIBERRAS: Well, yes, it does, and not just with Pure Land traditions, but with all schools of Buddhism, I believe. The question of whether the world is intrinsically good or not was the first question I tried to address in my studies of Buddhist philosophy, because if it isn't, then why bother with protecting it from climate change, say? Illness, accidents, partners, children, mistakes, and sins can all be grouped under the term *dukkha*—suffering—which is a result of *anicca*—impermanence. One of the key doctrines shared by all Buddhists is that nothing in this world lasts and that this very fact leads to suffering. So climate change is nothing new and to try to prevent our world from changing is misguided. My conclusion was that a Buddhist might consistently endeavor to protect the material world, not because of any inherent value it may have, but through concern about the flourishing of sentient beings. Is there anything similar in the Christian tradition, in which the environment is valuable as someone's *home*?

REVELEY: That is a really interesting question. There certainly are a lot of Christians who view the world as essentially a theater with humans as the main characters. I have always felt this view risks instrumentalizing and misvaluing the rest of creation, as well as making it seem as though we were somehow separable from, rather than intimately interwoven with, the rest of creation.

You also raise a fascinating distinction between caring about material existence because it is inherently valuable versus caring about sentient beings' flourishing, presumably because that flourishing is inherently valuable. I wonder to what extent the flourishing of another (in this case, "another" being sentient life form) is extricable from its material existence, particularly given that any being's physical existence is so deeply interconnected with the rest of creation.

SCIBERRAS: Interestingly, there is a "creation" story in the early texts, which is probably not meant to be taken seriously, but which reveals the inextricability of a being from its environment. The relation is one of interdependence, that is, what a being is depends on its environment and vice versa. It relates how in the beginning, beings had bodies of light and minds that were more elevated, but through the activity of feeding, both they, and their environment, including the food they fed upon, became coarser and degraded.[8] So this concept would seem to clash with the idea of eating as a finite glimpse of infinite goodness, which you argue for in your chapter. On the other hand, your ideas reminded me of the *ganacakra* tradition within Tantric Buddhism, which celebrates a meal, very often including meat, alcohol, and other conventionally frowned-upon substances, as an expression of the highest truth and love. Christianity similarly contains a notion of food becoming coarser and more difficult to obtain after the Fall, I believe?

REVELEY: Yes, in Genesis, growing food becomes much more toilsome and less reliable after God expels Adam and Eve from the garden. Interestingly, they were called to tend the garden prior to expulsion, so they had life-giving work to which they were called pre-fall; it's just presumably that their labor always

---

8. The story is part of a discourse in which the Buddha argues that it is not birth into one of the upper castes that makes one noble, but having a virtuous disposition. It is probably intended only as a parable because in every other scriptural instance in which the Buddha is asked about the beginning of the universe, he replies that this is not a useful question to ask, and that any definitive view one might hold is wrong (e.g., M i 483). In this sutra, however, the Buddha provides a rather fantastical account of how "in the beginning," that is, at the start of a new cycle of creation and destruction, beings dwell in the World of Radiance, "made of mind, feeding on rapture self-luminous, travelling the air, continuing in glory; and thus they remain for a long, long period of time." Reminiscent of Thales, Buddha goes on to explain that "earth" forms out of water, yet this "original" earth is like butter or honey. Eventually, some being of a "greedy disposition" tastes it and begins to crave it. Sooner or later all others join in, and their self-luminance begins to fade. The sun and moon are formed, and time begins, manifested as seasons and years. Clearly, this creation story is subject to the usual difficulties of explaining how the creative act could occur outside time. In any case, the story goes on that as beings continue to feed—on mushrooms, then creepers, and finally rice—the more solid their bodies become. They start to vary in beauty, and lust evolves. Houses are built to cover this lust, and then beings start to hoard food, rather than gather it daily. Crime becomes a reality and political systems arise as a defense. Gradually beings begin to regret the loss of that savory earth and of their self-luminance and the Buddha ends his parable by reiterating the claim that Dhamma—truth and virtue—is the highest good, in this world and the next. (D. iii 80–98; T.W. Rhys Davids and C.A.F Rhys Davids, trans., *Dialogues of the Buddha*, vol. 3 (Delhi: Motilal Banarsidass, 2000), 81–89.)

readily yielded fruit prior to the fall. Ultimately, though, having enough food to eat becomes much more difficult to secure when people operate sinfully—a truth that stands whether one takes Genesis 3 as recording of a historical occurrence or a poetic rendering of truths that have sadly recurred across time. On a different note, I've also always been very intrigued by the link we often make (in Christianity and it seems as with Buddhism as well) between permanence and goodness, as well as between impermanence and suffering. If we quote the Avett Brothers, it often seems taken as a given that "[t]here's nothing good, because nothing lasts, and all that comes here, it comes here to pass."[9] In other words, if something is finite, food or access to it, for instance, it cannot be good in any kind of ultimate sense. But I wonder if it is true that if something does not last it necessarily means (a) it cannot be intrinsically good, and (b) it results in *dukkha* (versus perhaps feeling grief when something good is lost, but also feeling a deep, attentive joy in finite goods that comes from not taking them for granted—precisely because one appreciates that they will not last forever)?

SCIBERRAS: This is the old, philosophical problem of essentialism, and the view that if something is truly good, then that goodness must be part of its inalienable nature. For example, Kant expressed this belief by pointing out that when an intention is good, it is unqualifiedly good, and that same intention can never turn into a bad one. The consequences of my intentions and actions, on the other hand, depend on multiple factors beyond my control, and what is good in particular circumstances may be harmful in others. This view is why finite goods are seen as lacking somehow, and why Buddha insists that all emotions are mixed with *dukkha*. Even the deep and attentive appreciation of an ephemeral good is tinged with a little sadness at the knowledge that it cannot last.

Not just goods, but all things in the world are finite and are therefore subject to the same critique that they have no essence, or that their essence is emptiness. Even the beings who want happiness have no essence. This belief is different, I think, from the Christian and Aristotelian understanding of what makes a species, particularly the eternal human soul.

REVELEY: One of the trickiest pieces in Christian traditions in regard to nonhumans is a view among some that people, and in particular our souls, are all that really matter (again, back to that question of impermanence, value, and happiness). However, I think things like (1) the scriptural declarations that creation is "very good," (2) God's incarnation and resurrection as part of this world, and (3) the bodily resurrection on Judgment Day all collectively point

---

9. The Avett Brothers, "Down with the Shine," in *The Carpenter*, American Recordings B001732802, 2012, compact disc.

to the truth that the material world has value and that all living beings—not just humans—have a form of flourishing that God intends.[10] This flourishing is deeply interconnected and interrelational. No creature could exist, let alone flourish, in isolation from others, with eating and nourishment being the most fundamental example of this fact. I'd be interested to hear more about what it means for all beings to want happiness from a Buddhist perspective.

SCIBERRAS: I'm glad you brought up the interconnections between beings. For Buddhists too this is an important fact, often described in metaphorical terms as the Net of Indra.[11] The interconnections between beings, that fact that nothing can be defined in essentialist terms, makes everything somewhat relative, including happiness, which depends on different things for different types of beings. An oft-repeated example is that of a glass of water, which might be a refreshing drink to a human, a home to a fish, a delicious nectar to a goddess, and a burning sensation to a hungry ghost.[12] So there is an understanding that with worldly flourishing, one being's meat is another's poison.

REVELEY: It has always seemed to me though that, even with the kind of differences you mentioned, there might still be some unifying aspect to "happiness" and to "good" (even if just linguistically and not in an ultimate unifying reality, such as God) that leads us use the same word for a refreshing glass of water for a person, a home for a fish, delicious nectar for whoever is capable of enjoying it, and *not* having one's throat burned. I realize my anchoring that unifying aspect in an infinite compassionate personal God is different from Buddhist perspectives, but I also wonder if there is some possible overlap between the concept of infinite Goodness and nirvana. In other words, isn't there something in quenching thirst, having a home, tasting delicious food, and being physically healthy that in some way connects with the joy of nirvana, even if we can't articulate the connection? Augustine mused along these lines in the 4th century in writing that even though loving God is not like loving anything he could see, hear, touch, taste, or smell, "I do love a kind of light, a kind of voice, a certain fragrance, a food and an embrace, when I love my God: a light, voice, fragrance, food and embrace for my inmost self, where something limited to no place shines into my mind, where something not snatched away

10. Passages like Revelations 4:11 also profess that God is worthy of praise because God intentionally created the material world for delight, both God's and creation's delight. See essays in *The Bible and the Pursuit of Happiness*, Brent Strawn, ed. (Oxford: Oxford University Press, 2012).

11. See Francis H. Cook, *Hua-yen Buddhism: The Jewel Net of Indra* (University Park: Pennsylvania State University Press, 1977).

12. Often depicted as the "Wheel of Life," traditional Buddhist cosmology adds to our familiar human and animal realms, the realms of gods (*deva-loka*), hungry ghosts (*preta-loka*), and hell (*niraya*). Cf. M i 73.

by passing time sings for me, where something no breath blows away yields to me its scent, where there is savor undiminished by famished eating, and where I am clasped in a union from which no satiety can tear me away."[13]

SCIBERRAS: Perhaps Augustine is the best example of a deeply spiritual man who also enjoyed worldly pleasures, even if he probably never reconciled these two goods. Could they be reconciled, and should they? Like you, I too think that there is some sort of connection between worldly and spiritual good. Despite the differences in the way various beings experience worldly things, like water, we all understand, in general, what it means to want happiness, even if most of us are deluded about where to look for it, or unsuccessful at obtaining it. The Buddha's teachings can be summed up as detailed directions through a graded path to true "happiness," which is beyond the duality of good and bad, happy and unhappy.

In Buddhism, there is the idea that although we cannot articulate what this ultimate goodness of nirvana is, we can know it. From one perspective of the Mahayana and Tantric traditions, it is deluded to worry about, say, whether eating meat is morally acceptable or not, or whether one should or shouldn't indulge in worldly pleasures. Such thoughts—like all other thoughts, and precisely *because* they are thoughts—belong to the conventional and to samsara, the reality in which we make divisions, form concepts, act upon their bases, and produce karma. Although conventional morality remains important in all traditions of Buddhism, nirvana is a state of mind that goes beyond all that, and the journey starts from a realization of interdependence—that nothing is good in and of itself, but everything in the universe depends on certain conditions. I think here we have touched upon an essential difference between Christianity and Buddhism.

Buddhism has many different schools, sects, and philosophies, and there are some texts that point explicitly to something that is intrinsically good. This is called Buddhanature and is the closest equivalent to the idea of a God. This is a nature that we all share, however, and is described in Mahayana texts as our very emptiness, which is inseparable from compassion.

I think our discussion has shown what I have personally come to believe: that there are more points of convergence between Buddhism and Christianity than there are differences. At least, there is much that is open to interpretation in both traditions. In my personal practice and study, I have found that a key difference is the unwillingness of Buddhist scholars and practitioners to attempt to express ultimate truth in words. This reluctance contrasts with the Christian tradition, in which, for a variety of historical reasons, various Churches have felt the need to write down an official creed.

---

13. Augustine, *Confessions* Bk X.6.8, Maria Boulding, trans. (New York: New City Press, 1997).

ANIMALS AND CARE

4 DAOISM, NATURAL LIFE, AND HUMAN FLOURISHING

David E. Cooper

In New York's Metropolitan Museum of Art there is a colored-ink handscroll by the 16th-century artist Qian Gu that depicts a famous gathering, held in 353 C.E., at the Orchid Pavilion in Shanyin. In the picture, a group of men sitting on the banks of a stream admire the natural surroundings, compose poems, drink wine, and talk. The painting beautifully communicates the perception of the Daoist calligrapher who organized this gathering that human lives, if they are to go well and flourish, should be led in intimate proximity to nature. This chapter is a sympathetic exploration of that Daoist perception.

Eudaimonia, Human Being, and Daoism

As a rendering of the ancient Greeks' notion of *eudaimonia*, "flourishing" has the advantage over "happiness" of drawing attention to the connection between *eudaimonia* and a conception of human life. If, as Aristotle held, *eudaimonia* is "living well and doing well" as a human being, it presupposes an understanding of the distinctive nature or "function" of human existence. For Aristotle, our distinctive "function" is "activity of the soul in accordance with reason": hence the flourishing life is the virtuous life, since, according to him, "virtue" refers to rational activities that are well conducted.[1]

The notion of human flourishing is easily extended to the many philosophical traditions, Eastern and Western, that concur with the Aristotelian thought that a human life flourishes—and is realized or fulfilled—through the exercise of virtues. Among these traditions, unsurprisingly, there are different views of the distinctive nature of

---

1. *Nicomachean Ethics* 1102, 1095ff.

human life and hence of what it is for this kind of life to flourish. In this chapter, my subject is the Daoist conception of how a life goes well and what this shows about, and implies for, people's relationship to the natural world of plants, animals, and environments.

The label Daoism comes from the term *daojia* (House, or School, of the Way) that, around 100 B.C.E., Han dynasty historians gave to a philosophical tendency discernible in a number of writings composed or assembled two or three centuries earlier. These writings include the *Daodejing* ("The Classic of the Way and Virtue"), attributed to the legendary Laozi (The Old Master), *The Book of Zhuangzi* (Master Zhuang), and the *Neiye* ("Inner Training").[2] A related term, *daojiao* ("Teachings of the Way"), was later applied to the beliefs and practices of a number of organized religious or "liturgical" schools that began to emerge at the end of the 2nd century C.E. Despite periods during which it was suppressed, Daoism has remained—alongside Buddhism and Confucianism—a main spiritual tradition in China.

The Greek conception of human beings as "rational animals" is not one that is found in the Daoist texts and schools. As in other Chinese traditions of thought, human beings are seen as essentially embodied creatures, but they are not categorized alongside animals in contrast to plants and other forms of inanimate life: rather, they belong with all of these as "living beings" composed of *qi* (vital energy or life force). Chinese texts are as likely to compare a human being with a plant as with an animal in order, for example, to explain how men and women grow and develop.[3] Human beings are distinguished from other living beings through a number of related capacities. The most crucial are the abilities to recognize, follow, and identify with the *dao* (Way) (D 23)—the mysterious, ineffable source or wellspring that is "the beginning of Heaven and Earth" (D 1) and holds sway over all things. This ability consciously to identify with the *dao* is, the texts emphasize, one that presupposes a capacity for cultivation

---

2. References to the classic works within the text use the abbreviations indicated for the following works: *Daodejing* (D), *The Book of Zhuangzi* (Z), *The Book of Liezi* (L), *Neiye* (N). References are to chapters of these works (e.g., D 25 refers to Chapter 25 of the *Daodejing*). I have drawn on various translations, but especially P.J. Ivanhoe, *The Daodejing of Laozi* (Indianapolis, IN: Hackett, 2002); B. Ziporyn, *Zhuangzi: The Essential Writings, with Selections from Traditional Commentaries* (Indianapolis, IN: Hackett, 2009); A.C. Graham, *The Book of Lieh-Tzu: A Classic of Tao* (New York: Columbia University Press, 1990); H. Roth, *The Nei-yeh*, www.stillness.com/tao/nei-yeh.txt (1999).

3. See Sarah Allan, *The Way of Water and Sprouts of Virtue* (Albany: State University of New York Press, 1997), 94ff. One important figure whom Allan discusses is the Confucian thinker Mencius, whose moral philosophy is informed by an analogy between humans and plants.

and, where necessary, transformation of the self. Self-cultivation enables a person, moreover, to discharge the uniquely human responsibility to help keep the world in good order—to "bring the world into harmony" (Z 33), or, in the words of a Han dynasty work, "to assist Heaven and Earth."[4]

In keeping with this conception of human being, the flourishing life, for Daoism, is a virtuous one in which, through bodily, mental, and spiritual cultivation, a person comes to identify with what he or she recognizes as the mysterious source and sustainer of the cosmos. This is a sketch of the flourishing life that probably all Daoists could accept, but it is a brief and vague one that masks considerable differences among tendencies in various schools of Daoism. This limitation becomes clear as soon as one delves further into the matter of what it is for a life to harmonize with the *dao*. In such organized religious movements as the Ways of Great Clarity and of Complete Perfection, there is a pronounced emphasis on the attainment of immortality, apparently on the ground that by never exhausting one's *qi*, a person thereby emulates the (eternal) *dao* itself. There is no similar emphasis, despite some remarks in the *Daodejing* on frugality and ensuring "long life" (D 59), in the older, classic texts. Again, in later Daoist religious dispensations, like that of the Way of the Celestial Masters, worship of Laozi—who is credited with the ability to intercede with Heaven—is a significant component in the spiritual life. There is no hint of the need for or appropriateness of religious worship of a sage in the *Daodejing* or the *Zhuangzi*.

My focus is on earlier or "philosophical" texts such as these two, and I do not discuss later religious doctrines and practices that are unlikely to have resonance for contemporary Western readers and that, in my judgment, have little basis in the foundational texts of Daoism. I do, though, occasionally cite later texts and briefly mention some extensions of ideas about human flourishing and the natural environment that were first indicated in the classic texts.

Virtue and Nature

For the time being, I set aside the heady question of how and why a person's life may be said to be in harmony with the *dao*, and instead consider the seemingly more tractable question of its harmony with nature. The two questions are closely related, since all things in the natural world, with the exception of errant human

---

4. Zhang Jiju, "A Declaration of the Chinese Daoist Association on Global Ecology," in *Daoism and Ecology: Ways within a Cosmic Landscape*, N.J. Girardot, James Miller, and Liu Xiaogan, eds. (Cambridge, MA: Harvard University Press, 2001), 367.

beings, act in accordance with *dao*-given "patterns" that govern "the course of their being."[5]

There are several reasons to think that in the flourishing life of the Daoist sage or "consummate person" an appropriate relationship to natural life—animals, plants, outdoor environments—is especially important. First, a human life is an embodied one whose connection with natural, physical environments is not irrelevant or merely incidental to spiritual fulfillment. Hence, one finds in Daoist tradition reflective attention to and management of the body's integration with nature. A well-known example is the practice of *fengshui* (wind-water) in architecture and landscape design. Second, an abiding theme in Chinese culture since ancient times has been that of natural environments as places where human beings may exercise freedom and find the tranquility essential to appreciative understanding of the *dao*. "Too long a prisoner, captive in a cage, / Now I can get back to Nature." These words from the 4th–5th century Daoist Tao Qian's poem "Returning to Live in the Country" were to be echoed by countless poets of the Tang era, including Li Bai and Wang Wei. Third, an important aspect of the responsibility that human beings have for maintaining good order and harmony in the cosmos is, as already noted, supporting "the myriad creatures in their natural condition" (D 64) and "nourishing" them (Z 33).

But in what, exactly, might harmony with the natural world consist? In popular Western writings on Daoism, at least three suggestions have been made. To begin with, we find the "primitivist" idea that harmony requires a "back to nature" style of life—one that seeks to retrieve some very ancient condition of humankind that supposedly existed prior to the emergence of technology, art, and even society. This idea, and its label, are indeed suggested by some remarks in the "primitivist" chapters of the *Zhuangzi*. Here we find calls to go back to our "uncontrived condition" and reference to carpenters as committing a "crime" in their "mutilation" of wood (Z 9). However, the considered Daoist position is not a "primitivist" one, and almost certainly the remarks that encourage this construal were not mouthed by Master Zhuang himself: the book attributed to him, like most ancient Daoist texts, were compilations, not single-authored works. The classic texts call, not for a return to "the state of nature," but for the conservation of simple agricultural societies in which people are literate, live in houses, dress well, and so on (D 80). Moreover, as we saw earlier, the life of virtue demands reflective understanding (though not necessarily of a kind that can be explicitly articulated): the virtuous Daoist is not a "noble savage." As one commentator

---

5. Han Feizi, "Returning to Live in the Country," in *A Source Book in Chinese Philosophy*, Wing-Tsit Chan, ed. and trans. (Princeton, NJ: Princeton University Press, 1963), 260.

puts it, virtuous Daoists become "*aware* that they are moved by the Way," an experience that is incompatible with "regression to an animal-like unity with nature."[6]

A second and related suggestion is that to seek harmony between human beings and nature is essentially to embrace and practice a "wilderness ideal," a maximally noninterventionist "letting be" of nature for the sake of "saving the earth." But there is no such wilderness ideal in Daoism. *Fengshui* and garden design, to take two obvious examples, are practices that Daoists have traditionally admired and engaged in, but ones that of course involve "intervention" in nature. Generally, too, the landscapes praised by the poets as places in which to find freedom and peace are not wild and remote ones, but "human landscapes," such as orchards and rivers on which people boat. Typically, the poets write not of wilderness, but of the countryside. It is true that there are texts—notably, the *One Hundred and Eighty Precepts,* followed by the early Celestial Masters—that forbid, among much else, disturbing birds and animals, poisoning lakes, and burning vegetation. But the purpose of such precepts is less to conserve pristine wilderness than to ensure that natural environments, cultivated or not, are suitable spaces—sacred ones, in effect—in which priests and other adepts may conduct their spiritual tasks.[7] Anyway, it would surely be a strange kind of harmony with nature that required human beings simply to leave nature alone. Such a policy is contradicted by the Daoist recognition of the intimate interconnections between the human and the nonhuman—by, for example, the emphasis in the *Neiye* (N 1) on how the *qi* that flows through everything unites heaven, earth, and human beings together. Hyperbolic expression is given to this interconnectedness when Zhuangzi proclaims that "Heaven and earth were born with me, and the myriad things and I are one" (Z 2).

Finally, there is the familiar suggestion that Daoist harmony with nature is, to borrow from current vernacular, to "go with the flow," be "laid back" or perhaps remain permanently "chilled out." The suggestion is encouraged, no doubt, by pictorial and literary images of Daoist sages as gently smiling, easy-going, sandal-wearing wanderers and, more seriously, by the analogy stressed in the *Daodejing* (e.g., D 8) between the sage and water. We should, the book urges, emulate water in its flexibility, the nonconfrontational way it goes around obstacles, its natural, steady flow, and so on. This analogy, together with remarks on the ideal of *wu wei* (lit. non-action), inspire a rhetoric of the sage as someone who works with, not against, nature. But it is difficult to know quite what this rhetoric enjoins by way

6. Eske Møllgaard, *An Introduction to Daoist Thought: Action, Language and Ethics in Zhuangzi* (London: Routledge, 2007), 124.

7. See Kristofer Schipper, "Daoist Ecology: The Inner Transformation; A Study of the Precepts of the Early Daoist Ecclesia," in *Daoism and Ecology*.

of actual relations with the natural world. It might seem obvious, for instance, that the Daoist gardener is one who will respect the innate natures of plants. Yet, later Daoists certainly regarded the ideal of *wu wei* as compatible with alchemy and other interventionist techniques. One commentator goes as far as to observe that the traditional Daoist "quest for transformation is alive and well in university laboratories" where work is done on genetic engineering and artificial intelligence.[8] This is hardly the kind of work suggested by phrases like "going with the flow" of nature, but the fact is that, without further elaboration and specification, this rhetoric, suggestive as it is, presupposes—rather than helps to explain—the notion of harmony with nature that it claims to articulate.

Various suggestions, then, as to the form taken by harmony with nature—an important dimension, we know, of the flourishing life for Daoists—have proved unilluminating. For some help, let us consider the sage figures that populate the classic Daoist texts, for these are held to exemplify harmony with nature.

Sages and Spontaneity

The Book of Zhuangzi in particular is crowded with characters who are regarded as manifesting or embodying *de*. This Chinese term is usually translated as "virtue," but in some contexts it is better rendered by such words as "power" or "efficacy." The *de* of a thing or creature is what enables it to become a good example of the kind of being it is. *De* should be "honored," according to the *Daodejing* (D 51), since it is what "nurtures," "rears" and "confirms" things. *De* in the case of human beings is virtue in the sense of the set of qualities or dispositions that enable people to live flourishing and authentically human lives.

Our word "virtue" has acquired a moralistic ring, but by no means are all of the qualities of *de* qualities that we would readily describe as moral virtues. Indeed, the classic texts are often suspicious of, or downright hostile to, morality when this is understood in terms of acting according to principles or out of a sense of duty. It is only when "the Way was lost," the *Daodejing* more than once reminds us, that people become preoccupied with "righteousness," "benevolence," moral conventions, and rites (D 38). In the *Zhuangzi*, this preoccupation—alongside ones with scholarship and technology—is regarded as a mark of a "contrived" and "entangled" way of living that harms the "inborn nature" we should instead be cultivating (Z 8).

In this suspicion of morality, scholarship, and clever technology there is an important clue to the Daoist conception of the *de* of human beings. It indicates

---

8. James Miller, *Daoism: A Short Introduction* (Oxford: Oneworld, 2005), 121.

the central place in this conception of *ziran*—a term that literally means something like "self-so-ness," but is usually rendered by "spontaneity" or "naturalness." This is not, however, the kind of spontaneity prescribed by Romantics, Existentialists, or hippies—"a surrender to passions," the performance of *actes gratuits*, or just "doing your own thing." Rather, as one commentator writes, it is "responsiveness in the impersonal calm when vision is most lucid."[9] The sage "uses [the] mind like a mirror" (Z 7), reflecting how things themselves are instead of viewing them through the distorting prisms of prejudice and self-interest. The sage then "follows along with the way each thing is of itself . . . without trying to add anything" (Z 5). Principles and norms of behavior then become redundant, for they are devices that are employed only by people whose vision is clouded or whose responsiveness to things is atrophied.

The various virtues of the sage are all connected with the ideal of *ziran*—whether as aspects, conditions, or consequences of it. One important virtue that is clearly an aspect of spontaneity is freedom—not in the sense of a license to act as one pleases, but in that of freedom from the contrivances, entanglements, prejudices, and fixed ideas that occlude attentive, mindful responsiveness to things. Something from which it is especially important to become free is what Zhuangzi calls the "characteristic inclination"—characteristic, at least, in complex and sophisticated societies—to *judge* things, to affirm this as right, that as wrong (Z 5). To view things in a manner distorted by the practical and other values that they have for *us* is to be blind to how the things themselves really are. It is this distorting vision that, more than anything else, confirms people's loss of the Way, their distance from the simpler and wiser ways of their ancestors. The obsession with rules, the relentless pursuit of "clever" technology, and the perpetual restlessness of urban life betray a failure any longer to perceive and respond to things as they really are.

Several Daoist virtues are, in effect, conditions for the exercise of spontaneity. Consider, for example, care and discipline of the body. Unless their "eyes and ears are acute and clear," and their bodies "supple," people will be unable to "mirror things" and to perceive and respond to them "with great clarity" (N 16). The same text talks of the "tranquility" necessary for clarity of perception and response, a theme that is also prominent in the *Daodejing*. The sage's mind must be "still" for, when "stirred-up," it becomes "muddied"—hence the sage "desires to be without [the] desires" that produce frustration, anxiety, and mental turbulence" (D 15, 64). A further condition for spontaneity is the virtue of humility. This is a virtue that anyway becomes necessary when we realize, as Zhuangzi continually urges

9. A.C. Graham, *Chuang-Tzu: The Inner Chapters* (Indianapolis, IN: Hackett, 2001), 14.

us to do, that we cannot really *know* many of things we claim to do: "nothing can be definitively called greater or lesser" (Z 17). More to the present point, overconfidence in beliefs and values, and a hubristic refusal to be open to new perspectives, are obviously obstacles to exercising the attentive flexibility that is a mark of spontaneity.

Then there are the virtues that we would expect to be practiced by the spontaneous person. For example, compassion or lovingkindness—one of Laozi's "three treasures" (D67)—will be the natural attitude adopted toward vulnerable people or other creatures once they are seen for what they are and not in a way distorted by personal preferences or hierarchical judgments about a creature's worth (Z 5, 17). We would expect, as well, that a spontaneous person's comportment in the world would be that of *wu wei*, defined by an early commentator on the *Daodejing* as "following what is spontaneous."[10] The many craftsmen and skilled practitioners in the *Zhuangzi* whom we are invited to admire—butchers, swimmers, carpenters, and so on—are people who do not impose themselves on, or contend with, their materials or environment. The consummate swimmer, for example, explains that he "follows the course of the water itself without making any private one of my own" (Z 19). Through mindful attention and flexible responses to things, such persons succeed in their aims economically, gracefully, and without friction.

But why, exactly, is *ziran* or spontaneity an ideal? For Daoists, recall, a human life is a flourishing one when it is led in conscious appreciation of its harmony with nature and hence the *dao*. The answer to the question must therefore be that the *dao* itself is *ziran*, "self-so": there is then a likeness between the virtuous person and the *dao*. This is an answer made explicit in the *Daodejing* (D 25), in which it is explained that people ultimately model themselves on the *dao*, which in turn "models itself on what is spontaneous." The *dao*, although it defies literal description, can be described in such figurative terms as "noncontending," "gentle," "self-reliant," "tranquil," "nurturing," "unbiased," "humble"—terms that help to register that the *dao* has nothing outside of itself to be controlled by or to impose itself on, and that in its unfolding it brings balance and nourishment to all things. In all of this philosophy, there is an analogy with the virtuous sage and skilled practitioner. The sage, swimmer, or carpenter, for example, who "follows the way each thing is . . . without bias" thereby helps to guarantee that "the world will be in order" (Z 7). The swimmer, through acting in keeping with his

---

10. Wang Bi, cited in David E. Cooper, *Convergence with Nature: A Daoist Perspective* (Dartington, UK: Green Books, 2012), 36.

appreciation of how to swim in harmony with the way of things, thereby makes his own small contribution to the harmony of the cosmos.

These answers to the questions of why certain qualities count for Daoists as virtues, and why a spontaneous way of being present in the world is an ideal, leave it fairly open, however, how in everyday practice people should conduct themselves in relation to the natural world. Perhaps this issue can be clarified by first considering what the texts have to say about our treatment of and attitudes toward animals.

"Living with the Birds and Beasts"

In the early 21st century, several statements have been made by Daoist organizations enjoining ethical treatment of animals: for example, by condemning the use in traditional medicine of animal extracts as aphrodisiacs. But these statements are often colored by a modern Western rhetoric of the rights and intrinsic value of animals that has no parallel in traditional Daoist texts. The attitude in these texts, moreover, is clearly a "speciesist" one, in the sense of attributing a special status to human beings, as creatures with a *dao*-given responsibility "to bring the world into harmony." With the significant exception of certain early texts, like *The One Hundred and Eighty Precepts* referred to above, there is relatively little material on animals in the literature of the organized religious schools. Especially among the remarks attributed to Zhuangzi and an earlier sage, Liezi, however, there emerges a clear and attractive account—condensed in the remark that "in the days of perfect virtue, the people lived together with the birds and beasts" (Z 9)—of how the virtuous person will relate to animals.

To begin with, we should admire and learn from many animals as models of the effortless spontaneity that human beings find it so hard to cultivate. Watching fish darting through a pond, for example, can be an object lesson in liberation from obsession with particular goals, in frictionless social relations, and in "allowing the flow of [our] lives to settle into stability" (Z 6). It is worth noting, in this connection, that many Daoist physical exercises and disciplines are inspired by the movements of animals, including cranes and monkeys.[11]

This natural admiration for animals is one reason that hunters, trappers, and fishermen should eschew technologically sophisticated trickery and contrivance when killing or catching animals. More importantly, the effect of such interventions in the natural world is to throw creatures into "great disorder" and

---

11. Kristofer Schipper, *The Taoist Body* (Berkeley: University of California Press, 1993), 137–138.

change their "inborn natures" (Z 13)—perhaps by turning them into purely noc-
turnal creatures, terrified to come out by day, or by upsetting a delicate ecological
balance. Whether or not there is truth to the claim, alluded to earlier, that genetic engineering of animals is a modern extension of the traditional alchemical
techniques of some religious Daoist schools, it is hard to conceive of Zhuangzi
endorsing such a practice.

That people are able to inflict on animals ingenious and cruel methods of
hunting is just one symptom of the estrangement from animals of people who
no longer "live together with the birds and beasts," people for whom there is no
longer any sense of communion with animals. We should try to redress this estrangement, urges Liezi, partly by recalling how similar to those of human beings
are the desires, intelligence, and wish to preserve their lives that animals have. But
we should try as well to restore close relations with animals by, for example, inviting them to "roam in [the] garden and sleep in [the] yard," so that the animals
will eventually regard their host as "one of themselves" (L 2). People should, more
generally, "walk side-by-side" with animals, for our own lives go better when we
exercise virtues like compassion toward animals. As the 4th-century C.E. work,
Baopuzi (the Master Who Embraces Simplicity), puts it, when railing against
those who "enslave the myriad things," by treating animals benevolently and even
with love "one becomes a person of high virtue and will be blessed by Heaven."[12]

The enslavement of animals that results from exploiting them for profit and
from the atrophy of communion with them both reflects and reinforces a failure
to see animals for what they are, a failure to exercise the mindful attention to
things and creatures that is a precondition of spontaneity. The *Zhuangzi*, in
particular, is full of examples whereby people ignore a creature's own nature—
whether through stupidity or indifference—and accordingly treat it in an inappropriate way. In one story, a well-intentioned, but ignorant, man feeds a captured
bird, not with "the wiggly things" it needs and likes, but with "the finest meats"
and other gastronomic delicacies, thereby ensuring that the creature wastes away
(Z 19). In another passage, horse trainers, determined to make the animals obe-
dient, brand, bridle, and fetter them, in violation of the "inborn nature of horses,"
which is freely to "prance and jump over the terrain" (Z 9). The trainers exemplify the entrenched tendency to view animals as put on earth in order to serve
human interests. In the *Liezi*, a courageous boy takes to task a visiting dignitary
who has thanked Heaven for providing—"for the sake of man"—the animals he
is about to feast upon. Mosquitoes, the boy reasons, might as well thank Heaven
for providing human blood to drink (L 8). Liezi would have welcomed early 21st

12. Jiju, "A Declaration," in *Daoism and Ecology*, 366–367.

century pronouncements of the China Daoist Association, such as its "Daoist Faith Statement," that criticize traditional Chinese medicinal practices in which rhinos, bears, and other animals are regarded as resources from which to extract ingredients that supposedly benefit human health or sexual potency.[13]

The emphasis on attention to and recognition of the natures of animals helps one to understand the many references in the classic texts to the virtuous person's "nurturing," "rearing," and "supporting" of things and creatures. As the *Daodejing* expresses it, what is "supported" by the sage whose desires are controlled and who does not impose on the world is "the own course (*ziran*)" of creatures and things (D 64). A world where animals are turned into materials for our use is one that is out of balance and discordant, for it is one in which the *dao*-given natures of natural beings are violated.

Compassionate, respectful, mindful, affectionate—these qualities of a person's attitude toward animals are paradigmatic of the exercise of virtue. As such, it is worth exploring how this relationship to animals may be indicative of the larger consonance with nature and the *dao* itself that, we know, is essential to human flourishing.

Nature, *Dao*, and Human Flourishing

Like a "Daoist animal ethics," a "Daoist environmental ethics" makes no appeal to notions like rights and intrinsic value. This omission does not mean, however, that it is a "shallow" or "anthropocentric" ethics that focuses solely on how human beings may materially benefit from a harmonious relationship to nature. (This focus is despite the several references in both ancient and contemporary texts to the "prosperity and longevity" we may hope to enjoy if we live in an appropriate relation to natural environments.) If the Daoist position has to be slotted into the categories of modern moral philosophy, it is best regarded as a form of "virtue ethics." Our attitudes and actions toward the natural world should be grounded in a conception of what makes a human life a virtuous or flourishing one.

A good way to understand what an ethical comportment toward nature might be like is to unpack the metaphor, inspired by references to human beings "nurturing" the myriad things, of Daoists as "gardeners of the cosmos."[14] It is a metaphor that helps to draw attention to several important aspects of this

---

13. "Daoist Faith Statement," included in Martin Palmer (with Victoria Finlay), *Faith in Conservation* (Washington, DC: World Bank, 2003). For a more extended version of my account of Daoist attitudes toward animals, see David E. Cooper, "Birds, Beasts and the *Dao*," *Philosopher's Magazine* 65 (2014): 84–90.

14. The phrase is James Miller's, in *Daoism: A Short Introduction* (Oxford: Oneworld, 2005), pp. 45–46, but it is one with precedents in Daoist literature. For a detailed exposition of the metaphor, see David E. Cooper, "Gardeners of the Cosmos: The Way of the Garden in East

comportment. For a start, it suggests—as we might expect on the basis of earlier remarks—that the environmental concern of Daoists is not solely or mainly with wilderness: for example, with protecting wild places from all human activity. Environmental concern, as we saw in the case of the *One Hundred and Eighty Precepts*, is more focused on places where human beings engage with nature.

The metaphor indicates next a number of analogies between the responsible gardener and people who conduct themselves appropriately in and toward natural environments. The good gardener nurtures and cares for plants and is attentive and responsive to the needs of what he or she is growing, and avoids forcing and rushing things. Like the farmer described by Zhuangzi (Z 12) who eschews a fancy newfangled irrigation device, the good gardener resists becoming entangled in technological "trickery" and "contrivance" and thereby losing contact with "the pure and simple and vital." Likewise, the attitude and comportment of people toward the natural environments that lie beyond the walls of their gardens should be caring, attentive, responsive, and free from the desire to submit them to technological control and exploitation. The virtuous Daoist extends to the landscape the kind of care shown by gardeners for their garden—and, indeed, the kind of concern for animals that Liezi and Zhuangzi proposed.

While gardening need not be solitary, it is typically "personal," for gardeners usually own the gardens in which they work and where they have their homes. To cultivate a garden is therefore to be fostering, at the same time, an individual, personal relationship with the garden. The Daoist emphasis on how we should relate to nature is a similarly "personal" one. In the books of Liezi and Zhuangzi, as in later works that perceive natural environments as theaters in which to seek health, peace of mind, and longevity, concern for nature is directed, in the first instance, toward the cultivation of one's own relationship to it. The Daoist is less likely to be found in the ranks of "eco-warriors," fighting against some global injustice, than among those—like responsible gardeners, farmers, and foresters— who care for the local places and creatures with which they are intimate and their lives are entwined. A text whose importance has been recognized only in recent times, the *Taiping jing* (Scripture of Great Peace), puts into the mouth of a sage-king a simple expression of what is itself a simple but moving message: "people should assist Heaven to produce living things and assist Earth by giving nourishment to form proper shapes."[15]

Asian Tradition," in *The Good Gardener: Nature, Humanity and the Garden*, Annette Giesecke and Naomi Jacobs, eds. (London: Artifice, 2015).

15. Jiju, "A Declaration," in *Daoism and Ecology*, 367.

Little needs to be added to this description of the virtuous Daoist's relations with animals and nature in order to understand how the life of this person is a flourishing one—a life, that is, "on the Way," in harmony with the *dao*. This harmony is because to be "on the Way" just is intelligently and reflectively to cultivate and exercise the virtues that inform right relations not only with one's fellow human beings, but also with natural environments and creatures. To be in harmony with the *dao* is not to stand in a certain privileged relation to a personal creator God, or—at the other extreme—is it to abandon one's humanity and seek to become, as Hegel put it, "sunk in nature." It is, rather, to live spontaneously, thereby aligning one's life to the nature of the *dao*, which is "modeled" on *ziran*. Exercising the virtues—spontaneity itself, and the qualities that flow into and from it—not least in relation to natural life, is the way that men and women are "on the Way" and lead lives that are flourishing.

5 ALL GOD'S CREATURES ARE COMMUNITIES LIKE YOU (QUR'AN 6:38)

PRECEDENTS FOR ECO-HALAL MEAT IN MUSLIM TRADITIONS

Sarah E. Robinson-Bertoni

People, eat what is good and lawful from the earth. . . . You who believe, eat the good things We [God] have provided for you and be grateful to God, if it is Him that you worship. (Qur'an 2:168, 2:172)

Introduction

Historian of religions Wendy Doniger wrote, "Animals and gods are two closely related communities poised like guardians on either threshold of our human community, two others by which we define ourselves."[1] Muslim identity can be expressed through practices in relation to animals, particularly by prohibiting meat that is not *halal*, or permissible. Designating spiritual, ethical, and ritual purity, this classification originated in the Qur'an and is interpreted worldwide, yet, it is particularly salient for diasporic or minority communities.[2] In response to ethical, ecological, social, and nutritional problems associated with factory-farming animals for meat, a variety of Muslims in the United States have forged innovative yet tradition-rooted ways for expressing religiosity through sourcing and eating "eco-halal" meat, instead of factory-farmed meat. The eco-halal movement roots in Islam, providing meaningful ethical expression for contemporary Muslims to counteract environmental and social ills through daily eating.[3]

---

1. Wendy Doniger, "The Four Worlds," in *Animals in Four Worlds: Sculptures from India*, Stella Snead, ed. (Chicago: University of Chicago Press, 1989), 3.

2. In Muslim majority regions, food may be assumed to be *halal*.

3. The author does not assert normative claims for Islam, but rather this scholarly assemblage represents existing articulations of Muslim ethics for restoring wholesome relations with animals, land, waters, farm laborers and farmers, and local food economies.

A variety of Qur'an passages, Muslim traditions, and contemporary Islamic scholarly conversations engage ethical commitments to land, nature, water, animal communities, and individual animals, commitments that together provide ample support for Muslim food and agriculture ethics expressed through eco-halal meat. First, in terms of earth care, Islamic ethicists have discussed the Qur'anic use of *khalifah*, which presents humans as viceregents responsible for tending God's creation. Earth's beauty offers signs (*ayat*) of God's work as creator of nature and its bounty. Nature's balance (*mizan*) also reflects God's creative hand, just as its imbalance reflects human ignorance and offense against God. All three terms, *khalifah, ayat*, and *mizan*, may be employed to critique and counteract agricultural practices that produce excessive pollution, diminish fertile topsoil, and exploitatively and unsustainably extract resources.

The Qur'an and *hadith* depict Islamic care ethics toward animals: animals live in *ummah*, or communities of their own; animals have languages of their own; kindness to animals results in God's forgiveness; animal cruelty results in hellfire; slaughter must be according to specifications; and animals should live naturally and eat their naturally adapted food. In eco-halal food movements, priorities for earth care combine with specific requirements for *halal* slaughter, which have traditionally been understood as more humane methods to reduce animal suffering.

Contemporary US Muslims navigate cultural coherence and assimilation in myriad ways; for example, choosing *halal* meat has been a key marker of identity in Muslim-minority regions. Although globally, Muslim identities and religious expressions vary, approximately 75% of North American Muslims choose to express their religion, in part, via *halal* meat consumption.[4] As eco-halal gains popularity as a further expression of Muslim identity and religiosity, its relative authenticity as a practice rooted in Muslim tradition gains importance.[5] This

---

4. Two similar statistics appear in this paper with citations for different authors, both of which are not verifiable: (1) 75% of Muslims keep *halal* standards as part of their religious observance (Mohammed Mazhar Hussaini, *Islamic Dietary Concepts and Practices*. [Bedford Park, IL: Islamic Food and Nutrition Council of America], 1993), and (2) 75% of Muslims in North America eat *halal* (B.T. Hunter, "More Consumers Ask: Is It Kosher?," *Consumers' Research Magazine* 80, no. 4 [1997]: 10–15). Karijn Bonne and Wim Verbeke, "Religious Values Informing Halal Meat Production and the Control and Delivery of Halal Credence Quality," *Agriculture and Human Values* 25 (2008): 35, 39. Mohammed Mazhar Hussaini, "Halal Haram Lists: Why They Do Not Work," web resource, accessed August 23, 2004 (by Hussaini), accessed September 15, 2015 (by Robinson-Bertoni), http://www.soundvision.com/info/halalhealthy/halal.list.asp. This webpage lists its content as deriving from Hussaini, *Islamic Dietary Concepts*.

5. I examined this notion of eco-halal meat eating as pious action in the following conference paper: "Sourcing Zabiha-Halal Meat as an Expression of Piety: Taqwa Eco-food Cooperative's

chapter takes the position of working within existing conditions, assuming that the majority of Muslims will continue to eat meat, despite a minority choosing to avoid some of these problems by abstaining from meat eating altogether.[6] Precedents in texts and traditions have become relevant for conscientious individuals and community groups to consider Islamic support for eco-halal meat sourcing and eating as a more *tayyib*, or wholesome, ethical and practical choice in comparison with factory-farmed meat, even when it is labeled *halal*.[7] Advocates of eco-halal meat wish to establish its legitimacy as a Muslim practice, in order to encourage at least some of the *halal* meat market to transition from factory-farmed *halal* meat to *tayyib* eco-halal meat.[8]

In the United States, even when food is labeled *halal*, globalized, industrial food systems present unique challenges for Muslims to eat ethically. Most food animals eaten in the United States live confined and unnatural lives in factory farms. Factory farms employ antibiotics both to assist in artificially fattening the animals and to combat unhealthy filth that characterizes the inhumanely cramped, indoor environment.[9] These practices pose ethical problems for

---

Care Ethics in Action," Global Halal Conference, Michigan State University, East Lansing, February 21, 2015.

6. Kecia Ali, "Muslims and Meat-Eating: Vegetarianism, Gender, and Identity," *Journal of Religious Ethics* 43, no. 2 (2015): 268–288.

7. Sarah Robinson-Bertoni, "Re-territorializing Religiosity in Wholesome Muslim Praxis," *Religions* 8, no. 7, Special Issue, *Religion and Nature in a Globalizing World*, Evan Berry, ed., July 22, 2017, http://www.mdpi.com/2077-1444/8/7/132.

8. Sarah E. Robinson (now Robinson-Bertoni), "Refreshing the Concept of Halal Meat: Resistance and Religiosity in Chicago's Taqwa Eco-food Cooperative," in *Religion, Food, and Eating in North America*, Benjamin Zeller, Marie Dallam, Reid Neilson, and Nora Rubel, eds. (New York: Columbia University Press, 2014), 274–293.

9. Antibiotics not only reduce and ideally eliminate disease-bearing bacterial infections for livestock animals, but also have been proven to enhance animal growth. Antibiotics have been included in livestock feed in small doses, which encourage animal growth but do not provide a high enough dose to eliminate harmful bacteria. Thus, when low doses of antibiotics appear in animal feed, not only do animals grow more quickly, but also strains of antibiotic-resistant diseases survive the low-dose environment. This peculiar scenario can be conducive to the spread of antibiotic-resistant diseases for animals. Both diseases and low-dose antibiotic use in livestock affect people's health: for example, via animal feces in waterways, which eventually return antibiotics to drinking water supplies. Eighty percent of antibiotics used in the United States per year are infused into the animal husbandry ecosystem, also mentioned below in the section "Protecting Water from Pollution." Natural Resources Defense Council, "Facts about Pollution from Livestock Farms," web resource, accessed September 18, 2015, http://www.nrdc.org/water/pollution/ffarms.asp. "Modern Meat: Is Your Meat Safe? Antibiotic Debate Overview," *Frontline*, PBS, web resource, accessed December 14, 2015, http://www.pbs.org/wgbh/pages/frontline/shows/meat/safe/overview.html.

Muslims seeking to adhere to religious values of humane treatment of animals and stewardship of the earth. For those who value interconnected human and animal flourishing, eco-halal meat is an improvement upon the majority of meat marketed commercially.

Earth Care

Inheriting the Earth

The Arabic terms *khilafah* (stewardship) and *khalifah* (steward, trustee, successor) appear in Islam's holy book, the Qur'an, as well as the *hadith*, or traditions. These terms imply that humanity acts in a role of guardian or trustee for the natural world through a covenant with God.[10] Trusteeship has a close parallel with the term sustainable, which involves a net-neutral relationship with resources, limiting extraction to what may be replenished.[11] The moral test for people lies in the balance between using the earth and relating to nature's resources as God's appointed trustee, to be eventually assessed and judged by God. The Qur'an narrative shows several other natural entities refusing the role as caretaker/ steward (*surah* 33:72), and humans agreeing to this role with some trepidation. The earth, sky, and mountains refused God's offer before humanity was entrusted with this serious responsibility. With God as true owner of God's work—the entirety of nature, including land, water, wild plants and animals, crops, and livestock—humanity takes responsibility to be liable for ensuring nature's health and wellbeing on behalf of the Creator. Rather than owners with rights to exploit, humans serve God as earth's temporary trustees, mindful of the consequences of breaking God's trust.

Early Islamic legal scholar Abu al-Faraj (897–967 CE) asserts that nature— land, trees, water, air—ultimately belongs to God, to be shared by people as a commons. He writes, "People do not in fact own things, for the real owner is

---

10. This Muslim tradition exists in parallel with discussions of stewardship among other Abrahamic religions. Some Muslim writers use the term stewardship in a similar way to that of Christian and Jewish environmental writers, indicating a divinely ordained requirement that people care for the land, water, and other natural resources with attention to their original or continuing ownership by God, and with awareness of future inheritors of the stewardship responsibility.

11. The common parlance and usage of the terms sustainability and sustainable development derive from a presentation at the World Commission on Environment and Development on April 27, 1987, commonly called the Brundtland Report, which states: "Sustainable development is development that meets the needs of the present without compromising the ability of future generations to meet their own needs." This pivotal work was later published: Brian R. Keeble, "Our Common Future," *Medicine and War* 4:1 (1988): 17–25.

their Creator; they only enjoy the usufruct of things, subject to the Divine Law."[12] Economics scholar Mohammed Ansari furthers this claim by invoking a particularly problematic offense in Islam, *shirk*, or attempting to share in God's unique identity. Ansari compares people's resource ownership with *shirk*, in order to encourage a greater sense of stewardship, or *khalifah*, of nature entrusted to humanity by God.[13]

The Qur'an has multiple references to the *khalifah*, such as *surah* 2:30: "[Y]our Lord told the angels, 'I am putting a successor on earth.'"[14] An alternate translation reads, "Thy Sustainer said unto the angels: 'Behold, I am about to establish upon earth one who shall inherit it.'"[15] Both of these translations give the sense of inheritance or trusteeship, a temporary responsibility, passed on from each generation to the next.[16] Similarly, visitors to the website for the Islamic Foundation for Ecology and Environmental Sciences have found this translation of *surah* 6:165, "He who has appointed you *guardians* on the earth and raised some of you above others in *understanding*, so He could test you regarding what He has given you" (emphasis mine).[17] This verse, from a chapter called "Livestock," names the

---

12. Usufruct laws define what can be taken, for example, from a fruit tree whose branches emerge from private property and reach across a public sidewalk. These branches are subject to usufruct, in which anyone may harvest fruit from the public leaning limbs, but not from the limbs that remain over private land. Abu al-Faraj in Al-Hafiz Masri, "Islam and Ecology," in *Islam and Ecology,* Fazlun Kahlid and Joanne O'Brien, eds. (New York: Cassell/World Wide Fund for Nature, 1992), 6–7.

13. M.I. Ansari, "Islamic Perspective on Sustainable Development," *American Journal of Islamic Social Sciences* 11 (1995): 400.

14. Full text of Qur'an 2:29–30: "[29] It was He [God] who created all that is on the earth for you, then turned to the sky and made the seven heavens; it is He who has knowledge of all things. [30] [Prophet], when your Lord told the angels, 'I am putting a successor on earth' they said, 'How can You put someone there who will cause damage and bloodshed, when we celebrate Your praise and proclaim Your holiness?' but He said, 'I know things that you do not.'" Translation by M.A.S. Abdel Haleem, in *The Qur'an* (New York: Oxford University Press, 2008), 7. As this passage shows, there may be further ambiguity in the ecological implications for this passage. Nonetheless, it is held up as an important example of ecologically potent Islamic sacral text.

15. Muhammed Asad, trans., *The Message of the Qur'an* (Bristol, UK: Book Foundation, 2003), 15.

16. M.A.S. Abdel Haleem, *The Qur'an* (New York: Oxford University Press, 2008), 7 *na.*

17. Fazlun Khalid founded the Islamic Foundation for Ecology and Environmental Sciences, whose website highlights this translation of the Qur'an passage, using contemporary, accessible language. "Charter," Islamic Foundation for Ecology and Environmental Sciences, web resource, accessed August 18, 2015, http://www.ifees.org.uk/charter. A more traditional translation reads, "It is He who made you successors on the earth and raises some of you above others in rank, to test you through what He gives you" (Haleem, *The Qur'an*, 93). Qur'an translator Muhammad Asad translates the same passage, "For, He it is who has made you inherit the

responsibility humanity faces, including tests of merit, in remaining accountable to God when caring for the earth as successors, inheritors, or guardians. In the end, humanity's role as steward points to each person's reckoning on the last day, or judgment day: the Creator will hold each individual accountable for his or her actions, with dire consequences for failure or corruption.

The human role as steward, under the Creator's scrutiny, has significant implications for the environmental and animal-welfare dimensions of food sourcing. Thus, this is a meaningful starting point for arguments in support of eco-halal food.

Learning from Nature's Signs

Islamic tradition and its interpreters recognize the teachings inherent in nature; humans may learn from it if they perceive it properly. As God's creation, all of nature has a "sacred aspect," meaning "the whole of it [is] as sacred and as clean as a mosque."[18] This belief connects to the concept of primordial unity; all is one in God.[19] The systems of nature and the creatures that participate in them already comply with the divine law. Some thinkers emphasize the notion that the whole of nature is "*muslim*" (small *m*), because in following the laws of nature, ecosystems and individual creatures are submitting to God.[20] Humanity, then, has much to learn from the natural world. Anything humans do that thwarts a creature's inherent nature—such as keeping livestock in confinement, feeding them a diet to which their bodies are unsuited, and many other practices to be examined below—violate God's laws.

It seems that humanity has a particular problem as the one earthly species responsible for choosing to live according to divine law—a skill, or more accurately a state of being, that comes "naturally" to the rest of living nature. Animals live according to divine will unless their natures are interrupted by human interventions. As stewards or guardians of nature, humans must consider natural habits of other-than-human animals, in order to properly manage livestock. Rather, good animal husbandry demands attention to an animal's inherent,

earth, and has raised some of you by degrees above others, so that He might try you by means of what He has bestowed upon you" (Asad, *The Message of the Qur'an*, 229).

18. Mohammad Yusuf Siddiq, "An Ecological Journey in Muslim Bengal," in *Islam and Ecology*, Foltz, Denny, and Baharuddin, eds. (2003), 452.

19. Siddiq, "An Ecological Journey in Muslim Bengal," 452.

20. Ibrahim Ozdemir, "Toward an Understanding of Environmental Ethics from a Qur'anic Perspective," in *Islam and Ecology*, Foltz, Denny, and Baharuddin, eds. (2003), 17. M.A.S. Abdel Haleem, *The Qur'an* (New York: Oxford University Press, 2008), 223–224.

muslim, nature, a demand that literally means submitting to the laws of nature as set by God.

Proper attention to the natural world entails learning divine balance, or *mizan*. Among people, *mizan* represents balance in behavior and use, moderation based on submission to God, avoiding waste or excess. Fazlun Khalid, the founder of the Islamic Foundation for Ecology and Environmental Science, describes *mizan* as the nature (essence) of all of nature (environment) as submitting to God. Khalid describes nomadic Tuareg communities in terms of *mizan*: they "had evolved a lifestyle unique to the environment in which they lived . . . in balance with their environment."[21] Unfortunately this balanced lifestyle was lost, a microcosm of what has happened to all people, according to Khalid: "We have lost the art of living in the *fitra* state, that is, the natural state, in balance and in harmony with creation."[22] In the words of influential scholar and former Pakistani government education advisor Saadia Khawar Khan Chishti, "Al-Qur'an and *Hadith* refer to Islam as *din al-fitra*, or literally, 'the religion of primordial nature.'"[23] Chishti considered the core of Islam reflecting the instinctive, natural, "life-giving nature" of things. The "order of nature" concept is central to the Islamic environmental scholarship of Seyyed Hossein Nasr, arguably among the earliest and most influential 20th-century scholars of religion and ecology.[24]

---

21. Fazlun Khalid, "The Disconnected People," in *Islam and Ecology,* Fazlun Khalid and Joanne O'Brien, eds. (New York: World Wide Fund for Nature, 1992), 103.

22. Ibid., 110.

23. Saadia Khawar Khan Chishti, "Fitra: An Islamic Model for Humans and the Environment," in *Islam and Ecology*, Foltz, Denny, and Baharuddin, eds. (2003), 67–82.

24. Since the 1960s, Seyyed Hossein Nasr has championed environmental thinking, and he may be counted among the first active religious scholarly voices concerned with planetary health. Nasr is a prominent Iranian American scholar of Islam in cross-cultural translation, particularly for European and North American audiences. In 1996, he published a comparative study of religious responses to the environmental crisis, entitled *Religion and the Order of Nature*. Nasr critiqued environmental problems as deriving from a secular, scientific worldview, offering a counter-narrative in a perennialist philosophy of religions, considering each religion to have environmental potential. His 1996 work preceded the first conferences on World Religions and Ecology at Harvard University (1996–1998). Under the leadership of scholars Mary Evelyn Tucker and John Grim, these original conferences collected contributions from religious, scientific, and other scholarly and vocationally relevant voices from major religions, defining the wider field of religion and ecology. Nasr participated in the original conference on Islam and ecology and offered a chapter to the published volume with the same name. Subsequent edited volumes emerged, collecting expert papers representing each major world religion in conversation with environmental themes. Seyyed Hossein Nasr, *Religion and the Order of Nature: The 1994 Cadbury Lectures at the University of Birmingham* (New York: Oxford University Press, 1996). Also, see the series of edited volumes on world religions and ecology by Harvard University Press.

These interpreters agree that humans may learn good stewardship through attention to the ways of nature: its balance, its natural order, and its inherent capacity to submit to God's will, defining the term *muslim*. Insofar as contemporary farming practices disrupt this balance, they may be critiqued; an effort for eco-halal food seeks food production in harmony with nature's God-ordained ways.

Protecting Water from Pollution

One of the most salient examples of good environmental stewardship in the Qur'an and hadith regards water: both sources prohibit water pollution and misuse.[25] Beyond its use for drinking, cooking, and agriculture, water has daily practical consequences in necessary washings before prayer.[26] Although much broader in scope, common cautions against greed and excess also apply to water use, encouraging moderation. According to Saudi Arabian environmental planner Othman Abd-Ar-Rahman Llewellyn, in Islam any source of water is common, rather than private property. Llewellyn delineates that a community of people's right of thirst takes precedence over cooking and washing, followed by water for livestock animals, then agricultural crops.[27]

Founding coordinator for Taqwa Eco-food Cooperative in Chicago, Shireen Pishdadi, named Qur'anic problems with polluting water as a key motivation to provide the community with education and access to eco-halal meat. In an interview with the author, Pishdadi emphasized the importance of water quality when thinking about a wider interpretation of *halal* meat:

> It's not *halal*, it is *haram* to pollute water, it is explicitly *haram* to pollute water, so if the food we're eating was raised in a way that pollutes water, is it *halal*? And nobody wants to answer that question . . . So basically the conversation's always about how the animal was slaughtered . . . are we looking at the letter of the law, black and white, or are we looking at the spirit of the law too? Islam is about principles, you know, and applying just principles, justice. It's not about blindly following the letter of the law. Even in the Qur'an it says, don't eat pork, but if you're starving and

25. Seyyed Hossein Nasr, "Islam, the Contemporary Islamic World, and the Environmental Crisis," in *Islam and Ecology*, Foltz, Denny, and Baharuddin, eds. (2003), 98.

26. In preparing for prayer, a notable exception is the prescription for washing when water is unavailable, in which case the prayerful may wash hands and face by using dust. (Qur'an 4:43, 5:6)

27. Othman Abd-Ar-Rahman Llewellyn, "The Basis for a Discipline of Islamic Environmental Law," in *Islam and Ecology*, Foltz, Denny, and Baharuddin, eds. (2003), 204.

you're going to die then eat it, you know what I'm saying? It's not black and white like that.[28]

Pishdadi appealed to the principles of justice in her interpretation, moving beyond the permissibility of meat. If water pollution is not permissible, then participating indirectly in such pollution via industrial food animal husbandry will follow as impermissible. Through the example of extreme hunger, she noted the flexibility of the Qur'an to meet real-life challenges faced by people attempting to live principled lives. Facing no shortage of food, Pishdadi saw a profound opportunity to deepen her religious expression through sourcing meats from small farmers, avoiding harmful effects from factory farms, which excessively pollute water.

Water pollution from factory farms is a significant problem. In California, 100,000 square miles of groundwater have been polluted by nitrates, which are linked to cattle farming. In Indiana in 1996, excessive nitrates in drinking water was associated with nearby feedlots, and the Centers for Disease Control found a link between nitrate pollution and "spontaneous abortions."[29] A 2015 study located nitrates in the drinking water of seven million people living in the United States.[30] Approximately forty diseases, including serious pathogens, are associated with livestock feces pollution, such as E. coli, Salmonella, fecal coliform, and cryptosporidium. Dairy-cow waste may have been central in Milwaukee's 1993 cryptosporidium outbreak, in which a hundred people died and 400,000 fell ill. Beyond pathogens, a wide majority of antibiotics used in the United States are given to livestock, in the range of twenty-nine million pounds, or 80% of all antibiotics dispensed.[31] As stated above, this generalized overuse of antibiotics for the purposes of fattening the animal, while artificially addressing filthy conditions for the animals, also contributes to an increase in antibiotic-resistant diseases, a hazard for nonhuman animals and people with bacterial infections.[32] Near concentrated animal feeding operations, animal waste "lagoons" can span the size of several football fields. In North Carolina in 1995, one such hog-manure lagoon leaked from its eight-acre trench, dumping manure into the New River to

---

28. Shireen Pishdadi, interview by Sarah Robinson, digital recording, October 2, 2010, Chicago, IL, transcript lines 819–828.

29. Natural Resources Defense Council, "Facts about Pollution from Livestock Farms," web resource, accessed September 18, 2015, http://www.nrdc.org/water/pollution/ffarms.asp.

30. Environmental Working Group, "State of American Drinking Water," web resource, accessed August 10, 2017, https://www.ewg.org/tapwater/state-of-american-drinking-water.php#.WY1JmXeGNmC.

31. Natural Resources Defense Council, "Facts about Pollution from Livestock Farms."

32. Ibid.

the tune of twenty-five million gallons, causing ten million fish deaths, as well as contaminating 364,000 acres of shellfish wetland on the coast. The Natural Resources Defense Council reported, "Ammonia, a toxic form of nitrogen released in gas form during waste disposal, can be carried more than 300 miles through the air before being dumped back onto the ground or into the water, where it causes algal blooms and fish kills."[33] Excessive algae decomposes in a way that interrupts oxygen access in the water, causing hypoxia, which kills or stunts growth of local marine animals or causes them to disappear, seeking clearer waters.[34] Thus, water pollution from factory farms poses serious health dangers to humans, fish, and riparian and ocean biosystems. Pishdadi's contamination concern is ecologically salient, as well as religiously significant.

Care for Animals

Scholar Richard Foltz writes that there is no consistent assessment of animals from an Islamic perspective across all authoritative texts, traditions, and leaders.[35] Islam's holy book, the Qur'an, contains many references to animals, including several chapters named for insects, livestock, and even an elephant. A variety of interpreters across history and geography have contributed to a complex reweaving of ethical meanings about animals and meat eating. Following is a collection of arguments for animal care, which leave a wide berth for interpretation, yet have been used to cite ethical and ecological content in Islam for animals.

Animal Communities and Animal Language

The Qur'an describes animals as members of communities, or *umam* (plural of singular *ummah*), akin to human communities (Qur'an 6:38), which some scholars cite as reason to give particular respect to animals. The passage preceding *surah* 6:38 shows the debate separating believers from unbelievers:

> (6:37) They also say, "Why has no sign been sent down to him from his Lord?" Say, "God certainly has the power to send down a sign," though most of them do not know: (38) all the creatures that crawl on the

---

33. Ibid.

34. Oliver Milman, "The Meat Industry Blamed for Largest-Ever 'Dead Zone' in Gulf of Mexico," *Guardian*, August 1, 2017, web resource, accessed August 10, 2017, https://www.theguardian.com/environment/2017/aug/01/meat-industry-dead-zone-gulf-of-mexico-environment-pollution.

35. "[T]here exists no unified Islamic or Muslim view of nonhuman animals," Richard Foltz, *Animals in Islamic Tradition and Muslim Cultures* (Oxford: Oneworld, 2006), 149.

earth and those that fly with their wings are communities [*umam*] like yourselves. We have missed nothing out of the Record—in the end they will be gathered to their Lord.[36]

Indicating the importance of signs of God to support belief, the narrative suggests that God created signs to exhibit God's existence, here through the resemblance between animal and human communities. The *ummah* is not only indicative of an otherwise secular understanding of social order but is also often the term for people's spiritual coherence in community. This passage refers to a divinely ordained order of nature, in which a variety of animals form groups according to the ways God made them, groups that by their very existence become another sign of God's existence. Further, this passage suggests that animal communities will return to God, as people endeavor to do through Islam.

As a Qur'anic scholar who focuses on animals, Sarra Tlili notices the apparent absence of certain categories in *surah* 6:38's communities: what about sea creatures, angels, and jinn?[37] Agreeing with the early Islamic scholar al-Qurtubi (d. 671), Tlili interprets this lack as an example of the Qur'an's emphasis on what is familiar to its intended human audience. (For example, God "'speaks [in the Qur'an] about wool, fur, and fleece but not cotton nor linen, because the latter items were not available in the lands of the Arabs.'") Taking the spirit rather than the letter of the law for creatures named in the Qur'an allows Tlili to advance her larger goal of peeling back anthropocentric interpretations, creating eco-centric possibilities for animals in the Qur'an's theocentric worldview.[38] Tlili also notes the absence of a distinct line between humans and nonhuman animals in this passage, instead seeing the capacity of various kinds of creatures to form communities comparable to human communities.

Qur'an scholar Muhammad Asad sees the communities named in *surah* 6:38 as both varied in type and indicative of God's ordering of the world.[39] Focusing

---

36. *Surahs* 6:37–38 in M.A.S. Abdel Haleem, trans., *The Qur'an* (New York: Oxford University Press, 2008), 82.

37. Sarra Tlili, *Animals in the Qur'an* (New York: Cambridge University Press, 2012), 9–10. Sarra Tlili, "The Meaning of the Qur'anic Word 'dābba': 'Animals' or 'Nonhuman Animals?'" *Journal of Quranic Studies* 12 (2010): 180–181. A *jinn* is a spirit being of lower rank than angels, which can possess people or appear in human or animal form.

38. Sarra Tlili, *Animals in the Qur'an*, ix, and thematic throughout the work.

39. Asad writes, "The word *ummah* . . . primarily denotes a group of living beings having certain characteristics or circumstances in common. Thus, it is often synonymous with 'community,' 'people,' 'nation,' 'genus,' 'generation,' and so forth. Inasmuch as every such grouping is characterized by the basic fact that its constituents (whether human or animal) are endowed with life, the term *ummah* sometimes signifies '[God's] creatures' (*Lisan al-'Arab*, with particular reference to this very Qur'an verse . . .). Thus, the meaning of the above passage is

on how natural communities can increase piety, environmental science and architecture scholar Attilio Petruccioli explains, "[W]hen an excited [Prophet] Muhammad describes the life of bees, it is not the 'marvelous mystery' of nature that moves him, but rather the perfect organization of a community he would like to transpose to the human Islamic *umma*."[40] A Classical jurist, Ahmad ibn Habit, took this verse to mean that "there never was a community (*umma*) without a warner [i.e., a prophet] having lived among them."[41] Richard Foltz deduced from this passage that animals also might become prophets among themselves, complexifying notions of anthropocentrism across the Abrahamic traditions.[42]

Underscoring continuity between human and animal communities, feminist vegetarian Muslim scholar Ghazala Anwar refers to "non-human muslim members of the *ummah*," to describe animals (recall that all animals can be considered *muslim* since they submit to God's laws in nature). In part on the basis of a reference to lactating and pregnant females (*surah* 22:2), Anwar asserts unity among mammals.[43] To cite continuity between human and other-than-human mammals, she references these and other Muslim traditions, defining vegetarianism as a non-obligatory sacrifice reflecting *tawhid*, or the oneness of God.

Considering, then, the Qur'anic notion that God made animals to live in communities as people do, and as God made them to do, Muslim farmers might embrace religious responsibility to maintain animals in indoor and outdoor spaces where they can freely engage in natural, community activities. Because the majority of contemporary eaters do not farm, it is incumbent upon eaters to

---

this: Man can detect God's 'signs' or 'miracles' in all the life-phenomena that surround him, and should, therefore, try to observe them with a view to better understanding 'God's way' (*sunnat Allah*)—which is the Qur'anic term for what we call the 'laws of nature'" (Asad, *The Message of the Qur'an*, 203).

40. Attilio Petruccioli, "Nature in Islamic Urbanism: The Garden in Practice and in Metaphor," in *Islam and Ecology*, Foltz, Baharuddin, and Denny, eds. (2003), 500–501. Please note that transliterations of Arabic words will be consistent with cited authors' usage, though their spelling may be inconsistent with the author's convention, such as *ummah*.

41. Richard C. Foltz, "'This She-Camel of God is a Sign to You': Dimensions of Animals in Islamic Tradition and Muslim Culture," *A Communion of Subjects: Animals in Religion, Science, and Ethics*, Paul Waldau and Kimberley Patton, eds. (New York: Columbia University Press, 2006), 151.

42. Ibid., 151.

43. Ghazala Anwar, unpublished conference paper, "From Animal Welfare to Animal Rights: The Basmalah of Vegetarianism," American Academy of Religion, national meeting in Atlanta, Study of Islam Section and Animals and Religion Group, Theme: To Kill or Not to Kill: Islamic Perspectives on Animal Ethics, November 22, 2015.

ensure that their food animals lived naturally in animal community.[44] This too may contribute to a holistic and wholesome (*tayyib*) eco-halal standard.

In the chapter entitled "The Ants," the Qur'an shows animals communicating not only with one another, but with people as well. King Solomon understands the ants' speech as one warns the others to stay out from under King Solomon's army's feet (*surah* 27:18).[45] King Solomon responds by smiling and offering thanks to God, renewing his commitment to act in ways that honor and please God.[46] In *surah* 27:20–28, a bird communicates in the role of servant to King Solomon, reporting on crucial political and religious ideas learned through visiting the Queen of Sheba's community. Bird language, though remarkable, here is instrumental politically, and the King threatens the bird's life when it is tardy in returning from its mission. Perhaps this passage indicates a harsher background to which many animal-care passages in the Qur'an respond, beyond anthropocentric ethical concerns, to the misuse of power, tyranny, and cruelty to animals. The Qur'an provides evidence of animal subservience and cruel treatment, contrasting with other passages depicting care and appreciation for animals, perhaps most compellingly by asserting animal and human communities as comparable.

Cruelty to and Kindness for Animals

Cruelty to live animals is unacceptable in numerous accounts. The *hadith Jihad Muwatta* depicts an appreciation for horses. In this *hadith*, the Prophet Muhammad uses his own cloth to wipe his horse's mouth. When someone wonders why, the Prophet responds, "Last night I was rebuked [by God] for not looking after my horse."[47] Tender care for animals appears here as a response to God's dissatisfaction with their neglect by the Prophet himself. As the Prophet presents the prime example of Muslim piety, this *hadith* gives the strongest support for compassionate care for animals, in this case, horses, which were crucial for transportation for centuries in varying geographies.

More commonly cited is the *hadith* narrative of a woman subject to hellfire because of abusing a cat: "a cat which she had imprisoned, and it died of starvation . . . God told her, 'You are condemned because you did not feed the cat,

44. Although some might assert variability in the notion of the natural, I offer a sense of coherence with interdependent living communities' needs grounded in history.

45. Surah 27:18, in M.A.S. Abdel Haleem, *The Qur'an* (New York: Oxford University Press, 2008), 240.

46. *Surah* 27:19, Haleem, *The Qur'an*, 240.

47. S. Nomanul Haq, "Islam and Ecology: Toward Retrieval and Reconstruction," in *Islam and Ecology*, Foltz, Denny, and Baharuddin, eds. (2003), 147.

and did not give it water to drink, nor did you set it free so that it could eat of the creatures of the earth.' "[48] The woman restricted the cat's "God-given" natural ability to find food and water, as well as neglecting to offer them. Islamic studies scholar S. Nomanul Haq suggested that this *hadith* is

> [r]ather well-known in the Islamic world . . . [and] forms the basis of the *fiqh*-legislation that the owner of an animal is legally responsible for its well-being. If such owners are unable to provide for their animals, jurists further stipulate, then they should sell them, or let them go free in such a way that they can find food and shelter, or slaughter them if eating their flesh is permissible. Given the requirement that animals should be allowed as far as possible to live out their lives in a natural manner, keeping birds in cages is deemed unlawful.[49]

Thus, this *hadith* supports the protection of animals' natural lives and wellbeing, even when kept to become food.

A 10th-century Neoplatonist Muslim text, *The Case of the Animals versus Man*, depicts an allegorical legal case supporting animal rights against enslavement.[50] This text addresses the question of whether animals exist for their own sake or to be helpful for people, and it explicitly encourages empathy and care for animals. For example, the mule presents his case against humans, who "forced us to these things [enslaved work] under duress, with beatings, bludgeoning, and every kind of torture and chastisement our whole lives long."[51] After a lengthy debate between a variety of representative voices from different animal groups, the text concludes that animals have been made for humans, but with a compelling twist. The process and the end product in *The Case* veil the important sub-theme of human identity in relation to the divine expression in nature's order, including care and appreciation for the lives and deaths of nonhuman animals.

Islamic studies scholar Zayn Kassam reflects on the implications of *The Case* for animal care, in that the text makes "the remarkable admission that the

48. M. Muhsin Khan, ed. and trans., *Sahih al-Bukhari* (Chicago: Kazi Publications, 1976–1979), 3:553, cited in Haq, "Islam and Ecology," 148.

49. Haq, "Islam and Ecology," 148.

50. Zayn Kassam, "The Case of the Animals versus Man: Toward an Ecology of Being," in *A Communion of Subjects: Animals in Religion, Science, and Ethics* (New York: Columbia University Press, 2006), 160–169.

51. Ikhwan al-Safa, *The Case of the Animals versus Man before the King of the Jinn: A Tenth Century Ecological Fable of the Pure Brethren of Basra*, with introduction and commentary by Lenn Evan Goodman, trans. (Boston: Twayne, 1978), 51, in Kassam, *The Case*, 160.

subjugation of animals to humans was not by virtue of human superiority in God's eyes, but a signal of His grace toward humans. . . ."[52] Thus, although *The Case* does not endeavor to dramatically change people's uses of animals, the conversation suggests a less anthropocentric and potentially exploitative view. Instead, the text encourages human humility and gratitude to God for myriad ways that animals improve the lives of humans, understanding that should, in turn, translate to kinder treatment. Beyond the clear message to care kindly for animals, Kassam asserts that the 10th-century text writers were addressing the meaning of being human, "a state in which one is on intimate terms with the universe that sustains life, life which is comprised with a sense of wonder, gratitude, compassion, and care."[53] By giving individual animals the chance to speak on behalf of each animal community, the text engages with animal personality, voice, community, and identity, all of which can lead to abhorrence of brutality.

The Case of the Animals versus Man opens up a conversation about the de-enslavement of animals in the 10th century, bolstering commitments to nourish and care for wild and domesticated animals, even as people relate to them as future food. Although the text does not release animals from servitude, it engenders values for compassionate care for animals, drawing attention to and highlighting opposition to exploitative use and abuse. Islamic norms of humane treatment of animals derive from multiple texts, as well as from the principles of respect for animal communities and appreciation for animals' adherence to God's laws.

Halal Meat

Given the above insights into human stewardship of creation and the duty to respect animals and treat them kindly, what then should be done about meat? Meat is the most heavily regulated food in the Qur'an.[54] Numerous *surahs* indicate the importance of ritual slaughter for any meat eaten by a Muslim, outlawing carrion, blood, pork, animals ritually slaughtered for another God or gods, plus animals killed with excessive beating (see *surahs* 2:173, 5:3, 6:145, 16:115). When Muslims engage in pilgrimage, hunting is forbidden (5:1). *Surah* 16:115 depicts God's forgiveness in situations of starvation, when impermissible foods are acceptable in moderation. Meat even appears as a reward in heaven (52:22, 56:21).[55] Thus, eating animal flesh is subject to a variety of injunctions and approbations.

---

52. Kassam, *The Case*, 165.

53. Ibid., 168.

54. Bonne and Verbeke, "Religious Values," 38.

55. Foltz, "She Camel," 151.

Among animals that are permissible, specific ritual slaughter techniques further prepare the animal for consumption. *Halal* slaughter prescribes a quick-cut method with a sharp knife that kills the animal by severing the throat. Blood is not *halal*, and the slaughter process involves removing the blood from the animal. After a prayer, and in some cases turning the animal to face Mecca, the slaughterer cuts the carotid artery, and the animal's heart beats the blood out of the cut. What blood is left in the meat should be washed away with water.[56] Following these requirements, permissible animals may be correctly prepared for consumption. Nevertheless, there is debate about the humaneness of traditional *halal* slaughter, as the animal bleeds to death, as well as the common use of stunning before slaughter, beyond the moral questions of whether and how to kill animals.[57]

The Qur'an expressly stipulates that no additional foods should be deemed *haram* (impermissible), yet, various Islamic jurists have interpreted *hadith* and other Qur'anic passages to exclude a variety of animals: birds of prey, carnivorous animals, rats, "land animals without ears, e.g., frogs and snakes,"[58] crocodiles, sea turtles, sharks, dolphins, and eels.[59] Interpreters of *halal* laws tend to conclude that beyond the traditionally defined *haram* foods, the Qur'an does not denounce other foods. To do so might be considered *bid'ah sayyi'ah*, or potentially harmful, problematic innovation.[60] Thus, reinterpreting ethical considerations, as in the case of eco-halal, is not simple, particularly when reinterpreters are not religious leaders. Nevertheless, contemporary Muslim scholars and laypeople work to balance tradition with current issues, which pose new challenges for religiosity in social, political, environmental, and religious locations.

---

56. Peter Heine, *Food Culture in the Near East, Middle East, and North Africa* (Westport, CT: Greenwood Press, 2004): 6–7.

57. Regarding animal pain, food ethics, and vegetarianism in Islam, see the work of Kecia Ali, Ghazala Anwar, Magfirah Dahlan-Taylor, Nuri Friedlander, and Sarra Tlili. Some European countries require stunning before slaughter, purportedly to reduce animal pain. Nevertheless, Muslims have sought religious exceptions to this rule because stunning sometimes kills the animal, bypassing and undermining *halal* slaughter requirements. Regarding European slaughter, see K. Bonne and W. Verbeke, "Religious Values Informing Halal Meat Production and the Control and Delivery of Halal Credence Quality," *Agriculture and Human Values* 25 (2008): 35–47.

58. Ibid., 38.

59. Ibid.

60. Both positive and negative valences of *bid'ah* exist, *bid'ah sayyi'ah* (problematic) and *bid'ah hasanah* (positive, worthy of praise). Islamic scholars assess a variety of innovative interpretations with attention to precedent and consistency with traditions.

Humane Questions of Halal

As already established above, the abuse of animals is unlawful for Islam. In the same spirit, the Qur'an warns against eating meat from animals that die violently: "You are forbidden to eat . . . any animal strangled, or victim of a violent blow or fall, or gored or savaged by a beast of prey, unless you still slaughter it [in the correct manner]."[61] This passage raises this question: Can an animal be slaughtered if it is already dead? If we assume, no, then an animal that dies by abuse and violence cannot be eaten. If we assume, yes, a dead animal can be ritually slaughtered, then a ritual may be expected to purify the meat from even an abused animal.[62]

What counts as abuse? A *hadith* narrated by Hisham bin Zaid in *Sahih Muslim* indicates that one should not even tie an animal before killing it: "Jabir b. Abdullah reported that Allah's Messenger (may peace be upon him) forbade that any beast should be killed after it has been tied."[63] Although the exact details that inspired this *hadith* may be obscured, it suggests in the most persuasive terms (the model of the Prophet Muhammad) that animals have rights to freedom of movement, even in slaughter. If an animal may freely move during slaughter, this condition may support the notion that violence against animals before slaughter is not acceptable, since any living being would avoid abuse when free to do so. Following this argument, abused animals—even tied up animals—cannot be ritually purified through *halal* slaughter. Unfortunately, nearly all factory-farmed animals are denied freedom of movement in confined spaces, among other potentially abusive issues.

Food industry writers Karijn Bonne and Wim Verbeke describe humane ways to treat animals according to Islamic principles, even during slaughter:

> Islam advocates humane treatment of animals before, during, and after slaughter. Animals should be treated as such that they are not stressed or excited prior to slaughter; they should be nourished and well rested and drinking water must be available in holding areas. In addition, the knife should not be sharpened in front of the animal and no animal should be able to witness the slaughter of another animal.[64]

---

61. Surah 5:3, Haleem, *The Qur'an*, 67.

62. As a scholar, rather than a jurist, I offer ideas and proposals, rather than interpretations.

63. *Sahih Muslim*, book 021, number 4817 in Bonne and Verbeke, "Religious Values," 41.

64. Bonne and Verbeke, "Religious Values," 41.

These guidelines prevent unnecessary suffering for the animal, such as excessive thirst or hunger, exhaustion, fear of the knife, and alarm to see a fellow animal killed. Although slaughter requires violence, specific *halal* guidelines assert the need to carefully contain violence, reducing animal pain.

Beyond *halal* slaughter, additional texts support the importance of care to avoid animal death. In the *Mishkat*, a saying of the Prophet Muhammad expresses further care for animals: "If anyone wrongfully kills [even] a sparrow, [let alone] anything greater, he will face God's interrogation."[65] In the *hadith Sahih Muslim*, Shaddid B. Aus offered a call to goodness, even in killing:

> Two are the things which I remember Allah's Messenger (may peace be upon him) having said: Verily Allah has enjoined goodness to everything; so when you kill, kill in a good way and when you slaughter, slaughter in a good way. So every one of you should sharpen his knife, and let the slaughtered animal die comfortably.[66]

Thus, wrongful killing is abhorrent, as well as killing done badly with a blunt knife. A sharp knife, cutting quickly through the windpipe, blood vessels, and throat, would shorten the suffering of a food animal. Meat requires death, but reducing harm and supporting animal comfort is valued, even while killing an animal. Although when the Qur'an was revealed, the quick-cut method may have been the most efficient and humane method, it is possible that further technological advances might improve upon the idea of humane slaughter. For example, stunning has been employed, particularly in Europe, to reduce animal suffering at slaughter. Currently, stunning is largely agreed to be impermissible for *halal* meats. Just as this innovation in agriculture poses problems for *halal* standards, so advocates of eco-halal see the wider practice of factory farming as problematic. Although communities have effectively mobilized for religious exemptions to some European laws requiring stunning, eco-halal movements have achieved a relatively small and dispersed but committed following, yet, both further personalize the act of slaughter as prayerful and tradition-laden.[67]

---

65. Haq, "Islam and Ecology," 149.

66. *Sahih Muslim*, book 21, number 4810, in Bonne and Verbeke, "Religious Values," 41.

67. Magfirah Dahlan-Taylor, "'Good' Food: Islamic Food Ethics beyond Religious Dietary Laws," *Critical Research on Religion*, 9 February 2015; K. Ali, "Muslims and Meat-Eating."

Factory Farming

In current animal husbandry, factory farming has replaced pastoral images of cows munching grass and chickens pecking awkwardly in the dust. Factory farms account for a staggering 99% of US farm animals. Between 1980 and 2011, pork producers reduced from over 650,000 farms to under 70,000 with nearly the same number of hogs at market. Although pork is not *halal* regardless of its agricultural method, this statistic gives a sense of the consolidation of food-animal farming from a smaller, more dispersed practice to an immense, concentrated phenomenon. Among US cattle "operations," 70% have 5,000 cows or more. In poultry, 90% is grown by ten giant businesses.[68] For example, in 2015 Hillandale, a large company that supplied eggs to the warehouse store Costco, had a chicken coop "the size of a football field," housing about 120,000 hens with six birds per cage.[69]

This concentrated animal husbandry situation means animals live in cramped buildings with thousands of other chickens, cows, or pigs, often standing in their own feces. Concentrated Animal Feeding Operations (CAFOs), also known as factory farms, have been challenged by journalists, animal rights activists, environmentalists, and other concerned people. Nonetheless, the status quo continues because of the market goal of cheap meat together with the silencing effects of "ag-gag" rules, which stifle journalists from reporting on inhumane and hazardous conditions in factory farms.[70] Animal agriculture lobbyists have introduced ag-gag legislation in over half of all US state legislatures, which criminalize documentation of farm conditions. These rules mean abuses are even more invisible.

Eco-halal Meat

The neologism "eco-halal" combines the ecological connotations of eco- and the religious connotations of *halal*.[71] Eco-halal combines "eco-" from the Greek root

68. Natural Resources Defense Council, "Facts about Pollution from Livestock Farms," web resource, accessed September 18, 2015, http://www.nrdc.org/water/pollution/ffarms.asp.

69. David Wright, Sally Hawkins, James Wang, Geoff Martz, and Lauren Effron, "Hillandale Farms Responds to Hidden Camera Footage Showing Decomposing Chickens at Pennsylvania Egg Farm," *ABCNews.com*, June 10, 2015, 9:07 pm ET, web resource, accessed December 15, 2015, http://abcnews.go.com/US/hillandale-farms-responds-hidden-camera-footage-showing-decomposing/story?id=31670059.

70. American Society for the Prevention of Cruelty to Animals, "Factory Farms: What Is Ag-Gag Legislation?," web resource, accessed December 15, 2015, https://www.aspca.org/animal-cruelty/factory-farms/what-ag-gag-legislation.

71. Although Arabic words are italicized here, such as *halal*, eco-halal represents a cross-cultural, hybrid notion. Appropriate to this neologism's location among Muslims living in majority European-language locales, the term appears with no italics.

oikos, or home, household, or dwelling place, with the Arabic word for lawful or permissible, *halal*. The Greek root has been employed toward the field of ecology, which scientifically studies the dynamic world of living nature, the dwelling place for humanity and all living beings on Earth. The term eco- also can imply a European-language location, for example, an English-language majority in the United States. The appropriately hybrid term represents a movement among Muslims in English-speaking areas, and other regions where the term ecology has influence.

Eco-halal meat connotes that the food animals lived a more natural, largely outdoor existence, which minimized soil and water pollution—thus meeting both environmental and Islamic stewardship standards. Usually, eco-halal also implies that the Islamic principles of respect, care, and humane treatment of animals were followed during the animals' lives. Eco-halal connotes that slaughter techniques maintained Qur'anic standards for humane care for animals immediately before, during, and after death. Within the eco-halal movement, specific individuals, families, and groups have worked to procure, educate about, define, and distribute eco-halal meat. They do so in order to more fully inhabit Muslim ethical traditions and act in accordance with their consciences, in the face of contemporary problems with factory farming.

Imam and educator Basheer Ahmad Masri (1914–1993) wrote the most comprehensive, contemporary Muslim consideration of human misuse of animals:

> To kill animals to satisfy the human thirst for inessentials is a contradiction in terms within the Islamic tradition. Think of the millions of animals killed, in the name of commercial enterprises, in order to supply a complacent public with trinkets and products they do not really need. And why? Because we are too lazy or too self-indulgent to find substitutes.[72]

Masri calls for traditional Muslim values like simplicity and moderation, avoiding greed, a stance particularly salient when considering animals tortured to provide people with cosmetics, for example. Richard Foltz interprets Masri's passage in terms of critiquing factory farming and testing on animals.[73]

Popular writer and community organizer Ibrahim Abdul-Matin connects food practices with religious tenets, as a divinely ordained expression of human ethics.

---

72. Al-Hafiz B. A. Masri, *Islamic Concern for Animals* (Petersfield, UK: Athene Trust, 1987), vii, in Foltz, "She-Camel," 155.

73. Foltz, "She-Camel," 155.

These practices should avoid injustice and embrace humane, natural lives for food animals:

> The factory farming industry treats animals the same way economic systems treat human beings—as units of production. In Islam we are commanded to treat animals with much more respect, for they are part of God's creation, which we have sworn to protect. Remember, everything is connected in the Oneness (*tawhid*) of Allah and His creation. Is this how we want to treat the food that we will put into our bodies?[74]

Abdul-Matin encourages readers to educate themselves about the horrors of factory farming and cites projects that embody Muslim ethics for livestock animal care. He writes, "[T]he [religious] principles require us to know where our food comes from and to place a premium on wholesome, ethical food sources."[75]

Eco-halal Farms

As the eco-halal movement has grown, farms reflecting these principles have begun to develop across the United States. Examples of Muslims inspired to farm organically, sustainably, and humanely include Zaid Kurdieh's chickens at Norwich Valley Farms in New York state,[76] Mukit Hossain's goat farm in Virginia,[77] and Taqwa Eco-food Cooperative in Chicago, which became Whole Earth Meats in 2009.[78] These are a few examples of a larger movement, represented also in community and online groups like D.C. Green Muslims and Beyond Halal.[79]

---

74. Ibrahim Abdul-Matin, *Green Deen: What Islam Teaches About Protecting the Planet* (San Francisco, CA: Berrett-Koehler Publishers, Inc., 2010), 147–148.

75. Ibid., 144.

76. Nadia Arumugam, "The Eco-halal Revolution: Clean Food for Muslims," *Culinate*, November 4, 2009, web resource, accessed September 18, 2015, http://www.culinate.com/articles/features/the_eco-halal_revolution.

77. Tara Bahrampour, "Muslim Immigrant Fills Niche Raising Goats on Virginia Farm," *Washington Post*, April 13, 2010, web resource, accessed September 18, 2015 http://www.washingtonpost.com/wp-dyn/content/article/2010/04/12/AR2010041204158.html.

78. Whole Earth Meats, web resource, accessed December 15, 2015, http://wholeearthmeats.com.

79. Green Muslims, web resource, accessed 15 December 15, 2015, http://dcgreenmuslims.blogspot.com and http://www.green-muslims.org. Beyond Halal, web resource, accessed 15 December 15, 2015, http://beyondhalal.com. Also worth mentioning is the Saudi Project for

In Chicago, Taqwa Eco-food Cooperative worked from 2001 through 2009 to educate about and source the most ethical meat available at that time, supported by the interreligious environmental nonprofit organization Faith in Place. Taqwa's goals were multilayered, finding alternatives to many interconnected problems in industrial agriculture: injustices to farmers and workers, mistreatment and abusive confinement of animals, overuse of antibiotics for livestock, water pollution, and poor land stewardship. Taqwa leaders worked to ensure a living wage for smaller-scale, family farms, cutting out the expensive "middle men" in industrial food distribution networks. The farmers carefully managed water and soil to ensure their long-term sustainability. Taqwa sourced meat from local, small-scale animal husbandry, where animals lived without antibiotics or growth hormones, grazing, foraging, and living a more traditional existence with room for normal animal social behaviors. Although these agricultural-ethical values might seem commonly held, unfortunately, the majority of these conditions are absent from industrial-scale factory farms. This stark reality sparked concern for founding coordinator Shireen Pishdadi, who organized the project as a cooperative, in order to foster a democratic leadership structure for the organization. The work of Taqwa continued in 2009 with the transformation of the organization from its nonprofit project status to a private business called Whole Earth Meats, run by Taqwa's last coordinator, Qaid Hassan.

In upstate New York, Norwich Meadows Farm grows organically and sells in New York City farmers' markets. Their website echoes Qur'anic injunctions against waste, while also warning against more contemporary issues such as genetically modified organisms, extreme weather disturbances, and the health dangers of industrial farming.[80] They call themselves "keepers of the earth," and pledge "to strive to preserve and not damage agricultural land, and to use it in a manner that is economically, ecologically and ethically sound."[81] Norwich Meadows Farm organically grows produce and chickens for meat and eggs for the local community. In an article about the Norwich Meadows Farm, entitled "The Eco-halal

Utilization of Hajj Meat (www.adahi.org), which seeks to distribute the meat from animal sacrifices from the *hajj*, pilgrimage. Kassam and Robinson encourage consideration of the opportunity to offer symbolic sacrifice, in order to reduce excess slaughter at *Eid al-Adha*, the pilgrimage feast, in which in 2011, nearly a million sheep and 3,000 cattle and camels were slaughtered. Z. Kassam and S. Robinson, "Islam and Food."

80. Norwich Meadows Farm website, "Our Farm," web resource, accessed August 11, 2017, http://www.norwichmeadowsfarm.com.

81. Norwich Meadows Farm website, "Our Promise," web resource, accessed September 17, 2015, http://www.norwichmeadowsfarm.com.

Revolution: Clean Food for Muslims," farmer Zaid Kurdieh expands the notion of *halal* to include care for the earth and humane, natural lives for animals:

> [Kurdieh] interprets Islam in a way that renders the environment and the manner in which an animal is raised from birth until death paramount. For him, it's not enough that the meat is emblazoned with a halal certification stamp. . . . The often neglected Islamic principle of *tayyib,* which he defines as meaning "wholesome" and "pure" . . . is the foundation upon which he has constructed his ethos toward food. That his chickens are fed on a purely natural diet, allowed to grow at a healthy rate, and given bug-filled pastures to explore are as crucial for him as the *"Bismallah Allah-u-Akbar"* he whispers before that final cut. . . .
>
> This drive for a more transparent and environmentally sound approach to halal meat reflects the natural juncture of Islamic dietary principles and the increasingly popular but almost entirely secular sustainable-food movement sweeping across the country.[82]

Although the sustainable food movement is arguably spiritual, if not "dark green religion," in the terminology of nature and religion scholar Bron Taylor, the above article does not attempt to make that case.[83] Instead, it depicts Kurdieh as a pious Muslim reinterpreting his tradition in support of a religiously inflected culinary purism toward practices that promote health and flourishing for humans, animals, and the environment. The interconnections between these levels of health means that a transparent food system is vital to those seeking ethical food, including those in the eco-halal movement. Rural ecosystems intertwine with urban dwellers hungry to participate ethically in natural systems through food. Such considerations and actions benefit from agricultural transparency, as opposed to ignorance encouraged by ag-gag rules.

The Prophet Ate Less Meat

Despite the existence of some eco-halal farms, challenges remain for maintaining an eco-halal diet. One is price: Abdul-Matin suggests that prices are lower for factory-farmed meat and higher for organic, grass-fed *halal* meat.[84] Another is

---

82. Arumugam, "The Eco-halal Revolution."

83. Bron Taylor, *Dark Green Religion: Nature Spirituality and the Planetary Future* (Berkeley: University of California Press, 2010).

84. Abdul-Matin, *Green Deen,* 147–148.

the cultural centrality of meat: it signifies hospitality, generosity, and prosperity, so eliminating meat entirely may be impractical or improbable in the near term. For Abdul-Matin, these challenges may be tackled, in part, by recalibrating cultural and financial expectations about meat. He encourages readers to see the film *Food Inc.* to educate themselves about factory farming.[85] Similarly, Islamic scholar, sheikh, and cofounder of Zaytuna College in Berkeley, California, Hamza Yusuf encouraged an audience to read Jeremy Rifkin's book *Beyond Beef: The Rise and Fall of Cattle Culture* (1993).[86] These non-Muslim sources may inform reinterpretations of tradition in light of contemporary challenges.[87]

Some suggest simply eating less meat for a variety of reasons, including the higher costs of eco-halal meat. Abdul-Matin cites conversations with "numerous scholars" who suggested that the Prophet Muhammad ate meat sparingly, rather than centrally, in his diet.[88] Islamic studies scholar Kecia Ali concurs with this notion in her article outlining reasons for Muslim vegetarianism, in which she writes that

American traditionalist Hamza Yusuf refers to the Prophet as a "semi-vegetarian" and lauds the early caliph 'Umar ibn al-Khattab (d. 644) for admonishing a man to eat meat every other day at most. 'Umar linked this prohibition to concern for those who went hungry while others feasted. In appealing to these precedents, Yusuf roots his advice about meat eating in a religiously authoritative history. If the Prophet and, as Yusuf puts it, the most Prophet-like of the post-prophetic Muslim figures ['Umar], ate meat sparingly, then not only is there nothing wrong with at least partial abstention from meat, indeed it is recommended. Ironically, this endorsement of limited meat consumption appears on a website for a purveyor

---

85. Robert Kenner, director, *Food, Inc.,* Magnolia Home Entertainment, 2008, 1h 34m.

86. Hamza Yusuf, "Excerpts from 'The Science of Shariah,'" web resource, accessed September 17, 2015, http://www.organic-halal-meat.com/article/hamza-yusuf.php. Jeremy Rifkin, *Beyond Beef: The Rise and Fall of Cattle Culture* (New York: Plume, 1993). Also, it is worth noting that Hamza Yusuf, born Mark Hanson, has repeatedly been named among the most influential Muslim leaders in the West: "The Muslim 500: The World's Most Influential Muslims," web resource, accessed August 11, 2017, http://themuslim500.com/profile/sheikh-hamza-yusuf-hanson). Jack O'Sullivan, "If You Hate the West, Emigrate to a Muslim Country," *Guardian,* October 8, 2001, web resource, accessed August 11, 2017, https://www.theguardian.com/world/2001/oct/08/religion.uk.

87. Ali, "Muslims and Meat-eating," 282–283.

88. Abdul-Matin, *Green Deen,* 155. Also mentioned by Ali, "Muslims and Meat-Eating," 272. Both appear to have been in conversation with scholars at Zaytuna College in Berkeley, California, who may have been a mutual source for this notion of the Prophet Muhammad eating meat in small quantities and not daily.

of "organic halal meat" (Abraham Natural Produce 2014)—perhaps suggesting the presence of commercial motivations: if one is going to eat less meat, then one can splurge on costlier organic meat.[89]

Yusuf outlines a lower-quantity meat-consumption paradigm as particularly Islamic, as detailed by Ali above, and particularly common, in his words below: "Meat is not a necessity in Shari'ah, and in the old days most Muslims used to eat meat, if they were wealthy, like middle class—once a week on Friday. If they were poor—on the Eids [or holiday feasts]."[90] Meat has historically been expensive and hard to access, particularly for the poor; thus, although meat is permissible, it is not plentiful. Yusuf suggests that the Prophet Muhammad and early Muslims, as well as *hadith* traditions, limit meat eating, even among the rich, to approximately once a week, or in the case of the *hadith* text of the *Muwatta*, never two days in a row.[91] In Yusuf's paraphrase, the *hadith* describes a resource-scarcity-charity issue: "It would be better for you to roll up your tummy a little bit so that other people can eat."[92] From the Prophet Muhammad to contemporary interpreters, reducing meat consumption is advisable, whether because of cost, access, resource consumption, charity commitments, or environmental concerns. Reduced meat consumption may be a complementary practice to the eco-halal movement.

Conclusion

Eco-halal is an integrated eco-religious approach to Muslim ethical eating, cohering standard understandings of *halal* together with additional layers of Islamic ethical expression. Factory farming is an ethically abhorrent situation for animals, as well as workers, who must endure daily abuses. Filthy, unnatural conditions for animals also affect nearby landscapes and waterways with excessive pollution, corrupting environmental health. Halal meats deriving from this unethical system may be considered *haram*, or impermissible, or at least questionable, for myriad reasons. Muslim sensibilities for biosystem, animal, and human health may be expressed through sourcing and eating eco-halal foods, including a balanced portion of ethically raised and slaughtered animals.

---

89. Ali, "Muslims and Meat-Eating," 272.

90. Hamza Yusuf, "Excerpts from 'The Science of Shariah,'" web resource, accessed September 17, 2015, http://www.organic-halal-meat.com/article/hamza-yusuf.php.

91. Ibid.

92. Ibid.

Muslims are called to be trustees of a divinely owned and created world, a commitment that includes caring for animals and being mindful of the environmental effects of farming practices. In Sarra Tlili's words, "The cosmos of the Qur'an is highly interactive with its Creator: It makes choices, experiences emotions, takes divine commands, prays, and hymns the praises of God."[93] Tlili emphasizes that not only people but also communities of animals and the living world are situated in supplicating and celebratory conversation with God. Although humans are uniquely situated as the recipients of the Qur'an's message, the text presents land, water, and communities of living creatures as valuable not as resources, but as relational beings with whom people's ethics are proven, hopefully, toward a God-pleasing end.

The eco-halal movement promotes more humane and ecological alternatives to factory-farmed meats, including sourcing meat more ethically and eating meat less often. For contemporary Muslims who endeavor to follow the example of the Prophet Muhammed and who reflect on people's roles as divinely appointed *khalifah*, eco-halal practices appear to be a Qur'anic and tradition-based duty, engendering respect for the specific animals who give their lives to become food and appreciation for the interconnected, creaturely communities with which people live.

---

93. Sarra Tlili, *Animals in the Qur'an*, x.

6 DIALOGUE

David E. Cooper and Sarah E. Robinson-Bertoni

There are salient differences, unsurprisingly, between Islam and Daoism, religions or spiritual movements that grew up centuries and great distances apart. Despite these differences, a number of themes relating to natural environments and animals emerge from our two chapters, and from the discussions between us, that interestingly connect the two traditions.

Differences

The most striking difference is that Islam is a theistic religion, whereas Daoism is not. The *dao* is the ineffable source of "heaven and earth" but, unlike Islam's one God, is not credited with intelligence, purposes, and moral concerns. It is worth noting, though, the existence of a tendency within Islam that regards personal descriptions of Allah that draw on human psychology as metaphorical or analogical, rather than literal, so that God, like the *dao*, is therefore ultimately mysterious and beyond human conception.

A second important difference flows from the one just mentioned. Islam proposes a rule- or principle-based ethics in which right and wrong, what we should and should not do, are determined by God's law. Daoists, by contrast, are skeptical toward rules, principles, rights, and duties, arguing that these are invoked only when human life has already gone badly wrong, when people have "lost the Way." Daoist morality has sometimes been described as a "virtue ethical" one, in which emphasis is placed not on principles of conduct or desirable outcomes, but on qualities of character, like compassion.

This difference should not, however, be exaggerated. Later Daoists do formulate "precepts," including ones that apply to our treatment of nature and animals. And Islam also emphasizes various virtues, such as kindness, mercy, and generosity, that the devout will manifest. Muslim piety cannot be reduced simply to obedience to rules and laws.

Affinities

Despite the differences between the traditions, significant affinities between Islamic and Daoist attitudes toward the relationship between humans and the natural world may also be discerned in our two chapters.

To begin, the Islamic emphasis on the task of human beings to tend God's creation is directly comparable to the Daoist one on humans' role in "nourishing the myriad things." This similarity is closely related to two others. First, Daoists and Muslims alike stress that the world manifests a natural balance or harmony—whether this is divinely designed or guaranteed by the *dao*-given rhythms of *yin* and *yang*—and that it is the role of human beings to maintain or restore this harmony. (It has been argued, perhaps unfairly, that these perceptions of nature as essentially a place of harmony are those of literate, urban elites more familiar with gardens and parks than with wilderness or nature in the raw.)

Second, both traditions locate human beings as nested in nature, though people alone can have a moral responsibility to care for nature, since they alone are capable of violating divine law or departing from the *dao*. Maintenance of nature's balance is in the hands of people who recognize and abide by its harmony. In Islam, living beings other than human are inherently *muslim*, in the original sense of the term, for they are beings that by nature "submit" or "surrender" to God's will. People must choose to live in balance with God's laws in nature, facing divine judgment for missteps. Likewise, in Daoism, it is only men and women among all living beings that can "lose the Way," and hence seek to rediscover it.

A further affinity between the traditions is the idea, present in each, that mindful experience of the natural world can be instructive and edifying. To begin with, nature is a repository of symbols or metaphors that help people who are alert to them in their understanding of religious truth and concepts. In Islam, as in medieval Christianity, nature is "a Book of God," replete with signs of the existence and creative force of God. In Daoism, the gentle ways of water and the growth of plants, for example, help people to acquire some sense of the workings of the *dao*.

Further, people can learn from nature how their own lives might better conform to God's will or to the Way. While in both traditions, human beings are unique, they do not belong to an order separate from other living beings. Observation of animals in particular—of bees, ants, and fish, for instance—can provide lessons on the ingredients of a good life: on sociability, industry, simplicity, frugality, and much else. Animals, in their own natural way, praise God, thereby providing an exemplary model for people to follow. For the Daoist, animals are models of the spontaneity or naturalness that we should cultivate in our own lives.

Animals

Both our chapters pay special attention to animals, to how they are understood, regarded, and treated in the two traditions. It will be useful here to make explicit some of the similarities in the attitudes adopted by Muslims and Daoists. First, both traditions emphasize that animals of many kinds are genuinely communal, social beings able to communicate with one other through their own languages. Partly because of this quality, second, animals have their own natures, goods, and perspectives, so that their lives can sensibly be described as flourishing or failing to flourish. Human beings should recognize and honor the natures, particular needs, sensitivities, and goods of the animals themselves, and not impose upon them peculiarly human tastes and practices. Animals should, for example, be fed what is good for them, not the food that people may happen to like.

Finally, men and women should not simply respect the natures of animals but feel and display compassion and kindness toward them. The idea familiar among some Christian writers that we may use animals as we please, since they exist only for our benefit, is rejected by various sources from Islam and Daoism alike.[1] A popular Muslim story tells of a woman going to hell for killing a cat by tying it to a post. By failing to ensure the animal's natural ability to find food and water, the person receives hellfire, a harsh judgment by God. More than one Daoist text tells the story of a boy admonishing a dignitary who gives thanks to heaven for providing animals solely for the purpose of being eaten by human beings. It is not surprising, in the light of such stories, that many followers of Daoist teachings have embraced vegetarianism. Though a select few Muslims embrace vegetarianism, concerns about environmental, social, and humane treatment of animals have spawned a larger movement toward careful sourcing of lawful meat that fits a "Green Deen," or environmentally friendly expression of Muslim religiosity.

That there are these similarities in attitudes toward animals does not mean, of course, that the attitudes are identical in the two traditions. One difference,

---

1. Subtleties of the subject of animal rights appear in an 10th century Muslim narrative, analyzed in the following article: Zayn Kassam, "The Case of the Animals versus Man: Toward an Ecology of Being," in *A Communion of Subjects: Animals in Religion, Science, and Ethics* (New York: Columbia University Press, 2006), 160–169.

perhaps, concerns the degree of closeness with animals that people should aspire to in their lives. In both traditions, we find nostalgia for a simpler, less techno-logically complex, and less consumerist society; in modern times, Muslims and Daoists throughout the world have felt the effects of industrial society. In the classic Daoist texts, moreover, one dimension of this nostalgia is a vision of times when, it is supposed, people and animals lived in close, friendly relationships. Similarly nostalgic notions emerge in texts of Islam, which encourage emulation of the Prophet Muhammed, who ate meat sparingly and lived in a non-industrial setting. The Qur'an, in particular, demonstrates the importance of nonhumans in the many chapters named for animals, and it offers a well-developed ethical stance on animal well-being, not only in life, but to minimize pain and fear at slaughter.

Concluding Reflection

What the dialogue based on our two chapters has demonstrated, perhaps sur-prisingly, are the considerable areas of affinity between Islam and Daoism in connection with views of and attitudes to the natural world, the animal world in particular. This coincidence between two traditions that emerged at very different times and in very different places prompts a more general reflection concerning premodern or non-industrial engagements with the natural environment—one that, we suspect, may be confirmed by considering other religious traditions and lifeways, like those of some indigenous, First Nations peoples in the Americas and Australia.

This reflection could be put in terms of stewardship. The idea that human beings are, or should be, stewards of nature has come in for criticism from some "deep" ecologists, on the ground that it implies that we humans are either sepa-rate from nature or especially important, privileged parts of it. Arguably, how-ever, what was recognized in the old traditions, including Islam and Daoism, is that human beings, while being continuous with nature, indeed have a special status and place in the order of things. This is not an easy idea to hold onto in our contemporary climate of thought, whether religious or scientific. For this climate is one in which human beings tend to be either elevated above nature or reduced to being "just another" part of nature like every other creature.

The older thought requires us to view human beings as creatures that belong to a natural order—one conforming to divine will or the *dao*—from which they are able, nevertheless, to deviate, and with destructive effect. But it is to view them, as well, as beings with a special responsibility—to restore and conserve what they have destroyed, to tend or nourish other living beings, and to ethically and responsibly engage with the natural world. If this is to regard human beings as stewards of nature, then Daoism, Islam, and other long-standing religious and spiritual traditions may rightly be described as urging participants to accept and exercise moral responsibility for the living world through acts of relational, re-storative care and stewardship, whereby interconnected lives may flourish.

III CLIMATE AND CULTURE

7 YOGA BODIES AND BODIES OF WATER

SOLUTIONS FOR CLIMATE CHANGE IN INDIA?

Christopher Patrick Miller*

Ancient techniques of introspection and self-control designed to transform one's orientation *away* from a false identification with the individual self and leading to a deep confrontation with one's existential condition, become instead optional methods for relieving daily stress and allowing individuals to cope better with the stresses and strains of the modern capitalist world . . . the goal is to align the employee's "personal mission" with that of the organization for which they work.[1]

—JEREMY CARRETTE AND RICHARD KING, *Selling Spirituality*

. . . [T]he meanings of rivers in religious exegesis and practice over time reflect in profound ways the eternal connections between humans and water. If these references erode or disappear in policy over time, their absence may signal the growing strength of other uses, such as hydropower and industry that may displace public needs.[2]

—KELLY ALLEY, *"The Paradigm Shift in India's River Policies: From Sacred to Transferable Waters"*

Poised under a tree, newspaper in hand, and with tea, books, and an animal by his side (see Figure 7.1), Narendra Modi elegantly portrays his vision of the modern yogi. Unlike his political predecessors who espoused an antagonistic relationship between modernity and

---

* Special thanks to artist Ryan Mills for providing the image for this chapter, and to Laura Hartman, Chuck Hamilton, and Christopher Chapple for their comments on previous drafts.

1. Jeremy Carrette and Richard King, *Selling Spirituality: The Silent Takeover of Religion* (London: Routledge, 2005), 135.

2. Kelly D. Alley, "The Paradigm Shift in India's River Policies: From Sacred to Transferable Waters," in *Water, Cultural Diversity, and Global Environmental Change: Emerging Trends, Sustainable Futures?*, Lisa Hiwasaki, Barbara Rose Johnston, Irene J. Klaver, Ameyali Ramos Castillo, and Veronica Strang, eds. (London and New York: Springer, 2012), 31.

FIGURE 7.1 Narendra Modi, Prime Minister of India, takes his ease, with an animal companion at his side. Image adapted from photographs in multiple online media sources. Illustration by Ryan Mills.

religion, the Indian Prime Minister creatively combines neoliberal[3] economic policies with religious traditionalism in ways that reify global capitalism as India's only viable path into the future.[4] Given its accelerating popularity and ascendancy

---

3. For the purposes of this chapter, like Carrette and King, I follow Robert McChesney, who defines the term as follows:

> Neoliberalism is the defining political economic paradigm of our time—it refers to the policies and processes whereby a relative handful of private interests are permitted to control as much as possible of social life in order to maximize their personal profit. Associated initially with Reagan and Thatcher, neoliberalism has for the past two decades been the dominant global political economic trend adopted by political parties of the center, much of the traditional left, and the right. These parties and the policies they enact represent the immediate interests of extremely wealthy investors and less than one thousand large corporations.

See Robert W. McChesney, "Introduction," in Noam Chomsky, *Profit Over People: Neoliberalism and Global Order* (New York: Seven Stories, 1999), 7. Also, for a detailed analysis and critique of the intersection of religion, spirituality, and neoliberalism, see Carrette and King, *Selling Spirituality*, 2.

4. See Thomas Bobbio, "Never-Ending Modi: *Hindutva* and Gujarati Neoliberalism as Prelude to All-India Premiership?," *Focaal: Journal of Global and Historical Anthropology* 67

over the center-left Indian National Congress political party, the present chapter considers the platform of Modi's right-wing Bharatiya Janata Party (BJP), specifically as it informs Modi's proposed solutions to climate change. I argue that two of the Modi's primary solutions—domestic yoga programming and India's recently revived river-linking project—undermine human flourishing and in fact reflect ambitions of a wider biopolitical strategy intended to support the global economic system that continues to perpetuate anthropogenic climate change. Though seemingly disparate solutions, both Modi's national yoga program and the national river-linking project are grounded in an environmentally deleterious political ideology that is inherited from India's colonial period and that seeks to erode the relationship between nature and the human body. As I show, however, alternative forms of yoga aimed at nurturing intimacy between the human body and the natural world are helping to prevent unnecessary climate-change-producing development activities in India, including the river-linking project.

Development Challenges

Following China and America, India is the third largest carbon-emitting nation in the world.[5] Despite the Trump administration's aggressive climate change denial in 2017, the international community's focus on the issue called all unsustainable global development plans into question via the ratification of the 2016 Paris Climate Agreement.[6] Nevertheless, India's attitude toward this international treaty has remained ambivalent. Invoking arguments of fairness as he responded

---

(2013): 125, 129. See also Ravinder Kaur, "Good Times, Brought to You by Brand Modi," *Television and New Media* 16, no. 4 (2015): 324. Previous to his election victory, from 2001 to 2014 Modi served as the Chief Minister of Gujarat, where he is remembered for his economic achievements, ability to oust corruption, and more infamously for his toleration of the Godhra riots. Modi has indeed been embroiled in human rights controversies surrounding his alleged provocation and toleration of the 2002 Godhra Riots, in which approximately a thousand Muslims were murdered at the hands of Hindu nationalists. Since his 2014 national election victory, Modi has necessarily adjusted his style of governance as he has stepped up from the state politics of Gujarat into the arena of international politics, where he must strike a balance between pleasing his Hindu nationalist support base in India and bolstering his tainted global reputation the world over. For a brief summary of the riot and the controversies that followed, see Manoj Mitta, "'Preplanned Inhuman Collective Violent Act of Terrorism': What Modi Got Away With in the Godhra Case," *Scroll*, February 27, 2017, accessed February 27, 2017, https://scroll.in/article/830319/preplanned-inhuman-collective-violent-act-of-terrorism-what-modi-got-away-with-in-the-godhra-case.

5. Tommy Wilkes, "India Says Carbon Emissions Will Grow as it Drives to Beat Poverty," *Reuters,* December 5, 2014, accessed December 5, 2014, http://www.reuters.com/article/2014/12/05/us-india-climatechange-idUSKCN0JJ1BS20141205.

6. "The Paris Agreement," United Nations Framework Convention on Climate Change, accessed March 11, 2016, http://unfccc.int/paris_agreement/items/9485.php.

to early carbon-emission negotiations, Prakash Javadekar, the BJP's Minister of State for Environment, Forest and Climate Change, made it clear that India would continue to emit carbon on its path toward development for the foreseeable future: "What cuts? That's for more developed countries. The moral principle of historic responsibility cannot be washed away."[7] Similarly, he stated less than two months later in response to the UN's climate talks in 2014 in Lima, "We need to grow. Our emissions will grow. . . . Our growth cannot be compromised."[8] While Modi's administration is justified in criticizing Western countries such as the United States for taking their unfair share of climate-emissions space as well as for backing out of the Paris Climate Agreement, is unrestrained economic growth really the path India should take to ensure human flourishing?

When discussing climate change in the international arena during his 2015 UNESCO speech, Prime Minister Narendra Modi encouraged a more conciliatory approach while subtly jabbing at the Global North's unsustainable consumption habits. Here, he proposed *yoga* and *clean energy* as the twin solutions to climate change:

> Too often, our discussion is reduced to an argument about emission cuts. But, we are more likely to succeed if we offer affordable solutions, not simply impose choices. That is why I have called for global public action to develop clean energy, that is affordable and accessible to all. And, it is for the same reason that I call for a change in lifestyle. Because, the emission reduction that we seek will be the natural outcome of how we live. And, it will also mean a different path to economic well being [sic]. It is with this vision that I had called the United Nations General Assembly last September to declare June 21 as the International Day of Yoga. Yoga awakens a sense of oneness and harmony with self, society and Nature. By changing our lifestyle and creating consciousness, it can help us deal with climate change and create a more balanced world.[9]

---

7. Coral Davenport, "Emissions from India Will Increase, Official Says," *New York Times*, September 24, 2014, accessed October 21, 2014, http://www.nytimes.com/2014/09/25/world/asia/25climate.ht ml?_r=1.

8. Wilkes, "Carbon Emissions," December 5, 2014. Despite Javadekar's defiance, India joined the international community in October 2016 by reluctantly submitting their ratification of the Paris Agreement. See Rebecca Hersher, "India Ratifies Paris Climate Change Agreement," NPR Capital Public Radio, October 2, 2016, accessed October 2, 2016, http://www.npr.org/sections/thetwo-way/2016/10/02.

9. "Narendra Modi's Speech at Unesco in Full," *Wall Street Journal*, April 10, 2015, accessed May 4, 2015, http://blogs.wsj.com/indiarealtime/2015/04/10/narendra-modis-speech-at-unesco-in-full.

Despite Modi's encouraging words, his government's actions indicate a more sobering reality. While yoga has become increasingly popular in India, the BJP has placed sanctions against international environmental organizations such as Greenpeace; continued to invest in coal; pursued environmentally destructive ventures, including the river-linking project; and diverted significant government funds away from projects intended to produce clean energy sources.[10] Why is there such a wide disparity between Modi's words and the actions undertaken by his government?

With Modi's 2014 election victory, the voting public of India revealed a tangible consensus regarding their desire for economic liberalization and the "good times."[11] That is not to say that anti-development sentiments do not persist, but it is to say that Modi's election and the activity that has followed demonstrate an ambitious effort to increase foreign direct investment and the flow of transnational capital at a pace heretofore unrealized. Modi's determination has materialized in his "Make in India Campaign,"[12] along with his optimism for renewed economic relations with the United States, China, Russia, member states of the European Union, and several other nations. Nevertheless, in addition to those who protest India's development, a number of other obstacles stand on the country's path toward becoming what the BJP perceives to be a developed modern country.

Two particular impediments to India's development are (1) its inefficient bureaucratic systems and (2) its dependence on an unreliable and intermittent supply of electricity that is largely produced from carbon-emitting coal. Both issues, which have challenged India for some time, will need to be addressed if the Modi government is to make any progress toward its development goals. The work efficiency of India's governmental employees, as part of the larger state mechanism that holds the door open for transnational capital, must be reformed and streamlined. This reform will allow for the expedient alteration of important

---

10. See, for example: Aditi Roy Ghatak, "Modi and Adani: The Old Friends Laying Waste to India's Environment," June 27, 2016, accessed June 27, 2016, http://www.climatechangenews.com/2017/06/27/modi-adani-old-friends-laying-waste-indias-environment. Also see Kumar Sambhav Shrivastava, "India Diverts Rs 56,700 Crore from the Fight against Climate Change to Goods and Service Tax Regime," *Scroll*, July 24, 2017, accessed July 24, 2017, https://scroll.in/article/844528/india-diverts-rs-56700-crore-from-the-fight-against-climate-change-to-goods-and-service-tax-regime.

11. Kaur, "Good Times," 324. In addition, Sonal S. Pandya from the University of Virginia writes, "Modi's party won May's national elections with an unprecedented majority. This victory was widely interpreted as a sweeping mandate in support of economic liberalization." See Sonal S. Pandya, "Why Foreign Investment Still Polarizes India," *Washington Post*, September 30, 2014, accessed August 4, 2015, http://www.washingtonpost.com/blogs/monkey-cage/wp/2014/09/30/why-foreign-investment-still-polarizes-india/.

12. See www.makeinindia.com.

environmental legislation as well as accelerated processing of environmental
clearances that stand in the way of large-scale development projects.[13] In regard to
electricity, a constant, reliable supply will permit industry to carry out its operations uninterrupted. With mounting global pressure surrounding anthropogenic
climate change, this supply will need to be sourced from increasingly renewable
sources.[14] Nevertheless, India will rely upon international funding in order to
develop a sufficient renewable energy budget, and Trump's withdrawal from the
Paris Agreement reduces this budget significantly.[15]

In order to address both of these overwhelming challenges, Modi and his regime are resuscitating old projects in novel ways. In the remainder of this chapter,
I problematize two of these projects and highlight a potential solution to both.
I first reflect upon Modi's promotion of yoga as a remedy for climate change as
proposed in his UNESCO speech along with his concurrent advancement of the
practice as a method for controlling Indian bodies in order to empower the neoliberal economy that contributes to anthropogenic greenhouse gas emissions.[16]

13. See "Six Green Law Amendments to Be Finalised by Oct: Javadekar," *Z News*, July 29,
2015, accessed August 8, 2015, http://zeenews.india.com/news/eco-news/six-green-law-
amendments-to-be-finalised-by-oct-javadekar_1638691.html. Also see All India Indo-
Asian News Service, "19 States Launch Online Platform for Environment Clearances,"
NDTV, July 2, 2015, accessed August 8, 2015, http://www.ndtv.com/india-news/
19-states-launch-online-platform-for-environment-clearances-777672.

14. According to "India's Intended Nationally Determined Contribution" report released before the 2016 UN climate talks in Paris, "With a vast potential of more than 100 GW, a number
of policy initiatives and actions are being undertaken to *aggressively pursue development of
country's* [sic] *vast hydro potential*" (my emphasis). See "India's Intended Nationally Determined
Contribution Working towards Climate Justice," accessed November 6, 2015, http://www4.
unfccc.int/submissions/INDC/Published%20Documents/India/1/INDIA%20INDC%20
TO%20UNFCCC.pdf.

15. See Annie Gowen and Simon Denyer, "As U.S. Backs Away from Climate Pledges, India
and China Step Up," *Washington Post*, June 1, 2017, accessed June 1, 2017, https://www.
washingtonpost.com/world/asia_pacific/as-us-backs-away-from-climate-pledges-india-and-
china-step-up/2017/06/01/59ccb494-16e4-4d47-a881-c5bd0922c3db_story.html?utm_
term=.b3721a392ebe.

16. I am taking the position that developmental, neoliberal capitalism is the cause of, and
not the solution to, unconstrained anthropogenic climate change. In a paper titled "The
Ultimate Crisis of Neoliberal Globalization: The Case of Climate Change," Gareth Greatrex
of Newcastle University succinctly argues that there are three causal links between the ideology
of neoliberal globalization and climate change. First, multinational corporations' emphasis
on profit alone inevitably leads to detrimental environmental costs. Second, multinational
corporations' geographical separation of the consumer and the sites of third-world production
obscures consumers' ability to understand the link between their consumptive behavior and
ecological degradation. And third, the process of neoliberal globalization spreads the "doctrine
of mass consumption" around the world. In sum, Greatrex writes that our "global malaise"
is an "epidemic of neoliberalism, which through globalization has committed global society
to economic growth and rampant consumerism, the principle obstacles to a stable climate."

By imposing health, work productivity, and the Indian economy as the primary objects of meditation for laborers on the home front, Modi and his regime seek to efficiently mobilize bodies to serve the climate-change-producing capitalist culture that he proposed to reform in his UNESCO speech. In this way, Modi's yoga facilitates an innovative form of Foucauldian biopower, or the "numerous and diverse techniques for achieving the subjugation of bodies and the control of populations" that remain essential for the expansion of capitalism.[17] Foucault's work provides a prism through which we might effectively understand the underlying agenda that fuels Modi's aggressive deployment of yoga.

Moving from yoga bodies to bodies of water, the next part of this chapter critiques India's river-linking project, a recently revived national undertaking that is intended to generate "renewable" and "clean" hydroelectric power while concurrently addressing the nation's ongoing drought challenges. Ironically, though touted by the Indian government as a panacea for India's increasing energy and irrigation needs in the face of climate change, the river-linking project will massively disturb India's deltaic flood plains and riparian forests and thereby contribute to, rather than eliminate, climate change. Considering Foucault's notion of governmentality, I demonstrate that the river-linking project also facilitates a form of biopower insofar as it subjugates divine bodies of water under the neoliberal economic framework. Finally, after problematizing the relationship between climate change, biopower, and human flourishing, I conclude the chapter with an alternative paradigm under which flourishing might be envisioned and realized in India.

See Gareth Greatrex, "The Ultimate Crisis of Neoliberal Globalization: The Case of Climate Change" (master's thesis, Newcastle University, 2014), 3, 15, accessed May 23, 2015, https://www.academia.edu/7526715/The_Ultimate_Crisis_of_Neoliberal_Globalization_The_Case_of_Climate_Change.

In another article, Glenn Fieldman argues that "the neoliberal *system* produces vulnerability to climate-induced (and other) changes and effectively incapacitates effective responses." Similarly, following other related scholarship, she highlights that "development as presently conceived and practised is itself maladaptive" (170). See Glenn Fieldman, "Neoliberalism, the Production of Vulnerability and the Hobbled State: Systemic Barriers to Climate Adaptation," *Climate and Development* 3, no. 2 (2011). I follow both Greatrex and Fieldman in asserting the causal links between neoliberal capitalism and anthropogenic climate change, as well as the inability of neoliberal economic policy to mitigate anthropogenic climate change.

17. See Michel Foucault, *The History of Sexuality Volume 1: An Introduction*, Robert Hurley, trans. (New York: Vintage Books, 1990), 140. Regarding the environmental implications of the BJP's economic agenda, see Ghatak, "Modi and Adani," June 27, 2016.

Yoga: A Brief History

The archaeological record provides evidence of potential yoga (from the verbal root *"yuj,"* meaning "yoke") practices dating as far back as 2,500 B.C.E. in the Indus Valley Civilization,[18] while later textual sources indicate the development of multiple, interpenetrating yoga systems throughout the history of South Asia. Nevertheless, the current manifestation of yoga as we experience it in modern yoga studios and retreat centers, that is, as a combination of therapeutic poses, stretching, breathing, chanting, and perhaps some anecdotal philosophy aimed at attaining health, happiness, and freedom however variously conceived, is largely a novel product that developed during India's encounters with modernity since the mid-19th century.[19] Indeed, rather than being part of an unchanging ancient tradition, "yoga" is a malleable set of heterogeneous practices that have been continually reconfigured to serve the particular needs of the socio-historical contexts in which they were developed.[20]

Given its malleability, yoga lends itself to creative uses in contemporary society. Nevertheless, there are some central metaphysical concepts and themes that, however restyled, remain influential in forms of modern yoga. One such influential concept relates to the fact that some yoga systems encourage the cultivation of a microcosmic-macrocosmic awareness wherein one develops an increasingly intimate understanding of the indissoluble link between the cosmos, the physical world, one's body, and one's emotional and mental experience.[21] These types of "open body" models of yoga became occluded when, from the late 19th century onward, transnational yoga gurus promoted universal, "closed model" systems that understood the yoga body to be a self-contained system hermetically sealed from the external environment.[22] "Closed body" models entered the modern yoga scene in the wake of earlier British translation projects

---

18. The evidence that leads to such dating is not without controversy, however, and has been discussed at length in: David Gordon White, *Sinister Yogis* (Chicago: University of Chicago Press, 2009), 48–58.

19. For an overview of the history of modern yoga, see Mark Singleton, *Yoga Body: The Origins of Modern Posture Practice* (New York: Oxford University Press, 2010), particularly page 16.

20. For an overview of some of the adaptations of modern yoga, see Andrea Jain, *Selling Yoga: From Counterculture to Pop Culture* (Oxford: Oxford University Press, 2015), particularly page 159.

21. Christopher Key Chapple, *Yoga and the Luminous: Patañjali's Spiritual Path to Freedom* (New York: State University of New York Press, 2008), 256, 259.

22. I am borrowing the "open" and "closed" models from David Gordon White, "'Open' and 'Closed' Models of the Human Body in Indian Medical and Yogic Traditions," *Asian Medicine* 2, no. 1 (2006): 1–13, doi:10.1163/157342106777996466.

undertaken during India's colonial period that strategically overemphasized world-negating spiritual philosophies conducive to colonial spatial imperatives. As David Haberman shows, for example, the disregard of world-embracing forms of *bhakti-yoga*, both from a textual and practical perspective, served first and fore-most as a colonial strategy intended to discourage religious practitioners' this-worldly orientation and, in its place, engrave a world-denying, Shankaracaryan theology that devalued the world as illusion.[23] Such a philosophical orientation was, as Haberman highlights, intended to undermine the authority of Indian roy-alty and displace Indian subjects from their land and resources. In colonial courts of law, Haberman writes, "the rites and practices of temple Hinduism that engage the body, mind, *and senses* in the worship of multiple forms of embodied divinity represent a popular corruption of and even dangerous deviation from the au-thentic tradition."[24] By overemphasizing the authority of the world-denying facets of Shankara's philosophy and even going so far as to *illegalize* world-embracing forms of religiosity, the British sought to divest Indian bodies of sensorial inti-macy with their surrounding environment. Ramakrishna was one such influential guru, who adapted to these colonial pressures by encouraging his lower-middle class disciples to develop a timeless and exclusively *inward-oriented* practice of *bhakti-yoga*. Closed systems of yoga like Ramakrishna's served as a refuge from an otherwise oppressive colonial reality, albeit by surrendering intimacy and agency with the external environment.[25]

This is not to say that open models of yoga have not persisted, of course, and a number of gurus and political figures have appropriated the mimetic, micro-macro theme in order to subvert hegemonic colonial ideologies. Perhaps most fa-mously, Gandhi organized nonviolent demonstrations involving yoga practices in order to nonviolently depose colonial rule. Veena Howard suggests that Gandhi's ascetic practices, which were thought to be conventionally deployed by yogis concerned solely with renunciation and enlightenment (*nivṛtti*), were in fact in-tended to affect the field of politics and everyday life (*pravṛtti*) by mobilizing the masses to produce an independent Indian nation state governed by the principles of *satyagraha* (truth-force), *swaraj* (self-rule), and *swadeshi* (self-sufficiency).[26]

23. See David L. Haberman, *River of Love in an Age of Pollution: The Yamuna River of Northern India* (Berkeley: University of California Press, 2006), 25–29.

24. Ibid., 28, my emphasis.

25. For details regarding Ramakrishna's deployment of yoga, see Sumit Sarkar, *Writing Social History* (Delhi and New York: Oxford University Press, 1997), chapter 8.

26. See Veena R. Howard, *Gandhi's Ascetic Activism: Renunciation and Social Action* (Albany: State University of New York Press, 2013). For an excellent comparison between Modi's yoga and that of Gandhi, see Sunila S. Kale and Christian Lee Novetzke, "The Yogic

Gandhi's practices sought to reestablish a relationship between citizens' bodies and the region that would soon become the country of India, in order to reclaim from the British the land and resources that had been subjected to imperial conquest for too long.

Yoga as Biopower: The Production of Neoliberal Yoga Bodies

Since taking office as India's Prime Minister in 2014, Narendra Modi has promoted two very different yogas tailored to the particular needs of the audiences with whom he interacted. As his UNESCO speech demonstrates, an open model was vaguely proposed as a solution to climate change on the international front by encouraging a change in lifestyle involving an appealing micro-macro awareness between "self, society, and Nature."[27] Concurrently in India, however, yoga became a means of training Indian bodies in order to improve the mental and physical health of the country's domestic labor force so as to bolster its neoliberal economy.[28] Indeed, Modi's domestic yoga encourages recognition of the micro-macro relationship between individual bodies and India's governmental and corporate entities. Rather than rely on a closed body model of yoga as India's former colonizers would have favored, he has retrieved the open model of yoga here to prepare India's bureaucracy to yoke neo-colonial foreign investment with the Indian nation state. As I show later in this chapter, the Prime Minister's practice, governance, and promotion of yoga in such a manner facilitates a form of Foucauldian biopower that has the potential to strengthen the economic systems that support the proliferation of anthropogenic climate change that his UNESCO speech sought to obviate.

In *The History of Sexuality*, Michel Foucault identified biopower as the "power over life"[29] that was

> without question an indispensable element in the development of capitalism; the latter would not have been possible without the controlled

Ethic and the Spirit of Development," *Political Theologies and Development in Asia*, Giuseppe Bolotta, R. Michael Feener, and Philip Fountain, eds. (Under Review at Duke University Press).

27. "Narendra Modi's Speech," *Wall Street Journal*, April 10, 2015.

28. For an excellent discussion on the potential uses of yoga to produce neoliberal subjectivity, see Farah Godrej, "The Neoliberal Yogi and the Politics of Yoga," *Political Theory* (2016): 1–29, doi:10.1177/0090591716643604.

29. Foucault, *Sexuality*, 139.

insertion of bodies into the machinery of production and the adjustment of the phenomena of population to economic processes.[30]

Foucault identified two interlinked forms of biopower, both of which help illuminate the underlying utility of Modi's yoga as he endeavors to use the practice to support India's efficient integration into the space of global neoliberalism. The first, which was developed in his earlier work *Discipline and Punish*, views the body as a machine that can be supervised, disciplined into docility, and optimized for efficient use in economic systems. Foucault presents systems of incarceration and rehabilitation as examples of such disciplinary measures.[31] The second, more subtle form focuses on the maintenance of the life of the human species itself. Unlike Europe's medieval period during which bodies were managed from the top down by the lethal brutality of political sovereigns, and wherein illness perpetually held out the threat of death, decentralized biopower required that neoliberal nation-states work from the bottom up, focusing on the production of a healthy, self-regulating, and docile citizenry capable of holding the door open for the flow of transnational capital.[32]

Though biopower ultimately results in the control of bodies, it does so by seizing and maintaining the most indispensable aspect of those bodies, that is, *life itself.* Finally and perhaps most significantly, biopower necessarily operates much more efficiently, subtly, and pervasively than mere coercive force, as it quietly permeates everyday life in order to achieve and reinforce novel forms of bodily subjugation.[33] Modern biomedicine and organizations such as hospitals and mental health institutions are specific manifestations of biopower. This is a concept that is difficult to grasp, as most of us were born in hospitals and rely upon biomedicine to maintain our vitality so that we might live a prosperous, healthy life. While it is hard to argue with the benefits of such institutions and practices, what Foucault wishes to highlight is that they subject our individual bodies, as well as populations at large, to a wider network of subtle power relations. That is to say, health-supporting institutions and practices often implicate citizens' bodies in political and economic systems in which they may not

---

30. Ibid., 140–141.

31. Michel Foucault, *Discipline and Punish: The Birth of the Prison* (New York: Vintage, 1977).

32. For a detailed genealogy of the intensification of power in Foucault's work, see Jeffrey T. Nealon, *Foucault beyond Foucault: Power and Its Intensifications since 1984* (Stanford, CA: Stanford University Press, 2008).

33. See Foucault, *Sexuality*, 140–143.

otherwise wish to participate had they full knowledge of the wider social and environmental implications of their involvement.

As the British sought to extend their colonial grip across India, for example, they offered medical support and biomedicine to their colonial subjects in an effort to eradicate various diseases. Nevertheless, Indians were not naive to the fact that the British intended to create a dependency on Western medicine and to integrate Indian bodies into the colonial economic order. By refusing treatment from the British and by relying upon indigenous forms of medicine, many colonial-era Indians were able to subvert biopower, thereby holding the colonial economic order at arm's length.[34]

While I acknowledge the potential pitfalls of bringing Foucault's political theory into the Indian context,[35] I would argue that the current global economic system of which Modi, the BJP, and an increasingly growing section of the Indian population feverishly wish to be an integral part permits us to do so.[36] Within this neoliberal context, Modi's domestic brand of therapeutic yoga does in fact serve as an instrument of biopower, as it primarily focuses on the production

---

34. For an extended discussion concerning the relationship between colonial medicine and imperialism, see David Arnold, *Colonizing the Body: State Medicine and Epidemic Disease in Nineteenth-Century India* (Berkeley: University of California Press, 1993).

35. Because the concept of biopower is derived from European history and economics, we may be limited regarding the extent to which we might apply Foucault's theoretical model into a cultural framework such as that of an increasingly Hindutva-oriented India. As Joseph Alter rightly points out with regard to yoga specifically, Foucault's theory, which emphasizes the production of *docile* bodies alone, does not always translate one to one into the Indian context. Using the yoga exercises disseminated by the rajah of Aundh in the early 20th century as a case study, Alter suggests that Indian sovereigns often instead sought to inculcate their subjects' bodies with a "*dharmic* orientation toward life." For example, rather than merely reducing his citizens into docile subjects for integration into the British economic order, Alter argues, the rajah of Aundh used yoga to give his subjects the capacity to independently administer education and other forms of civic duty and governance on their own terms. See Joseph S. Alter, *Gandhi's Body: Sex, Diet, and the Politics of Nationalism* (Philadelphia: University of Pennsylvania Press, 2000), 109–111. See also Joseph S. Alter, *Yoga in Modern India: The Body between Science and Philosophy* (Princeton, NJ: Princeton University Press, 2004) wherein Alter demonstrates that pre-independence Indian nationalists such as Sri Yogendra and Swami Kuvalyananda stripped yoga of its magic and mystique by conflating yoga with science and therapeutics in order to prepare the practice to "colonize the West" (106). As Alter shows, rather than merely reducing yoga to a therapeutic practice, Yogendra and Kuvalyananda, as well as other individuals and organizations in India, were in fact subtly disseminating "*Indian* visions of what is possible in the field of human experience" (74–75, my emphasis) that subverted the hegemony of empirical scientific epistemology and ontology.

36. For a summary of yoga and India's neoliberal aspirations, see Andrea Jain and Michael Schulson, "The World's Most Influential Yoga Teacher Is a Homophobic Right-Wing Activist," *Religion Dispatches*, October 4, 2016, accessed October 4, 2016 http://religiondispatches.org/baba-ramdev.

of an efficient, healthy, docile, and stress-free labor force, the qualities of which Modi himself embodies.

A flurry of media releases following Modi's 2014 inauguration and leading up to the first International Day of Yoga in 2015 suggest that this focus is indeed the case. As Lance Price wrote in *The Modi Effect*, "When he does something that isn't directly work-related—as with his daily yoga and meditation routines—it is simply to make him more productive and effective for the rest of the day."[37] Similarly, according to *Hindustan Times*, Modi's work day "begins early—at 5am—with a cup of tea followed by pranayama (an alternate breathing technique) and some yoga. Barring two 30-minute breaks for lunch and dinner, PM Modi works late into the night and ends the day around midnight."[38] Similarly, *Business Times* wrote, "Prime Minister Narendra Modi is an avid yoga fan who credits his strict regime of exercise and meditation for his ability to work long hours on just four or five hours sleep a night."[39] In his own words, Modi said, "I am equally energetic from morning till night . . . I guess the secret behind it is yoga and breathing exercises. Whenever I feel tired, I just practice deep breathing and that refreshes me again."[40] Lakshmanan Gurukkal, Narendra Modi's former campaign masseur, confirmed this strategy while giving me an ayurvedic massage in Auroville in 2015 as he recalled his time spent with the Prime Minister:

> Modi works long hours on his campaign and is very disciplined. He meets one person after the other late into the night. To keep his energy, he practices yoga everyday, and I give him ayurvedic massage in the evening.[41]

---

37. Lance Price, *The Modi Effect: Inside Narendra Modi's Campaign to Transform India* (London: Hodder and Stoughton, 2015), 2–3.

38. Anirudh Bhattacharyya, "PM Modi's Yoga, Ascetic Lifestyle Save His Doctors Unease," *Hindustan Times*, April 24, 2015, accessed April 24, 2015, http://www.hindustantimes.com/india-news/pm-modi-s-yoga-ascetic-lifestyle-give-relief-to-his-team-of-doctors/article1-1338139.aspx. Compare this statement with other statements Modi made about his morning routine. For example, in *The Modi Effect*, he also says, "I am up daily by five a.m. and do not need any time to settle down before I am online checking my messages. It's a mechanical process for me to reach out for my iPad within the first four to five minutes after I wake." Modi effectively blurs the lines between yoga and work (Price, *Modi Effect*, 137).

39. "Yoga to Turn Round Indian Civil Service," *Business Times*, March 23, 2015, accessed March 23, 2015, http://www.bdlive.co.za/businesstimes/2015/03/22/yoga-to-turn-round-indian-civil-service.

40. Harriet Alexander, "India's Yoga Minister Aims to Reclaim Practice from West," *Telegraph*, December 3, 2014, accessed December 3, 2014, http://www.telegraph.co.uk/news/worldnews/asia/india/11271782/Indias-yoga-minster-aims-to-reclaim-practice-from-West.html.

41. Lakshmanan Gurukkal, personal interview, September 7, 2015.

To provide the opportunity for civil servants to reap similar benefits, the Indian government announced that it would provide free daily yoga classes for its three million employees and their families in March 2015.[42] Soon thereafter in April 2015 in New Delhi, a yoga camp was established, the objective of which was, according to the *Times of India*, "to help Members of Parliament channelize their energy for the betterment of their constituency and society as a whole and make them stress free so they can work in a better way."[43] Similarly, Air India, a government-owned commercial airline, began to require pilots to take part in morning yoga sessions. According to one airline official,

> [w]e have introduced yoga for the first time in our training module for pilots and cabin crew, as we believe that yoga brings in a sense of discipline as well as helps cope better with the stress of the job. This is true for each one of us.[44]

Prakash Javadekar, India's Minister of State for Environment, Forest and Climate Change with whom I began this chapter, also supported this strategy. According to a May 2015 newspaper article, Javadekar "practices yoga to keep fit while working long hours and travelling" and his ministry provides these benefits for their staff.[45] In addition to these civil servants, Modi has also targeted police, military, and railway personnel with his yoga programming.[46]

42. "Yoga to Turn Round," *Business Times*, March 23, 2015.

43. "Special Yoga Camp for Parliamentarians," *Times of India*, April 24, 2015, accessed April 24, 2015, http://timesofindia.indiatimes.com/india/Special-yoga-camp-for-parliamentarians/articleshow/47034567.cms.

44. Mihir Mishra, "Air India Introduces Yoga Sessions for Its Newly-Recruited Cabin Crew and Pilots," *Economic Times*, June 1, 2015, accessed June 1, 2015, http://economictimes.indiatimes.com/industry/transportation/airlines-/-aviation/air-india-introduces-yoga-sessions-for-its-newly-recruited-cabin-crew-and-pilots/articleshow/47494757.cms.

45. Richa Sharma, "Yoga Gets Green Signal from the Environment Ministry," *New Indian Express, Sunday Standard*, May 10, 2015, accessed May 10, 2015, http://www.newindianexpress.com/thesundaystandard/Yoga-Gets-Green-Signal-From-the-Environment-Ministry/2015/05/10/article2806037.ece.

46. Deshman Akshay, "Government Planning to Make Yoga Mandatory Soon for Cops, Paramilitary," *Economic Times*, March 14, 2015, accessed March 14, 2015, http://articles.economictimes.indiatimes.com/2015-0314/news/60111647_1_international-yoga-day-morarji-desai-national-institute-defence-staff. Also see Saubhadra Chatterji, "Narendra Modi's Imprint on Suresh Prabhu's Railway Budget Speech," *Hindustan Times*, February 26, 2015, accessed February 26, 2015, http://www.hindustantimes.com/india-news/prabhu-stamps-modi-name-in-railway-budget-speech/article1-1320937.aspx.

Shripad Naik, the BJP's Minister of the Department of Ayurveda, Yoga and Naturopathy, Unani, Siddha and Homoeopathy (AYUSH), the governmental Ministry currently charged with the oversight of yoga education and research, sums up the BJP's civil-service yoga programming as follows:

As for government workers, Mr. Naik said, they will become more productive and less corrupt. "There will be a definite change in the way the bureaucracy functions," he said. "When they are thin, all their energy will go into producing better work. There is no need to do it forcefully, once we have put them on the right path."[47]

Significantly, AYUSH also provides the following definition of yoga on its website:

The science of Yoga and its techniques have now been *reoriented to suit modern sociological needs and lifestyles*. . . . The practice of Yoga prevents psychosomatic disorders and *improves an individuals* [sic] *resistance and ability to endure stressful situations.*[48]

Following this interpretation of a modernized, secularized yoga, Shripad Naik later commented that

[y]oga is [an] ancient Indian heritage and has its roots in myriad spheres of Indian culture and traditions and is being promoted by [the] Ministry of AYUSH as health promotive [sic], disease preventive and rehabilitative drugless therapy without any consideration of caste and creed.[49]

Leading up to the Isha Foundation's unveiling of a 112-foot Shiva statue in Coimbatore in February 2017, Modi reiterated Naik's comments, assuring

---

47. Ellen Barry, "Modi's Yoga Day Grips India, and 'Om' Meets 'Ouch!,'" *New York Times,* June 15, 2015, accessed August 8, 2015, http://www.nytimes.com/2015/06/16/world/asia/india-modi-yoga.html?_r=0.

48. AYUSH, "Yoga," Ministry of Health and Family Welfare, Government of India, accessed March 15, 2015, http://www.indianmedicine.nic.in/searchdetail.asp?lang=1&lid=33, my emphasis. I have cited the sections of AYUSH's definition salient to our discussion. To see the definition in its full context, visit http://www.indianmedicine.nic.in/searchdetail. asp?lang=1&lid=33.

49. "Yoga Is Ancient Therapy, Not Promoted on Lines of Caste or Creed: Govt," *Zee News,* December 9, 2015, accessed December 9, 2015, http://zeenews.india.com/ayurveda/yoga-is-ancient-therapy-not-promoted-on-lines-of-caste-or-creed-govt_1829571.html.

his audience, "There is ample evidence that practicing yoga can help chronic conditions. It helps create a beautiful temper. That is why I call Yoga a passport to health insurance."[50] By repeatedly publicizing such statements in popular media, the BJP has effectively co-opted yoga into biopolitical discourse. Its governmental yoga programs seek to non-forcefully reduce stress and improve health so as to allow employees to work longer, harder, and more efficiently. Through the rehabilitation of the bodies of civil servants, so too, we can assume, will the health and functioning of India's bureaucratic institutions improve.

Outside of his direct influence within India's governmental bureaucracy, Modi has also celebrated the use of yoga to increase worker productivity in the private sector. In March 2015, he wrote on Twitter, "interesting article on yoga & meditation at workplace," praising a *New York Times* piece that celebrated Aetna's success in increasing employee productivity and lowering company costs through its free on-site yoga program.[51] The use of various forms of yoga and meditation in the corporate environment is a popular trend to which Modi appeals, and indeed studies have shown that participation in these types of programs tends to increase one's productivity and resilience to workplace stress.[52] A publication from Modi's own home state of Gujarat indicates that yoga can produce "stress-free employees" who "perform better, work harder, feel happier, and have a long term commitment to the organization as compared to their counterparts."[53]

India's business leaders are also enthusiastically aware of the potential benefits of incorporating yoga into the private sector. Shortly after yoga practitioners around the world joined Modi to celebrate the first UN-sanctioned International Day of Yoga on June 21, 2015, the Federation of Indian Chambers of Commerce and Industry (FICCI), a nonprofit organization that serves as the "voice for India's business and industry" and has celebrated Modi's ability to implement a new economic vision, partnered with AYUSH to encourage India's businesses

---

50. ANI, "Yoga a Passport to Health Insurance: PM Modi," *Business Standard,* February 24, 2017, accessed February 24, 2017, http://www.business-standard.com/article/news-ani/yoga-a-passport-to-health-insurance-pm-modi-117022400991_1.html.

51. "Why PM Modi Tweeted a New York Times Article Today," *India Today,* March 4, 2015, accessed March 4, 2015, http://indiatoday.intoday.in/story/narendra-modi-tweet-new-york-times-article-yoga-meditation/1/422204.html.

52. See, for example, Ned Hartfield, Jon Havenhand, Sat Bir Khalsa, Graham Clarke and Anne Krayer, "The Effectiveness of Yoga for the Improvement of Well-Being and Resilience in the Workplace," *Scandinavian Journal of Work, Environment and Health* 37, no. 1 (2011): 70–76.

53. Revati C. Deshpande, "A Healthy Way to Handle Work Place Stress through Yoga, Meditation, and Soothing Humor," *International Journal of Environmental Sciences* 2, no. 4 (2012): 2151.

to integrate yoga into their employee wellness programs.[54] According to Dr. A. Didar Singh, FICCI's Secretary General,

> "Business houses should increasingly introduce Yoga under their employee wellness programs. . . . FICCI's National Wellness Committee promotes benefits of implementing Preventive Healthcare measures including yoga, among corporates to improve productivity and efficiency among employees. Workplace wellness initiatives, including yoga, can lead to a better performance of an organization."[55]

Partnered with the government, FICCI promotes corporate yoga along the same lines as Modi and his ministry affiliates, prioritizing the mimetic correspondence between employee and organizational health.

Modi's yoga and the authorities and institutions that promote it frame yoga as a stress-reducing, health-optimizing practice intended to create employee bodies capable of enduring the increasing demands of both the governmental and corporate work pace. As Shripad Naik admitted, compulsion is not a necessary counterpart to the yoga programming, as laborers who have been put on the "right path" will, we can deduce from his comments, realize these benefits for themselves. Furthermore, Modi's successful execution of the International Day of Yoga in 2015, 2016, and 2017, coupled with the overwhelmingly positive global response and the increased local interest that has ensued, surely invests yoga with renewed popularity in India.[56]

---

54. See "Welcome to FICCI.COM," FICCI Industry's Voice for Policy Change, accessed August 8, 2015, http://www.ficci.com/about-ficci.asp. Also see "Modi Will Focus on Implementation, says FICCI Prez," Moneycontrol.com, February 27, 2014, accessed August 8, 2015, http://www.moneycontrol.com/news/economy/modi-will-focusimplentation-says-ficci-prez_1048789.html.

55. Rani Singh, "International Yoga Day and What It Means for India," Forbes, June 29, 2015, accessed August 8, 2015, http://www.forbes.com/sites/ranisingh/2015/06/29/international-yoga-day-and-what-it-means-for-india/.

56. Responding, for example, to the demand for yoga after the second International Day of Yoga held in Chandigarh in 2016, the Ministry of AYUSH proposed to build fifty yoga camps there in October 2016. See Adil Akhzer, "Health Department to Start 50 Yoga Camps in Chandigarh Next Month," Indian Express, October 23, 2016, accessed October 23, 2016, http://indianexpress.com/article/cities/chandigarh/health-department-to-start-50-yoga-camps-in-chandigarh-next-month-3098014.

In some cases, yoga was made compulsory. In Rajasthan alone, almost 50,000 schools made the sun salutation, a popular yoga exercise, a mandatory part of the school curriculum in 2015. See "Surya Namaskar Made Compulsory in 48,000 Schools in Rajasthan," Times of India, February 4, 2015, accessed February 4, 2015, http://timesofindia.indiatimes.com/india/Surya-namaskar-made-compulsory-in-48000-schools-Rajasthan/articleshow/46114163.cms.

It is in the sense heretofore described that Modi's yoga, functioning as a subtle disciplinary measure intended to improve worker health and efficiency while cloaked in the facade of an ancient spiritual tradition, constitutes an instrument of biopower. By suggestively positing a correlation between health, employee productivity, and organizational success, the Prime Minister reframes yoga as a practice that increases one's "resistance and ability to endure stressful situations"[57] within various workforce contexts. That is to say, through a regimen of psychosomatic discipline, yoga "cures" laborers of any potential "abnormal" physical or mental illnesses that might prevent optimal participation in their employment undertakings.[58] Such subtle disciplinary measures have far-reaching implications, as they encourage laborers to singularly devote their minds and bodies to support the institutions that serve the development of the neoliberal economic system that lies at the root of anthropogenic climate change.

River Linking as Biopower: The Production of Neoliberal Water Bodies

Like Modi's yoga, India's river-linking project (RLP) also seeks to subjugate bodies to fulfill India's economic aspirations. Rather than controlling employee bodies, however, Modi's government seeks to subjugate India's divine bodies of water via a massive river diversion project intended to provide the country with clean energy and a host of other alleged benefits. To position the RLP within our broader discussion, a brief return to Foucault will be useful here.

In some of his later lectures, Foucault transitions his focus from the control of the *individual* body to the ways in which biopower operates within the wider context of governmentality, or the present mode of government, which relies upon economic knowledge and security apparatuses in order to manage a stable and

---

57. AYUSH, "Yoga," http://www.indianmedicine.nic.in/searchdetail.asp?lang=1&lid=33.

58. This strategy is not unlike some varieties of modern Buddhist mindfulness practices, which, as Slavoj Žižek has argued, serve to allow practitioners to "participate in the frantic pace of the capitalist game" while creating the impression that they are somehow unaffected by it. Žižek writes, "The 'Western Buddhist' meditative stance is arguably the most efficient way for us to fully participate in capitalist dynamics while retaining the appearance of mental sanity." However different this "Western Buddhist" ontology of detachment might be from the mimetic, micro-macro metaphysics emphasized in Modi's yoga, Modi's version might well give Western Buddhism a run for its money. See Slavoj Žižek, "From Western Marxism to Western Buddhism," *Cabinet Magazine*, Spring 2001, accessed June 9, 2015, http://www.cabinetmagazine.org/issues/2/western.php.

healthy *population*.[59] In *Security, Territory, and Population*, Foucault draws our attention to the milieu, or a "field of intervention" that, rather than implicating individuals alone, indeed affects an entire population and the geographical context to which they are bound:[60]

> The milieu is . . . a set of natural givens—rivers, marshes, hills,—and a set of artificial givens—an agglomeration of individuals, of houses, etcetera . . . who are and fundamentally only exist biologically bound to the materiality within which they live.[61]

Within the milieu, security is deployed

> . . . at that point of connection where nature, in the sense of physical elements, interferes with nature in the sense of the nature of the human species, at that point of articulation where the milieu becomes the determining factor of nature.[62]

With a tone of environmental determinism, Foucault suggests that governments maintain a healthy and happy state at the level of population by controlling the material forces with which society must interact. State intervention is rationalized and carried out on these material forces, which include "natural resources," via the government's production of a "domain of knowledge" built upon statistical data.[63] Ramachandra Guha, Tariq Banuri, and Frédérique Apfell Marglin have shown, for example, how India's methods of scientific forestry, which are largely founded upon Western systems of knowledge, create a dominant epistemological paradigm that, coming into direct conflict with forest dwellers' alternative ways of knowing, justifies the state's systematic decimation of forests and sacred groves.[64]

---

59. Michel Foucault, "Governmentality," in *Power: Essential Works of Foucault 1954–1984*, James D. Faubion, ed., Robert Hurley, trans. (New York: New Press, 1997), 219–221.

60. Michel Foucault, *Security, Territory, Population: Lectures at the Collège de France 1977–1978*, Michel Senellart, ed., Graham Burchell, trans. (New York: Palgrave Macmillan, 2009), 21.

61. Ibid.

62. Ibid., 23.

63. Ibid., 315.

64. See Ramachandra Guha, *The Unquiet Woods: Ecological Change and Peasant Resistance in the Himalaya, Expanded Edition* (Berkeley: University of California Press, 2000), and Tariq Banuri and Frédérique Apfell Marglin, eds., *Who Will Save the Forests? Knowledge, Power and Environmental Destruction* (London: Zed Books, 1993).

In the context of governmentality, biopower thus moves its preoccupation with the health and well-being of individuals alone to a preoccupation with the scientific management of the health of the entire population via the rationalized manipulation of material reality at large. The outcome of such state interventions, however, is often environmentally destructive and, consequently, does not necessarily support the flourishing of human life in the long run. In similar fashion and concurrent with its commitment to economic liberalization, such practices nevertheless work through the government of India as the BJP continues to transform the subcontinent's material reality into "natural resources" for human utility and consumption.

Another apt example of this phenomenon, and one that I focus on for the purposes of this chapter, comes from the way in which the BJP continues to appropriate India's rivers into neoliberal discourse. In countless religious contexts throughout India, rivers are otherwise revered as sacred embodiments of the goddess. The Ganges, for example, whose source at Gangotri in the Himalayas creates a river that runs the length of India's northern plains until meeting the ocean at the Bay of Bengal, is worshipped as a goddess of divine origin. Overtaken by her beauty in the *Mahābhārata*, the royal Shantanu persuades the goddess of the Ganges River, who is manifest in the form of a beautiful maiden, to be his wife. Today, the river remains an important site for religious devotion and pilgrimage. Similarly, in South India, the Cauvery River plays an important role in the religious lives of those who worship her. The Tamil *Kantapuranam* relays the story of the god Shiva, who sent the sage Agastya into the south of the Indian subcontinent with the Cauvery River in a pot. Here, the pot was eventually overturned by Ganesha disguised as a crow in order to let the river loose to bring much needed water to Indra's drought-ridden garden downstream.[65] To this day, the life-giving Cauvery is worshipped as a goddess in various forms along her banks and is often revered as the Ganges of the south. Sacred rivers abound in India, and the Cauvery and the Ganges represent but two that testify to their divine nature.

Despite these rivers' divinity, in their interactions with the modern state, politicians prioritize these same waterways for their economic and utilitarian value. With regard to development specifically, Chris Deegan and William Fisher have highlighted the ways in which pragmatic development plans, including the construction of the massive hydroelectric Sardar Sarovar Dam, have disrupted religious practice along the Narmada

---

65. Indira Viswanathan Peterson, "The Kaveri in Legend and Literature," in *Eternal Kaveri: Historical Sites along South India's Greatest River,* George Michell, ed. (Mumbai: Marg Publications, 1999), 36–37.

River.[66] In her book about the Ganges, Kelly Alley has elucidated the complex interactions between coexisting religious and political-scientific ontologies that have resulted in the river's pollution, obstruction, and diversion, ultimately suggesting that religions alone might not necessarily have all of the resources to prevent the river's ecological degradation.[67] Contra Alley, David Haberman has argued that the influence of Vaishnava devotional practice along the Yamuna River reveals the central role that religious devotion and metaphysics must play in India's efforts to mend its degraded rivers and protect them from development.[68] Similarly, George James shared the story of Sunderlal Bahuguna, the environmental activist who dedicated years of his life to nonviolently protesting the construction of the Tehri Dam on the sacred Bhagirathi River in Uttarakhand in the name of spiritual values.[69] As we will later see, I share the opinion of Haberman and James, namely, that religious values and spiritual practice can contribute to the preservation and protection of India's rivers.

Each of the works cited above details the individual consequences of the encounter between economic agendas and India's sacred rivers. Today, however, these rivers face an unprecedented collective threat, which brings us to Narendra Modi's second UNESCO solution for climate change, *clean energy*. Like countless other rivers around the world, many of India's waterways are used to produce "clean" hydroelectric power. Hydropower, along with several other perceived benefits that I am about to mention, provides the justification for India's recently revived RLP, a project by which the BJP intends to dramatically alter the entire subcontinent's sensitive hydrological cycle via the interlinking of India's major rivers.

Like the popularity of world-negating spiritual philosophies mentioned previously, the RLP has its roots in India's colonial period. Prior to British colonization, localized water management techniques were put to use throughout the

66. See Chris Deegan, "The Narmada: Circumambulation of a Sacred Landscape," in *Hinduism and Ecology: The Intersection of Earth, Sky, and Water*, Christopher Key Chapple and Mary Evelyn Tucker, eds. (Cambridge, MA: Harvard University Press, 2000); also see William F. Fisher, "Sacred Rivers, Sacred Dams: Competing Visions of Social Justice and Sustainable Development along the Narmada," in *Hinduism and Ecology,* Chapple and Tucker, eds.

67. See Kelly D. Alley, "Separate Domains: Hinduism, Politics, and Environmental Pollution," in *Hinduism and Ecology;* also see Kelly D. Alley, *On the Banks of the Gaṅgā: When Wastewater Meets a Sacred River* (Ann Arbor: University of Michigan Press, 2002).

68. See David L. Haberman, *River of Love*, 179, 189. Also see Haberman, "River of Love in an Age of Pollution," in *Hinduism and Ecology*.

69. George Alfred James, *Ecology Is Permanent Economy: The Activism and Environmental Philosophy of Sunderlal Bahuguna* (New York: State University of New York Press, 2013).

subcontinent. In South India, for example, the Pallavas (*c.* 300–900 C.E.) ritually managed their hydrological environment with numerous interconnected rainwater tanks and irrigation canals, the success of which was believed to have depended upon the moral character and proper ritual praxis of the king who built them.[70] The Cholas (*c.* 900–1300 C.E.) introduced additional water management innovations such as the Grand Anicut Dam in order to transform lowland flooding into gentle flush irrigation for agriculture in the fertile Cauvery Delta.[71] Inheriting the work of the Pallavas and the Cholas, the Vijayanagara empire (*c.* 1300–1500 C.E.) promoted, managed, and manipulated locally maintained water tanks and canal irrigation networks for storing and releasing rainwater for agriculture.[72] During the colonial period, local tank irrigation systems such as these were nationalized and neglected. Consequently, these ancient systems slowly deteriorated as the British shifted their focus to large-scale, maladapted irrigation techniques, including river linking.[73] Indeed, as a potential remedy to India's uneven monsoonal rain distribution, British engineer Sir Arthur Cotton first proposed to interlink some of India's rivers in the 1850s on a scale theretofore unimagined. Despite the warnings of soil specialists, Cotton made this proposal under the pressure to increase the area of irrigated farmland so as to earn additional revenue. In South India, the distinguished engineer Sir Visveswaraya made similar proposals prior to independence and supervised major projects such as the Krishnarajasagara Dam in Karnataka. In a grand post-independence scheme that moved beyond both Cotton and Visveswaraya's plans, Captain Dinshaw Dastur and K.L. Rao suggested the interlinking of India's perennially fed Himalayan northern rivers with their seasonally fed counterparts in the peninsular south.[74]

Though initially deemed unworthy of consideration, the north-south idea found its way back into India's water policy in 2002. Acting on the president's plea to network the country's rivers after China initiated their own south-north water diversion project in November 2002, the Indian government created the

70. Anne Monius, "Ecologies of Human Flourishing: A Case from Precolonial South India," in *Ecologies of Human Flourishing*, Donald K. Swearer and Susan Lloyd McGarry, eds. (Cambridge, MA: Harvard University Press, 2011), 51–53.

71. Christopher John Baker, *An Indian Rural Economy, 1880–1955: The Tamilnad Countryside* (Delhi and New York: Oxford: University Press, 1984), 27, 465.

72. Venkatesh B. Athreya, Göran Djurfeldt, and Staffan Lindberg, *Barriers Broken: Production Relations and Agrarian Change in Tamil Nadu* (New Delhi and Newbury Park: SAGE, 1990), 65–68.

73. Ibid.

74. Binayak Ray, *Water: The Looming Crisis in India* (Lanham, MD: Lexington Books, 2008), 89.

Task Force on Interlinking of Rivers.[75] Under current plans, thirty rivers will be connected in one of the largest, most expensive, and highly disputed water development projects in recorded history.[76]

Disregarding the potentially enormous ecological costs, the RLP Task Force has endorsed the project's undertaking on four major grounds:

(i) to augment irrigation potential by 35 million hectare . . . which would increase the production of food for our growing population;

(ii) to fulfil[l] the growing needs of water . . . the domestic and industrial needs of water is expected to grow steeply. . . .

(iii) to generate about 34,000 MW of additional power through hydroelectricity to meet the increasing need of energy in the country; and

(iv) to facilitate transportation in the country through inland waterways.[77]

The specific plans for the RLP continue to undergo modification and negotiation. In July 2014, the Union Cabinet approved the Ken-Betwa river link while the BJP's Water Resources Minister, Uma Bharti, proposed that the remaining twenty-nine links should be completed over the course of the next ten years.[78] In April 2015, Bharti also initiated a new task force to continue to try to bring some consensus around the highly contested project, and in February 2016 Modi himself declared to the nation, "We must shed our differences and make-up our minds to link rivers."[79] Nevertheless, environmental organizations have delayed

75. Kelly D. Alley, "India's River Linking Plan: History and Current Debates," Harvard Center for Middle Eastern Studies, 2008, 6, http://cmes.hmdc.harvard.edu/files/alleyharvardwater.may08.doc.

76. See Jayanta Bandyopadhyay and Shama Perveen, "The Interlinking of Indian Rivers: Questions on the Scientific, Economic, and Environmental Dimensions," in *Interlinking of Rivers in India: Issues and Concerns*, M. Monirul Qader Mirza, Ahsan Uddin Ahmed, and Qazi Kholiquzzaman Ahmad, eds. (Boca Raton, FL: CRC, 2008), 53–76. The Indian RLP is estimated to cost approximately US $125 billion (Bandyopadhyay and Perveen, "Interlinking," 58). In terms of its breadth and ecological impact, we might compare the Indian RLP with China's recently completed south-north water diversion project: http://www.bloomberg.com/bw/articles/2014-12-15/world-s-largest-river-diversion-project-now-pipes-water-to-beijing.

77. "Interlinking of Rivers: Addressing Ecological Concerns," *Economic and Political Weekly*, April 24, 2004, accessed May 4, 2015, http://www.epw.in/editorials/interlinking-rivers-addressing-ecological-concerns.html.

78. Vishwa Mohan, "Cabinet Okays Linking Ken, Betwa Rivers," *Times of India*, July 25, 2014, accessed May 4, 2015, http://timesofindia.indiatimes.com/home/environment/developmental-issues/Cabinet-okays-linking-Ken-Betwa-rivers/articleshow/38984990.cms.

79. See Express News Service, "Govt's Task Force on River Inter-linking," *New Indian Express*, April 15, 2015, accessed April 15, 2015, http://www.newindianexpress.com/nation/Govts-Task-Force-on-River-Inter linking/2015/04/15/article2765004.ece. See also "Shed

the Ken-Betwa link, arguing that portions of the Panna Tiger Reserve would be flooded. These organizations have also demanded that the government's scientific data, which allegedly supports the RLP's implementation, be released to the public (the government of India has, to date, kept this data out of the public domain). In a desperate response in June 2016, Bharti threatened to go on a hunger strike if the project was delayed any further.[80] Replacing Bharti in 2017, new Water Resources Minister Nitin Gadkari has attempted to fast-track clearance for several of the RLP's individual linking projects.[81] As of the writing of this chapter, the RLP nevertheless remains delayed.

Though the RLP is intended to assist India as it confronts the various challenges presented by climate change,[82] each of the action items listed above bears the potential to contribute to its anthropogenic proliferation. As such, insofar as each plays a role in Modi's clean energy solution to climate change, it must be scrutinized. With regard to points (i) and (ii), advocates of the RLP intend for the project to deliver "surplus" water from flood-prone areas to drought-prone "deficit" areas, all the while preventing river water from reaching the ocean. Doing so, however, will prevent floods from performing their role in recharging groundwater, flushing silt and minerals to land for agriculture, supporting the

Differences, Help Link Rivers, Modi Tells Parties," *Deccan Herald*, February 28, 2016, accessed February 8, 2016, http://www.deccanherald.com/content/531520/shed-differences-help-link-rivers.html.

80. "Uma Bharti Threatens Hunger Strike over Ken-Betwa Project Delay," business-standard.com, June 7, 2016, (accessed June 7, 2016), http://www.business-standard.com/article/news-ians/uma-bharti-threatens-hunger-strike-over-ken-betwa-project-delay-116060701096_1.html.

81. "Government mulling 'large fund' for river inter-linking projects: Nitin Gadkari," *Economic Times*, October 10, 2017, (accessed October 10, 2017), https://economictimes.indiatimes.com/industry/transportation/shipping-/-transport/government-mulling-large-fund-for-river-inter-linking-projects-nitin-gadkari/articleshow/61021859.cms.

82. Several sources discuss the complexity of the river-linking project as it pertains to climate change. See, for example, Murari Lal, "Implications of Climate Change in South Asia on the Interlinking Project of Indian Rivers," in *Interlinking of Rivers in India: Issues and Concerns*, 187. See also Upali A. Amarasinghe, Tushaar Shah, and R.P.S. Malik, eds., "India's Water Futures: Drivers of Change, Scenarios and Issues," in *Strategic Analyses of the National River Linking Project (NRLP) of India, Series 1, India's Water Future: Scenarios and Issues*, Upali A. Amarasinghe, Tushaar Shah, and R.P.S. Malik, eds. (Colombo, Sri Lanka: International Water Management Institute, 2008), 23. See also Rathinasamy Maria Saleth, "Water Scarcity and Climatic Change in India: The Need for Water Demand and Supply Management," *Hydrological Sciences Journal* 56, no. 4 (2011): 685. See also P.R. Shukla, Subodh K. Sharma, Amit Garg, Sumana Bhattacharya, and N.H. Ravindranath, eds., "Climate Change Vulnerability Assessment and Adaptation: The Context," in *Climate Change and India: Vulnerability Assessment and Adaptation*, P.R. Shukla, Subodh K. Sharma, Amit Garg, Sumana Bhattacharya, and N.H. Ravindranath, eds. (Hyderguda, India: Universities Press, 2003), 14.

development and movement of fish and other aquatic life, and pushing sediment flows into the deltaic plains that prevent coastal erosion and groundwater salinization.[83] The dramatic changes that will be made to India's hydrological cycle may also disturb the subcontinent's monsoon cycle.[84] Furthermore, as transferred water is put to use for agriculture as indicated by item (i), the amount of cultivated land will increase to such an extent so as to cause a significant increase in greenhouse gases such as methane.[85] Likewise, as water is diverted to urban areas to serve expanding industrial needs, it will support the polluting system that currently produces vast amounts of unregulated greenhouse gases in India's urban settings.

Point (iii) pertains specifically to Modi's UNESCO speech solutions for climate change, as the RLP is expected to generate "clean" hydropower from the 200 dams related to the project.[86] Though hydropower is apparently "cleaner" than India's extensively exploited coal power, it too has the potential to exacerbate climate change. Significantly, studies by the World Bank indicate that large dam projects may have considerably unfavorable effects on both vegetation and climate.[87] For the RLP specifically, these effects include the submersion of close to

---

83. All of these consequences are further explained in Bandyopadhyay and Perveen, "Interlinking"; Ray, *Water,* 97–99; and Lal, "Implications," 211.

84. See Radhakrishnan Kuttoor, "River-Linking Will Lead to Climate Change," *Hindu,* April 1, 2015, accessed April 1, 2015, http://www.thehindu.com/news/national/kerala/riverlinking-will-lead-to-climate-change/article7055933.ece. See also Indo-Asian News Service, "River Linking Could Alter Rainfall, Hit Monsoons: Expert," NDTV, December 6, 2014, accessed May 4, 2015, http://www.ndtv.com/india-news/river-linking-could-alter-rainfall-hit-monsoons-expert-709209.

85. Lal, "Implications," 211. Methane, a greenhouse gas far more potent than carbon dioxide, is released into the atmosphere as a consequence of a number of agricultural activities, including the propagation of rice, India's domestic food staple and major export (according to the World Bank, India is the world's second largest supplier of rice). According to Fred Pearce, contributing author to the *Yale Environment 360* magazine, "Now that the world has a strategy—agreed to in Paris last December—for combating CO_2 emissions, it badly needs a similar plan for climate enemy No. 2: methane. The Paris agreement to keep warming 'well below two degrees C' will be unachievable without it." Pearce points to research that indicates that reducing the duration of time during which rice paddies are flooded can in fact significantly reduce methane emissions, although as others point out, incentive must be created for farmers dealing with seasonal rain variability in India to do so. See Tim Searchinger, "More Rice, Less Methane," *World Resources Institute,* December 16, 2014, accessed July 30, 2017, http://www.wri.org/blog/2014/12/more-rice-less-methane. See also "India: Issues and Priorities for Agriculture," *World Bank,* May 17, 2012, accessed July 30, 2012, http://www.worldbank.org/en/news/feature/2012/05/17/india-agriculture-issues-priorities. See also Fred Pearce, "What Is Causing the Recent Rise in Methane Emissions?," *Yale Environment 360,* October 25, 2016, accessed July 30, 2017, http://e360.yale.edu/features/methane_riddle_what_is_causing_the_rise_in_emissions.

86. Ray, *Water,* 90.

87. Ibid., 108.

80,000 hectares of forests,[88] a situation that threatens human and other biological life that depends on these areas for survival. Depending on the role these forests play in mitigating climate change, the effects of such a loss could be substantial.

Finally, point (iv) on the Task Force's list seems to speak for itself. Facilitating "transportation in the country through inland waterways," as the list notes, will undoubtedly require carbon-emitting vessels, further contributing to climate change along India's altered riparian systems.

Like the neoliberal bodies Modi intends to discipline and direct with yoga, the RLP, a project that serves to control and redirect sacred water bodies, will disrupt necessary ecological functions that mitigate climate change, all the while supporting and expanding the industrial processes that contribute to greenhouse gas emissions. Thus, although the Indian government may intend to create a flourishing, healthy, and happy society, the RLP has the potential to rebound and produce, in the long term, harsher climatic conditions.

Climate Change as Biopower: The Production of Neoliberal Solutions

If human flourishing entails the need to protect and nurture the welfare, health, and happiness of citizen subjects, then the Foucauldian perspective presented in this chapter affirms the pervasive grip of biopower to this end. Subtle and persistent, biopower operates on *life itself* as it holds our mortality in its grasp. This concept raises difficult questions with regard to our individual and collective dependencies on all of the institutions and practices that serve to protect and nurture our lives. As humans, we want to live and flourish, and we want our loved ones to do the same. But natural limits may demand limits to human flourishing. Whose flourishing should be limited? Who should make such a sacrifice? These are some of the difficult questions the concept of biopower forces us to confront as we deliberate flourishing within the context of environmental ethics, both within India and elsewhere.

Using Narendra Modi's 2015 UNESCO speech, I have shown how two particular forms of biopower are at work in India. Modi's yoga, playing on modern themes of health and wellness and appropriating the micro-macro dynamics of yoga philosophy, seeks to maximize the health of employee bodies so as to increase the efficiency of environmentally destructive bureaucratic and corporate organizations. The RLP, which seeks to divert the water of all of India's major river systems for hydropower, industry, agriculture, and transportation, attempts to

---

88. Ibid., 90.

seize India's sacred water bodies in order to place them in service to the neoliberal economic logic to which the country is rapidly opening its doors. Paradoxically, to the extent that both of these projects are contributing to the acceleration of the flow of transnational capital and foreign direct investment, the disposal of critical Indian environmental legislation, and the deleterious alteration of India's sacred riparian bodies and other ecological systems, both Modi's yoga and the RLP inadvertently defy biopower insofar as they are feeding the industrial machine that produces anthropogenic climate change and poses a threat to planetary life. Nevertheless, by justifying both of these projects as solutions to the greater global challenge of climate change in his UNESCO speech, Modi harnesses and perpetuates the rhetorical force of global biopower, which, seeking to protect global life, renders climate change a threatening yet governable situation that justifies "global management of spaceship Earth in the name of the survival of life on Earth."[89] When positioned as a threat to human life, climate change empowers the politicians who deploy the issue from the helm of neoliberal governance with the deceptive authority to sanction its solutions. Thus, by situating yoga and clean energy projects as the twin solutions to climate change, Modi subtly transforms both into technologies by which global neoliberal governance can allegedly clean up its own planetary mess. Though Modi has proposed solutions that suit his position as the doorkeeper for the flow of transnational capital and unrestrained economic development, I conclude this chapter with an alternative solution to human flourishing that is already well under way in India.[90]

Conclusion: Local Biopower and the Production of an Alternative Paradigm

In 2015, Rajendra Singh, the "Water Man of India," was recognized for his innovative efforts to restore water, livelihoods, and ecological systems in drought-ridden areas in Rajasthan when he was awarded the Stockholm Water Prize

---

89. Angela Oels, "Rendering Climate Change Governable: From Biopower to Advanced Liberal Government?" *Journal of Environmental Policy and Planning* 7, no. 3 (2005): 185. Oels continues in her abstract, "Since the mid-1990s, climate change has been captured by advanced liberal government, which articulates climate change as an economic issue that requires market-based solutions to facilitate cost-effective technological solutions" (185).

90. With regard to flourishing, Foucault began to develop notions of self-care in some of his later ethical work, resulting in his "aesthetics of existence." Nevertheless, considering our discussion on yoga, the RLP, and climate change in India, I would like to conclude by citing the case of one particular figure who, standing at the nexus of philosophy, water, and the environment, offers local solutions for flourishing that defy the homogenizing tendencies of neoliberal economics.

Laureate. Working with local communities, Singh has revived rivers, recharged groundwater, restored traditional methods of rainwater harvesting, and averted threats from flooding.[91] Likewise, Singh is also an outspoken critic of India's RLP who underscores the dangers the project poses for the environment, as well as the government's intentions to centralize water management for industrial and urban purposes.[92]

Significantly, prior to beginning his water work, Singh studied ayurveda, the Indian system of medicine that shares close ontological affinities with many systems of yoga. In an interview following his receipt of the Stockholm Water Prize, Singh said,

> My education was in Indian traditional medicine. And the goal of this system is the safeguarding of health. Safeguarding health is only possible when everybody gets pure and clean water. . . . I agree I didn't use that particular system [ayurveda], but the work I have done fulfills the objective of Ayurveda. With my work the area that was filled with salt water, by filtration through the ground, became fresh and sweet water. Hence the people of that region became healthier. . . . People who were ill, unemployed and displaced, were able to become healthy and return to their areas again.[93]

As I conclude this chapter, there are two important features of Singh's remarks that I wish to highlight here. First, though concerned with the health of the villagers with whom he worked, Singh indicates that his efforts actually provided the opportunity for displaced residents to return to their villages. Subverting global biopower, these individuals gain an increased level of autonomy from compulsory urban dwelling and the normalizing processes of neoliberalism.

Second, Singh, though not practicing ayurveda in a clinical setting, credits his work as an accomplishment of ayurveda nonetheless. Indeed, many of India's ontological systems, including ayurveda and yoga, but additionally those yoga

---

91. "The Water Man of India Wins 2015 Stockholm Water Prize," Stockholm International Water Institute, accessed August 9, 2015, http://www.siwi.org/prizes/stockholmwaterprize/laureates/2015-2.

92. Press Trust of India, "Linking Rivers Won't Make India Drought Free: Rajendra Singh," *Business Standard*, June 16, 2015, accessed August 8, 2015, http://www.business-standard.com/article/pti-stories/linking-rivers-won-t-make-india-drought-free-rajendra-singh-115061600743_1.html.

93. "Long Interview with 2015 Stockholm Water Prize Laureate," SIWI Media Hub, accessed August 8, 2015, http://siwi-mediahub.creo.tv/prizes-and-awards/stockholm-waterprize/long_interview_with_2015_stockholm_water_prize_laureate.

systems espoused by texts of the Jain, Buddhist, Hindu, and Muslim variety,[94] recognize the five gross elements of earth, water, fire, air, and space to be the fundamental and indispensable building blocks of material reality. In many cases, these open yoga systems emphasize the cultivation of an awareness of the direct correspondence between one's body, which is comprised of these elements, and the elemental world at large.[95] Singh's assertion that he has done the healing work of ayurveda is a recognition of this mimetic correspondence, and in particular of the indissoluble link between human bodies and bodies of water. His comments in a later interview provide further confirmation. According to Singh,

> [i]nstead of linking rivers, the Government should try to link mind and hearts of people to rivers, so that the rivers which have dried can be resurrected.... [t]he way we did it in Rajasthan. Drought will end only when society associates itself with water.[96]

As Singh's work and comments here suggest, those who deploy the epistemological and ontological insights found in systems such as ayurveda or classical yoga are well situated to create alternative solutions to ecological challenges, solutions that defy the hegemony of reductionist national science. These solutions manifest when alternative ways of knowing are used to encourage the cultivation of an ever-expanding awareness of the micro-macro correspondence between one's self and the local environments in which one finds oneself. Local solutions informed by such worldviews allow both human and nonhuman life to flourish while simultaneously downscaling biopower's influence from the level of national and state governmentality to a bioregional, and (following Joseph Alter) perhaps bio-*moral*,[97] form of

---

94. For case studies and translations in each of these traditions, see, for example, Christopher Chapple, "The Sevenfold Yoga of the *Yogavāsiṣṭha*," and Carl W. Ernst, "A Fourteenth-Century Persian Account of Breath Control and Meditation," in David Gordon White, *Yoga Sutra of Patanjali: A Biography.* (Princeton, NJ: Princeton University Press, 2014), 117–139, and Christopher Chapple, "*Mahābhūta Dhāraṇas* in Subhacandra's *Jñānārṇava* and the Practice of *Kasiṇas* in Buddhagosa's *Vishuddimagga*," in *Buddhist and Jaina Studies: Proceedings of the Conference in Lumbini, February 2013*, J. Soni, M. Pahlke, and C. Cüppers, eds. (Lumbini, Nepal: Lumbini International Research Institute), 205–217.

95. In ayurveda, writes T.S. Rukmani, nature is "not just part of an ecological outlook but is embedded in an intimate relationship with the general well-being, both physical and mental, of humans." See T.S. Rukmani, "Literary Foundations for an Ecological Aesthetic," in *Hinduism and Ecology,* Chapple and Tucker, eds., 104.

96. Press Trust, "Linking Rivers," June 16, 2015.

97. Alter, *Gandhi's Body*, 28.

governance.[98] That is to say, to the extent that these solutions are grounded in holistic Indian metaphysical systems that define the flourishing of the human being in direct relationship to the flourishing of the immediate ecological systems of which they are an integral part, life can flourish according to the constraints that such bioregional knowledge endows and permits. Recognizing that this is by no means a perfect solution,[99] it nevertheless offers an alternative way of being in the world that retrieves climate change and its potential solutions from the grip of global neoliberalism's hegemonic discourse, relocating climate change's solutions within bioregional contexts.

However much Modi seductively suggested yoga as an effective technology for addressing climate change at UNESCO, I have suggested that he is deploying the practice as an instrument of biopower in order to manufacture a microcosmic-macrocosmic association between employee bodies, their work, and the organizational devices of the neoliberal state. While many of India's pre-independence yogis deployed yoga practices as a means to liberate citizens' bodies from the grips of colonial power and restore the subcontinent to its inhabitants, Modi's yoga reflects an ambitious attempt to prepare India's bureaucracy to receive neo-colonial foreign investment into the Indian nation-state. We should continue to monitor Modi's efforts, as well as the efforts of his affiliates, as they endeavor to expediently authorize and implement environmentally deleterious and climate-change-producing projects such as the RLP from their stations in Delhi.

---

98. In April 2017, the Yamuna and Ganges rivers were granted legal status as living entities, a step that may further complicate the implementation of India's river-linking project and grant important legal protection to India's holy rivers. Nevertheless, the Supreme Court order was made at the national level, which continues to promote the national government's ability to manage local resources. See Omair Ahmad, "A Court Naming Ganga and Yamuna as Legal Entities Could Invite a River of Problems," *Scroll*, April 3, 2017, accessed April 3, 2017, https://scroll.in/article/833069/a-court-naming-ganga-and-yamuna-as-legal-entities-could-invite-a-river-of-problems.

99. Mangala Subramaniam of Purdue University published an article that demonstrates the local problems that ensue as a result of the partnerships between Rajendra Singh's Non-Governmental Organization (Tarun Bharat Sangh) and the villagers with whom it works, arguing that even as state market commodification of water is subverted, the local work nevertheless creates "local neoliberalisms" as communities' caste and gender characteristics create power struggles and uneven local resource management. See Mangala Subramaniam, "Neoliberalism and Water Rights: The Case of India," *Current Sociology* 62, no. 3 (2014): 393–411.

Another potential pitfall in a scenario that attempts to subvert biopower arises in Joseph Alter's *Yoga in Modern India,* wherein Alter demonstrates how Nature Cure/Yoga inadvertently destabilizes biopower's structure, while ultimately establishing itself as a form of "mutated biopower." This is so, as Alter argues, because individuals willingly submit their bodies to the socially constructed and state funded "will of nature." See Alter, *Yoga in Modern* India, 112–116, 141. As movements like Singh's continue to gain popularity, it will be important to monitor how national entities intervene to support his efforts, and therefore potentially re-globalize biopower.

Finally, despite the fact that "climate change" might emerge out of neoliberal discourse as an exercise of biopower, both literally in the sense that this discourse is the result of industrial systems that continue to create an abundance of harmful emissions and figuratively in the sense that it uses climate science to produce and govern "climate change" as global enemy number one, it is hard to deny that the elemental world is reflecting back to us a dire need for some form of effective reconciliation between itself and *homo oeconomicus*.[100] Yoga, if deployed in a manner that emphasizes an increasingly holistic microcosmic-macrocosmic awareness within particular localities does bear the potential to mediate this reconciliation, to subvert global neoliberal biopower, and, ultimately, to help the collection of bioregions that we call "India" to flourish in our shared times of climatic uncertainty.

---

100. With the rise of biopower, economic science produced a form of rationality by which a happy, free, and healthy human life could be calculated, managed, and lived. Foucault called this human "*Homo oeconomicus*," a self-absorbed individual who could become "an entrepreneur of himself." See Michel Foucault, *The Birth of Biopolitics: Lectures at the Collège de France 1978–1979*, Michel Senellart, ed., Graham Burchell, trans. (New York: Palgrave McMillan, 2008), 226.

8 UNDERSTANDING A "BROKEN WORLD"

ISLAM, RITUAL, AND CLIMATE CHANGE IN MALI, WEST AFRICA

Dianna Bell

Introduction

One evening, while sitting in the courtyard of the compound I lived in during my field research in Ouélessébougou, Mali in 2011, I listened as Djègèni, the great-aunt of residence, and Yirigoi, the grandmother, loudly scheduled a fishing trip for the following afternoon. The two Muslim women agreed that they would leave after the day's third prayer, a plan that would give them enough time to net their fish and return home before the fourth prayer. Adja, a twenty-year-old girl who also lived in the household, begged the two old women to forego their plans. Djègèni and Yirigoi deliberately ignored Adja's pleas, and their preparations culminated as they brought their fishing nets outside for inspection. Upon seeing their equipment, Adja began to cry and continued to plead with them not to go fishing.

I finally asked Adja to explain her objection, and she said, "People will see them! Then they will tease me, saying my family is so poor that we send our old women out to find food!"

Suddenly, Djègèni and Yirigoi began to laugh and assured Adja they had no real plans to go fishing. Their preparations had been a joke to chide her for having acted so shallowly about the importance of money and image in recent months.

As the women laughed together, I considered the inadequate amount of protein in meals in our residential compound and decided that a fishing trip would, in fact, be beneficial to our diets. Yet, although this conversation took place in the middle of the rainy season, no water flowed under any of the town's bridges.

"We would love to fish," the old women told me after Adja left, pointing to their unused fishing gear as evidence of their desire. "But the river has dried up."

As Djègèni and Yirigoi drew my attention to their arid environment I recalled that a number of other people had similarly complained during interviews on religious life, in what I originally dismissed as non sequitur remarks, that Mali's climate had become increasingly inhospitable in their lifetimes. I decided to include in field research a documentation the ways people in Ouélessébougou defined and dealt with environmental changes and pressures in their community. Although I saw this subject as a departure from my research on religion, I soon found myself looking at how the problem of climate change in Mali informed religious practice.

As it happens, ethnographic vignettes serve to relate the environmental changes people in Ouélessébougou confronted during their lifetimes, and explain how residents managed and assessed the causes of climate change through religion. Throughout this chapter the personal accounts of Malians show that in southern Mali, residents' religious beliefs and practices played a central role in shaping their interpretations of what has caused local climate change and supporting their criticisms of the moral state of the world. Muslims in Mali also tended to make use of religious rituals in their efforts to cope with the problems that climate change created. The common view of Muslims in Mali is that God exclusively controls the environment. The many international agencies and scientific groups that recommend measures to counter major climate effects in the Sahel often neglect this reality. This chapter features the voices and authority of people whose participation in sedentary farming and nomadic pastoral activities has made them exceedingly vulnerable to hostile changes in their environment but who have remained underrepresented in discussions on climate change in Africa.[1]

As many Malians alongside foreign interlocutors worry about the fate of future generations in West Africa, it is increasingly necessary to address local interpretations of climate change in order to effectively assess declines in agricultural production and food security. James Clifford recently observed that ongoing political and economic insecurity in developing countries has become increasingly compounded by seemingly unmanageable ecological threats.[2] Take Mali, for instance, where economic development and security have been severely

1. See Jonathan A. Patz and R. Sari Kovats, "Hotspots in Climate Change and Human Health," *British Medical Journal* 325, no. 7372 (2002): 1094–1098; Harri Englund and James Leach, "Ethnography and the Meta-Narratives of Modernity," *Current Anthropology* 41, no. 2 (2000): 225–248.

2. James Clifford, "Feeling Historical," *Cultural Anthropology* 27, no. 3 (2012): 417–426.

compromised since 2012 because of a coup and continued fighting between the south and Islamic militants in the north. In his remarks Clifford continued to provocatively wonder, "What happens when the supplies run out?"[3]

Because of increased consumption by Mali's burgeoning population and to land denudation in the Sahel, the future of many of the natural resources on which Malians rely on for their livelihood has recently become ever more in question.[4] In the mid-20th century Garrett Hardin evaluated the fate of people who consume and depend on shared finite resources.[5] Hardin offered a dooming prediction for "the commons," such as the forest where Malians grazed domesticated animals, gathered wood, hunted, picked fruit, and farmed, and he forecast that shared and ungoverned resources are destined for ruin, as people inevitably overuse them in pursuit of their interests.[6] Hardin consequently called for either increased, centralized governmental control over or the privatization of the commons in order to preserve and determine who, when, and how people can access shared resources.[7]

As concerns over both climate change and the danger of overusing scarce resources have increased environmental consciousness, governments worldwide have taken ostensible initiatives to protect and control their resources. In Mali, the Ministry of the Environment and Sanitation (*Le ministre de l'Environnement et de l'Assainissement*) officially advocated the sustainable use of Mali's resources. Governmental regulations pertaining to the forest, however, were weakly enforced and largely dismissed, and most rural residents instead assigned authority over "the commons" to God. Roy Rappaport, of course, who spearheaded efforts to join ecological and cultural studies, would have been unsurprised that many Muslims in Mali believed that God controls the forest above any government

---

3. Clifford, "Feeling Historical," 426; see also Andrea Muehlebach, "On Precariousness and the Ethical Imagination: The Year 2012 in Sociocultural Anthropology," *American Anthropologist* 115, no. 2 (2013): 297–311.

4. A 2012 World Bank report, "Turn Down the Heat," forecasts that predicted warming and population growth (estimated at 3.01% in Mali) throughout West Africa will combine to result in significantly drier conditions that will lead to decreases in agricultural output and to water scarcity across the Sahel. Journalist Max Follmer summarized the World Bank report: "Africa Will Starve in 30 Years" (Max Follmer, "Africa Will Starve and Asia Will Drown in 30 Years Due to Climate Change: Report," *Take Part*, June 19, 2013).

5. Garrett Hardin, "The Tragedy of the Commons," *Science* 162 (1968): 1243–1248.

6. Hardin, "The Tragedy of the Commons," 1243–1245; see also Elinor Ostrom, *Governing the Commons: The Evolution of Institutions for Collective Action* (Cambridge: Cambridge University Press, 1990), 2–3.

7. Hardin, "The Tragedy of the Commons," 1245–1248; see also Ostrom, *Governing the Commons*, 9–10.

entity.[8] Rappaport treats consciousness and the selfish behaviors that it inevitably produces "as a malady for which ritual regulation is the cure" and affirmed religion as a potential defense against environmental degradation.[9] Likewise, this chapter shows how Islam mediates the relationship that Malians have with their environment and that religion stood as the most salient lens through which local people examined and addressed the challenges they faced.

Despite a growing ethnographic literature on Islam in West Africa[10] and interrelated anthropological studies on ecology in West Africa that address how residents manage climate change in their communities,[11] no definitive account from either side satisfactorily addresses the significance of Islam in understanding and dealing with environmental changes in West Africa. This chapter offers a more nuanced approach, first by focusing on social experience in managing local environments by accounting for the way Muslims concepts link a deteriorating social, political, and material world to local ideas about the environment[12]; and second, by attending to practical outcomes wherein studies of this nature begin to form a baseline for incorporating Muslim beliefs and rituals into international efforts to manage climate change in West Africa.

These issues are taken up in three sections. The first section describes the personal observations on how people in southern Mali viewed that the environment had changed during their life span. From here, the chapter details the reasoning Malians frequently invoked for ascribing climate change to a willful act of God. The final section reviews how people coped with the slow deterioration of their

---

8. Roy A. Rappaport, *Pigs for the Ancestors: Ritual in the Ecology of a New Guinea People* (New Haven, CT: Yale University Press, 1984); Roy A. Rappaport, *Ecology, Meaning, and Religion* (Berkeley, CA: North Atlantic Books, 1979).

9. Gillian Gillison, "Reflections on *Pigs for the Ancestors*," in *Ecology and the Sacred: Engaging the Anthropology of Roy A. Rappaport*, Ellen Messer and Michael Lambek, eds. (Ann Arbor: University of Michigan Press, 2001), 296.

10. See, e.g., Robert Launay, *Beyond the Stream: Islam and Society in a West African Town* (Berkeley: University of California Press, 1992); Adeline Masquelier, *Women and Islamic Revival in a West African Town* (Bloomington: Indiana University Press, 2009); Geert Mommersteeg, *In the City of the Marabouts: Islamic Culture in West Africa* (Long Grove, IL: Waveland, 2012); Benjamin F. Soares, *Islam and the Prayer Economy: History and Authority in a Malian Town* (Ann Arbor: University of Michigan Press, 2005).

11. See, e.g., James Fairhead and Melissa Leach, *Misreading the African Landscape: Society and Ecology in a Forest-Savanna Mosaic* (Cambridge: Cambridge University Press, 1996); Stephen Wooten, *The Art of Livelihood: Creating Expressive Agri-Culture in Rural Mali.* (Durham, NC: Carolina Academic Press, 2009).

12. Thomas J. Csordas, "Notes for Cybernetics of the Holy," in *Ecology and the Sacred: Engaging the Anthropology of Roy A. Rappaport*, Ellen Messer and Michael Lambek, eds. (Ann Arbor: University of Michigan Press, 2001), 227–232; see also Rappaport, *Ecology, Meaning, and Religion*, 157–159.

environment and the religious rituals that Muslims in Mali used to attempt to restore the temperate climate of their past.

Reflecting on Climate Change

The town of Ouélessébougou lies in the Guinea Savannah in an ecosystem positioned between the semi-arid north and the wet southern rain forest and savannahs of West Africa. Plains of discontinuous and wiry grasses used for both farming and grazing cattle, sheep, goats, and donkeys surrounded the outskirts of Ouélessébougou. In 2013 the local mayor's office estimated the population to be approximately 7,000 inhabitants, 90% of whom identified as Muslim (the majority of whom identified themselves broadly as Sunni, although Salafi and Wahhabi currents are gaining popularity), 5% are Christian (there is one evangelical Protestant church and one Catholic church), and the remaining 5% are either unreligious or practice a form of African worship. There were no longer any permanent rivers in Ouélessébougou, but a large aquifer beneath the town gave inhabitants dependable access to open well and hand-pump water. Bambara speakers identified three main annual seasons: a rainy season (*samiya*), hot season (*futeni*), and cold season (*nènèma*). The mean elevation stood at about 1,100 feet above sea level, and temperatures ranged from 50°F during the cold season to above 100°F in the hot season. June, July, and August were typically the rainiest months of the year in Ouélessébougou, with August ranking as the wettest. Annual rainfall usually varied from thirty to forty inches. A cold and dry season lasted from November until February, followed by a three-month hot dry period from March through May.[13]

As a growing town astride both rural communities and near Mali's sprawling capital of Bamako, Ouélessébougou offers unique insight into both rural and urban ways of life. For example, exposure to media and other information sources has undoubtedly shaped how residents understand environmental degradation in local and global contexts. As is typical in urban cities, most residents in Ouélessébougou either owned or had regular access to televisions and radios. Both technologies popularly featured cases of extreme weather worldwide and global environmental pressures in their programming, giving residents a sense that others internationally shared in their struggles with the environment.

---

13. "Country Data: Mali," *World Bank*, 2013, accessed March 17, 2014, http://data.worldbank.org/country/mali.

"Climate Change Knowledge Portal," *World Bank*, 2013, accessed March 17, 2014, http://sdwebx.worldbank.org/climateportal/index.cfm?page=country_historical_climate&ThisRegion=Africa&ThisCCode=MLI.

Despite access to technology and other urban influences in town, subsistence in Ouélessébougou was similar to rural settlements in Mali, and most residents relied on local faming or herding pursuits for their livelihood to some degree.

Elderly people in Ouélessébougou especially spoke often of the way that the hot season had increasingly intensified in temperature and duration, while the rainy and cold seasons had become progressively more meager. This section relates the observations of town residents on how their local environment had changed and the disruptions these shifts had on their welfare. The accounts presented focus on the disappearance of the town's river by the end of the 20th century, the impact that drought has had on residents who either farmed or raised livestock, and how people noticed that heat impaired the overall well-being of residents.

Koniba Doumbia, a sixty-five-year-old welder, described his memories from the nearby river and its shores. As a child, Koniba and his friends took swims during the hot season. The river was reliably full all year round. Koniba recalled that while swimming, he kept watch for freshwater crocodiles, which were known to float in the slow-moving currents of the river. The river was also full of large fish, which his parents caught and cooked for their family. Similarly, as a young woman, Yirigoi Konaté, who was in her seventies during my research, used to fish at the river by casting a net into the water from its banks. While fishing, she would visit with her neighbors who were washing clothes, taking a restful dip in the water, or similarly fishing by the river. She recalled that pulling up a net with a fish led to merriment, and onlookers cheerfully sang to the successful angler, *"Jègèba filè! Jègèba filè! I ye jègèba minè koyi!"* ("Look at the big fish! Look at the big fish! You really caught a big fish!").

During the presidency of Modibo Keïta, Mali's first president from 1960 through 1968, residents in Ouélessébougou reported that they began to notice lower amounts of precipitation causing the river's level to recede.[14] The river had entirely dried out by the turn of the century. People took the loss personally. Yirigoi anthropomorphized the event, recollecting that the river had "run away" (*bòlila*) from the people of Ouélessébougou, as though it had stood up and relocated to a more deserving group. With the river's disappearance, the

---

14. Most people did not give numerical dates when certain events occurred and rather indicated which president held power at the time of an experience. In speaking about the onset of erosion and the loss of rivers during Modibo Keïta's administration, people were directly referencing a massive series of Sahelian droughts that lasted from 1968 to 1974 (with only partial recovery since). See Michela Biasutti and Alessandra Giannini, "Robust Sahel Drying in Response to late 20th Century Forcings," *American Geophysical Research Letters* 33, no. 11(2006): L11706, doi:10.1029/2006GL026067, and Compton J. Tucker, Harold E. Dregne, and Wilbur W. Newcomb, "Expansion and Contraction of the Sahara Desert from 1980 to 1990," *Science*, n.s. 253, no. 5017 (1991): 299–301 for assessments of the many studies on the causes and consequences of the severe drying of the Sahel from the 1950s onward.

population lost their principal source of protein: free fish. Residents' diets were consequently filled with more carbohydrate staples and less animal protein. Women from outlying villages with rivers regularly traveled to Ouélessébougou's market to sell their catch to residents. Fresh fish were priced at between 2,000 and 2,500 francs CFA per kilogram—a cost well beyond the budgets of most residents, who typically earned under 1,000 francs per day.[15]

The slow desiccation of Ouélessébougou's environment had negative consequences beyond the dried riverbed. During interviews, elderly residents concluded that farming and herding had become more difficult and less dependable and profitable during their lifetimes. Farmers in the region, who normally harvested millet, corn, and peanuts, have always worked without sprinkler irrigation systems. Yielding a successful crop therefore depended solely on ample rainfall, but in the late 20th and early 21st centuries, high heat and humidity alongside infrequent rainstorms damaged the quality and quantity of their harvests. The people in Ouélessébougou primarily ate locally produced food, so the problems that farmers faced concerned the entire town. People continually said that the population of Ouélessébougou might die at any time from thirst or hunger. Anxieties about residents' uncertain future and susceptibility to the environment arose in every interview I conducted about local ecology in Ouélessébougou. People readily recalled deceased friends and family members whose deaths had been attributed to undernourishment or dehydration, especially noting that malnutrition had made people more susceptible to developing fatal cases of malaria.

Many families in Ouélessébougou owned and herded domestic animals as their primary occupation, but some had abandoned or scaled back their work because the drying pastures around Ouélessébougou made their income dangerously undependable. Herders reported that less fresh grass was available and that their stock grazed in dry pastures filled with coarse wild grass with low nutritional value. Finding water in Ouélessébougou's neighboring forest had also become difficult. Typically, neither animals nor herders had access to water until they returned home in the evening. Given the harshness of the forest, some animal owners in the region were far more resigned and lenient and allowed their animals to ingest contaminated garbage and latrine run-off, which of course compromised livestock health and contributed to the spread of disease.

---

15. The West Africa CFA franc, a common currency throughout Francophone West Africa, Guinea-Bissau, and Equatorial Guinea, was freely convertible during the time of my research into Euros at a fixed rate of 1 Euro = 655 CFA francs (see Jean A.P. Clément, *Aftermath of the CFA Franc Devaluation* [Washington, DC: 1996], 1–3). Someone who earned fewer than 1,000 francs per day, then, would be surviving on under 1.5 Euros daily.

Because of the changes in the environment, farmers and herders in Mali who remained committed to their occupations adjusted their techniques in order to continue their pursuits.[16] For example, fresh water for animals had once abounded in Mali's forests but had now disappeared. So, to supply water, herders drew it by hand from wells for their stock. Those responsible for large herds regularly overused their wells and thus caused many wells to temporarily dry out. Once their wells were dry, people first relied on their neighbors' wells. As a second option, residents made use of freshwater hand-pump wells that had been installed throughout the town by the municipal government. But, depending on the location of one's compound, the pumps could be more than a mile away. Using the pumps required time and preparation. Women gathered all the buckets and water containers in their household that they could and rented a handcart before leaving. Once they had arrived, they waited for their turn at the pump before pushing the heavy water-filled handcarts back home. Herders reported that Mali's desiccation had increased the number of livestock deaths, and animals that did survive grew less than cattle formerly did. Because of poor nourishment, the brindled cows in southern Mali produced less milk, with lower nutritional quality, and butchered animals yielded meat that was tough and stringy.[17]

Wooten has highlighted the ways that Malians reflected on and negotiated their livelihood and subsistence, and I similarly observed that people in Ouélessébougou made changes to their lives in response to the drying environment while reflecting on its causes.[18] As fraught residents in Ouélessébougou saw their earnings dwindle from farming and herding, many had no choice but to either migrate to cities or find low-paying jobs as laborers in town.

Meanwhile, for those who stayed in Ouélessébougou the nights were no cooler than the days. Amadou Diallo, a man in his mid-seventies in 2011, often had difficulty sleeping because of the sultry heat. So did his two-year-old grandson, for whom Diallo and his wife had assumed the responsibility of raising. Diallo's grandson often stayed up late at night during hot spells and cried because he was too uncomfortable to fall asleep. Diallo and his wife, Nouhouba, took turns manually fanning their grandson until he fell asleep. The young boy often woke up several times in a single night, calling to be cooled again. Exhausted by restless nights, Diallo often found his job making rope by hand

---

16. See Fairhead and Leach, *Misreading the African Landscape,* and Wooten, *The Art of Livelihood.*

17. K.T. Wagenaar, A. Diallo, and A.R. Sayers, *Productivity of Transhumant Fulani Cattle in the Inner Niger Delta of Mali* (Addis Ababa, Ethiopia: International Livestock Center for Africa, 1986).

18. Wooten, *The Art of Livelihood.*

near Ouélessébougou's central market too tiring. Like many others who worked near him, including schoolteachers who frequently canceled afternoon sessions because the classrooms were too hot, Diallo regularly stopped his work to take short naps and complained about the excessive heat and the "broken world" *(diɲè tiɲè)* that Malians now inhabited.

Understanding Change

If the world had been broken, what, or who, was responsible for its ruin? In sum, religious teachings and practices were the primary way that Malians joined their material world to ideals for how to understand and manage recent climate change. This section explores the range of explanations Muslims offered as to why God had decided to alter the local environment upon which they were so highly dependent. It purposively focuses on the three most common answers encountered during fieldwork: first, God periodically changes the natural world without reason and that Muslims should accept the challenge of living in a new environment; second, depraved locals had brought the changes on; and third, international political conflicts, corrupt world leadership, and warfare were responsible for the disastrous environmental transformations in their community.

People in Ouélessébougou explained that since the creation of the world, God had continually involved Himself in the affairs of people by periodically altering their environments. For example, God provided Malians with ample rain in good years but in subsequent years, in order to create balance, God might take the precipitation and replace it with a prolonged period of dry and cold weather. Muslims asserted that people should always anticipate such changes while remaining mindful that God never allows the world to stay for too long in one condition. This explanation was very popular, and numerous collaborators in this project used the same phrasing when explaining the link between God and climate change. Hearing this common stance in conversations prompted me to begin asking residents where they had learned about the divine cause of environmental change. This inquiry surprised people, who all declared that God's role in designing and altering their world was a self-evident fact of life—no one had taught them. One old man kindly answered by shaking his head and posed a question in return: how had I failed to notice God's work? Without pausing for my response, he reminded me that during my visit in 2010 the grass in the forests had been shorter than it was in 2011. The old man confidently attributed this change to God, demonstrating the close involvement between religious cognition and the material environment that pervaded among Muslim residents in Ouélessébougou.

Some residents resolved to avoid feeling upset about the changes God had recently made to their local environment. Rather, they classified their compromised environment as a responsibility, describing climate change and the desertification of the Sahel that they observed as "God's work" (*Ala ka baara*). One middle-aged herder offered his insight that people primarily change in response to alterations in their environment, adding that all cultures would become mindless and empty without the need to adapt to new conditions. When Malians faced warmer years, they looked for new ways to care for the crops and animals that they depended on in order to ensure future food supply. Rather than ruing the severe climate as an affront, some people in Ouélessébougou understood their challenging conditions as an opportunity to improve their community. Many Malian Muslims also viewed living in a desert as a fact of life. After all, Islam was founded in the desert and the Qur'an makes continual reference to the challenging environment that surrounded early Arab Muslims, and concern over natural resources, especially water, fruit trees and livestock, is reflected throughout the Qur'an.[19] The Qur'an teaches the impossibility of absolute dominion over nature, given the difficulty of the desert landscape, and rather affirms through vivid imagery that that God will give righteous Muslims a garden in the afterlife in return for their earthly remorse.[20] Accordingly, a great number of Muslims in southern Mali had dutifully accepted that one day the Sahara would finish "swallowing up" (*kunu*) the Sahel and that they would manage in this new barren environment as a show of piety.[21]

Others resented Ouélessébougou's difficult environment and described the changes as a consequence, inflicted by God, for immoral human behavior. Chérif and Greenberg have similarly detailed how elsewhere in West Africa, climate change and population pressures in Côte d'Ivoire have been ascribed to the abandonment of tradition, the growing influence of "outside" religions such as Islam and Christianity, and the denigration of traditional beliefs.[22] Thus, across

---

19. See, for example, Qur'an 7:130; 9:90, 101; 24:39; 33:20; 56:73. Jonathan Benthall, "The Greening of Islam?," *Anthropology Today* 19, no. 6 (2003): 10.

20. Benthal, *Greening of Islam*, 10–11.

21. Scant and largely anecdotal estimates on the rate of the Sahara's southward expansion in the late 20th and early 21st centuries vary between one to thirty miles annually. Such approximations, and the anthropomorphic imagery of the Sahara "swallowing" the Sahel that people commonly used, tend to misinterpret erosion in the Sahel by presenting it as the result of the Sahara spreading outward, while ignoring how internal local activity (overgrazing, increased cultivation, and firewood cutting) exacerbates climate change (see Tucker et al., "Sahara Desert.")

22. Sadia Chérif and Joy H. Greenberg, "Religious Perspectives on Climate Change in the West Ivoirian Mountainous Region," in *How the World's Religions Are Responding to Climate Change: Social Scientific Investigations*, Robin Globus Veldman, Andrew Szasz, and Randolph Haluza-DeLay, eds. (London: Routledge Press, 2014), 130–136.

West Africa people frequently used the environment metaphorically to express their dissatisfaction with both local community relations and global politics. In Mali some opined that their neighbors had committed sins (*jurumuw*) that led to changes in the local environment. People listed stealing and lying as the most prevalent and problematic sins in their community. For example, Amadou Diallo recounted that during the 1980s he worked by selling grains and sugar in a marketplace near Ouélessébougou. One day a woman who looked familiar asked him to lend her ten kilograms of sugar so she could make flavored ice to sell, promising Diallo she would pay him back as soon as she had sold her product. Diallo trusted the agreement and gave the woman his sugar. Several weeks passed without Diallo seeing his debtor, and he began to ask residents of her whereabouts. He learned that she had moved to Mopti, a city more than 700 kilometers north of Ouélessébougou. Diallo identified this type of deceit—which he noted had become endemic in West Africa—as the direct cause for the climate problems Malians faced.

While not condoning the misdeeds of their neighbors, various residents rather opined that the conduct of high-ranking politicians had prompted God to change the earth's climate. One afternoon in 2011 I overheard two farmers commiserating with each other that the lack of rain had decimated their harvest. I offered the men a sympathetic smile as I walked past them. The farmers drew me into their conversation, and one yelled in frustration, "George Bush and Barack Obama are breaking the world!" ("*George Bush ani Barack Obama be diɲè tiɲè!*"), while sweeping both arms across the front of his body like a referee signaling an unsuccessful goal. People who owned radios and televisions had limited access to channels and programming, and news programs produced by Mali's national broadcaster ORTM (*Office de radiodiffusion et de télévision du* Mali) were among the most popular and consistent shows available. Accordingly, most adults in the region, especially those who understood French, had a respectable understanding of both local and global politics. From a Malian perspective, leaders in Europe and North America had unlimited money at their disposal but used it selfishly. Some testified that God saw the US government's use of its power and wealth for wars against poorer countries as unforgivable because it effectuated a change in the earth's climate. Muslims in Ouélessébougou also accused militant Islamist organizations of threatening world security, placing the responsibility for climate change on these organizations' attacks on civilians. Muslims in southern Mali habitually ascribed blame for climate change to any person or group who threatened world peace.

Most of the time, when discussing the impacts of foreign social, political, and military issues on the local environment, residents focused on the world's major economies, but African countries were also occasionally criticized for their fighting. One morning in early 2012 Fousseyni Soumaré, a shopkeeper and farmer, spoke with the director of a local *medersa*. Fousseyni singled out Libya and Sudan as the most violent countries in Africa. The school director countered that Fousseyni should not ignore Mali's southern neighbor Côte d'Ivoire, saying that the country's 2010 post-election political crisis—in which President Laurent Gbagbo and opposition candidate Alassane Ouattera both claimed victory—and the country's subsequent war had upset God. Fousseyni nodded and, after a long pause, noted the lingering violence in Côte d'Ivoire, adding that these reflections gave him a clearer idea as to why his field had been so dry in recent years. The blame for Mali's dry environment has recently further internalized to include Malians, as ongoing fighting between the military and its allies against Islamic fundamentalists in the north has deeply divided the country and compromised its security.

Many associated politics with spectacles of deceit and violence that were directly responsible for the negative environmental changes in their town. Some responded to the drying of their ecosystem by paying close attention to local politics and carefully considering the merits of candidates before casting their vote in each election, in the hope that their candidate would represent their morals and interests after election. Other Malians lamented the actions of national and local politicians, who, they complained, abandoned their supporters for their own interests after winning public elections. Numerous Malians told me that voting in their republic was worthless and that they had vowed to no longer vote or otherwise participate in politics. For instance, one elderly man had voted in every election since Mali's independence in 1960 but said he would no longer vote in elections. For him, politicians had caused the slow drying of southern Mali's climate and, moreover, jeopardized the spiritual security of Muslim voters. He warned his friends against the religious dangers of voting for politicians who acted unethically, saying that, in the afterlife, God holds voters responsible for the innermost sins of the politicians they supported. This eternal condemnation made any type of political involvement too risky.

In short, people in Mali commonly described erosion as either a natural challenge for Muslims or as the result of divine punishment, and moreover it determined parties that were directly responsible for upsetting God. This blame ranged from sinful neighbors to corrupt political leaders. Climate change consequently impacted the way that Malians dealt with members of their community and participated in politics. Although it is difficult to precisely quantify how much rural West Africans have contributed to recent changes in their local environment, research on land denudation in the Sahel collectively recognizes that the degradation in the Sahara's southern fringe is compounded by both the local mismanagement of resources and the increased global emissions of greenhouse gases.[23] Yet, most believed that only God could generate significant changes to their climate. Accordingly, Muslims in southern Mali expressed concern for the climate by participating in religious practices designed to mollify and appeal to God for a better environment.

Managing the Misfortune

As people insisted that God had changed their climate as a punishment for human depravity, they turned to religious rituals to plead for God to have mercy and deliver them from their hard climate. This section accounts how Muslims in Ouélessébougou sought to regulate environmental changes through religious practices such as group prayer meetings and personal sacrifices.

People depended on rain during the summer months to replenish the forest, but the weather during August 2011 brought terrible heat and humidity to the town and very little rain. As the month ended and turned to September, residents worried over the irregular and inadequate rainfall. On the evening of Sunday, September 2, elderly Muslim men organized a special prayer meeting for the following day in which they planned to appeal to God for rain. The men assembled in the mosque Monday morning to pray, recite benedictions, and listen while the town's imam read passages pertaining to the environment from the Qur'an in Arabic. The assembly lasted for well over an hour and although women were not invited to attend, the entire meeting was broadcast over the mosque's sound system so that all people near the mosque could hear the petitions.

Monday and Tuesday went by with the same blue skies, sunshine, and sultry air that had tormented residents during earlier summer months. Muslim leaders scheduled a second prayer meeting for Wednesday morning, but this time they invited the women to join them. Wednesday's meeting concluded at eleven o'clock, and by one o'clock storm clouds began to gather over Ouélessébougou. It rained lightly all afternoon and at dusk the storm intensified. Rather than visiting with friends and neighbors, families passed the night at home, listening as the rain rattled against their metal roofs. It was one of the biggest storms of the wet season. Women were overjoyed, taking public credit for the sudden rainfall—after all, God had supplied rain only after women had been included in the prayers. On Thursday morning, they returned to the mosque, deliberately

23. See Biasutti and Giannini, "Robust Sahel Drying"; Gerald C. Nelson, Elena Bennett, Asment A. Berhe, Kenneth G. Cassman, and Ruth DeFries, "Anthropogenic Drivers of Ecosystem Change: An Overview," *Ecology and Society* 11, no. 2 (2006): 29; UNEP (United Nations Environment Programme), *Status of Desertification and Implementation of the United Nations Plan of Action to Control Desertification* (Nairobi: UNEP, 1991).

coordinated in white dresses and headscarves, to offer formal thanks to God through prayer. Some men resented that the women attributed the storm to their participation in the prayer meeting. For example, one middle-aged man named Bourama said he had no personal ill feeling toward the women but suggested that Muslim ritual had not brought rain in this particular case. In 2011 the Malian government subsidized cloud-seeding operations to create rain, and Bourama pointed out that a cloud-seeding aircraft had flown over Ouélessébougou two days before the storm.[24]

The rain created a momentary feeling of hope, but rejoicing in the town subsided shortly thereafter as residents agreed that a single storm could not fix the forest. Meanwhile, elderly residents said that droughts had become less fatal than in the past, largely because imported food and water are now more readily available. As the sixth poorest country in the world, Mali received myriad international aid and food donations. Some Malians welcomed the assistance, but others had misgivings about consuming food from overseas—whether complimentary or sold in the market. One elderly man, for example, said that he preferred to eat only food grown within Ouélessébougou and its surrounding villages and expressed suspicions about international products. He added that malaria had become more deadly in his lifetime and theorized that the Maggi bouillon cubes that women used daily to flavor the sauces they served with rice were to blame.

One day this man asked several friends where Maggi products were produced. "Hong Kong? Germany?" he asked rhetorically. "How can we eat something that we know nothing about? It is making us sick!"[25]

This man was among many Ouélessébougou residents who preferred food grown in their home region, making the drying climate a particularly frustrating

24. Although cloud seeding was practiced widely in the mid-20th century, recent analyses of regions of cloud seeding have concluded that it does not enhance precipitation; Levin Zev, Noam Halfon, and Pinhas Alpert, "Reassessment of Rain Enhancement Experiments and Operations in Israel Including Synoptic Considerations," *Atmospheric Research* 97, no. 4 (2010): 513–525. Even so, Mali was one of the few countries that continued to utilize cloud seeding in an effort to augment rainfall in the early 21st century.

25. Although there is currently no evidence that Maggi cubes (which are produced by Nestlé) actually intensify malaria, this man was right to worry about their impact on consumers' overall health. Maggi cubes are extremely high in sodium, hydrogenated oils, and MSG. A report from the Slow Food and the United Nation's Food and Agricultural Organization highlights that deforestation in the Sahel has made more nutritious local ingredients that have traditionally thickened and added flavor to West African sauces (such as *sounbareh*) increasingly less available in urban and semi-urban areas and that Maggi cubes have consequently increased in popularity (Slow Food Foundation for Biodiversity, "Promoting Origin-Linked Quality Products in Four Countries (GFT/RAF/426/ITA)," *Food and Agriculture Organization (FAO)*, 2012, accessed October 15, 2013, http://www.fao.org/fileadmin/templates/olq/documents/documents/Midtermreport3.pdf.

and complicated problem. Although climate change affects all human societies, rural residents in underdeveloped countries are especially vulnerable to reduced food production during droughts.[26] In West Africa, Hoffman has predicted that agricultural yields will very likely decrease by as much as 50% by 2020.[27] Those who preferred eating locally or depended on local food production for earnings often turned to personal religious sacrifices (*saraka*) to seek rain and cooler temperatures. People listed domesticated animals as the preferred sacrificial objects, although income restraints prevented this ideal in most cases. Consequently people seeking changes in weather typically bought either fresh milk or beans to offer God in sacrifice. To consecrate the sacrificial offering, people prayed privately with the object before dispensing it to individuals within their ethnic and social communities. Such sacrifices incorporate an overtly Islamic practice with long-standing local rituals. Islam valorizes acts of sacrifices, especially when sacrificial items are distributed to one's community, as meritorious. Yet, these sacrifices also have strong indigenous elements, as the practice extends across Christian, Muslim, and indigenous religious currents in Ouélessébougou and were often instigated on the suggestion of non-Muslim sorcerers (*soma*), who are commonly consulted by Muslim clients. For Muslims, prayers containing both Arabic portions of the first *surah* of the Qur'an and local languages were used to explain to God why the sacrifice was being offered and the outcome that the sacrificer would like to obtain from such openhanded charity. Some people reported that they always included a passage of adoration in their sacrificial prayers in which they expressed that their request seemed impossible and would come to fruition only by the generosity of God. Following their prayer, the person making the sacrifice visited selected friends and neighbors to distribute the sacrificial item. Beneficiaries in sacrifices demonstrated their knowledge of Islam by reciting from the Qur'an and *hadith* literature to affirm to the sacrificer God's potential to offer solutions to seemingly unmanageable problems. Numerous farmers and herders reported that they had used sacrificial rituals before the onset and during the rainy season to try to ensure their prosperity.

Muslims in Ouélessébougou widely understood climate change as connected to God, and in this section I have shown that people accordingly used religious rituals such as prayer and sacrifice to petition God for a more favorable

26. See Veldman et al., *How the World's Religions,* 3–5.

27. Ulrich Hoffmann "Assuring Food Security In Developing Countries Under The Challenges Of Climate Change: Key Trade And Development Issues Of A Fundamental Transformation Of Agriculture," UNCTAD Discussion Papers 201, United Nations Conference on Trade and Development, 2011. accessed October 15, 2013, https://ideas.repec.org/p/unc/dispap/201.html.

environment. Many times these pursuits were reported to be ineffective, but those who participated in such practices said that unsuccessful prayers and sacrifices did not lessen their faith in God or their Islamic beliefs. Rather, people said that God's refusal to provide them with better environmental conditions deepened their understanding about the gravity of the impiety that had caused local climate change.

Conclusion

In the early 21st century Muslims in southern Mali were impacted in their daily lives by destructive environmental changes and found Islam to be a key source for theorizing about the causes for local climate change. Interviews with residents revealed that people commonly reasoned that climate change was due to both inevitable periodic changes in the natural world and to the immoral actions of humans, with blame assigned to groups ranging from fellow Malian citizens to international political leaders. Although Muslims appealed to God for a better climate through religious rituals, most residents of Ouélessébougou ultimately accepted that they now lived in a harder environment than their ancestors.

In conclusion, it is worth noting that interviews with people aged twenty to forty years old revealed that residents are largely inheriting the beliefs of their grandparents and parents, and young adults shared the same understandings of the causes for environmental changes as the town's elderly populace. This research indicates that religious factors and ritual activity will very likely continue to characterize how Malians experience and manage the worsening climate. Accounting for such outlooks, efforts to promote the long-term conservation of the environment in the Sahel may find it useful to develop programs based on considering both Muslim and local indigenous teachings, beliefs, and practices that promote long-term environmentally sustainable behavior. Ideally, such programs would incorporate the relevant knowledge and recommendations of scientists, development experts, and government officials on the local and global dimensions of climate change while also honoring the long and successful history of pastoral and agricultural pursuits in West Africa alongside prominently held Muslim sensibilities.[28] This research highlights the way that forming alliances between influential Muslim leaders in Mali and scientific communities stands as the most productive tactic to help Malians better subsist in and begin to restore their "broken world."

---

28. See Bron Taylor, "Kenya's Green Belt Movement: Contributions, Conflict, Contradictions, and Complications in a Prominent ENGO," in *Civil Society in the Age of Monitory Democracy*, Nina Witoszek, Lars Tragardh, and Bron Taylor, eds. (Oxford and New York: Berghahn, 2013), 195.

9 DIALOGUE

Christopher Patrick Miller and Dianna Bell

By looking at India and Mali, two countries on the climate frontline, our chapters demonstrate the growing international recognition of the need to establish meaningful and sustainable relationships between humans and nature. We both show how such concerns have left many people in both nations vacillating between religious leaders and government regulations alike for guidance. When religious leaders take the reins, the way that ecology stands in as a reflection of social values becomes especially apparent. Despite such a meaningful grounding, we each show that in both Mali and India religious leaders have become bit-part players in comparison to the power that bureaucrats wield in creating environmental regulations. Such a state of affairs leads to questions of whether religious leaders would ultimately be more effective than politicians in leading people to observe sustainable environmental directives, should they have the resources and support to do so, and to what extent the two types of leaders can effectively work together.

In the case of India, I (Chris) take us through an analysis of popular Indian news media to demonstrate the way that the national government continues to construct climate change as a nationally governable project in their ongoing advancement of economic liberalization. Nevertheless, as *New Indian Express* laments, "India is still found struggling to find the right laws to fight climate change."[1] This high-level, bureaucratic approach regarding India's relation to the environment reflects wider projects to bring the management of almost *all* environmental phenomena under the hegemony of the

---

1. "Soaring Pollution, Crippling Floods, Laws Awaiting Implementation: India's Environment in a Fix," *New Indian Express,* December 28, 2015, accessed December 28, 2015, http://www.newindianexpress.com/nation/Soaring-Pollution-Crippling-Floods-Laws-Awaiting-Implementation-Indias-Environment-in-a-Fix/2015/12/28/article3200012.ece.

national government's "objective" and scientific eye.[2] By controlling the discourse surrounding the environment, India's government ensures the ongoing exploitation of resources that not only promotes India's growing middle class, but even more so benefits foreign investors and shareholders. When reading Dianna's chapter, I was intrigued to find that the government of Mali exercises similar procedures to manage the environment.

When considering Mali, I (Dianna) too notice the similar ways by which the government ministry officially controls and protects Mali's forests and resources. Such bureaucrats are not only a joke in the eyes of many who live in Mali's hinterlands, but the aims of the government are moreover often seen as blasphemous. Historically, in Mali the state of the forest has been linked to ancestors and, as Islam has made inroads throughout the rural countryside, to God. Thus, local leaders and ritual specialists, not government officials and their cronies, best manage the forest. In speaking with Malians about the forest, it quickly becomes apparent that nature holds not only physical resources but has its own spiritual life force, too. Without taking such ideologies into consideration, governments worldwide run the risk of losing local credibility and thus can lead to further destruction of forests. For example, disregard for national regulations in Mali often culminates in pastoralists setting illegal fires to the forest in order to get fresh shoots to quickly grow for their herds. Pastoralists justify such destruction by claiming that governmental regulations favor commercial farming operations over raising livestock, and that the current state of affairs in Mali increasingly desacralizes the forest. Local and national officials could very likely more effectively curb such practices if residents took their efforts and policies to preserve the environment more seriously. Incorporating the expertise and religious ethos of those who work in the forest is one such tactic for states to use.

As we have shown, despite the current hegemony over environmental discourse held by national political leaders, both chapters also feature the prominence of religious leaders who recommend alternative paradigms for improving human relations to the environment and solving local water challenges. Indeed, I (Chris) illustrate that local activists and organizations continue to challenge the government's efforts to monopolize environmental discourse at the national level. As my chapter shows, India's political conservatism has evoked passionate reactions from "Water Man" Rajendra Singh, who passionately argues for the

---

2. The Ministry of Environment and Forests only recently added "climate change" to its increasingly long title. See ETR Bureau, "Ministry of Environment and Forests Undergoes a Nomenclature Change: Government Serious to Tackle Climate Change," *Economic Times*, May 28, 2014, accessed December 28, 2015, http://articles.economictimes.indiatimes.com/2014-05-28/news/50149634_1_climate-change-navroz-dubash-climate-action-network.

re-localization of solutions to India's water woes.[3] Singh, though willing to work with the government, is part of what Kelley Alley has referred to as the "broken spheres of expert debate," a community of nongovernmental scientists and activists who, often finding themselves marginalized from governmental decision-making information and processes, nevertheless challenge the execution of government water management projects via the production of alternative epistemic systems.[4] I wonder, how might closer cooperation between leaders like Singh and the government lead to more effective and sustainable water management? Can the concerns of neoliberal governance come into harmony with the needs of local constituencies without subordinating one to the other?

Speaking to Chris's concerns, I (Dianna) encourage that national and local governments and international organizations alike would benefit from working more closely with religious leaders to effectively improve Mali's environment. My ethnography recounts the memories of people who have witnessed, in a single lifetime, the transition from subsistence farming to cash cropping to rapid urban migration. Changes to religion have accompanied such transformations and indigenous deities and ancestors have been increasingly pushed out of the picture in favor of Islamic cosmology. Although critics of religion may single out "world" religions like Islam as a mask that legitimates capitalistic economies, my work helps us to see the way that Malians draw from Islamic doctrine to understand and ensure that all forms of life continue to flourish. Similarly, Chris's chapter demonstrates that Rajendra Singh attempts to use yoga metaphysics to challenge reductionist scientific environmental management, despite the fact that India's prime minister also strategically capitalizes on yoga's global rhetorical force in order to streamline India's labor force and harness foreign direct investment.

Combined, these chapters explore questions of epistemology and advocate that environmental conditions can improve when national-level officials incorporate religious and local knowledge into their initiatives. Both Mali and India offer examples of religious leaders producing knowledge that involves a commitment to localized, indigenous metaphysics in lieu of the Cartesian-Baconian-Newtonian worldview that informs the postcolonial governance of both countries. As we have shown, both chapters propose rebalancing the relationship between postcolonial bureaucracy and the bio-spiritual, with attention to the way local environmental knowledge is so often valorized only to the extent to which it matches up with reductionist scientific understanding. Combined, we hope to have illustrated that

---

3. Kelly D. Alley, "The Making of a River Linking Plan in India: Suppressed Science and Spheres of Expert Debate," *India Review* 3, no. 3 (2004:) 231. Here, Alley invokes Peter Haas's notion of the epistemic community.

4. Ibid., 231–232.

national governments can benefit from taking the religious or spiritual beliefs that factor into local knowledge and resource management more seriously. Thus, in closing, we would like to briefly offer one successful example that demonstrates how a national government has actively incorporated indigenous knowledge grounded in a holistic cosmology as an alternative approach to environmental protection and management. Highlighting such an example will give us a sense of what to look for and envision as we consider how national and bio-spiritual knowledge might effectively collaborate to ensure human flourishing.

In 2008, to illustrate the practicality of such ideas, the Australian government initiated a program known as "Working on Country" (WOC) to provide job opportunities to aboriginal people whose indigenous knowledge, mythology, and values would be put in service to protect the country's environment, all the while providing job opportunities for those who were chosen to participate. WOC rangers manage the 20% of land owned by Australia's indigenous population, as well as certain portions of the land that they do not own, effectively handling fires, feral animals, and weeds while also protecting biodiversity and threatened species. Some have criticized efforts to include aborigines in the government workforce via the WOC program for potential hidden intentions to absorb indigenous people into the national economic workforce. But the partnership nonetheless represents a large-scale effort to incorporate localized ways of knowing into environmental protection and management programs and should be considered exemplary to the extent that indigenous land and sea managers are "empowered to pursue their own aspirations—and not those imagined for them behind closed doors in Canberra."[5] We suggest that if programs such as WOC are adequately funded, closely monitored for accountability of all parties involved, and designed to acknowledge and appreciate indigenous ways of knowing, more fruitful alliances might be made between indigenous cultures and national governments in other parts of the globe. This is one way to ensure that life and knowledge both continue to flourish in their many forms.

---

5. K. May, "Government Support for Indigenous Cultural and Natural Resource Management in Australia: The Role of the Working on Country Program," *Australian Journal of Social Issues* 45, no. 3 (S2010): 395–416, 409. For those interested in learning more, this article provides an excellent background summary of the Working on Country program.

IV TEXTS AND TRADITIONS

10 INTERTEXTUALLY MODIFIED ORGANISMS

GENETIC ENGINEERING, JEWISH ETHICS, AND RABBINIC TEXT

Rebecca J. Epstein-Levi

Ben Bag Bag says [of Torah]: Turn it, and turn it again, for everything is in it;
examine within it, and grow old and worn out in it; never deviate from it, for there
is no better trait you can have than this.

—MISHNAH AVOT 5:22

And while it's killing you dead, it will mess with your head
And it's the light in the dark that will guide you
It's the pages and pages of what you are like
In the giant book that's hidden inside you

—JONATHAN COULTON, *"That Spells DNA"*

"An Objection Was Raised": The Problem

The contemporary debate about whether it is acceptable to genetically engineer food crops revolves around two main questions: whether the effects of such technology will be helpful or harmful, and whether the direct alteration of an organism's genetic code constitutes "playing God."[1] Despite heated public debate, the scientific consensus on the first point is fairly clear: genetically engineered (GE) crops pose no more threat to human or animal health than conventionally bred ones.[2] Depending on how they are managed, the use of these crops

1. I thank Laura Hartman for the opportunity to contribute to this project. Conversations with Mark Randall James and Peter Ochs were of great help to me in clarifying key points of my argument; in particular, I am grateful to Mark for pointing out the importance of *qere/ketiv*. Jeremy Epstein and especially Tim Smith graciously double-checked my understanding of the relevant biology and my use of scientific sources; if I have avoided causing any biologists to weep and gnash their teeth because of this chapter, it is thanks to their efforts. Finally, Sarah Epstein-Levi's input on the chapter's overall flow and clarity is, as always, invaluable.

2. See Committee on Identifying and Assessing Unintended Effects of Genetically Engineered Foods on Human Health, *Safety of Genetically Engineered Foods: Approaches to Assessing Unintended Health Effects* (Washington,

may actually be a net benefit to the environment, especially with regard to the reduction of pesticide use.[3] However, scientific consensus alone is ill equipped to address the second point—even if the technology is harmless or even beneficial, it may still be morally problematic if we understand it as overstepping our bounds as members of a divinely created order.[4]

Rabbinic traditions of reading Scripture can shed some light on this latter point. Rabbinic readings take as a fundamental hermeneutical presupposition that written Torah is the binding, authoritative, revealed word of God. Yet, they employ several interpretive techniques that seem to modify or outright reverse the meaning of a given unit of scripture to a greater or lesser extent. Further, this modification often occurs in response to a problem—either textual or real world. Indeed, one instance in which a *takkanah* (an act of rabbinic legislation) is justified is when "it is time to act for Adonai." In certain circumstances, an abrogation of a specific part of God's word may be needed to preserve the larger divine order.

The question, then, is "what constitutes respectful engagement with divine language?" I argue that these textual techniques provide a useful model for thinking about ways of reinterpreting and modifying divine language—which

DC: National Academies Press 2004), accessed July 16, 2015, http://www.nap.edu/openbook. php?record_id=10977&page=8; American Medical Association, "Labeling of Bioengineered Foods," accessed July 16, 2015; Alessandro Nicolia, Alberto Manzo, Fabio Veronesi, and Daniele Rosellini, 2014, "An Overview of the Last 10 Years of Genetically Engineered Crop Safety Research," *Critical Reviews in Biotechnology* 34, no. 1 (2014): 77–88, accessed July 16, 2015, doi:10.3109/07388551.2013.823595; A. L. Van Eenennaam and A. E. Young "Prevalence and Impacts of Genetically Engineered Feedstuffs on Livestock Populations," *Journal of Animal Science* 92, no. 10 (2014): 4255–4278, accessed July 16, 2015, doi:10.2527/jas.2014-8124.

3. In general, consensus seems to be that genetically engineered (GE) varieties can give greater yields and reduce pesticide usage. Herbicide usage tends to increase with the adoption of herbicide-tolerant GE crops; however, such crops also allow the more widespread use of relatively less toxic herbicides. See Wilhelm Klümper and Matin Quaim "A Meta-Analysis of the Impacts of Genetically Modified Crops." *PLOSOne* 9 (2014):11, accessed July 16, 2015, doi: 10.1371/journal.pone.0111629; Jorge Fernandez-Cornejo, Seth Wechsler, Mike Livingston, and Lorraine Mitchell, "Genetically Engineered Crops in the United States" USDA Economic Research Service Report 162 (2014), accessed July 16, 2015, www.ers.usda.gov/publications/err-economic-research-report/err162.aspx.

4. Indeed, one might argue that, precisely because of our relative lack of omniscience, we are actually not in a position to know the relative harms and benefits. However, this line of argument, since it is fundamentally about the *nature* of human knowledge rather than the specifics of accumulated data on any given issue, potentially forestalls practical determinations of risk regarding any number of technological innovations. Because of our relative lack of omniscience, how do we truly know that the risks of vaccination, modern sanitation, or sterile surgical technique do not, on a cosmic level, outweigh the benefits? While such questions make for important (truly!) philosophical and theological reflection, they effectively paralyze practical ethics when deployed inappropriately.

category, I argue, includes both scripture and DNA—that are at once responsive to contemporary needs and respectful of their origin. The reasonings behind particular instances of textual modification shed light on the ways people have modified and continue to modify their environment, and on the ways in which people can be disciplined, flourishing participants in a divine order.

For the purposes of this essay, I am specifically considering the case of modifying food crops by using genes borrowed whole from other species or subspecies of organism. The potential scope of genetic technologies is far broader than this case; we can, for example, engineer bacteria or plants to produce pharmaceutical compounds, or engineer lab rodents with genes that have been modified from their source to produce entirely new traits for research purposes. Scientists are developing the ability to edit individual genes with increasing precision, perhaps eventually rendering transgenesis—that is, the transfer of whole genes from one species to another—obsolete. It may be that some of these other technologies and their potential applications fit within the defense of GE crops that I articulate in this chapter, while others may not. What I hope to offer here is the beginning of a religiously and textually attentive ethical framework with which to evaluate genetic technology, a framework that takes into consideration the ways it is and is not appropriate to engage divine language, whether that language is textual or genetic.

"For Everything Is in It": The Shared Character of Life and Text

The arguments I make in this chapter rest on the claim that DNA, like scripture, is a form of divine language. On a basic level, this claim is intuitive. If we understand God to be the creator of all life, then it stands to reason that the genetic sequences that determine the characteristics of every life form are the language through which God describes God's living creation. Beyond this basic level, however, genetic language and scriptural language share certain structural and performative similarities. Genetic language and scriptural language are similar in the ways they build meaning, embody tradition, and suggest certain kinds of expression.

There will not be an exact parallel between every aspect of scriptural language and every aspect of genetic language, and I do not wish to become hung up on mapping out every single structural similarity or disjunct. For the purposes of this chapter, it is enough to argue that the basic sequences of building meaning function similarly enough that it makes sense to compare their overall structures, as well as techniques for modifying individual expressions within them.

The genetic code of all living things, in all their variety, is made up of various combinations of four nucleotide bases (guanine, cytosine, thiamine, and adenine.) The multiplicity of genetic variation we see is a result of endless permutations of those four bases. Similar to the example of DNA, there are a limited number of units (verses, words, even letters) of written Torah. As is the case with all alphabetical languages, biblical Hebrew forms meaning from a finite set of phonetic symbols—twenty-two consonantal letters and, later, a series of vowel markers (fifteen, according to the now-standardized Tiberian Masoretic system.) From this small set of basic components comes a larger set of words, and from words are formed verses; it is these basic combinations that are, according to rabbinic tradition, the fundamental building blocks of the Written Torah. The inexhaustible world of meaning of the interpretive tradition derives from combinations of a finite set of components. Combinations—that is, interactions or relations—are the generators of variations of meaning.

We can, then, make a loose analogy regarding the ways these languages build meaning: the letters of the Hebrew alphabet are roughly comparable, in function and obvious finitude if not in number, to DNA's nucleotide bases. Words and verses—sequences of letters—are roughly comparable to genes: while any given Hebrew letter, though pregnant with meaning in its own right, is like any other instance of the same letter, the particular combinations of letters and spaces that form words and verses begin to give texts distinctive characteristics, and make it possible at the very least to sort them into rough groupings. Just as a gene for the production of chlorophyll, for example, tells us that we are probably dealing with a photosynthesizing organism, a phrase like *Vaydabeir Adonai el-Moshe leimor* ("The Lord spoke to Moses, saying") lets us know that we are probably dealing with a legal text from the Pentateuch.

Scripture, like DNA, is a blueprint for a living, embodied organism. Like DNA, scripture must be embodied, performed, and activated if it is to be a real, living worship of its maker. And, like DNA, which set of scripture's possible meanings is in fact expressed depends in part on the circumstances of its embodiment. Finally, genetic language and scriptural language both encode within them the marks of their history. We can trace the genetic history of organisms by following patterns in the DNA of related species. Genetic sequences tell us where they have been, what they have done, and what they might do in the future; this narrative helps us figure out how to interact with these sequences. Similarly, scriptural sequences give us clues as to their redactional, ritual, and interpretive histories; in doing so, they suggest which modes of interaction with and performative expressions of them have traditional precedent or make structural sense. These clues continue to condition our present and future interactions with the text.

"Turn It, and Turn It Again": Interpretive Techniques

If DNA and scripture are both forms of divine language, we may learn much about what constitutes respectful engagement with divine language by looking at the classic modes of engagement with scripture of a tradition that venerates it as divine language. Rabbinic hermeneutical traditions offer several techniques of reading scriptural language that evince a deep respect for the divine origins of that language while nevertheless creatively modifying it in ways ranging from the subtle to the absurdly obvious. For examples, I want to discuss three distinct cases of interpretive modification—the phenomenon of *qere* and *ketiv* (in which a biblical word or phrase is pointed such that a reader pronounces it differently from the way the letters would indicate), the mechanics of classical rabbinic midrash, and the phenomenon of *takkanah* (acts of rabbinic legislation). These cases hail from different eras in Jewish history and affect different textual corpora in different ways. My purpose in using these three cases is not to elide distinct interpretive phenomena, but rather to showcase the variety of ways in which Jewish tradition, writ large, has consciously tweaked an inviolable text, all the while retaining a deep sense of that text's very inviolability.

Qere and Ketiv

There are a number of cases in which the written consonantal text (*ketiv*) of a word in the Hebrew Bible differs from the way it is traditionally recited (*qere*); the institution of the *qere* is traditionally attributed to the biblical figure of Ezra. These discrepancies, and their standard treatment, were codified between the 7th and 10th centuries C.E. by a group of scribes known as the Masoretes, who attached a standard vowelization[5] to codices of the Hebrew Bible (Torah scrolls meant for ritual use are unvowelized.)

Thus, for example, the consonantal text of Genesis 12:8 reads, "From there, he [Abram] moved on from the mountain east of Bethel, and pitched *her* tent (*ohalah*)." However, the Masoretic text vowelizes this last word such that it reads *ohaloh*—*his* tent. Or, in Leviticus 23:42–43, in which the Israelites are commanded to dwell in booths (*succot*), the two mentions of booths in verse 42 are written without a penultimate *vav*, such that they could be vowelized as either *succot* (plural) or *sucat* (singular), while in verse 43 the penultimate *vav* is present, rendering the word unambiguously plural. The Masoretic text vowelizes the two

---

5. Hebrew letters are consonantal, with the vowel sounds inferred by context and word construction. The Masoretes attached a set of standard vowel symbols that instructed the reader as to their preferred pronunciation.

ambiguous cases in verse 42 such that their pronunciation is identical to that of the unambiguous case in verse 43: *succot*, or booths.

These discrepancies can have significant interpretive consequences, even in matters of practical *halakhah*, or Jewish law. The example of *sucat/succot* noted above is the basis of a debate about the requirements for a valid *sucah* in B.T Succah 6a and Sanhedrin 4a. There, the number of *succot* mentioned in the verses is the basis for determining the number of walls a *succah* must have; the sages hold to the *ketiv* and count four total instances (*sucat, sucat, succot*), which translates to three walls plus a hand's-breadth, while Rabbi Shimon holds to the *quere* and counts six instances (*succot, succot, succot*), which translates to four walls plus a hand's breadth.

It is important to note that while the verse is *recited* according to the *qere*, and while the Masoretic vowelization is rendered according to the *qere*, the actual vowels written *always* follow the *ketiv*. The inconsistencies in the written text must be modified in practice, but the original written text is inviolable and must be preserved as well.[6] The codification of *qere* and *ketiv* thus represents a type of textual modification that is at once concretely obvious and very subtle. It visibly and directly modifies a physical manifestation of the divinely given text, in a way that both reflects previous oral performative tradition and conditions future oral performance of the text. At the same time, the modification is made precisely in order to reinforce the text's sense of inviolability: the idea that either the oral tradition or the written text had picked up errors somewhere in its tradition was, as Halivni puts it, "religiously unpalatable . . . as soon as corrective and expository traditions were received by the people . . . the idea ascended that these instructions emanated from the holy scriptures themselves."[7] For the sake of the overall inviolability of the text itself, the *qere* and *ketiv* traditions, codified by the Masoretes, had to modify the text in order to save it.

Rabbinic Midrash

Rabbinic midrash refers both to a broad genre of rabbinic literature, and to the set of interpretive techniques the rabbis used to read the Hebrew Bible and generate

---

6. As David Weiss Halivni puts it, ". . . the problem of *qere* and *ketiv* demonstrates the principle of the inviolability of text. Even as altered readings (*qere*) effectively superseded the scriptural orthography, these readings did not displace the written words themselves. . . . The scriptures maintained their form, and the divergent readings were transmitted as an oral tradition, adjunct to the preserved holy text." "Rabbinic Hermeneutics," *Proceedings of the American Academy for Jewish Research* 62 (1996): 38, accessed May 19, 2015.

7. Halivni, 40.

this literature; unless I note otherwise, when I say "midrash" I mean the latter sense. Midrashic interpretation, while varying according to hermeneutic style, geography, time period, and subgenre (the techniques for generating *halakhic,* or legal midrash, differ from those for generating *aggadic,* or narrative midrash), nevertheless has a set of notable identifying characteristics.

First, midrash begins with the assumption that God is the implied author of biblical text. This divine authorship means that the text is not only inviolable, but that it is also fully sufficient. This claim, as Daniel Boyarin puts it, "is not a theological or dogmatic claim but a semiotic [one] . . . [I]f God is the implied author of the Bible, then the gaps, repetitions, contradictions, and heterogeneity of the biblical text must be *read,* as a central part of the system of meaning production of that text. In midrash the rabbis respond to this invitation and challenge."[8] Both the impetus for interpretation and all necessary resources for generating it are to be found within the text itself.

Second, midrash understands scripture in atomistic terms. The verse, or even the individual word, is the Bible's "basic unit" and the target of the midrashist's interpretive energies.[9] Further, verses are not just basic units but are also independently significant, mobile units; they, not the chapters or books, are the Bible's basic organizing principle. Thus, any verse can potentially interact with any other verse in interpretively significant ways.[10] As such, midrashic interpretive methods are often deeply intertextual, using elements from one part of scripture to interpret a completely different part, even a different genre. Indeed, as Daniel Boyarin argues, "The repetition of the narrative in the Torah sets up an interpretive gap; this gap must be read, if the unity of the text is to be maintained."[11] The unity of the text can be maintained only through total atomization of its verses—atomization both in the sense of examining verses as basic units *and* in the sense of mobilizing those verses.

Third, midrash is generated in response to problems in the biblical text. We have already seen, with the example of *qere* and *ketiv,* one such "problem."

8. Daniel Boyarin, *Intertextuality and the Reading of Midrash* (Bloomington: Indiana University Press, 1994), 40.

9. James Kugel, "Two Introductions to Midrash," in *Midrash and Literature,* Geoffrey H. Hartman and Sanford Budick, eds. (New Haven, CT: Yale University Press, 1986), 93.

10. As James Kugel puts it, ". . . it might be said that there is simply no boundary encountered beyond that of the verse until one comes to the borders of the canon itself. . . . One of the things this means is that each verse of the Bible is in principle as connected to its most distant fellow as to the one next door; in seeking to illuminate a verse from Genesis, the midrashist is as likely to have reference (if to anything) to a verse from the Psalter as to another verse in the immediate context—indeed, he sometimes delights in the remoter source" (ibid.).

11. Boyarin, *Intertextuality,* 56

But there are other "surface irregularities," as Kugel puts it—grammatical discrepancies, apparent omissions or contradictions between two texts, or even dissonance between the apparent meaning of a text and an observed social reality. Thus, by putting the problem verse in conversation with other verses—often from entirely different parts of the Hebrew Bible—the midrashist exposes in the problem verse a layer of meaning that addresses that problem. Of course, the interpretation might create other problems in turn. So the midrashist continues the interpretive process, and in doing so remains in live, engaged, and respectful conversation with the divine word. [12]

Take, for example, Genesis Rabbah 8:1, which deals with a problem of number in Genesis 1:26: "And God said, let us make the human creature in our image, after our likeness. . . ." God, singular, creates the human creature, singular, in *our* image, after *our* likeness, plural. The midrash asks, what are these multiple creations? [13] For the sake of space, I do not present the entire passage, but one example should be sufficient to demonstrate the mechanics:

> *And God said: let us make the human creature, etc.* (Gen. 1:26) R. Yohanan opened [the discourse]: *You have hemmed me in behind and before* (Ps. 139:5) Said R. Yohanan: If a man is worthy enough, he enjoys both worlds, for it says, *you have molded me for a later* [world] *and an earlier* [world.] But if not, he will have to account [for his misdeeds], as it is said, *and set your hand upon me.* (Ps. 139:5)

The midrash opens by quoting the beginning of the verse in question; immediately, R. Yohanan jumps in to interpret the verse, by way of another verse from Psalms: *You have hemmed me in behind and before.* He goes on to explain that this verse, in juxtaposition with the lemma verse from Genesis, actually refers to creation and, with a bit of wordplay, can answer the initial question: what are these multiple creations? Here, R. Yohanan reads the word *tzartani*—translated at first as "you have hemmed me in," from the root *tzadi-reish-reish*, "to bind, be restricted"—as being from the root *yod-tzadi-reish*, "to create, to form"; thus, "you have molded me." Therefore, the two creations are the two worlds for which humanity is formed; whether individuals achieve their full potential depends on their behavior. Thus, a verse from all the way across the canon explains an apparent problem in the lemma; conversely, when the verse from Psalms is put in

---

12. Kugel, "Midrash," 92.

13. The questions the midrash asks are conditioned by its basic theological assumptions, chief among which is that of strict monotheism. Thus, the midrash's question is about a multiplicity of creations, rather than of creators.

conversation with the verse from Genesis, the midrashist can tweak the valence of a key verb and unlock a new level of meaning that was not apparent from the original context within the Psalm.

Takkanah

A *takkanah* is an act of rabbinic legislation; it articulates a new rule that did not previously exist in the *halakhic* code and often overturns or extensively modifies a biblical commandment. *Takkanot* issued during the Talmudic era are considered binding for all Jews, while *takkanot* issued after the rabbinic era are generally considered binding only for particular communities.[14] *Takkanot*, as Byron Sherwin puts it, are issued in order "to cope with a new socioeconomic or historical situation or to improve compliance with existing halakhah. . . . The goal of a *takkanah* is stated by the meaning of the term itself—'to set aright.'"[15]

Perhaps the iconic *takkanah* of the Talmudic era is the *prozbul*, a legal innovation attributed to Rabbi Hillel, which allows for the public takeover of loans during the sabbatical year. The *shmita*, or sabbatical year instituted in Deuteronomy 15, stipulates, among other things, the cancellation of all debts in that year. However, the Mishnah relates the following:

> A loan made with a *prozbul* is not remitted [in the sabbatical year.] This is one of the rulings that Hillel the Elder instituted, for he saw that the people refused to lend to each other, and transgressed what is written in the Torah: "Beware, lest there be a wicked thought in your heart, etc." (Deut. 15:9). So Hillel instituted the *prozbul*. (m. Shvi'it 10:3)

The *prozbul* itself consists of a kind of promissory note by which the creditor gives control of his loans to a rabbinic court:

> This is the body of the *prozbul:* "I transmit [my loans] to you, so-and-so and so-and-so, who judge in thus-and-such place, so that I may collect any loan in my possession at whatever time I want [i.e., even after the sabbatical year]." And the judges, or the witnesses, sign below. (m. Shvi'it 10:4)

---

14. Laura Hartman helpfully suggests a parallel here with genetic modification: the same mechanism that was applied earlier and is now considered part of the tradition may be viewed with greater suspicion when it is applied contemporarily. Personal correspondence, October 13, 2015.

15. Byron L. Sherwin, *In Partnership with God: Contemporary Jewish Law and Ethics* (Syracuse, NY: Syracuse University Press, 1990), 40.

The full verse in Deuteronomy quoted above reads, "Beware, lest there be a wicked thought in your heart, saying, 'The seventh year, the year of remittance, approaches!' and you look wickedly upon your brother in need, and you do not give to him; and he cries out against you to Adonai, and it is a sin in you." Thus, according to the Mishnah, Hillel saw that precisely the situation that the biblical rule warned against had come to pass—because creditors feared the cancellation of their debts, they would no longer lend to those in need. The very people the biblical law was designed to protect were being hurt by the law's specific form. In order to preserve the law's authority and power, the law itself had to be modified.

The act of *takkanah* itself actually violates a set of biblical prohibitions regarding the interpretation of Torah: Deuteronomy 4:2—"You shall not add to the word which I command you, nor shall you take away from it"—and Deuteronomy 13:1—"you shall not add to it, nor diminish from it"—both inveigh against adding to or subtracting from the words of God's commandments; these were codified as the legal-interpretive principles of *bal tosif* ("do not add") and *bal tigra* ("do not subtract.") These prohibitions emphasize how critical it is to maintain the integrity and inviolability of scripture.

However, the rabbis also interpreted certain passages from the Hebrew Bible to mean that in specific circumstances, it would become necessary to add to or subtract from its own specific words, precisely in order to maintain its integrity. For example, several instances in the Talmud in which a biblical law is abrogated make reference to a midrash on Psalms 119:126: "It is time for Adonai to act; they have dissolved Your Torah." In Mishnah Berakhot 9:5, Rabbi Nathan translates the verse thus: "They dissolved Your Torah, for it is time to act for Adonai."[16] If the Torah is in radical danger, even acts that are explicitly forbidden become permitted, by the words of the Torah itself, in order to preserve its existence as an internally dynamic, living, flourishing system. Indeed, one could suggest that because this internal dynamism is so integral to Torah's particular character, it is precisely the judicious and paradoxical permission of what is forbidden that preserves the Torah's integrity: allowing Torah to become self-destructively static is a greater violation than is any one instance of modification.

The *takkanah* is the clearest example of outright rabbinic modification of a biblical law. It occurs when a rabbinic actor observes in the lives of those who are bound by Torah a concrete problem that makes a particular law as it is currently written unlivable, and chooses to exercise their expertise and professional discretion to address the problem. This modification seems like a grave overreach—an

---

16. Also see Tosefta Berakhot 6:24, BT Berakhot 54a and 63a and Yoma 49a, and *Sifrei Zuta* on *parshat Pinchas.*

obvious and literal case of "playing God," of usurping the role of the Lawgiver to play legislator. But *takkanah* has caution built into its very mechanics. The rabbis were careful to restrict the act of *takkanah* to rabbis—those who were expert in the law as it already stood. And they grounded the mechanics of *takkanah* back into the law itself, so that the law was directly amendable only by its own explicit permission, and only for reasons—such as its own preservation—that it itself articulated.

Commonalities

Again, *qere-ketiv*, rabbinic midrash, and *takkanah* are distinct phenomena that have different effects in different textual spheres. However, they all have in common three points: (a) that they are all what appear, at least, to be explicit modifications of a text that is, by the rules of the very people who are doing the modifying, divine and inviolable; (b) that upon closer examination, the mechanics of and resources for the apparent modification are present within the broad body text that is being modified (with the partial exception of *takkanah*, wherein the mechanics are part of the tradition, but the substance of the modification may not be); and (c) that they all arise in response to some kind of problem.

Further, these problems can be both intertextual and extratextual—that is, meaning is generated in response to problems resulting from the interaction between text and the outside world. If individual instances of interpretive modification arise in response to particular textual problems, midrash as a whole entity exists as the result of an overwhelming problem. The centrality of rabbinic interpretive techniques to Judaism as we know it today was the result of a crisis. When the Temple was destroyed, in 70 C.E., Jews needed a different way to relate to the texts and rituals that had been handed down, generation to generation, and that were their spiritual livelihood. To remain relevant and alive, these old texts had to be approached in a new way.

Yet, even so, for the rabbis, the "new approach" was not so new. As Boyarin puts it, "The [Bible's] heterogeneity—the multivocality of the biblical text itself, its hiatuses and gaps, creatively but not open-endedly filled in by the midrash—allows it to generate its meanings—its *original* meanings—in ever new social and cultural situations."[17] Regardless of how radical their interpretive techniques might seem to an outside observer, it is important to note that the rabbis understood themselves as part of an interpretive tradition. They understood their

---

17. Boyarin, *Intertextuality*, 39

techniques as ways to discover meaning *already present* in the Written Torah, which text was handed down generation to generation.

"To What May We Compare This?": Genetic Techniques

In the previous section, I argued that rabbinic interpretive techniques that appear, at first glance, to be outright—even outrageous—modifications of the original language of Torah are, upon closer examination, at least formally grounded within that very language; that, in other words, the language being modified authorizes and provides the mechanical framework for its own modification. This understanding of the mechanics of rabbinic interpretation would seem, at first, to trouble my argument that there is a parallel between such interpretation and the genetic modification of plants. However, if we make a closer examination of the mechanics and natural history of plant genetics, it turns out that the genetic modification of plants is likewise less radical than it initially appears.

To genetically engineer a plant, farmers or scientists identify a problem that might be solved by tweaking a plant's genetic code—for example, a widely grown variety of rice is susceptible to a common plant disease. Second, scientists identify a source of a gene that may solve the problem—perhaps a wild species of rice that is resistant to that particular disease. The gene of interest in this second species is isolated by breaking down the plant's cell wall by using a soapy solution, separating out the DNA, and using a special enzyme to "cut" out a particular genetic sequence. It is then "pasted" into bacterial DNA that also carries a "marker gene" of some kind that will help identify which cells have been engineered successfully. The bacterial DNA is introduced to some mechanism of transfer—often, a species of bacterium, *Agrobacterium tumefaciens*, which has the ability to facilitate horizontal gene transfer between other species. These engineered bacteria can then transform specially prepared cells from the target species with the gene of interest. The successfully engineered cells, which also have a "marker gene" from their carrier DNA, are identified by using the traits conferred by the marker gene; these cells are then propagated into whole plants, which in turn are field tested to see if disease resistance has been successfully engineered into the organism.[18]

---

18. Pamela Ronald and Raoul Adamchak, *Tomorrow's Table: Organic Farming, Genetics, and the Future of Food* (Oxford: Oxford University Press, 2008), 49, fig. 4.4. The example I use here, of engineering domestic rice for disease resistance by using a gene from a wild species, is a loose synopsis of an experiment that Pamela Ronald actually carried out and that she describes in her book.

While the description of this procedure may sound sterile and far removed from the earthy, age-old picture of a farmer cultivating his strongest, best-producing plants from year to year, the farmer and the plant biologist are actually working toward the same end—ever since people first noticed that specific traits were passed down through generations of breeding, farmers have been selecting for hardiness, output, disease-resistance, drought or flood tolerance, and quality of product. Even before the modern understanding of genetics, farmers understood that when they crossed a fragile tomato plant that produced especially tasty fruit with a hardy plant whose fruits were mediocre, they were introducing something to each plant that the other lacked, in hopes that the offspring would retain the best qualities of each. Similarly, even before the advent of genetic engineering, scientists and farmers have used other methods to introduce desirable genetic changes to crops. Since the early part of the 20th century, when Lewis John Stadler discovered it was possible to induce mutations in plant genomes by bombarding plants with ionizing radiation and breeding plants whose mutations proved desirable, crops have been improved through the use of radiation mutagenesis.[19] Later in the 20th century, plant breeders also began to utilize chemical mutagens to the same end. Genetic engineering works toward the same goal of introducing desirable genetic traits to a target species; it simply does so more precisely.

Furthermore, the transfer of genes between different species is not an originally human endeavor. Bacteria engage in horizontal gene transfer on a regular basis (this is one way they can adapt so quickly to resist various antibiotics). Indeed, this capacity among bacteria is critical to humans' ability to engage in genetic engineering—as we saw above, *Agrobacterium tumefacens* is one vehicle for transferring the gene of interest from the source species to the target species. Transgenesis also occurs in more complex species. Horizontal gene transfer occurs among fungi and between insects, nematodes, amoeba, and asexual animals, and it even occurs between kingdoms: fungus has been known to transfer genes to aphids, humans transfer genes to the bacteria that infect them, and plants transfer genes to silkworms.[20] A number of species in the tobacco family contain DNA structures of probable bacterial origin—specifically, from species of

19. For a more detailed explanation of the process of radiation mutagenesis, see International Atomic Energy Agency, "Mutation Induction: Creating Novel Genetic Diversity Using Radiation," accessed July 16, 2015, http://www-naweb.iaea.org/nafa/pbg/mutation-induction.html.

20. Caihua Gao, Xiaodong Ren, Annalies S. Mason, Honglei Liu, Meili Xiao, Jiana Li, and Donghui Fu, "Horizontal Gene Transfer in Plants," *Functional and Integrative Genomics* 14, no. 1 (2014): 23–29, accessed July 16, 2015, doi:10.1007/s10142-013-0345-0.

Agrobacterium—that may have modified the plants' growth and influenced their evolutionary trajectory.[21] Bdelloid rotifers—a class of microscopic animals—have genes of bacterial, fungal, and even plant origin; some of these foreign genes seem to be functional in the rotifers.[22] Recently, researchers have targeted another potential case: most land ferns have a photoreceptor called neochrome that helps them photosynthesize in low-light environments. This photoreceptor, it turns out, is not found in ferns' nearest common ancestor; instead, it may have been acquired by way of horizontal gene transfer from an unrelated plant called hornwort.[23]

In fact, human participation in genetic text had already produced new species, long before we had access to sophisticated gene splicing techniques—indeed, before we had the concept of genes themselves! *Canis lupus familiaris* (the domestic dog) and *Zea mays mays* (maize) are two genetic innovations whose breaks from their parent subspecies were complete well before Gregor Mendel began observing patterns of heritability in garden peas. The closest wild ancestor of maize is a grass called teosinte, whose tiny seeds are hidden within an indigestible seed coat. Long before Europeans colonized the New World, Mesoamerican peoples selectively bred modern maize from teosinte until they achieved the nutritious, high-producing plant we have today. Indeed, a strain of maize that has had a pest-resistance gene from a species of bacterium inserted into its genome may have more in common, genetically speaking, with heirloom, open-pollinated varieties of maize than *any* variety of maize has with teosinte. As we have learned more about genetics and refined our techniques, the organisms we modify retain

21. Alessandra Pontiroli, Aurora Rizzi, Pascal Simonet, Daniele Daffonchio, Timothy M. Vogel, and Jean-Michel Monier "Visual Evidence of Horizontal Gene Transfer between Plants and Bacteria in the Phytosphere of Transplastomic Tobacco," *Applied and Environmental Microbiology* 75, no. 10 (2009): 3314–3322, accessed July 16, 2015, doi:10.1128/AEM.02632-08; Tatiana V. Matveeva and Ludmilla A. Lutova, "Horizontal Gene Transfer from *Agrobacterium* to Plants," *Frontiers in Plant Science* 5 (2014): 326, accessed August 24, 2015, doi:10.3389/fpls.2014.00326.

22. E. A. Gladyshev, M. Meselson, and I. R. Arkhipova "Massive Horizontal Gene Transfer in Bdelloid Rotifers," *Science* 320 (2008): 1210–1213, accessed August 24, 2015, doi: 10.1126/science.1156407.

23. Fay-Wei Li, Juan Carlos Villarreal, Steven Kelly, Carl J. Rothfels, Michael Melkonian, Eftychios Frangedakis, Markus Ruhsam, Erin M. Siegel, Joshua P. Der, Jarmila Pittermann, Eric Carpenter, Yong Zhang, Zhijian Tian, Li Chen, Zhixiang Yan, Ying Zhu, Xiao Sun, Jun Wang, Dennis W. Stevenson, Barbara J. Crandall-Stotler, A. Jonathan Shaw, Michael K. Deyholos, Douglas E. Soltis, Sean W. Graham, Michael D. Windham, Jane A. Langdale, Gane Ka-Shu Wong, Sarah Mathews, and Kathleen M. Pryer, "Horizontal Transfer of an Adaptive Chimeric Photoreceptor from Bryophytes to Ferns," *Proceedings of the National Academy of Sciences* 111, no. 18 (2014): 6672–6677, accessed July 2, 2015, doi: 10.1073/pnas.1319929111.

more genetic commonality with their predecessors than those we have selectively bred over generations of trial and error.

It is likely that, as genetic techniques become more sophisticated, the de novo creation of gene sequences will become more widespread; such technology has the potential to accomplish in agriculture what transgenesis can, with even more precision and efficiency. While it is more difficult to justify such de novo sequence creation by way of comparison to intertextual midrash, it may be possible to do so by comparing it to *takkanah*. If such sequence creation proves critical to solving a serious or even potentially deadly problem—and food supply problems, it should be noted, often have the potential to become deadly—one could make the case that the genetic code of a given food plant as it currently stands threatens to become unlivable for those who depend on it.

Genetic engineering, then, shares the key characteristics I have identified in my examples of rabbinic interpretive techniques. First, like the rabbinic techniques, genetic engineering appears, from an initial description, to be an outrageous and ungrounded modification of a divine language from an initially "given" form to a novel and unrecognizable one. Second, like these techniques, genetic engineering proves on closer examination to be part of a tradition of interpretation of and engagement with the genetic "text" whose mechanics are derived from and authorized by the content and formal structure of the text itself. Several organisms, from bacteria to plants, are known to have in effect transgenically modified themselves. And any number of species have engaged in slower, longer-term symbiotic relationships with humans that have involved modifying their DNA through selective breeding, to the benefit of both members of the partnership. As with the rabbinic understanding of scriptural verses as atomistic, intertextually mobile units, genes also seem to be atomistic and "intertextually" mobile—and, as the Written Torah itself already seems to have realized this potential even before rabbinic midrash made use of it, so to have other organisms realized the intertextual potential of genes before it occurred to humans to do so.

Finally, like these interpretive techniques, genetic engineering responds to problems, on both micro and macro levels. As individual midrashim, for example, arise in response to particular textual difficulties, individual genetic modifications have, thus far, been made in response to particular problems with a staple crop. This result applies whether or not that problem is internal to the crop itself or occurs in the context of the crop's primary usage; thus, rice's relative lack of vitamin A becomes a problem when rice forms the bulk of a population's diet—hence, golden rice, which is modified to produce significantly higher levels of vitamin A. And, as the institution of rabbinic midrash became central to Judaism because of the existential crisis that was the destruction of the Temple, the existential crisis of climate change—combined with a booming human population that must eat under growing conditions that climate change will render less and less amenable to agriculture—will very likely render genetic engineering central to our continued relationship to the age-old institution of agriculture.

"You Shall Live By Them": Obligations of Justice and Care

What, then, *does* respect for divine language look like? I have been arguing that there are deep and significant *formal* similarities between DNA and scriptural text. I want now to go further: *the formal similarities between the two also indicate normative similarities.* That is, the fact that the language of biology and the language of Scripture are structurally similar can tell us something about the proper mode of engagement with both languages. If it is already in the character of DNA to engage in such a way with other DNA, how much more so is this kind of engagement permitted when it has the potential to alleviate considerable suffering? Jewish patterns of text interpretation *and* Jewish ethical obligations to pursue justice converge here.

Integral to justice as it has been articulated in the Jewish tradition is the obligation to repair the world—to make things better than they are now. Put a different way, to act justly is to participate in rebuilding the world as a place where all may flourish, where all may participate fully in the life of the created world, in good relationship with one another and with God. In times of crisis, this reparation often involves taking risks. We might assume that the obligation to pursue justice means avoiding risks—after all, those who are already disadvantaged are likely to bear the greatest burden should a risky technology, for example, fail to live up to its promise. Indeed, the precautionary principle—often interpreted, in this context, as meaning that "a new technology should never be introduced unless there is a guarantee that no risk will arise"[24]—holds considerable rhetorical power in the public conversation on genetic engineering. However, in the astute words of Melvin Kranzberg, "people seek a zero-risk society. But as Aaron Wildavsky has so aptly put it, 'No risk is the highest risk of all'. For it would not only petrify technology but also stultify developmental growth in society along

---

24. Nuffield Council on Bioethics, "The Use of Genetically Modified Crops in Developing Countries: A Follow-up Discussion Paper" (London: Nuffield Council on Bioethics, 2003) 57, accessed December 1, 2015, http://nuffieldbioethics.org/project/gm-crops-developing-countries/. In contrast to this strict interpretation of the precautionary *principle,* the Nuffield Council recommends a more nuanced and flexible "precautionary *approach,*" concurring with Kranzberg (below) that doing nothing is also a risky action and advising that the risks of *any* scenario be weighed on a case-by-case basis.

any lines."[25] Doing things differently from the way they have been done in the past can mean shaking up the conditions, both material and social, by which some groups of people have been oppressed by others—and that upheaval often involves great risk.

If great risk, and great breaks with past means of doing things, are sometimes required for the pursuit of justice, how much more so is it required to take reparative actions that are, comparatively speaking, neither all that risky nor all that new? Genetically engineered crops seem, at first glance, like a scary new thing, like something out of our wildest science fiction nightmares. When we look at its actual processes and goals, however, we find that genetic engineering is not, as Laurie Zoloth so eloquently articulates, "an answer to science fiction (to pigs who chew the cud or designer pets); it is an answer to the world right now, with the poor right now, waiting their turn in our harvest."[26] If used rightly, GE crops have the potential to allow for greater, more reliable harvests from less land area, for greater drought or flood tolerance, for resistance to disease, and for less intensive use of environmentally destructive agricultural inputs like fertilizer and pesticides. They can, in short, allow more humans to access the basic material conditions necessary for flourishing, and allow them to do so in a way that puts less stress on ecosystems, rather than more. And this is to say nothing of the lifesaving drugs—modern insulin, to take just one case—that have been made possible or more widely available thanks to non-agricultural uses of genetic engineering.

As I have noted above, an act of legislation—a clearly novel disruption of the received word—can be justified on the grounds of "acting for God" and preserving the integrity of the very text being disrupted. This apparently paradoxical justification offers an insight about the character of scriptural text and about humanity's proper posture toward it: *Scripture is that text toward which a proper posture of respect includes dialogical engagement.* Dialogical engagement of this sort will *always* modify all parties engaging in it. It is impossible to engage Scripture as Scripture without modifying in in various ways.

I believe it is similarly impossible to engage with living organisms without causing, over time, their modification on a genetic level, whether actively, through genetic engineering or selective breeding, or passively, by influencing the shared environment in ways that cause certain traits to be more favorable than others.

---

25. Melvin Kranzberg, "Technology and History: 'Kranzberg's Laws,'" *Technology and Culture* 27, no. 3 (1986): 553, accessed May 21, 2014, doi: 10.2307/3105385.

26. Laurie Zoloth, "When You Plow the Field, Your Torah Is with You," in *Acceptable Genes: Religious Traditions and Genetically Modified Foods*, Conrad Brunk and Harold Coward, eds. (Albany: State University of New York Press, 2009), 110.

Further, Scripture shows this character by intertextually modifying itself *within* its canon. And DNA, the genetic code common to all organisms, displays similar characteristics. If the possibility of massive famine as agricultural resources are strained further and further does not count as a time to "act for God," what does? And if an act of legislation—"uprooting the law"—is justified in order to "act for God," how much more justified is a *less* radical modification such as intertextual midrash, to which I would argue the genetic engineering of crops is more closely comparable?

None of this is to say that such engagement is completely unproblematic. Engagement and interpretation are by nature risky enterprises, and there will always be methods of engagement—and ways of using the results of that engagement—that are better or worse than others. I have not, here, addressed questions of just implementation: how, for example, to ensure that humanitarian uses of these technologies, such as biofortification, drought- or flood-resistant staple crops, or the efficient production of lifesaving pharmaceuticals, take priority in funding, or how to prevent profiteering and predatory patenting of new plant varieties. While I suspect that the specific policy details of how to accomplish this safeguarding are beyond the scope of this particular approach,[27] it is worth noting that there are a number of episodes in rabbinic literature that may help us distinguish between problematic uses of textual interpretation and the activity of risky interpretation itself.[28]

It is of course a good and holy thing to cultivate humility and *yira*—awe— toward God's Torah, and it is similarly a good and holy thing to cultivate humility and *yira* toward God's creation. But we delude ourselves if we believe that the best way to develop these virtues is a policy of static, perceived noninterference. Rapport and understanding are developed through mutual engagement, and such engagement always transforms all participants.

---

27. Zoloth. "When You Plow," 81–114, makes some important moves in the direction of policy and implementation.

28. One example would be the well-known "Oven of Akhnai" narrative in Bavli Bava Metzia 59 a–b. This episode famously establishes the legitimacy of human interpretation of the divine word—after God Godself intervenes in an interpretive debate, Rabbi Joshua retorts that the life of the text is "not in heaven!" (Deut. 3:12). God then seems to authorize the claim, laughing and exclaiming, "My children have defeated me!"

Yet, the aftermath of the debate is catastrophic: Rabbi Eliezer, who argued against Rabbi Joshua and the academy, is excommunicated, and the power of his hurt and humiliation over the insult lead to storms, crop failures, and the death of his brother-in-law, Rabban Gamliel. The Bavli's discussion of these disasters makes clear that it is not (at least primarily) Rabbi Joshua's audacious interpretive move that caused them; rather, it is the use of the argument as a pretext for shaming and exiling Rabbi Eliezer that constitutes the failure of justice.

If, on the other hand, we persist in the delusion that there are methods of living on this planet *without* altering it, we shall always find ourselves relating to a static and distorted picture of our world, of the creator who brought it forth, and of one another. And that will be a true shame—both because we will persist in engaging with a falsehood, and because we will jettison critical weapons in the in reducing land, water, and pesticide use and condemn scores of people to perish of malnutrition for the sake of our preferred fantasy.

11

FLOURISHING IN CRISIS

ENVIRONMENTAL ISSUES IN THE CATHOLIC SOCIAL TEACHINGS

Jennifer Phillips

At the time of this book's publication, humankind faces an ecological reckoning for centuries of aggressive development. While mainstream culture argues causality and policy, some religious leaders attempt to cut through the noise. Perhaps most notably, in terms of global influence, the Roman Catholic head, Pope Francis, speaks decisively on the matter. His encyclical *Laudato Si'* condemns both ecological and economic crises, exposes the weakness of technocratic thought, and offers a theological paradigm to replace it.[1] In doing so, he adds to the canon of Catholic social teachings, both drawing heavily from its authority and updating it to address contemporary needs.

As a body of theological ethics, the social teachings are typically dated to Leo XIII's 1891 encyclical, *Rerum Novarum*. That text is a sweeping theological analysis of the relatively new industrial economy—asserting the dignity of work and workers, criticizing conditions belying that dignity, and making a case for human rights in the modern economy. Future pontiffs were to reassert *Rerum Novarum*'s themes and assumptions, both deploying its arguments and extending its logic. Not only do the social teachings retain remarkable consistency across many decades, but they also evolve to encompass a broad range of concerns, such as political unrest, war, capital punishment, capitalism, communism, poverty, consumption, and, most recently, environmental degradation.

---

1. Francis, *Laudato Si': On Care for Our Common Home* (Vatican, 2015), http://w2.vatican.va/content/francesco/en/encyclicals/documents/papa-francesco_20150524_enciclica-laudato-si.html. Given the frequency of citations for this source, this chapter employs parenthetical paragraph references for *Laudato Si'*.

In keeping with this pattern, a theory of interconnectivity coalesces assertively in Francis's *Laudato Si'*. While the word "interconnected" also finds its way into the writings of his predecessor, Benedict XVI, Francis employs it with a uniquely decisive tone. He explicitly affirms the interconnected nature not only of all creation, but also of contemporary crises, their causes, and their solutions. Referencing the authority of Genesis, he writes, "These ancient stories, full of symbolism, bear witness to a conviction which we today share, that everything is interconnected, and that genuine care for our own lives and our relationships with nature is inseparable from fraternity, justice and faithfulness to others" (70). He draws this conclusion from biblical authority and the robust resources of the Catholic social teachings, specifically referencing the 1987 Conference of Dominican Bishops (92). He concludes lyrically, "Everything is related, and we human beings are united as brothers and sisters on a wonderful pilgrimage, woven together by the love God has for each of his creatures and which also unites us in fond affection with brother sun, sister moon, brother river and mother earth" (92).

This development creates new space for robust environmental consideration within the Church's largely anthropocentric ethic, and it enables the Catholic social teachings to dialogue with environmentalists who scrutinize the Christian tradition.[2] However, there remains a significant gap between Francis's theory of interconnectivity and a more robust framework of intersectionality.[3] In this chapter I examine the social teachings on flourishing, those doctrines' pertinence to environmental care, and the Church's response to the contemporary ecological crisis. Finally, I suggest two concerns that merit intersectional consideration both within the social teachings and in dialogue with non-Catholic environmentalists: animal welfare and population growth.

Flourishing in the Catholic Social Teachings

Creation theology is at the heart of the social teachings on flourishing, particularly the foundational concepts of *imago Dei* and *telos*. The former, humanity's

2. A good example of such criticism was leveled in the 1960s by Lynn White, who wrote, "Christianity is the most anthropocentric religion the world has seen . . . [it] not only established a dualism of man and nature but also insisted that it is God's will that man exploit nature for his proper ends. . . . By destroying pagan animism, Christianity made it possible to exploit nature in a mood of indifference to the feelings of natural objects. Man's effective monopoly on spirit in this world was confirmed, and the old inhibitions to the exploitation of nature crumbled." Lynn White, "The Historical Roots of Our Ecologic Crisis," *Science* 155, no. 3767 (March 10, 1967): 1205.

3. I am grateful to this volume's editor, Laura Hartman, for her input and assistance in clarifying this idea.

creation in God's image, tethers the social teachings to a basic ethical priority: the inalienable dignity of every human being. The latter, God's plan to unite human beings in solidarity with one another, all creation, and God himself, describes the final end that will fulfill the seeds of *imago Dei* in each person. These tenets promote a commitment to flourishing—in particular, *human* flourishing—that honors both the image of God and its promised fulfillment.

Paul VI outlines this commitment in his 1967 encyclical *Populorum Progressio*, in which he calls for an "authentic development" that aims at the whole person.[4] Human flourishing, he explains, "is destined for a higher state of perfection. United with the life-giving Christ, man's life is newly enhanced; it acquires a transcendent humanism which surpasses its nature and bestows new fullness of life. This is the highest goal of human self-fulfillment,"[5] and it is more ambitious than mere economic growth or material prosperity.

Authentic development aligns with Catholic orthodoxy; in particular it reflects the contemplation of happiness found in Thomas Aquinas's *Summa Theologica*. The opus begins its outline of human ethics with an assertion that humanity has an ultimate end, which is happiness. Aquinas rejects worldly happiness, such as wealth, honor, fame, power, or created goods, in favor of spiritual happiness.[6] He argues that happiness is God, the seed of whom is within all humans and desires fulfillment. "In the first sense, then, man's last end is the uncreated good, namely, God, Who alone by His infinite goodness can perfectly satisfy man's will. But in the second way, man's last end is something created, existing in him, and this is nothing else than the attainment or enjoyment of the last end."[7] In other words, humanity's *telos* will be in God and the fulfillment of God's image within us.

Admittedly, this framework is anthropocentric, and it explicitly favors the transcendent over the earthbound—two aspects that should be red flags for environmentalists. On the other hand, in refusing to overvalue material wealth, the social teachings challenge a paradigm that prizes economic prosperity at any cost. In addition, the social teachings have evolved to incorporate other doctrines, which expand the tradition's concept of human flourishing, connect it to nature's

---

4. PaulVI, *Populorum Progressio: On the Development of Peoples* (Vatican, 1967), 14, http://www.vatican.va/holy_father/paul_vi/encyclicals/documents/hf_p-vi_enc_26031967_populorum_en.html.

5. Ibid., 16.

6. Thomas Aquinas, *The Summa Theologica of St. Thomas Aquinas*, online ed., Fathers of the English Dominican Province, trans. (New Advent, 2008), I–II, 2, 1–8, http://www.newadvent.org/summa.

7. Ibid., I–II, 3, 1.

flourishing, and, ultimately, support arguments for environmental care. I turn now to one such doctrine: the option for the poor.

The Option for the Poor

In determined calls for solidarity, the social teachings assert that *universal* authentic development is paramount; one person's fulfillment is incomplete if others lack human needs, are in conflict with one another, or suffer other injustice. Aquinas writes, "If there were but one soul enjoying God, it would be happy, though having no neighbor to love. But supposing one neighbor to be there, love of him results from perfect love of God. Consequently, friendship is, as it were, concomitant with perfect Happiness."[8] On this authority, the tradition insists that each person should promote authentic development for all persons. Paul VI exhorts, "It is not just certain individuals but all men who are called to further the development of human society as a whole. . . . The reality of human solidarity brings us not only benefits but also obligations."[9] In other words, flourishing is a fundamental requirement of human dignity, not an elite privilege. This important qualification challenges mainstream norms, institutions, and social structures, most notably those framed by capitalist economics. Constructively, it establishes the preferential option for the poor, which requires special concern for the poor and vulnerable.

The option for the poor finds theological purchase not only in the core beliefs regarding *imago Dei* and *telos*, but also in paschal redemption, which unravels merit-based thinking in favor of universal dignity.[10] As described above, humanity's creation in God's image promises that every person has dignity. All humans bear the likeness of God, and the promise of its fulfillment. This principle finds root in scripture, where Matthew attests, "The king will reply, 'Truly I tell you, whatever you did for one of the least of these brothers and sisters of mine, you did for me'" (Matthew 25:40). It also emerges in the Beatitudes, in which Christ specifically blesses, among others, "the meek" (Matthew 5:5). The social teachings carry these ideas into the modern era, calling on Christians to

---

8. Ibid., I–II, 4, 8.

9. Paul VI, *Populorum Progressio*, 17.

10. For a lengthy analysis of the ideas and primary sources presented in this paragraph, see my doctoral dissertation. Jennifer Phillips, "Ethics and Economic Life: The Catholic Social Teachings and Microeconomics" (PhD diss., University of Virginia, 2013), 50–53, http://gradworks.umi.com/35/70/3570388.html.

recognize Christ in the poor neighbor.[11] Finally, paschal redemption models and makes incarnate the option for the poor. In his death, Christ *becomes* vulnerable on the cross, and he *demonstrates* Christian love through the cross. Importantly, his sacrifice takes place on behalf of a sinful humanity, which does not merit salvation. Christ's resurrection liberates us—not only from personal sin, but also from sinful paradigms that assign more and less dignity to certain individuals or peoples.

The option for the poor is significant to environmental ethics for three reasons. First, it illuminates the incompatibility of environmental degradation and human flourishing. Second, it challenges the self-interest of NIMBY (not in my backyard) environmentalism, insisting instead on an approach that supports universal human thriving. Third, it confronts the unjust economies that simultaneously exploit both the poor and the natural world. Francis exemplifies all three of these in *Laudato Si'*, in which he articulates particular concern for the outsized effects of climate change on the poor. He writes, "Its worst impact will probably be felt by developing countries in coming decades. . . . Sadly, there is widespread indifference to such suffering" (25). Francis goes on to scrutinize water quality and availability, condemning unequal access to safe drinking water (27–31). He argues, on the basis of the option for the poor, that wealthy individuals and nations have an "ecological debt" to the poor and "differentiated responsibilities" in light of ecological crisis (51–52).

The Universal Destination of Goods

Notwithstanding such remarks, environmentalists may worry that the option for the poor is predominantly anthropocentric. This concern is exacerbated by the doctrine of human dominion, which remains an important component of the Catholic tradition. As John Paul II wrote as recently as the last decade of the 20th century,

> [t]he Book of Genesis . . . places man at the summit of God's creative activity, as its crown, at the culmination of a process which leads from indistinct chaos to the most perfect of creatures. Everything in creation is

---

11. For example, John Paul II writes, "I exhort every Christian . . . to evidence his personal conversion through a concrete sign of love toward those in need, recognizing in this person the face of Christ and repeating, as if almost face to face: 'I was poor, I was marginalized . . . and you welcomed me'"; John Paul II, "Message for Lent 1998" (Vatican, September 9, 1997), http://www.vatican.va/holy_father/john_paul_ii/messages/lent/documents/hf_jp-ii_mes_09091997_lent-1998_en.html.

ordered to man and everything is made subject to him: 'Fill the earth and subdue it; and have dominion over every living thing" (1:28); this is God's command to the man and the woman.... We see here a clear affirmation of the primacy of man over things; these are made subject to him and entrusted to his responsible care, whereas for no reason can he be made subject to other men and almost reduced to the level of a thing.[12]

This excerpt represents a traditional Catholic assertion of human dominion, and it is rightly subject to scrutiny from environmentalists. Without nuance, the doctrine of human dominion provides theological legitimacy to those who would dismantle environmental care. It raises these questions: What limits humanity's dominion over nature? Does this framework subjugate the natural world to human whim, under the guise of obedience to God? How can such an approach make theoretical room for environmental protection?

In *Laudato Si'*, Francis engages this challenge directly by rejecting interpretations of dominion that condone or facilitate "unbridled exploitation." He writes, "We must forcefully reject the notion that our being created in God's image and given dominion over the earth justifies absolute domination over other creatures" (67). Constructively, the social teachings condition dominion by referring to the universal destination of goods, the doctrine that creation exists on behalf of the common good. This doctrine makes humanity's uses of nature, including private property, subordinate to God's intent for creation.

Specifically, the universal destination of goods inhibits human dominion in two ways. First, it constrains dominion by the sheer scope of universal flourishing, made exponential by "intergenerational solidarity," which, according to Francis, "is not optional, but rather a basic question of justice" (159). It condemns misuse of nature as a theft from the poor and future generations, thereby issuing a vital challenge to "blank check" interpretations of dominion. For example, on this authority, Francis conditions private property rights, which the social teachings posit are socially necessary, but only inasmuch as they support the common good:[13]

Every ecological approach needs to incorporate a social perspective which takes into account the fundamental rights of the poor and the

---

12. John Paul II, *Evangelium Vitae: On the Value and Inviolability of Human Life* (Vatican, 1995), 34, http://www.vatican.va/holy_father/john_paul_ii/encyclicals/documents/hf_jp-ii_enc_25031995_evangelium-vitae_en.html.

13. For detailed analysis of private property ethics in light of the universal destination of goods, see my doctoral dissertation. Phillips, "Ethics and Economic Life," 37–47.

underprivileged. The principle of the subordination of private property to the universal destination of goods, and thus the right of everyone to their use, is a golden rule of social conduct and "the first principle of the whole ethical and social order." The Christian tradition has never recognized the right to private property as absolute or inviolable, and has stressed the social purpose of all forms of private property (93).

Second, the universal destination of goods affirms the necessity and goodness of creation, thereby reframing dominion as a responsibility not to hoard, destroy, or otherwise damage nature's role in sustaining human life. In the Catholic tradition, the natural world is God's creation, and he deems it "good" (Genesis 1:31); this is the first judgment God makes in scripture. God created the natural world *before* humans and *for* humans—all humans. According to this design, the bountiful natural world is a precondition for human life. Because nature's flourishing is essential to human flourishing, it must be an ethical priority.

Covenant

In addition to the universal destination of goods, a second theological device establishes this interconnectivity: the social teachings assert that God, the natural world, and humanity exist in covenant with one another. God's participation in this covenant is absolute and perfect; he is creator, sustainer, and savior. Nature nourishes God's creation, including humanity, in all its aspects. Human beings are God's co-creators, participating in both his image and his work. The covenant is ordered to fulfilling God's *telos* for creation, which, as described earlier in this chapter, will culminate in perfect communion among all human beings, creation, and God.

Like human flourishing, the covenantal relation of humanity and nature conveys the authority of Catholic orthodoxy. Specifically, Aquinas's *Summa* outlines a theology of ordered creation:

We shall find, first, that each and every part exists for the sake of its proper act, as the eye for the act of seeing; secondly, that less honorable parts exist for the more honorable, as the senses for the intellect, the lungs for the heart; and, thirdly that all parts are for the perfection of the whole, as the matter for the form, since the parts are, as it were, the matter of the whole. Furthermore, the whole man is on account of an extrinsic end, that end being the fruition of God. So, therefore, in the parts of the universe also every creature exists for its own proper act and perfection, and the less noble for the nobler, as those creatures that are less noble than man exist for the sake of man, whilst each and every creature exists for the perfection of the entire universe. Furthermore, the entire universe, with all its parts, is ordained towards God as its end, inasmuch as it imitates, as it were, and shows forth the Divine goodness, to the glory of God. Reasonable creatures, however, have in some special and higher manner God as their end, since they can attain to Him by their own operations, by knowing and loving him. Thus it is plain that Divine goodness is the end of all corporeal things.[14]

In this passage, Aquinas argues that all life, whether human or nonhuman, is ordered to God and "the perfection of the entire universe."[15] Nearly 750 years later, Francis both affirms the special status that Aquinas affords human beings and maintains Aquinas's argument for nature's special purpose. Francis writes in 2015, "All creatures are moving forward with us and through us towards a common point of arrival, which is God. . . . Human beings, endowed with intelligence and love, and drawn by the fullness of Christ, are called to lead all creatures back to their creator" (83).

In fact, Francis deepens the idea to convey a spiritually significant relationship between humanity and nature, which results in not only mutual benefit, but also mutual enjoyment. He writes, in a passage that evokes the intimacy of marriage, "When we speak of the 'environment,' what we really mean is a relationship between nature and the society which lives in it. Nature cannot be regarded as something separate from ourselves or as a mere setting in which we live. We are part of nature, included in it and thus in constant interaction with it" (139). Like married partners (a special status in Catholic tradition), humanity and nature, however unique, are permanently entwined "in constant interaction." One party cannot thrive in isolation; both must flourish or wither. This depiction, alongside the tradition's emphasis on covenant, underscores the holy nature of the relation between humanity and nature. Francis uses the phrase "integral ecology" to describe the full realization of this bond (137–142).

Nature participates in this covenant in three ways.[16] First, it enables the biological fact of human life. Nature is the source of shelter and nourishment for the whole of God's creation—including not only human beings, but also the dazzling array of nonhuman life. Second, nature bears an aesthetic energy described in the teachings as "a deep restorative power" that draws humanity closer to God. This

---

14. Aquinas, *Summa Theologica*, I, 65, 2.

15. Ibid.

16. Phillips, "Ethics and Economic Life," 133–134.

phrasing comes from John Paul II's 1990 World Day of Peace message,[17] but the idea belongs to the entire tradition—for example, the following affirmation from John XXIII in 1961: "Bread it [nature] was for the body, but it was intended also to foreshadow that other bread, that heavenly food of the soul, which He was to give them on 'the night before He suffered.'"[18] Fifty years later, Benedict XVI was to be recognized for describing the "sacramental character of the world" and thereby affirming nature's power to unite humans with God.[19]

In addition to biological and spiritual nourishment, nature's third covenantal role is to inspire humans to care for one another, in particular the poor and vulnerable. John Paul II asserts during his 1990 World Day of Peace message, "There is an order in the universe which must be respected, and . . . the human person, endowed with the capability of choosing freely, has a grave responsibility to preserve this order for the well-being of future generations."[20] The very fact that the World Day of Peace has become an occasion for ecological considera-tion highlights the relation between society and ecology in the Catholic social teachings. Nature's beauty bestows a renewed awareness of God,[21] which in turn strengthens the beholder's understanding and determination for a moral society.

Humanity's covenantal responsibilities are seeded in the *imago Dei* that all human beings share. As described earlier in this chapter, this design assigns hu-manity a unique dignity among God's creatures; it also assigns human beings a vocation as collaborators alongside God and nature. Specifically, that vocation is stewardship of the earth, on behalf of universal flourishing. According to the Vatican's International Theological Commission (ITC):

> Created in the image of God to share in the communion of Trinitarian love, human beings occupy a unique place in the universe according to the divine plan: they enjoy the privilege of sharing in the divine governance

---

17. John Paul II, "Peace with God the Creator, Peace with All of Creation (Message for the Celebration of the World Day of Peace)" (Vatican, January 1, 1990), 14, http://www.vatican.va/holy_father/john_paul_ii/messages/peace/documents/hf_jp-ii_mes_19891208_xxiii-world-day-for-peace_en.html.

18. JohnXXIII, *Mater et Magistra: On Christianity and Social Progress* (Vatican, 1961), 5, http://www.vatican.va/holy_father/john_xxiii/encyclicals/documents/hf_j-xxiii_enc_15051961_mater_en.html.

19. Jame Schaefer, "Celebrating and Advancing Magisterial Discourse on the Ecological Crisis," in *Environmental Justice and Climate Change: Assessing Pope Benedict XVI's Ecological Vision for the Catholic Church in the United States*, Jame Schaefer and Tobias Winwright, eds. (Plymouth, UK: Lexington Books, 2013), xxi.

20. John Paul II, "Peace with God the Creator, Peace with All of Creation," 15.

21. Ibid., 14.

of visible creation. This privilege is granted to them by the Creator who allows the creature made in his image to participate in his work, in his project of love and salvation, indeed in his own lordship over the universe. Since man's place as ruler is in fact a participation in the divine governance of creation, we speak of it here as a form of stewardship.[22]

However, notwithstanding this privilege, humanity embodies it imperfectly. Every human being bears the imprint of original sin, which the ITC describes as "a disfigurement of the *imago Dei*" within us.[23] This "disfigurement" mirrors the damage that human beings inflict on the earth, and it corrupts humanity's participation in the creative covenant with God and nature (2). Benedict XVI describes this phenomenon in his 2010 World Day of Peace message:

> The harmony between the Creator, mankind and the created world, as described by Sacred Scripture, was disrupted by the sin of Adam and Eve, by man and woman, who wanted to take the place of God and refused to acknowledge that they were his creatures. As a result, the work of "exercising dominion" over the earth, "tilling it and keeping it," was also disrupted, and conflict arose within and between mankind and the rest of creation (cf. Gen 3:17–19). Human beings let themselves be mastered by selfishness; they misunderstood the meaning of God's command and exploited creation out of a desire to exercise absolute domination over it. But the true meaning of God's original command, as the Book of Genesis clearly shows, was not a simple conferral of authority, but rather a summons to responsibility.[24]

The social teachings assert that human beings have transcendent aspects, being created in the image of God. However, humans are also creatures, brought to life only by the grace of the creator. Thus, humanity exercises dominion over nature on the authority of God's image, rather than any autonomous power. Ultimately, God's sovereignty directs, limits, and assigns divine ambition to humanity's

---

22. International Theological Commission, "Communion and Stewardship: Human Persons Created in the Image of God" (Vatican, 2004), 57, http://www.vatican.va/roman_curia/congregations/cfaith/cti_documents/rc_con_cfaith_doc_20040723_communion-stewardship_en.html.

23. Ibid., 6.

24. Benedict XVI, "If You Want to Cultivate Peace, Protect Creation (Message for the Celebration of the World Day of Peace)" (Vatican, January 1, 2010), 6, http://www.vatican.va/holy_father/benedict_xvi/messages/peace/documents/hf_ben-xvi_mes_20091208_xliii-world-day-peace_en.html.

stewardship of nature. When we human beings fail to exercise dominion within these parameters, we forget that "we ourselves are dust of the earth" (2, from Genesis 2:7). Uses that are not in accord with God's sovereignty are symptomatic of broken covenant and humanity's inherited sin. John Paul II mourns this failure bluntly, stating, "I wish to repeat that the ecological crisis is a moral issue."[25]

Confronting Ecological Crisis

John Paul II's 1990 World Day of Peace message represents the social teachings' first explicit condemnation of ecological crisis as a crisis in human morality.[26] He continued to develop the message, and future pontiffs carried it forward with an intensity to match growing urgency among scientists and environmentalists.[27] Benedict XVI, then Cardinal Joseph Ratzinger, collaborated closely on the development of the 1990 message; it became his mantle to carry when he assumed the papacy fifteen years later. He did so aggressively, speaking more frequently on the topic than any pope before him and contemplating ecological ethics at length on three occasions: his 2010 World Day of Peace message, the encyclical *Caritas in Veritate*, and a noteworthy 2006 talk on stewardship.[28]

Benedict XVI's successor has also embraced the emphasis. In fact, Francis began by selecting a papal name that signals his commitment to ecological leadership. He explained the choice to media representatives as follows:

I was seated next to the Archbishop Emeritus of São Paolo and Prefect Emeritus of the Congregation for the Clergy, Cardinal Claudio Hummes: a good friend, a good friend! . . . And he gave me a hug and a kiss, and said: "Don't forget the poor!" And those words came to me: the poor, the poor. . . . That is how the name came into my heart: Francis of Assisi. For me, he is the man of poverty, the man of peace, the man who loves and protects creation; these days we do not have a very good relationship with creation, do we? He is the man who gives us this spirit of

---

25. John Paul II, "Peace with God the Creator," 15.

26. Jame Schaefer, ed., "Introduction," in *Confronting the Climate Crisis: Catholic Theological Perspectives* (Milwaukee, WI: Marquette University Press, 2011), 9.

27. Ibid.

28. Jean-Louis Bruguès, "The Urgency of a Human Ecology," in *The Garden of God: Toward a Human Ecology*, Morciano Milvia, ed. (Washington, DC: Catholic University of America Press, 2014), xiii–iv.

peace, the poor man. . . . How I would like a Church which is poor and for the poor![29]

This explanation punctuates the interconnectivity of ecological concerns and concern for the poor. Francis carries the theme forward, culminating (as of this writing) with an extended treatment in the encyclical *Laudato Si'*. As described above, Francis hopes to strengthen the integral ecology, which includes the natural ecology, as well as human life, society, institutions, and culture. He describes a single "global crisis," which encompasses both the ecology and an array of human concerns, including poverty, political corruption, urban decay, overconsumption, and unchecked individualism (137–162). "Every violation of solidarity and civic friendship harms the environment" (142), Francis asserts, quoting Benedict XVI.[30] "It cannot be emphasized enough how everything is interconnected" (138).

Because of this interconnectivity, both Francis and the broader social tradition point to deep, cultural roots of the global crisis. Explanations cannot be simple; nor can solutions. Francis recommends no less than total collaboration, new thought paradigms, and spiritual conversion. Although the social tradition assigns responsibility to humanity without ambiguity,[31] it also examines a broad range of complex ethical, theological, and institutional considerations. These include a theology of life, legal frameworks, sin, charity, consumption, anthropocentrism, and individualism. Though each of these is essential, they are all complex and deserving of more space than this chapter allows. I focus here on another aspect, also essential, which Francis himself examines closely: technology and the dominant paradigm that corrupts its use.

The Technocratic Paradigm

Before parsing Francis's condemnation of technocratic mindsets, it is important to understand the tradition's ethical assessment of technology itself. The social teachings' treatment of technology is perhaps more nuanced than the casual observer would expect, and it aligns fully with the theological paradigm we have

---

29. Francis, "Audience to Representatives of the Communications Media: Address of the Holy Father Pope Francis" (Vatican, March 16, 2013), https://w2.vatican.va/content/francesco/en/speeches/2013/march/documents/papa-francesco_20130316_rappresentanti-media.html.

30. Benedict XVI, *Caritas in Veritate: On Integral Human Development in Charity and Truth* (Vatican, 2009), 51, http://www.vatican.va/holy_father/benedict_xvi/encyclicals/documents/hf_ben-xvi_enc_20090629_caritas-in-veritate_en.html.

31. For example, see Francis, *Laudato Si'*, 101.

examined thus far in this chapter. Specifically, technology—like all human-made phenomena—has extrinsic value to the extent that it supports universal flourishing. In other words, it is good insofar as it aligns with humanity's vocation to collaborate with God on behalf of the *telos* described earlier in this chapter (131). Technology is essential to the modern exercise of dominion; it must be subject to similar limits and goals (136). Such parameters are essential because, where technology extends humanity's power, it can also extend its harm.[32]

This line of thinking is present throughout the social teachings, and the Holy See's attention to it has intensified with the pace of technical development. Francis affirms the tradition in *Laudato Si'*:

> Technoscience, when well directed, can produce important means of improving the quality of human life.... Yet it must also be recognized that nuclear energy, biotechnology, information technology, knowledge of our DNA, and many other abilities which we have acquired, have given us tremendous power. More precisely, they have given those with the knowledge, and especially the economic resources to use them, an impressive dominance over the whole of humanity and the entire world. Never has humanity had such power over itself, yet nothing ensures that it will be used wisely (103–104).

In other words, it is critical to beware false equivalence between technological progress and human progress. Francis sounds an alarm, describing the mistake as dangerous—particularly where technical development outpaces the development of ethical frameworks to manage it. "We stand naked and exposed," he warns, "in the face of our ever increasing power, lacking the wherewithal to control it" (105). Technological interventions can be beneficial and may be necessary, but they are perilous in the absence of adequate ethical frameworks.

Unfortunately, that peril is status quo. Satisfactory deliberations are either absent or too complicated to keep pace with technological developments. Francis illustrates this point with an investigation of genetic modifications, illuminating the issue's complexity and outlining the type of analysis that should take place. He considers whether the interventions respect creation, how they support or undermine human flourishing, how they iterate throughout the ecosystem, whether they oppress or empower, and, finally, whether they invite the manipulation of human embryos. He calls for rigorous ethical analysis that incorporates not only scientific insight, but also the concerns of all stakeholders, for example in

---

32. Phillips, "Ethics and Economic Life," 136–137.

this case "farmers, consumers, civil authorities, scientists, seed producers, people living near fumigated fields, and others" (135). This case study demonstrates that modern technologies' complexity and rate of change present a serious challenge to humankind—a problem exacerbated by what Francis calls an "undifferentiated and one-dimensional" technocratic paradigm (136).

The technocratic paradigm fails in two aspects. First, rather than a synthesis of the many ideas, research, perspectives, and concerns of modern life, it offers us only narrow specializations. Francis writes,

> Fragmentation of knowledge proves helpful for concrete applications, and yet it often leads to a loss of appreciation for the whole, for the relationships between things, and for the broader horizon. . . . This very fact makes it hard to find adequate ways of solving the more complex problems of today's world (110).

Second, by exalting the scientific method and economic profitability, the technocratic paradigm has severed material development from ethics (106). It "tends to absorb everything into its iron-clad logic" and has thereby marginalized theological and ethical considerations (108). This effect occurs to the great detriment of the integral ecology (107–109).

The unmitigated sway of technocracy is incompatible with Catholic ideas of flourishing in four ways. First, its logic overrides the preferential option for the poor. A system that calculates worth wholly on the basis of quantitative advantages, such as efficiency and profitability, cannot also comprehend a love for the poor that transcends merit. Second, fetishization of quantity promotes hyper-consumption.[33] Like his predecessors, Francis condemns current levels of consumption as contributing directly to ecological crisis and, in particular, the suffering of the poor (51).[34] Third, technocracy legitimates ecological degradation. Because nature has no intrinsic value in this paradigm, it is valued only inasmuch as it is profitable. Mystery, awe, beauty, and revelatory power—the intrinsic value of nature as God's creation—are worthless currencies in a technocratic system. This view invites inordinate anthropocentrism and outsized

---

33. John Paul II outlined an ethic of consumption that employed Gabriel Marcel's distinction between "having" and "being," according to which the former is insufficient justification for consumption, especially when it undermines the latter. Gregory Beabout and Eduardo Echeverria, "The Culture of Consumerism: A Catholic and Personalist Critique," *Journal of Markets and Morality* 5, no. 2 (Fall 2002): 348. See also Phillips, "Ethics and Economic Life," 142–143.

34. See also paragraphs 25 and 55.

dominion, both of which unravel the compact between humanity and nature (117). Finally, the technocratic paradigm assigns no importance to communion with God, the highest good in the Catholic tradition. Its assessments of value are strictly earthbound. Each of these incompatibilities is related to the others—an interconnection that results in the complex web of crises humanity faces today.

A Call to Action

In response, Francis condemns the technocratic paradigm and calls for "a bold cultural revolution" (114):

> Ecological culture cannot be reduced to a series of urgent and partial responses to the immediate problems of pollution, environmental decay and the depletion of natural resources. There needs to be a distinctive way of looking at things, a way of thinking, policies, an educational programme, a lifestyle and a spirituality which together generate resistance to the assault of the technocratic paradigm (111).

More concretely, the pontiff criticizes the "weak responses" of wealthy nations (54), the abuse of political power to obstruct environmental healing (56), and the avoidance of urgent ecological realities (59). "Such evasiveness," he chides, "serves as a license to carrying [sic] on with our present lifestyles and models of production and consumption" (59). Constructively, he urges individuals to make lifestyle changes that will add political and economic pressure in favor of a flourishing integral ecology. He reminds consumers of his predecessor's wisdom: "Purchasing is a moral—and not simply economic—act" (206).[35] Further, he asks that believers educate others and themselves about the covenant between humanity, nature, and God—"at school, in families, in the media, in catechesis and elsewhere" (213).

However, Francis reserves the most prescriptive space for a discussion of the forms of dialogue that will be necessary to assess and solve the current crisis. He delineates five "major paths of dialogue" (163), listed here verbatim:

- Dialogue on the environment in the international community (164–175),
- Dialogue for new national and local policies (176–181),
- Dialogue for transparency in decision-making (182–188),

---

35. Benedict XVI, *Caritas in Veritate*, 66.

- Politics and economy in dialogue for human fulfillment (189–198), and
- Religions in dialogue with science (199–201).[36]

The last recommendation, religion in dialogue with science, returns us to the significance of technology in response to ecological crisis. Francis advises against the extremes of both those who embrace "the myth of progress" without qualification and those who reject all technical interventions with equal stubbornness (60). He calls for investment in research and a robust debate that incorporates fields of scientific knowledge, theological frameworks, and ethical theories (42, 60–61). Finally, he asks the media to facilitate this exchange of ideas (47).

Catholic Social Teachings in Dialogue

Francis's chapter on dialogue—the centerpiece of his constructive recommendation—concludes with the following wisdom: "The gravity of the ecological crisis demands that we all look to the common good, embarking on a path of dialogue which demands patience, self-discipline and generosity" (201). He calls scientists, theologians, and the representatives of ecological movements to engage in robust debate among themselves and with each other—always with the common good in mind. It therefore seems appropriate, as I conclude this chapter, to offer two suggestions for extending the Catholic social teachings in dialogue on flourishing.

Animal Welfare

First, the Church and Catholic scholars must employ the social teachings to better defend animal welfare. The tradition tempers human dominion with stewardship responsibilities, and it therefore offers some protection to nonhuman species. This teaching helps answer criticisms that the tradition's ethical framework is overly anthropocentric and therefore ecologically harmful. However, though the teachings consistently defend biodiversity and the preservation of nonhuman habitats, animal welfare concerns are less visible. While Francis gives an unambiguous condemnation of "needless" animal suffering (130), his analysis

---

36. Not only must religions be in dialogue with science, but the religions and the sciences must also dialogue among themselves. Francis issues this call for both interreligious and interdisciplinary dialogue: "The majority of people living on our planet profess to be believers. This should spur religions to dialogue among themselves for the sake of protecting nature, defending the poor, and building networks of respect and fraternity. Dialogue among the various sciences is likewise needed, since each can tend to become enclosed in its own language, while specialization leads to a certain isolation and the absolutization of its own field of knowledge" (201).

is brief, it does not address factory farming, and it fails to connect animal cruelty to the social teachings' larger critique of economic injustice.[37]

Fortunately, the social teachings contain seeds for deeper engagement on this issue. First, the historical inspiration of Francis of Assisi models a genuine fellowship with animals, according to which one may observe and enjoy the light of creation in each creature. The Holy See writes, "His response to the world around him was so much more than intellectual appreciation or economic calculus, for to him each and every creature was a sister united to him by bonds of affection. That is why he felt called to care for all that exists" (11). This joyful care can be an antidote to stewardship models that are strictly utilitarian, thereby protecting animals against cruel implementations. Second, the social teachings already examine the economic significance of farming and the special dignity of agricultural work.[38] In affirming the importance of farming and calling for farmworkers' rights, the tradition is logically able to—and should—address animal welfare in that context. Third, the social teachings' criticism of the technocratic paradigm should expand to incorporate agricultural industry. The scale of food production required for the world population is daunting, and the need for efficient solutions is real. However, it will be impossible to address this challenge in a meaningful way if profitability is the primary means of assessment. Nutritional quality, sustainability, accessibility, and both human and animal suffering must find a way into discourse about the future of agriculture.[39]

Population Growth

Population growth represents a second target for improved dialogue—and a challenging one, given its theoretical proximity to sexual ethics. Specifically, it is difficult to engage in dialogue on population growth without debating contraception, abortion, and non-procreative sexuality. However, sexual ethics do

---

37. This aspect of the social teachings has also surfaced in mainstream press. For example, animal rights activist Brian Friedrich, director of policy for Farm Sanctuary, uses the social teachings to make a case for vegetarianism. Brian Friedrich, "Does Pope Francis Practice What He Preaches? I Am Watching," *USA Today*, September 16, 2015, sec. Opinion, http://www. usatoday.com/story/opinion/2015/09/16/pope-francis-encyclical-meat-eat-planet-column/ 31858967/.

38. See John XXIII, *Mater et Magistra*, 123–156, and John Paul II, *Laborem Exercens*, 21.

39. Benedict XVI addresses the need for better methods of assessing agricultural technologies, but he includes a general call for respect rather than specific concern for animal welfare. He writes, "It could be useful to consider the new possibilities that are opening up through proper use of traditional as well as innovative farming techniques, always assuming that these have been judged, after sufficient testing, to be appropriate, respectful of the environment and attentive to the needs of the most deprived peoples." Benedict XVI, *Caritas in Veritate*, 27.

not encompass the Church's entire argument against a zero population growth (ZPG) solution. The social teachings also offer an important caution that population control alone will not mitigate the suffering of the poor, because it does not address the economic inequalities that are interconnected with the ecological crisis. Further, ZPG solutions may unfairly shift environmental responsibility to communities with both the least culpability for the current crisis and the least power to influence outcomes.

The Catholic Church will better sustain this discourse when it leads with the insights above, employing the preferential option for the poor as an entry point. Indeed, a subtle shift can be detected in the way Francis frames his response to population control in *Laudato Si'*. Whereas Benedict XVI's contemplation of the issue invokes arguments against non-procreative sex,[40] Francis steeps his argument in the language of economic justice (50). He writes of the ZPG movement, "It is an attempt to legitimize the present model of distribution, where a minority believes that it has the right to consume in a way which can never be universalized" (50). In doing so, he levels a forceful critique against population control movements, and his argument retains its persuasive impact with or without agreement on matters of sexual politics.

If the Church develops this line of argument, it can engage in productive discourse with liberative theories that criticize tensions between the option for the poor and Catholic sexual ethics. For an example relevant to ZPG, it is important to consider how the Catholic ban on contraceptive intervention impacts the poor, in particular women in developing nations. Katha Pollitt makes this point at *The Nation*, where she writes,

> The world, unlike Vatican City, is half women. It will never be healed of its economic, social, and ecological ills as long as women cannot control their fertility or the timing of their children; are married off in childhood or early adolescence; are barred from education and decent jobs; have very little socioeconomic or political power or human rights; and are basically under the control—often the violent control—of men.[41]

Pollitt's criticism points to a weakness in the option for the poor; namely, it must expand further to incorporate the full scope of oppression. The social teachings address both sexual ethics and the option for the poor, and they

---

40. Benedict XVI, *Caritas in Veritate*, 44.

41. Katha Pollitt, "If Pope Francis Really Wanted to Fight Climate Change, He'd Be a Feminist," *Nation*, September 9, 2015, http://www.thenation.com/article/the-popes-blind-spot.

articulate a theological connection, but they do not yet acknowledge any tension between them.

Intersectional considerations—analysis of the manifold and overlapping forms of oppression—would facilitate that expansion and promote the option for the poor in meaningful ways. In addition, an intersectional perspective would enhance both the content and the form of Catholic dialogue. However, at this time the Church remains burdened by its own marginalization of women, homosexuals, and transgendered persons. There exists a profound need for intersectional consideration *within the Vatican itself*, in order for the Church to fulfill the promise of its own ethic. This step would prepare the Church for the important and challenging work of developing intersectional analyses that are consistent with the Catholic theology of life.

In 2013, as Benedict XVI stepped down and Francis emerged as the new leader of the Church, I wrote, "Sexual ethics have . . . become a dominating controversy. This situation is particularly dire in the political sphere, where the sidelining of economic justice precludes the Church's full embodiment of its own principles, most notably the preferential option for the poor."[42] It has been exciting to witness Francis as he catalyzes a reorientation of sorts, insisting that Catholics—and all citizens of the world—view poverty and ecological degradation as urgent and related crises. Francis's theory of interconnectivity signals a theoretical opening for important intersectional considerations, which I hope the pontiff will incorporate in both his teaching and his institutional leadership. Not only do those considerations deserve priority, but focusing on them also opens doors for collaborative solutions from a more diverse group of participants. Differences will persist, and they will require, as Francis warns, "patience, self-discipline and generosity" (201). This is the hard work of discourse needed to solve complex problems, including flourishing in crisis.

---

42. Phillips, "Ethics and Economic Life," 171.

12 DIALOGUE

Rebecca J. Epstein-Levi and Jennifer Phillips

EPSTEIN-LEVI: One thing that our initial meeting brought out is that for both of us, our feminist commitments are major factors in shaping what each of us wrote in our respective chapters. Neither of us makes this particularly explicit in the chapters themselves—here, can we talk a bit more about how these feminist commitments play in?

For me, it has long been clear that ecology is a feminist issue, in that ecological catastrophes are likely to affect marginalized groups sooner and more severely. I also think about technology in feminist terms, and I strongly believe that, all other things being equal, technological advancements have been good for women as a class. This progress is directly true in terms of medical technology—modern obstetrics, for example, has made childbirth routinely survivable in a way that it simply wasn't previously, and modern birth control has allowed women to determine if and when to bear children. It is also true in a more indirect way: the more technology can reduce the drudgework needed to live day to day, the harder it is to saddle any one class of people with the brunt of that drudgework—something I think that Shulamith Firestone in *The Dialectic of Sex* (1970),[1] for example, articulated quite well.

PHILLIPS: I agree. However, I am also wary of the economic logic behind technology's development and use. For example, market-based pricing can restrict patient access to many life-saving drugs. Agricultural technologies entrench the power of corporate producers, to the detriment of small farmers and their communities. And the large-scale suffering of farm animals is ignored, in the name of efficiency. As I see it, the work of feminism

1. Shulamith Firestone, *The Dialectic of Sex: The Case for Feminist Revolution* (New York: William Morrow and Co., 1970; reprint, New York: Farrar, Straus, and Giroux, 2003).

is to name and uproot unjust power, in order to correct such injustices, and I consider the Catholic social teachings' critique of technocracy to be an example of such naming. With that critique and its constructive alternatives (the option for the poor, the universal destination of goods, and covenant), the Church directly challenges unjust economics.

At the same time, however, I feel a responsibility to declare the limits of a feminist alliance with the Catholic Church. This is an institution that has accumulated massive wealth, systematically marginalized women, offered calculated protection to abusers, and guarded its power at the expense of children. These problems strike me as critically important, because they exemplify the urgency of intersectional discourse, both *for* Church and *alongside* it.

EPSTEIN-LEVI: I think Jennifer's critiques of the technocratic paradigm are well taken, although I would argue that they are primarily economic claims rather than strictly technological ones. What we are really discussing here, then, is a question of just implementation. If we have technologies that we know can increase flourishing and reduce suffering, it's all the more appalling that they're being hoarded by the powerful and used against the marginalized. However, the most effective ways to challenge that power can sometimes turn out to be counterintuitive.

The case of genetically engineered (GE) crops is actually rather interesting here. The major economic critique of GE is that new varieties are increasingly controlled by a few large corporations, control that in turn affects the direction of research: modifications to already profitable large-scale, first-world crops are prioritized over and against modifications that would benefit the marginalized, like biofortification or engineering for drought or flood resistance. Ironically enough, however, the way in which the regulatory structure for GE crops has shaken out in the United States—in response, in part, to pressure from people who were concerned precisely about the potential risks of the technology—means that it's largely those corporations, rather than universities and other nonprofits, that have the means to pursue GE projects on a large scale. To me, that is an object lesson in the pitfalls of targeting a technology in and of itself rather than targeting the economic and social structures that control the technology's distribution and parameters of use.

I agree that the work of feminism is to name and disrupt unjust power structures. But I also think that we should be very careful about rejecting what are potentially very helpful tools for disrupting those power structures because others have wielded them unjustly. If the ill-use of technology has served to reinscribe disparities of power and wealth, it is also the case that the proper use of technology can help bridge them.

PHILLIPS: I appreciate Rebecca's reasoning here, particularly her caution that focusing overly on the *possibility* of unjust implementation may obstruct essential research. As the GE example illustrates, we should be skeptical of regulation that, however well meaning, hinders beneficial innovation. Further, because uncertainty is inherent to creative process, asking scientists and engineers for specific outcomes will almost certainly circumscribe their work. These errors, as Rebecca rightly points out, inhibit technology's potential for good.

The Catholic social teachings represent one approach for addressing the ethics of implementation without resorting to a restrictive technophobia. They distinguish between technology and a *technocratic paradigm*, the latter of which exalts development that is unexamined, or too closely aligned with business interests. The tradition rejects technocratic measures of value and calls for just production and distribution, but it does not censure technological development per se. This distinction creates space for the new, while protecting the priority of just implementation.

EPSTEIN-LEVI: Speaking more generally about just implementation, I think the pairing of my piece and Jennifer's is quite fortuitous, because each piece draws out something in the other that helps address that question more comprehensively. The methodology of my piece is primarily oriented toward the appropriate ways of interacting with units of meaning, and it can seem like a bit of a leap to go from there to questions of economic justice without any intermediate steps.

PHILLIPS: And this approach is very well done. Rebecca's chapter is a valuable example of how one might engage a religious tradition both to protect the creative impulse of science and assert its ethical context. She finds strong parallels within Judaism for the claim that technology is necessary (and good for women), and she defends them through close examination of her tradition. This methodology empowers her to advocate freely for technological development. For readers like me, working outside the Jewish tradition, it raises an important question: how can we, or should we, advocate for open-ended scientific development? Specific to the Catholic tradition (and particularly its condemnation of embryonic-stem-cell research), this question reinforces the need for intersectional discourse around the social teachings and the Catholic theology of life. Finally, in light of Rebecca's reasoning, Francis's appeal for dialogue between religion and science resonates as loudly as ever.

EPSTEIN-LEVI: Jennifer's piece, in contrast to my own, starts from broader questions of justice and moves from there into particular issues. I think that her account of Francis's critique of the "technocratic paradigm"—despite my own hesitations about some of the ways that critique is couched—is a good place to start bridging the gap between our respective foci: technology is good when it is put in the service of just goals, but that the adulation of technological progress for its own sake has serious moral pitfalls and can slide into idolatry if technological progress gets confused with human progress. So Jennifer's framework opens up a way to ask "why" questions about a given technology— to what ends are we interacting with units of biological meaning?

As it happens, I'd push back, at least mildly, against some of the critiques of what's referred to as the technocratic paradigm: I would note, for example, that the path between initial research and life-saving interventions is not always straightforward. It can be difficult to know how to incentivize the technologies that will help the most disempowered among us, because we often don't know which technologies those are until after we've done the research and development! Some of the technological advances that have had significant positive effects on human flourishing have occurred as a result of so-called pure research that didn't start out with an explicitly humanitarian goal in mind. I would also note that giving substantial weight to what Jennifer refers to as "qualitative advantages" is often essential to figuring out exactly *how* we're going to serve disadvantaged populations as best we can.

The important thing, though, is that Jennifer's framing puts my more narrow methodological focus into a broader moral context, in which we can start having that back-and-forth. This step is crucial, because I think it is absolutely true that we are susceptible to tunnel vision. For technophiles, that narrow view can mean failing to engage with broader questions of *telos*, or of who's serving whom. For justice-oriented critics of technology, tunnel vision can mean giving insufficient attention to the mechanics of exactly how, practically speaking, to achieve flourishing. We need to ask, on the one hand, "Why? For whom?" and, on the other hand, "How, exactly, is this going to work?"

PHILLIPS: The social teachings answer those questions by urging humanity to promote a deeper, theological purpose for technologies. They also warn that the relation between business and science is too closely bound, an "alliance" (*Laudato Si'²*, 54) that stands between science and its potential for good. Practically speaking, Francis calls for a robust dialogue between religion and science (199–201), in support of advances that are not only useful and justly distributed, but also implemented with care for unanticipated externalities.

As I have mentioned, I do not present the social teachings as the only approach to the challenge Rebecca describes. Instead, I offer them as a

---

2. Francis, *Laudato Si': On Care for Our Common Home* (Vatican, 2015), http://w2.vatican.va/content/francesco/en/encyclicals/documents/papa-francesco_20150524_enciclica-laudato-si.htm.

model. I admire their stubborn insistence on the centrality of economic justice, and I appreciate Francis's careful work to create positive, if conditioned, space for technology. This juxtaposition strikes me as a useful bridge between the errors of technophiles and technophobes. More concretely, I wonder, can they help us untangle the practical difficulty of just implementation? I appreciate that Rebecca presses on that idea; unfortunately, I don't have clear answers. Regardless, I agree with her emphatically on the question's importance. Practical implementation is as ethically significant as ever, and perhaps even more so, in the absence of concrete solutions.

EPSTEIN-LEVI: To be honest, I don't have an answer for how to address that difficulty, either—only that it has to be part of both ethical and technological discourse. I think the complications inherent in that question also point to the need for more and better dialogue between researchers/engineers and ethicists. The people who are actually working with the technologies we interrogate are the ones who are able to discuss the "nuts and bolts" that ethicists may elide. Conversely, ethicists, by the very nature of our discipline, can zoom out and remind researchers and engineers of the range of possible social consequences of their projects. But—and this is critical—those different foci will remain an unproductive dualism if genuine conversations don't actually occur.

PHILLIPS: I recently participated in a discussion on the academic (re-)engagement of religious studies PhDs who, like myself, work outside the Academy. This initiative strikes me as promising. PhDs working outside the Academy are uniquely qualified to facilitate the kinds of conversations that Rebecca and I both wish to see. They share a vernacular with those producing new scholarship, they understand applied context intimately, and they have influence in other sectors.

EPSTEIN-LEVI: I fully agree, and I think that science and technology research is an important site for this collaboration. Along the lines of hospitals employing ethics consult services, I think there could be a similar role for bioethics scholars in research labs.

PHILLIPS: Absolutely. I also see a glaring need for this kind of translation between ethical theory and business praxis. How might we claim meaningful roles for ethicists within the companies funding that research? Seats in venture capital boardrooms? Ethical expertise needs better traction at every stage of the business process, from research and development, to production, to pricing, to distribution, and so forth.

EPSTEIN-LEVI: As long as those conversations don't happen, or don't happen enough, more just implementation will continue to elude us.

V COMMUNITIES AND HUMAN AGENCY

13   FLOURISHING IN NATURE RELIGION

Chris Klassen

This chapter explores contemporary Pagan concepts of nature and proposes some suggestions for how Pagans may understand an ethic of flourishing. As a set of self-declared nature religions, contemporary Paganisms understand humans to be part of, rather than separate from, the natural world. Human flourishing is possible only in the larger context of the flourishing of all life. This concept does not, however, lead to clear rules on environmental ethics or social justice. Contemporary Pagans are typically suspicious of dogmas and rules. It is the cultivation of particular kinds of virtues that allow for cooperation and interdependence that is emphasized. By looking at how Pagans understand the natural world, what it means to see nature as sacred—to be a nature religion—we can begin to see the multiple ways that flourishing can be articulated and engendered.

A number of years ago I was involved in a research project in which I facilitated focus groups within contemporary Pagan communities on the topic of nature. Contemporary Paganism, sometimes called Neo-paganism, is a set of religious and spiritual traditions that draw inspiration from pre-Christian European ritual and mythology. These communities include groups trying to reconstruct modern versions of Norse, Celtic, Greek, and other European religions. Paganism also includes those who use elements from a variety of these pre-Christian traditions to create something admittedly new. Because of the variety of groups under the umbrella of Paganism, I often use the term Paganisms. Because of the agricultural base of pre-Christian Europe, most contemporary Pagans try to reclaim a connection to the earth and the seasons. They typically see their traditions as nature religions.

My project was motivated by the desire to find out from Pagans themselves what nature means to them in their practice of a nature religion—a topic that has been discussed frequently by scholars of contemporary Paganism. Because Paganisms overall privilege subjective experience and personal spiritual choice over sacred text and traditional doctrine, interviews and participant observation are the most effective ways to get a clear picture of Pagan belief and practice. I utilize Bron Taylor's category of dark green religion to explore some of the differing ways these contemporary Pagans understand nature and how nature is sacred.[1] I argue that though Taylor's typology is useful in charting out the variety of Pagan approaches to nature religion, ultimately, it is missing an important component: the relationship of human technological constructs to the rest of the natural world. By looking at how Pagans understand this relationship we can begin to understand their ideals of flourishing for human and other-than-human beings.

The focus groups I conducted were all held in southern and eastern Ontario, Canada. I led a number of discussions with groups consisting of people from the same tradition and a number consisting of people from a variety of traditions. In this chapter, I present discussions that come from a British Traditional Wiccan coven, a group of Reclaiming Witches, and a small group of feminist women who name themselves atheist Witches. I also draw on three multi-tradition groups, all of which were conducted at a pan-Pagan conference. One of these groups included two Wiccans and a Druid. Another group consisted of a Druid and a Goddess woman. The third group consisted of a Thelemic Wiccan, a Feri Witch, and a Druid. Some explanation of these traditions is in order.

British Traditional Wicca (BTW) is the term given to those who practice Gardnerian and/or Alexandrian Wicca.[2] Gerald Gardner is credited with the development of Wicca as a new religious movement in the 1950s in Britain. Alex Sanders was one of his students who branched off to slightly alter the tradition. In both Gardnerian and Alexandrian Wicca, tradition and lineage are very important. One must be initiated into the tradition and follow the ritual practice, as handed down from teachers with a line stretching back to Gardner. Both have various degrees of initiation, a practice that Gardner adapted from Freemasonry. Wicca, in this traditional sense, is focused on fertility in nature and humanity, emphasizing a balance of femininity and masculinity as idealized in the duotheism of Goddess and God. The term BTW is commonly used in Canada to refer to covens that follow these teachings, as a way to differentiate from those who use the term Wicca less specifically to refer to any kind of Pagan Witchcraft. Also, in Canada is the Wiccan Church of Canada, which is an Odyssean Wiccan tradition. Odyssean Wicca is an offshoot of Gardnerian Wicca. One of the

1. Bron Taylor, *Dark Green Religion* (Berkeley: University of California Press, 2010).

2. For readers who wish to learn more about Gardnerian, Alexandrian, and the other traditions and individuals mentioned in this section, I refer them to Rosemary Ellen Guiley, *The Encyclopedia of Witches, Witchcraft, and Wicca*, 3rd ed. (New York: Checkmark, 2008).

Wiccan participants in the multi-tradition focus groups followed this tradition. Thelemic Wicca is an incorporation of Wicca with the philosophy of "Thelema" proposed by Aleister Crowley: "Do What You Will." Thelemic Wicca also utilizes the practices of Hermetic Kabbalah and other Western magical traditions with presumed origination in ancient Egypt. All of these "traditional" forms of Wicca have similar beliefs about Goddess and God and highly structured ritual practices.

Feri Witchcraft, a form of initiatory witchcraft that is not based in Wiccan lineage, developed in the 1940s from the spiritual experiences of Americans Victor and Cora Anderson and focuses on an ecstatic experience of the divine. Feri Witchcraft is not to be confused with Fairies, though it does have a strong sense of the reality of the "fey."

Reclaiming Witchcraft, the tradition associated with popular author and Pagan teacher, Starhawk, developed in California in the 1980s as an amalgamation of Wiccan beliefs about deity and ritual, Feri experiences of ecstasy, feminist politics, anti-militarism, and environmentalism. Unlike traditional Wicca, Reclaiming is based on a non-hierarchical consensus-driven organizational structure and has developed theology that has moved away from dualistic feminine/ masculine ideas. Many feminist Goddess worshippers have also been highly influenced by Reclaiming, such as the Goddess woman in one of my focus groups, but they stick with the ideals of the feminine divine.

Druidry is a tradition that draws on pre-Christian Celtic traditions as well as the romantic movement of the 1800s that reintroduced druidry to the popular imaginary in Britain. It is focused on traditional virtues such as honor, as well as seasonal and other natural cycles. Druids value direct interaction with nature and the spirit(s) of nature. In many ways, modern Druidry is a reclamation of a British shamanism.

Flourishing and Dark Green Religion

All of the contemporary Pagan traditions mentioned above name themselves "nature religion." This focus on nature implies a concern for more than simply human flourishing, but a flourishing that encompasses the larger natural world. If flourishing involves a recognition of non-instrumental value, then for Pagans the other-than-human natural world deserves flourishing regardless of its value to human life. This belief does not mean flourishing cannot be valuable to human life, but that it is more than its relationship to humans. At the same time, our conception of our relationship to the rest of the natural world shapes our identities and our ethical framework. For example, Chris J. Cuomo's feminist ecological flourishing requires a consideration of "who we *are* in the world," not just what we do.[3] Our interactions with others (human and other-than-human nature) are determined by our perception of our being-in-relationship. This concept is key within many Pagan worldviews in which, like in Cuomo's philosophy, humans are part of, or interdependent upon, other parts of the natural world. This human flourishing is dependent upon that of the rest of nature.

Cuomo suggests relooking at feminist theorist Donna Haraway's thought project of the cyborg. Haraway is well known for her argument that who we are in the world is an integration of human and other-than-human, be it animal, plant, machine, microorganism.[4] Facing that knowledge of integration, or permeability, pushes us to consider a larger arena of flourishing. Recognizing our permeability limits our ability to see humans as distinct beings apart from the rest of nature. Environmental humanities scholar Stacy Alaimo names this permeability "trans-corporeality."[5] Alaimo draws on the work of Harold Fromm, who writes, "The 'environment,' as we now apprehend it, runs right through us in endless waves, and if we were to watch ourselves via some ideal microscopic time-lapse video, we would see water, air, food, microbes, toxins entering out bodies as we shed, excrete, and exhale our processed materials back out."[6]

Focusing our ethical standpoints solely on human flourishing is not only insufficient for sustaining our planet, but it is also insufficient for sustaining ourselves as permeable and trans-corporeal. Of course, Cuomo points out, there is no purity in this flourishing. In other words, "nature" is not ever, nor has ever been, pristine. This feminist ecological flourishing does not require a withdrawal of human intervention from the natural world. That very notion suggests that humans themselves are not part of the natural world. Political ecologist Thomas Crowley suggests the term ecosocial flourishing as one that avoids this false sense of separation and potential purity.[7] Human social justice is about ecological flourishing, even as ecological ethics is about human flourishing.

---

3. Chris J. Cuomo, *Feminism and Ecological Communities: An Ethic of Flourishing* (New York: Routledge, 1998), 81.

4. See Donna Haraway, "A Cyborg Manifesto: Science, Technology, and Socialist-Feminism in the Late Twentieth Century," in *Simians, Cyborgs, and Women: The Reinvention of Nature*, Haraway, ed. (New York: Routledge, 1991), 128–149.

5. Stacy Alaimo, *Bodily Natures: Science, Environment, and the Material Self* (Bloomington: Indiana University Press, 2010).

6. Fromm quoted in Alaimo, *Bodily Natures*, 11. See Chris Klassen, "Honoring the Duallium: Disability, Environmental Ethics, and the Religion of Gardening" *Cultural Studies* 16, no. 3 (2015): 243–252 for further discussion of Stacy Alaimo's concept of trans-corporeality and permeability in the context of nature and disability.

7. Thomas Crowley, "From 'Natural' to 'Ecosocial Flourishing': Evaluating Evaluative Frameworks," *Ethics and the Environment* 15, no. 1 (2010): 69–100.

Table 13.1 Chart to Clarify Bron Taylor's Four Categories

Supernaturalist Animism (Spiritual Animism): spiritual intelligences within natural entities	**Naturalistic Animism**: the importance of kinship with natural beings
Supernaturalist Gaian (Gaian Spirituality): the biosphere or universe has consciousness	**Naturalistic Gaian**: agnostic or nontheistic awe and wonder for the whole

Bron Taylor's concept of *dark green religion* ties this ecosocial flourishing with the sacred. According to Taylor, dark green religion flows "from a deep sense of belonging to and connectedness in nature, while perceiving the earth and its living systems to be sacred and interconnected." Dark green religion is further characterized by "a felt kinship with the rest of life," a "critique of human moral superiority," and a "metaphysics of interconnection," all drawing on elements of contemporary science.[8] Taylor divides his dark green religion into four categories, albeit loosely organized and with blurred boundaries (Table 13.1) These categories include two supernaturalist and two naturalist ways of approaching nature, as well as two different levels of talking about nature: animistic and Gaian. The animistic approach "refers to perceptions that natural entities, forces, and nonhuman life-forms have one or more of the following: a soul or vital lifeforce or spirit, personhood (an affective life and personal intentions), and consciousness, often but not always including special spiritual intelligence or powers." Supernaturalist versions of animism, or what Taylor calls Spiritual Animism, is about understanding there to be "some immaterial, supernaturalistic dimension" or spiritual intelligences within natural entities. Naturalistic Animism, on the other hand, is "skeptical of any immaterial dimension underlying the life-forms or natural forces" but is still an approach that sees kinship with the rest of the natural world as elementary and sacred.[9] An example Taylor gives of Spiritual Animism is Gary Snyder's animistic Buddhism, along with his focus on bioregionalism. Naturalistic Animism is more akin to the work of Jane Goodall with the chimpanzees.

Gaian approaches to dark green religion are more holistic and organicist than the animistic approaches. It is characterized by a belief that "the biosphere (universe or cosmos) [is] alive or conscious." The supernaturalist version, which

---

8. Bron Taylor, *Dark Green Religion* (Berkeley: University of California, 2010), 13.

9. Ibid., 15.

Taylor calls Gaian Spirituality, sees the biosphere or universe as having conscious-ness, "whether this is understood as an expression or part of God, Brahman, the Great Mystery, or whatever name one uses to symbolize a divine cosmos." The naturalistic version, Gaian Naturalism, is limited to a sense of "awe and wonder when facing the complexity and mysteries of life and the universe."[10] There is still a concern for the whole, and often a use of metaphors of the sacred, but overall an agnostic or nontheistic approach. An example Taylor gives of Gaian Spirituality is the ritual process of the Council of All Beings, developed by Buddhists Joanna Macy and John Seed. This process involves participants speaking for the earth and, at times, feeling possessed by the spirit of the Earth, or some other natural entity, and thus speaking in the earth's voice. Gaian naturalism is exemplified by the work of James Lovelock and his famous Gaian theory "which asserts that the biosphere functions as a self-regulating organism."[11]

In looking at Taylor's four categories: Spiritual Animism, Naturalistic Animism, Gaian Spirituality, and Gaian Naturalism, it seems obvious that con-temporary Pagans would qualify in one or more of these categories. In fact, on the basis of my analysis of the focus groups I conducted, I have found contemporary Pagans in Canada who fit in each of these four categories, making Taylor's dark green religion a powerful and essential tool for understanding Pagan concepts of nature and the sacred. Dark green religion, as defined by Taylor, in many ways is analogous to Crowley's ethical framework of ecosocial flourishing, whereby the flourishing of human and other-than-human nature is equally significant in the contemplation of ethical behavior. I now turn to some examples of how Pagans fit in these categories. These examples come from my interviews with Pagans in southern Ontario. While not representative of all Pagans, these voices show some of the variety found in Pagan discourses about the flourishing of nature, including humanity.

Pagan Examples of Dark Green Religion

Spiritual Animists see a sacred connection between humans and other species or life forms in the natural world. I see this category of dark green religion best exemplified by the discussion between Wiccan Bythor and Druid Holly[12] about "the spirit of place." Holly particularly emphasized that specific places have

---

10. Ibid., 16.

11. Ibid., 35.

12. Participants were given a choice to use their legal name, their Pagan name, or a pseudonym. The names used in this paper reflect those choices. All interviews took place in 2007 and 2008.

specific spirits, and even if one doesn't know the name of that spirit, it is important to "be respectful of the spirit of place." Bythor picked up on this theme and talked about the spirit of his garden that he honors both by working with the dirt and plants, and also by erecting a figurine to allow for a more direct, if symbolic, focus of devotion. Naturalistic animists also are concerned with place, but instead of giving specific places spiritual personalities, they tend to focus on the ecological significance and life force of beings in that place. For example, Reclaiming Witch Sumac talked about a "sense of place" that, for her, involved being ecologically literate, connecting to specific places and using spiritual practice as a way to do that. She further clarified that this connection involved "being conscious of the impact that certain decisions you make have on the earth, and to make that one of the important factors around making decisions." She did not see "spirit" or necessarily "consciousness" in the trees, for example. Yet, she recognized them as alive and playing a part in her life as much as she played a part in their lives and survival.

When we move to the Gaian examples, we get more concern with the whole organism of the earth, or even the whole cosmos or universe. An example of Gaian Spirituality in a Pagan perspective can be seen in Wiccan John's description of nature as "the cycle of things," including "day and night, the moon cycle, cycle of the year," which holds consciousness. While he also sees this consciousness in a more animistic way—he says, "the rivers, the forests are alive, they are part of nature and their consciousness is distinct from one another"—yet, he continues, "at the same time, together they form a greater consciousness along with us because we are part of nature too." An example of Gaian Naturalism would also focus on the whole but limit the sense of consciousness or connection to deity. For example, atheist Witch Margie talks of a spiritual connection to "the wonder inherent in the universe, scientifically." That wonder is amazing in itself; it doesn't need "jazzing up," as she says. Goddess woman Linnéa and Druid Judith also tended toward a Gaian naturalistic perspective in their discussion of nature as a "living organism" or "living dynamic" with which they interacted or were embedded.

We can see here examples of Pagans in each of Taylor's categories. However, keeping with the amorphous nature of these categories it is important to point out that the use of them is not exclusive. That is, even though, for example, Druid Holly definitely talks about the spirit of place in a way that fits nicely into Taylor's Spiritual Animism, that does not mean she does not fit into other categories as well. She also uses naturalistic animism at times to discuss her connection to birds, for example, as providing "an understanding of where I fit in the universe" rather than as spiritual beings themselves. And Wiccan Bythor, also clearly fitting within the Spiritual Animism category, also uses Gaian Spirituality in his emphasis on universal cosmology. So individual Pagans may use both Animistic and

Gaian approaches to nature as well as spiritual and naturalistic approaches. All of these approaches acknowledge the importance of the flourishing of nonhumans and they do so by according non-instrumental value to the other-than-human natural world.

Technology

While I like Taylor's typology for its usefulness in investigating differing approaches to nature, there is one element of inquiry that I find to be missing in his discussion. He emphasizes that dark green religion is characterized by a sense of kinship with the rest of the natural world, a recognition of human embeddedness in nature rather than separation from and particularly superiority over the rest of the natural world. However, he does not adequately address the question of the relationship between nature and culture and how one's perception of that relationship fits within the varying categories of dark green religion. In other words, from a dark green religious perspective, if humans are assumed to be a part of nature, then what parts of human invention fit within nature?

This question was central to my project as I directed the discussion to the relationship between nature and technology. I found a lot of difference of opinion here. But these differences can loosely be arranged in three categories: (1) technology as a human construct is also part of nature, as humans are part of nature; (2) technology and nature are definitely related, but there are important differences in how we talk of and relate to that which is human-processed and that which is not; (3) technology is not nature and is in fact at war with nature.

Those in the first category, who saw technology (any human-made tool or product) as part of nature, did not necessarily see technology as good. However, as Wiccan John pointed out, "I say we definitely are *in all aspects* part of nature. It's only our arrogance that makes us think we're not." Further to this, he says, "technology is just an outgrowth of us" using our "big brains and opposable thumbs." Thus, he sees technology "as being our children, in the same sense as we are the children of the gods." Wiccan Brigid and Druid Carol, in discussion with John, disagreed. Carol first defined nature as "everything which is not manmade." She waffles on this opinion, though. She later says that nature is everything, including the human and also something distinct from the human-made world, a response that would put her in the second category. "It is both," she stated. Brigid, in the third category, was clearer in her disagreement: "the definition of nature does, to a certain extent exclude humans, what humans have produced ... otherwise why have a separate word?" Furthermore, she states, "I definitely don't feel a spiritual connection to technology, whereas I feel a spiritual connection to nature." In the discussion with the BTW group I found the same kind of disagreement. Whereas Nuhyn claims that technology is not natural, "because it is manmade" and Jennett says the relationship between nature and technology is "a war," Oakwyndhr, Conleth, and Awnhy disagreed. Oakwyndhr states, "everything's nature" and thus, he also says all religions must be nature religions; the difference is in one's attitude toward nature. Furthermore, for Oakwyndhr, then, "technology is from the planet, therefore it is natural." Awnhy does not quite take as strong a position as Oakwyndhr on the naturalness of technology. However, she does see nature and technology in a sort of symbiotic relationship, though she sees that "for the moment [technology is] doing more harm than good."

If Taylor's dark green religion requires a perspective that humans be embedded in nature, then it seems logical that those of the dark green persuasion should also see human-made objects and tools as part of nature. However, it seems that many of the examples Taylor gives of dark green religion in fact have a hard time with this logical conclusion, as technology is typically demonized and nature deified or at least the "natural" is seen as morally superior to the processed. Taylor points specifically to the legacy of figures such as Henry David Thoreau and John Muir as forerunners of today's dark green religion, with their sympathetic position toward the wild and skeptical, and at times antagonistic, approach to human civilization. I do not believe that Taylor adequately addresses the inconsistencies these positions create.

I would like to propose an additional schema of categorization to augment Taylor's. Let us further define the greenness of dark green religion. Those whose perspectives follow the logic of human embeddedness and allow for technology or human products to be part of nature could be seen as dark metallic green religion. Those who deny technology any place within nature or see the two at war, and particularly favor the wild, are not metallic but rather a dark translucent green religion (more in character of the green places of the ocean). Those who see technology and nature as related, but with important differences in how we talk of and relate to that which is human processed and that which is not, are a more dark murky green. Thus, we could expand Taylor's categories from four to twelve: dark-metallic-green spiritual animism, dark-murky-green spiritual animism, dark-translucent-green spiritual animism, etc.

While this proposal is somewhat tongue in cheek, there is a need to make sense of this difference in ways of approaching the human place within the natural world, especially in light of human constructions of varying kinds of technologies. Without such contemplations, the possibilities of flourishing are stunted. The way human technology is understood ties to the understanding of the relationship between humans and the rest of nature. How we make and use technology points to how we understand ourselves, both ontologically and ethically. These understandings affect what we see as virtuous being and behavior. Elsewhere I have explored these virtues as articulated by these Pagan focus groups.[13] I used Louke van Wensveen's ethical typology as "a hermeneutical key to improve our understanding of the ways in which nature is rendered morally operative in existing eco-discourse."[14] The categories for understanding nature that I discovered in this analysis were Divinity, Living Organism, Seasonal Cycles, and Life and Death. These differing images of nature lead to a multiplicity of ethical virtues. I discuss these further in "Nature Religion and the Ethics of Authenticity."[15] One of these virtues is recognition of connection: the very basis of Taylor's dark green religion. For example, Goddess woman Linnéa framed this virtue in this way: "the thing that I'm dancing with right now, in terms of daily living, is to . . . not only make those kinds of [ecologically sustainable] choices, but to hold a consciousness in my mind about . . . what I have thought. Oh, 'this must be the nature of the world.' Oh well, okay, so now do more than think it; hold it there. Look through this, and see us all as alive with not gas in between us but living energy."

This connection, though, at times is in tension with a virtue of balance. As BTW Jennett suggests, "it's a delicate balancing act to live well and not pollute, but you're still at some point going to have to pick and choose what you do. You try your hardest to keep everything in balance and not use too much of the wasteful products like [Oakwyndhr] says, the water bottles, and recycle and everything. But it's still a hard road, because you can't always be 100%." Further, if connection is romanticized, then it comes into conflict with the virtue of knowledge. This contradiction was articulated by a number of my participants in their critique of some Pagans who think of nature as all good and loving. The most poignant articulation of this critique came from Druid Judith, who recounted her experiences of talking with "fairly urban, fairly young, fairly middle-class people that talk about . . . run[ning] through the woods naked. You can hurt yourself! You're going to trip and your feet are going to hurt and the branches flick into your genitals!" The image of nature as Life and Death is highly relevant

13. Chris Klassen, "The Role of Nature in the Construction of Ethics: A Study among Contemporary Pagans in Ontario, Canada," *Journal for the Study of Religion, Nature, and Culture* 7, no. 1 (2013): 49–64.

14. Louke van Wensveen, *Dirty Virtues: The Emergence of Ecological Virtue Ethics* (Amherst, NY: Humanity Books, 2000), 147.

15. Chris Klassen, "Nature Religion and the Ethics of Authenticity: 'I Won't Speak for All of You,'" *Environmental Ethics* 33 (2011): 295–305.

here. Both Judith and Linnéa emphatically point out that "nature kills." Without knowledge about nature, in a scientific sense, a naive pursuit of connection with nature can lead to problematic behavior.

Conclusion

Flourishing of nature, including the human, cannot ignore the position of human-made technology as a significant player within an ecosocial ethical framework. Including this technology as a part of nature, by extension, limits the automatic assumption of the moral good of any parts of nature. Excluding this technology from an understanding of nature, while not necessarily leading to applying a moral position to nature, does tend to come from a more romantic place in which "nature" is pure. Both Haraway and Alaimo, as we have seen, prefer a more complex, blended, permeable view of the human, nature, and technology. The ethical virtues articulated by the contemporary Pagans in my focus groups tended toward a recognition of the permeability of all of nature (connection) and the importance of understanding the rest of the natural world (knowledge) in realistic and scientific ways. But they did not lead to universal agreement on technology, evidence perhaps of this issue's complexity and the intractability of dualistic thinking. In the end, Pagan reflection on this issue did not lead to specific ethical rules. Pagans do not like being told what to do. It does, however, lead to ethical frameworks, and an operative ethos or worldview, which seems to help Pagans think beyond themselves as they make daily decisions about how to *be* in the world. Ecosocial flourishing requires a deliberation on the context of the moment and possibilities of the future; it does not start from the position that non-mediated nature (if there is still, or ever was, such a thing) is morally superior to human-mediated nature. My discussions with contemporary Pagans in Ontario show that there are various ways Pagans see their place, as humans, in the natural world and the interaction between their human actions and the rest of nature. Seeing technology as natural does not mean seeing technology as good or having an anthropocentric worldview. It does, however, lead to differing approaches to thinking about possible moral issues, compared with a perspective that sees technology as always already unnatural.

14 INTERFAITH ENVIRONMENTALISM AND UNEVEN OPPORTUNITIES TO FLOURISH

Amanda J. Baugh

On Wednesday nights in 2010, six women—five members of a suburban Chicago Unitarian Universalist congregation and a friend who attended a Catholic church—came together to till the earth their community garden. Calling themselves the Purple Radishes, the women quietly greeted one another as they arrived, before heading to the shed to collect tools they would need for that evening's work.[1] Having already discussed their tasks over email, each week the women spent the next hour completing their assigned duties—pulling weeds, planting seeds, harvesting lettuce, thinning carrots—in relative silence. Then they put away their tools, brought coolers of food and bottles of wine from their cars, and gathered around a picnic table to enjoy an evening of conversation and friendship in their community garden.

Twenty miles away from the garden, in the village of Bridgeview, members of the Mosque Foundation washed their hands for daily prayer by using water heated by the sun. They prayed in a room that featured natural light and recycled carpet, and they periodically heard sermons highlighting connections between environmental sustainability and the teachings of Islam. Recycling bins and energy-efficient light bulbs were bountiful throughout the building, and the congregation's Green Committee ensured that sustainable living tips appeared in each of the mosque's monthly newsletters.

The Purple Radish gardeners and members of the ecofriendly mosque both enacted religious environmental projects through partnerships with Faith in Place, a Chicago-based interfaith environmental nonprofit. Established in 1999 as a project of the Center for

---

1. The names of all individuals interviewed (and the gardening group itself) have been changed to respect their privacy.

Neighborhood Technology, an urban sustainability think tank, Faith in Place incorporated as an independent nonprofit in 2003. Its stated aim was "to help religious people become good stewards of the earth."[2] The organization was expressly interfaith, listing Protestants, Catholics, Muslims, Jews, Hindus, Buddhists, Baha'is, and Zoroastrians among its congregational partners. It achieved great acclaim among community partners because it had successfully integrated participants who were diverse in terms of race, ethnicity, and class into its environmental projects. Faith in Place aimed to help congregations develop a "culture of conservation" in which people across the community would understand earth stewardship as an important issue that was also a matter of faith.[3] Focusing on food, energy, water, and policy, it offered worship resources, educational programming, and practical support for green infrastructural projects. Faith in Place leaders wanted participants to make the environment a fundamental concern for their congregations throughout the year—not just on Earth Day—by connecting environmental degradation to matters of faith and presenting earth stewardship as central to religious life.[4]

Between 2006 and 2011, I conducted ethnographic research among Faith in Place leaders and participants in order to investigate whether and how Chicago religious groups were "going green." Within the organization, I spent hundreds of hours volunteering in the office; attending meetings with the staff, board, and collaborators; preparing for fundraisers; and helping with database management, filing, correspondence, and other office duties. Between 2009 and 2011 I also conducted extensive fieldwork outside the office, attending worship services and meetings of "green teams" at partner congregations, participating in earth-themed Bible studies, visiting community gardens, and joining Faith in Place staff members at every meeting and event where I was welcome. My research also included recorded, semi-structured interviews with thirty-six people involved with Faith in Place.

In this chapter I discuss the religious environmental projects of two Faith in Place partners, the Purple Radish gardeners and the Mosque Foundation participants, to consider how different groups might flourish through their involvement with interfaith environmentalism. As they combined principles of

---

2. http://www.faithinplace.org.

3. Clare Butterfield, "Book Proposal for *Faith in Place, Faith in Practice: A Field Guide to Bringing Congregations into Right Relationship with the Earth*" (April 30, 2007), 30.

4. The first of Faith in Place's "Ten Tips" for organizing environmental ministries, summarized in an introductory talk staff members presented to new congregations, was "connect green efforts to your faith." When elaborating this point, staff members emphasized the importance of connecting environmental values to the central worship life of the church so that the environment was on people's minds throughout the year (field notes August 26, 2008).

environmental stewardship and justice, along with interfaith cooperation by virtue of working with Faith in Place, these projects seem to represent interfaith environmentalism at its best. But closer examination demonstrates that the outcomes of interfaith environmentalism do not always center on the environment, and the opportunity to flourish is not shared equally by all.

Community and Meaning in a Unitarian Garden

The Purple Radish gardeners met at "Menu for the Future," a discussion class on sustainable food held in 2009 at their Unitarian church.[5] As one of Faith in Place's original partners, the congregation supported a range of projects to advance environmental sustainability in the church's operations and among its members. The community hosted the "Menu" discussion group to help participants learn about the negative effects of modern industrial agriculture on communities, health, and the environment. As the class was drawing to a close, six participants wanted to initiate a project that would respond to the problems they had discussed over the previous weeks, so they decided to establish a community garden. Unlike the format of many community gardens, which are divided into separate, individually managed plots, the Purple Radishes decided to work collaboratively, planting together and sharing the work and the harvest. They worked out an arrangement to use the backyard space in an alley behind a local cafe, and began meeting to work together in the garden on Wednesday nights. Throughout the rest of the week the women took turns coming to the garden to water, harvest, or take care of any other time-sensitive matters, and some liked to come to the garden just to hang out. After meeting two of the Purple Radishes through my research at Faith in Place, I inquired about conducting fieldwork in their garden. They invited me to join their weekly gardening rituals in the spring and summer of 2010. I also conducted formal interviews with five of the women.

When I asked the Purple Radishes about their reasons for starting the garden, they all pointed to food concerns they had discussed during "Menu for the Future." Two of the women, Doris and Andrea, wanted to grow their own food because it was overwhelming to get all the information they sought before purchasing commercially produced food. Teresa, a mother of four, joined the garden because it was related to her passion for providing healthy, fresh food for her

5. The class, called "Menu for the Future," was one of nine discussion courses created by the Northwest Earth Institute (NWEI). Although the class was hosted at a church, the curriculum was not specifically designed for religious congregations. Intended for groups at workplaces, schools, neighborhoods, community centers, and faith communities, NWEI courses include a workbook with readings and discussion guides for self-facilitated small groups.

family, and Jean participated in the garden because she did not want to support corporate food production.

As I spent time with the Purple Radishes, however, I saw how the garden offered them much more than sustainable food. When the women described their religious environmental project, they spoke as much about creating community as they did about growing food, and I saw how their time in the garden became a source of community, identity, and meaning. Both Marilyn and Teresa signed up for the "Menu" class not really to gain new insights about food, they revealed, but to make connections with people. Marilyn had already taken the course two times, but she was relatively new to the Chicago area and she signed up to meet others, "knowing the class would attract like-minded people."[6] Teresa, the group's only Catholic, learned about the class from a friend who attended the Unitarian church. Teresa already had extensive knowledge about sustainable food and even ran a small organic grocery store before her children were born, but she took the class because she wanted to find people as concerned as she was about food quality. Doris expressed great joy for the community that unexpectedly grew out of the garden, telling me that the garden offered "an amazing sense of camaraderie and purpose, and sort of a joy of life."[7]

All six Purple Radishes were middle- to upper-middle class, college-educated, and white. They were cognizant of their privileged social locations, and they wanted to help others through their work in the garden. As a former activist in the feminist, civil rights, and urban renewal movements, Marilyn hoped the garden could become an extension of those social-justice-oriented endeavors, and Jean told me that the group planned to donate some of their harvest to a local food bank. In addition to providing food for the hungry, the Purple Radishes sought to share their knowledge and experiences through educational outreach. In 2010 they offered a free gardening class at the YMCA, set up an information booth at a local street festival, and shared gardening lessons through a blog. The Purple Radishes recognized that they had privileges that were unavailable to those who were less fortunate, and part of their experience in the garden involved a desire to share its bounty with others.

Garden Spirituality

The garden was not officially tied to the women's church, but five of the six gardeners shared a church community and religious worldview, and those five

---

6. Interview September 29, 2010.

7. Interview September 14, 2010.

women generally understood their gardening as an extension of their religious worlds.[8] "Respect for the interdependent web of all existence of which we are a part" is one of the seven principles that Unitarian Universalist congregations affirm, and the women referenced that principle as they told me about their experiences in the garden. Jean explained that the garden was related to her religion because it expressed Unitarian principles: "It's about respecting the earth and dignity for all, and that we are all entitled to the goodness of everything, the goodness of the earth, the goodness of the experience that we get, with no judgment about what that is for people."[9] Marilyn invoked the Seventh Principle in her description of an improved world. The benefit of being in the garden, she explained to me, "is in that little seed. So if we nurture the place for that little seed to grow, it grows in us as well. That, to me, is the Seventh Principle of Unitarianism, that we're completely connected to this."[10]

The other Unitarians also tied the garden to the Seventh Principle of Unitarianism. But they spoke more in terms of a spiritual experience that developed in the garden, related to making things right in the world and being a better person. In an overview of the garden that she wrote for a community newsletter, Andrea explained that the group was "not officially linked to any religion or organization." But the women did meet at a class through their church, she conveyed, "and we do consider gardening a nondenominational spiritual experience."[11] The spiritual experience the Purple Radishes described stemmed from an understanding of nature in general, and the garden in particular, as something greater, an expression of what's "really real."[12] As Doris explained it succinctly, the garden "transcends the silliness of human struggles, whatever they might be."[13] Marilyn talked about the garden in almost animistic terms, describing it as representative of something greater, and Andrea said the nature she experienced in the garden was "a manifestation of the mysticism of the universe."[14] Adding their own

---

8. Teresa saw it as an expression of her spirituality but adamantly did *not* see it as part of her Catholic faith.

9. Interview April 13, 2010.

10. Interview September 29, 2010.

11. "Galaxy Café" Newsletter, June 2010.

12. Anthropologist Clifford Geertz describes the "really real" as a wide reality that corrects and completes the realities of everyday life. A defining concern of religious perspectives is to accept those wider realities. Clifford Geertz, *The Interpretation of Cultures* (New York: Basic Books, 1973).

13. Interview September 14, 2010.

14. Ibid.

sense of spirituality to the expressly environmentalist language of the Seventh Principle, Doris, Marilyn, and Andrea all described the garden as a sacred space where they experienced something greater than themselves.

If the garden offered the Purple Radishes a place to create and maintain their spiritual selves, they ensured that their garden spirituality did not include the aspects of traditional religion they rejected. The five Unitarian Purple Radishes all found their religions as adults, after rejecting their cradle religions and engaging a process of religious seeking. The spirituality they created in the garden was shaped by their negative memories of the religions they rejected. Jean, a devout Lutheran as a child and young adult, found her way to Unitarianism after dabbling in Wicca and "back to the earth" spirituality.[15] When she told me that the principles of the garden were "very Unitarian," she qualified her statement by saying, "but we're not out to recruit. We don't really say. We're just the Purple Radishes."[16] Implicit in this statement is her association of "bad religion" with evangelizing. Andrea also brought negative associations with conservative Christianity to her experiences in the garden. Andrea's most vehement criticism of Christianity had to do with people who purported to be religious but whose Christianity was superficial, and she wanted to ensure that she did not replicate that hypocrisy in the garden. To align her daily practices with the values she cultivated with the Purple Radishes, Andrea quite smoking and drastically reduced her reliance on beauty products because, as she explained, "If anyone ever saw me smoke then I'd be the biggest hypocrite on the face of the planet. And worse than what people think of me, I'm living with a conflict in my values." Andrea and the other Unitarian gardeners combined their Unitarian principles with both positive and negative memories from the past to construct the garden as a sacred space where they came together and flourished.

Inspiration without Invitation

As they explained their mission of growing food and modeling an alternative lifestyle of spiritual attunement with nature, the Purple Radishes expressed hope that their project would lead others to challenge the mainstream food supply. "I hope we're an example to others and we inspire them," Andrea told me during an interview. But the actual experience of gardening became a sacred ritual exclusive to these six women, and this was not a component of their experience that they were willing to share. When the Purple Radishes came together in their garden

15. Interview April 13, 2010.
16. Ibid.

on Wednesday nights, they created a shared world that counteracted the negative trends they saw in mainstream American society. During the rest of the week, the women themselves participated in some of those negative trends, as they were caught up in the mundane activities of daily life—commuting to work, caring for children and grandchildren, watching television, running a business, preparing meals for their families. But in the garden they experienced a different world, where neighbors knew intimate details of one another's lives, where communities shared values and lived in harmony, and where hearty, healthy food came straight from the ground. By returning to that ideal world each Wednesday night, the women supported one another in their endeavors to live more sustainably and create an ideal world in the larger community.[17]

But even as they wanted to serve as a model for an ideal world that included everyone, the Purple Radishes' gardening experience was also marked by physical and social isolation. The garden was physically bounded on three sides: a wooden fence to the north, a chain-link fence to the south, and a building to the east. On Wednesday nights the women's cars lined the edge of the alley immediately adjacent to the garden so that their group was fully closed off from the surrounding neighborhood. To be sure, this physical separation of the garden was a matter of practicality and not specifically designed to isolate the Purple Radishes. The fence surrounding the garden fulfilled the very important function of protecting fragile produce from unwanted critters. The wall of cars that isolated the women from traffic in the alley was simply a matter of convenience. Nonetheless, these physical features contributed to the production of the garden as a particular kind of space. In contrast to many community gardens that are designed to be welcoming to passersby, the location of the Purple Radish garden created a more private experience for the women.[18]

In addition to the physical separation of the garden from surrounding space, through their gardening ritual the women socially isolated themselves from the rest of the local community. While they occasionally welcomed a visitor to stop by to talk or take some tomatoes from the garden, full membership in the group was closed to outsiders. When the garden emerged from the "Menu for the Future" course, all twelve class members were invited to participate. After that, when others expressed interest in joining the group, the Purple Radishes turned them away. Even my involvement as a researcher posed problems for the group's self-understanding and

---

17. My discussion of the gardening ritual is influenced by Adam B. Seligman, *Ritual and Its Consequences: An Essay on the Limits of Sincerity* (Oxford and New York: Oxford University Press, 2008).

18. Laura J. Lawson, *City Bountiful: A Century of Community Gardening in America* (Berkeley: University of California Press, 2005), 3.

helped highlight their exclusionary boundaries, which they reluctantly admitted to themselves after experiencing my presence for two weeks. Originally, the group had invited me to join them in the garden every week. But after two weeks they requested that I join them once a month instead. "We don't want to be cliquish," Jean told me as she hesitantly shared their decision over the phone, "but actually we kind of are." They welcomed me to continue spending time with them because that advanced their mission of education and sharing their vision with others. But my interrupting presence clarified for them some boundaries for the group, and they were a group of six women who functioned best on their own.

The Purple Radish gardeners created a religious environmental project that enabled them to experience a flourishing world as they wished to see it, at least for a few hours every week. While the ostensible purpose of their project was to create a source of sustainable food, the women returned to their garden every week to engage in a sacred ritual in which they could reinforce their ideal selves— in the company of a like-minded community whose experience were marked by privilege—and cultivate visions of community that they wished to maintain during the rest of the week.

Connecting Environmentalism and Civic Identity

While the Purple Radishes sought to distance themselves from certain aspects of mainstream society through their time in the garden, religious environmentalism at the Bridgeview Mosque Foundation was connected to community efforts simply to fit in as "good" Americans. Located in the village of Bridgeview, thirteen miles southwest of Chicago's Loop, the Mosque Foundation served more than 50,000 Muslims. Mosque leaders developed a set of environmental initiatives in close partnership with Faith in Place, beginning in 2008, when they installed a solar water heating system and became the first solar-powered mosque in the United States. Building on community enthusiasm around the solar panels, the mosque developed additional environmental initiatives in the following years, establishing a "green team," developing environmental programming for youth, introducing practices for a "green Ramadan" and incorporating ecofriendly meas-ures in their renovations. The mosque's greening initiative received significant coverage in the local media, including stories on public radio and in the *Chicago Tribune*, and garnered the attention of then Lt. Governor Patrick Quinn, who honored the mosque with an "environmental hero" award in 2008.[19] I learned about the mosque's environmental programming through my fieldwork at Faith

19. Alexandra Salomon, "Bridgeview Mosque Gets Solar Panel," WBEZ91.5, August 1, 2008; Heidi Stevens, "Remarkable Woman: Clare Butterfield," *Chicago Tribune*, April 6, 2012; "Lt.

in Place, and participated in meetings where the Muslim outreach coordinator discussed her plans to work with the mosque. Additionally, I attended events that Faith in Place cosponsored with the mosque and conducted interviews with community leaders.

Although populated primarily by second- and third-generation Americans, the Mosque Foundation experienced widespread prejudice and suspicions of terrorism after 9/11, and in 2008 *The Wall Street Journal* published an article that characterized the mosque as "fundamentalist-controlled."[20] The mosque's environmental programming was featured prominently in the community's response. In a post on the political blog 538, Rany Jazayerli, a respected member of the mosque community, responded:

> The consensus of the vast majority of Muslims in Chicago is that the mosque is not a fundamentalist anything, which is why it has such a large membership. Some of the mosque's more recent projects include donating a riverfront garden to the city of Chicago and becoming the first mosque in the country to run on solar power.[21]

Jazayerli offered the mosque's greening projects as evidence in the informal cultural court. While *The Wall Street Journal* projected an image of the mosque as engaged in political activity that promoted violence, Jazayerli suggested that the mosque's participation in environmentalism offered self-evident proof that its leaders could not be fundamentalists.

In a similar rhetorical move, Ibrahim Abdul-Matin, author of *Green Deen: What Islam Teaches about Protecting the Environment*, offered a related piece of advice at an event for Muslim youth that Faith in Place co-sponsored in 2011: "When people talk about terrorism, change the subject to water."[22] Rather than allowing fears of terrorism to dominate discussions about Islam, Abdul-Matin advised, the youth needed to demonstrate they were just like other Americans and shared their concerns about major environmental issues that affected every human. Similar to Jazayerli, Abdul-Matin proposed that Muslims could embrace environmental identities as a way to challenge discourse that

---

Governor Quinn Honors 26 Residents with Environmental Hero Awards," http://www.scarceecoed.org/about-us/awards/81-lt-governor-quinn-environmental-hero-award.html.

20. Glenn R. Simpson and Amy Chozick, "Obama's Muslim-Outreach Adviser Resigns," *Wall Street Journal,* August 6, 2008.

21. Rany Jazayerli to FiveThirtyEight: Politics Done Right, August 8, 2008.

22. Field notes February 27, 2011.

linked Islam and terrorism. He instructed youth to share their environmental concerns with others as a positive way of relating to those who continued to perceive Muslims as un-American.[23]

The mosque leaders I interviewed also discussed the solar panels in the context of a positive civic identity, but that was not their primary explanation. When I asked about the mosque's environmental programming, the leaders first told me about passages from the Qur'an and *hadith*. Dr. Tahir Haddad, a member of the mosque's board of directors, explained that numerous Islamic sources supported caring for the earth. On the basis of the Qur'an, he told me, "We believe that we are the descendants of Adam and Eve, and one of our main responsibilities on earth is to protect earth, protect creation, and not to shed blood or to ruin the earth."[24] Haddad went on to offer numerous examples from *hadith* that emphasized protecting trees, conserving water, and avoiding overconsumption.[25] Sheikh Eshaal Karimi, an imam at the mosque, also told me that environmental concerns were central to his faith. "I just need to go and bring out the references in the Holy Quran and the tradition of the Prophet, and compare it with what is happening around us," he explained. "And you see it's matching in all aspects."[26] Aligning their viewpoints with constructive scholarship in the area of Islam and ecology, mosque leaders indicated that environmental values lay at the very heart of Islam.[27] A desire to live out what they considered basic religious teachings offered one explanation for these men's religious environmental involvement.

When I asked about the origins of the mosque's greening initiative, however, conversations revealed an additional set of motivations. It is no surprise that Jazayerli offered the mosque's solar panels and lakefront garden as evidence

---

23. Interestingly, Abdul-Matin goes to great lengths in his book to establish himself as an American. He writes, "I am an American whose roots go back to the Revolutionary War, and this book is therefore inevitably centered on people and places in North America. . . . I am simply presenting the perspective I know from being born and raised in the United States, and I hope these domestic examples will resonate with people living in other countries as well." Ibrahim Abdul-Matin, *Green Deen: What Islam Teaches about Protecting the Planet*, 1st ed. (San Francisco: Berrett-Koehler, 2010), xxii.

24. Interview March 3, 2011.

25. Ibid.

26. Interview June 4, 2010

27. See, for example, Seyyed Hossein Nasr, *The Encounter of Man and Nature: The Spiritual Crisis of Modern Man* (London,: Allen and Unwin, 1968); Mawil Y. Izzi Dien, "Islamic Environmental Ethics, Law, and Islam," in *Ethics of Environment and Development*, J. Ronald Engel and Joan Gibb Engel, eds. (London: Bellhaven, 1990). Although Haddad and Karimi offered viewpoints that aligned with constuctive "Islam and ecology" scholarship, both men indicated that they developed these ideas straight from Islamic sources, not from secondary literature. Karimi, moreover, indicated that he rarely read material about Islam written in English.

to counter accusations of fundamentalism, because the mosque's leadership developed its green projects with their community's public image in mind. When I asked Haddad about the origins of the mosque's greening initiative, he immediately spoke of the September 11th terrorist attacks. Before 9/11, he told me, the mosque prioritized issues typical of immigrant communities such as maintaining certain values and taking care of their youth. As they experienced prejudice in the aftermath of 9/11, however, they sought ways to expand their focus and demonstrate that they were "good neighbors" who cared about Muslims and non-Muslims alike. To that end, the mosque opened a food pantry to serve both Muslim and non-Muslim families in need, joined an Illinois coalition to work on comprehensive immigration reform, and developed an interfaith relationship with the Chicago archdiocese. In addition, the board discussed taking steps to protect the environment as another way for the Muslim community to "be more relevant, and take more of a leadership role in general affairs of the community at-large, not only focused on what's happening within the congregation, but also focused on issues that touch every American."[28] Karimi offered a similar explanation for the origins of their green initiative as an effort to participate in projects important to many Americans: "When Dr. Haddad started as president, this idea came in reference to the movement that was taking place nation-wide."[29] Both of these men talked about environmentalism in terms of participating in a movement that was important to a broader American community.

Complicating "Pure" Intentions

Toward the end of my interview with Haddad, he asked me what I planned to write about Muslims. I told him that I wanted to convey the complex motivations that different people brought to their environmental practices, so I found it interesting that he had immediately talked about 9/11 when I asked about the origins of the mosque's green programming. Having encountered a wide variety of motivations that contributed to green behavior in other settings, I was not surprised that he offered reasons that extended beyond concern for the earth. But Haddad wanted to assure me that his community's greening initiative was motivated by pure intentions. He paused for a moment as he thought about a way to clarify his remarks. "Maybe it started with that [being a good neighbor]," he finally responded, "but it's not like that anymore. I'm against showing people that we are 'good Americans,' and because of that we are taking care of the

28. Interview February 3, 2011.

29. Interview June 4, 2010.

environment. This is not something that I believe in. I believe that unless you are genuine and you believe that this is your role in society, then it will not be successful."[30] Haddad explained to me that intentions are of utmost importance in Islam, and good deeds are nullified if not undertaken with positive intentions. If you give charity to the poor because you want people to say you are generous, or if you pray to God just to look pious, those actions do not count. Actions with impure intentions, Haddad told me, "may succeed for a certain period of time, but eventually you will not be successful. People will discover that you are not genuine, you are a hypocrite, if your intention is not right. And secondly, God will not accept your work, and that's the most important thing."[31]

Haddad wanted to assure me of his community's environmental authenticity: they were not simply using environmentalism for the instrumental purpose of generating positive civic identity. But members of the Mosque Foundation engaged with religious environmentalism in particular ways that had to do with the interests and needs of their own community, as did every other community that engaged with the movement. For the Purple Radishes, working in a community garden offered a way to advance environmental sustainability while *also* helping them achieve ideal formations of themselves. And for members of the Mosque Foundation, installing solar panels and promoting green practices offered a way to decrease their carbon footprints while *also* marking them as civically engaged Americans.

Flourishing in Interfaith Environmentalism

The contributors to this book have grappled with questions about flourishing among humans and nonhumans, and the possibilities of mutual flourishing for each group. It would seem that religious environmental projects through an organization like Faith in Place are aimed at achieving such a balance—finding a way for humans and the rest of the earth community to flourish at the same time. But closer examination of the goals and outcomes of these projects seems to indicate that the flourishing of the earth community is more of a byproduct than the primary goal. In a major sociological investigation of American religious environmental groups, Stephen Ellingson finds that the primary goal of these groups is to help people live out their religious values more faithfully, while actual environmental outcomes are somewhat beside the point.[32] On the basis of its mission

---

30. Interview February 3, 2011.

31. Ibid.

32. Stephen Ellingson, *To Care for Creation: The Emergence of the Religious Environmental Movement* (Chicago: University of Chicago Press, 2016).

statement of "help[ing] religious communities become good stewards of the earth," Faith in Place seems to align with that model. The organization's primary work, and its measurable outcomes, focus primarily on religious communities, not the earth itself. In a report for GuideStar, Faith in Place leaders wrote that their long-term success would be measured on the basis of the degree to which environmental activities became mainstream among faith communities.[33] This measure of success does not hinge on the environmental efficacy of such activities, but instead focuses on the engagement of the individuals undertaking them. Participants undertook these measures with some recognition that they might not actually matter at all, but they were important nonetheless because taking care of the earth was part of being a good person.[34]

To be sure, the Purple Radishes cultivated the soil by using organic techniques and promoted plant diversity by using endangered heirloom seeds, so they did help the earth flourish in their small patch of suburban Chicago. But the primary flourishing had to do with the women involved. The garden contributed to a sense of self that longed to reject the mainstream society of which they were part. Their vision involved dreams of cultivating that ideal world for everyone, especially those who did not share their own privileged status. But in practice such ideals would have to be cultivated without their direct help, because the Purple Radishes' flourishing in the garden entailed a retreat into a "like-minded" community, structured by their geography of race, ethnicity, and class.

The Mosque Foundation's environmental projects also helped the earth flourish in a small way, or at least slowed its destruction by reducing the carbon footprint of its members. But consideration of their motivations indicate the challenges Muslims face in their efforts to simply fit into mainstream American society, and the need to intentionally perform certain identities in order to quietly live their lives. Whereas the Purple Radishes' religious environmentalism was part of an effort to diverge from the mainstream by creating an alternative food system and community, the Mosque Foundation's religious environmentalism was part of an effort to blend in.

The disparity in these two groups' experiences with religious environmental projects points to broader challenges as we consider the possibilities of mutual flourishing among humans and the larger earth community. In short, the varied experiences of the mosque community, the Purple Radish gardeners, and other Faith in Place partner congregations who inhabit the racially segregated terrain

---

33. Faith in Place, "Guildestar Exchange Charting Impact Report" (2013).

34. Amanda Baugh, *God and the Green Divide: Religious Environmentalism in Black and White* (Oakland: University of California Press, 2017).

of greater Chicago underscore the extreme diversity in the category of "human" that must be acknowledged when we consider the flourishing of humans and the rest of the earth. Structural and environmental factors that enable humans to flourish are not shared equally by all. The experiences of the Mosque Foundation can serve to illustrate that point. At one level, their solar panels are an exciting example of an innovation that allows a human community and the earth to mutually flourish. But that analysis fails to appreciate the societal forces that led the mosque to install the solar panels in the first place. Rather than leading a quiet life as they raised their kids, went to work, and worshipped their God, mosque community members woke up many mornings to learn that another sister was yelled at in the grocery story, another neighbor was subjected to intense interrogation by the FBI, and another mainstream newspaper marked their community members as dangerous and Other. Installing solar panels is a great way for the Mosque Foundation to reduce its carbon footprint, and the community's "green Ramadan" and other environmental programs surely inculcate ecological values among its members. But to what extent do these outwardly positive features cover up something much darker that is going on? To what extent do they hide a clear failure of certain humans to flourish?

15

DIALOGUE

Chris Klassen and Amanda J. Baugh

Both of us approach this topic by observing and analyzing how others think about ethics, rather than doing ethical constructions of our own. Neither of us considers herself an ethicist. This, of course, does not mean we leave our own ethics at the door when we do our work. Our own beliefs and ideas inform our study in who we choose to talk with, what we choose to ask, and what theories we choose to use to analyze the conversations we were privileged to participate in. In all of this, however, neither of us is in a place to suggest what flourishing *should* look like in these traditions. Nor could we do this analysis on behalf of the informants we've met. I (Amanda) most definitely consider myself to be a "sympathetic outsider" among the participants I encountered through Faith in Place, and my aims tend not to be constructive.

In thinking about the Pagans I (Chris) spoke with, flourishing is a term they would very likely find appealing, though none used it. Flourishing implies living well, rather than just surviving. Human flourishing, for Pagans, would require the flourishing of other life as well. All the Pagans I spoke with saw a necessary interrelationship between all species of nature, including human and nonhuman. The most profound question would be "how might flourishing of all species happen?" The three categories I use in my paper, those who see human technology as natural because humans are part of nature, those who see some distinction between human technology and natural processes, and those who see human technology as detrimental to natural processes, would see flourishing happening in different, often competing, ways.

In terms of their ideas about flourishing, I (Amanda) think both the Purple Radishes and the mosque participants from my research would also support the general idea that human flourishing should not unnecessarily interfere with the flourishing of the rest of the earth community. They all expressed environmental commitments, so

I do not think they would disagree with that general proposition. The mosque participants I interviewed explained their environmental commitments on the basis of the Qur'an, such as a comment that humans are part of the earth because they came from clay and water. One informant told me there were more than fifty references in the Qur'an that told Muslims to contemplate nature. The Purple Radishes frequently referenced the Seventh Principle of Unitarian Universalism, which calls for "respect for the interdependent web of existence of which we all are part." In an additional measure to recognize their oneness with the earth, the Purple Radishes told me about their church's child dedication ceremony, in which the pastor prayed that the child would "come to know yourself as a piece of the earth conscious of itself." Whether or not my informants took significant measures to actually promote nonhuman flourishing in the context of their everyday lives, they at least would have identified that as a worthwhile goal.

The Purple Radishes seem to have a very similar outlook to the Pagans who were suspicious of human technology. Their suspicion of technology showed in their preference for small-scale, "low tech" gardening techniques. In interviews, several described genetically modified organisms such as "Franken-fish" as "insane." In terms of their gardening techniques, the Purple Radishes seem to fit in Chris's category of those who see human technology as detrimental to natural processes. Rather than looking to improve the technology, the gardeners saw the very use of high levels of technology as the problem. It would seem that we, as humans, need to get our hands dirty to be able to flourish ourselves and to help our neighboring species, including our food, to flourish as well.

The Muslims, on the other hand, seem much more interested in using technology to help improve their environmental practices to align with a larger earth flourishing. When I (Amanda) asked Dr. Haddad about the environmental measures he had enacted in his daily life, his responses all involved technological fixes: he started by going online to calculate his carbon footprint, and then he retrofitted his house with storm windows and insulating materials and replaced his gas-guzzling car with a hybrid. While they may not be motivated by the "naturalness" of technology in the way some Pagans are, the impact is similar. The thought, it seems, is "let's draw on the technology we have created (using our God-given abilities?) to solve the environmental problems we have also created." The use of technology to shape our world is a necessary human practice. However, how much technology, and how it helps the larger natural world flourish, is debated within Paganism, as well as the larger environmental movement.

But, of course, it's more complicated for both groups. In my (Amanda) interview with Sheikh Karimi, he told me that he embraced certain aspects of technology, but he worried that technology took people too far away from nature and needed to be used in moderation. And even though the Purple Radishes rejected agricultural technologies, a different type of technology actually was central to their gardening experience. All six of the Purple Radishes participated in online gardening and sustainable agriculture communities, including listservs and an online network through the Seed Savers Exchange. One of the gardeners also maintained an active blog about their group, posting updates on plans for the season, bountiful harvests, failed experiments, and vignettes about shared meals. The women discussed that blog frequently, and it seemed important to them that their gardening experience was part of a larger, global movement. I did not directly discuss attitudes toward technology with the Purple Radishes, so I do not know how they might explain their embrace of some forms of technology in contrast to their rejection of other forms.

A similar dynamic is present among Pagans. Pagans also use the internet frequently to build community and learn from one another. Even those who are suspicious of technology do so, although to a lesser degree than those who embrace technology. It seems, at times, a contradiction. But then, there are many contradictions, or competing narratives, that are involved in all our participants' environmental activities. I (Chris) really appreciate Amanda's focus on motivation. She points out multiple, and possibly even conflicting, motivations for environmental practices among the people she talks with. Are the Muslims motivated by environmental consciousness, a desire to protect the earth, or are they motivated by a desire to be seen as civically conscious Americans just like any other Americans in the face of Islamophobia and racism? Are the Purple Radishes motivated by their desire to get close to nature and be a positive influence on others, or are they motivated by a desire to be part of a group that provides personal identity and support?

The Pagans I (Chris) talked with were certainly motivated by spiritual and religious ideals. But they were also motivated by a common civic discussion about environmentalism. For example, the British Traditional Witches were very clear to point out their recycling practices, which were slightly above the expectations of average Canadians. I also remember a conversation in which one member of that group indicated that she was very careful to pick up garbage and not throw her Tim Horton's cup out the car window. What motivated this statement? A desire to show civic responsibility? Or a desire to show care for the earth? If the latter, one could question why one is buying a disposable cup of coffee from a large-chain non-organic, non-fair-trade company and driving a gasoline-fueled car. And some other Pagans I talked with would certainly ask those questions. But I wonder if participating in the discourse of recycling and environmental civic responsibility, regardless of the actual motivation, is a necessary first step for many people who previously had never contemplated what earth flourishing might mean.

While there might be significant areas of overlap in terms of ideas about flourishing among the Pagans, Unitarian Universalists, and Muslims that we met through our research, the possibilities for them to interact through interfaith dialogue at Faith in Place actually would be limited due to some strategic decisions made by that organization. On the basis of Pagans' embrace of nature religion, they would seem to be a natural fit for an interfaith environmental group like Faith in Place. Surprisingly, this was not the case. Some who identified as Pagan were actively involved with Faith in Place, but the organization did not include Pagans in the list of traditions it worked with and took no active measures to involve them. When I asked Faith in Place leaders about that decision, they explained that they did not specifically welcome Pagans because they worried that a Pagan presence could alienate some adherents of some of the organization's more conservative traditions, especially Muslims.

Perhaps we shouldn't be surprised by this. Paganism is held with suspicion by a number of institutional religious groups, not just Muslims. On the flip side, Pagans don't typically trust institutional religious groups either. They believe (and sometimes it is actually true) that Christians and Muslims, particularly, are antagonistic towards them and see them as evil. They look to both the Bible and the Qur'an as texts that condemn polytheism and as such the traditions that hold these texts as sacred could be a threat to them. It would take much work building trust on both sides to get these groups to work together. We as scholars can have a fruitful dialogue, but it would be much harder for practitioners of these traditions to build enough trust to engage in such interfaith efforts.

VI RESPECT AND RELATIONALITY

16

DEVELOPING A MENGZIAN ENVIRONMENTAL ETHIC

Cheryl Cottine

In *The River Runs Black*, Elizabeth Economy tells the story of the Huai River, one of the most polluted rivers in China. According to Economy, the Huai River Valley is a fairly prosperous region: "Long known for its rich supply of grain, cotton, oil, and fish, the river basin has over the past twenty-five years become home to tens of thousands of factories."[1] Additionally, around 195 dams have been constructed on the Huai. Between dam collapses and the frequent opening of sluice gates, river pollution has had devastating effects on the eco-system and human communities. Reflecting more broadly on the history of China's environmental issues, she remarks, "China lacked any compelling ethos of conservation. Rather, attitudes, institutions, and policies evolved from traditional folk understanding and philosophical thought, such as Confucianism, which most often promoted man's need to use nature for his own benefit."[2] While she acknowledges that some early sources suggest that a good ruler must preserve various ecosystems, by and large, Economy sees the philosophical underpinning of Chinese human-nature relations as predominantly anthropocentric and destructive.

Whereas Economy sees Confucian philosophy as leading to a de-structive environmental ethic, scholars such as Mary Eleven Tucker and others working within the Confucianism and ecology movement[3] have sought out new ways to interpret Confucian and Neo-Confucian

---

1. Elizabeth Economy, *The River Runs Black: The Environmental Challenge to China's Future* (Ithaca, NY: Cornell University Press, 2004), 17.

2. Ibid.

3. The Confucianism and ecology movement is part of a larger religion and ecology movement, which was born from the Yale Forum on Religion and Ecology. The Forum was established by John Grim and Mary Evelyn Tucker in the 1990s.

texts that depict them in a more favorable light. While these scholars agree that Confucian texts are anthropocentric, they do not deem it to be a destructive anthropocentrism. Tucker and John Grim, for example, suggest that the Confucian conception of personhood aligns closely with pragmatic social ecology. This ecological vision recognizes "the necessity of forming human institutions—both educational and political—for a stable society."[4] Their primary interest in human relations and institutions, however, is set against a backdrop that takes nature to be ethically normative and that sees the transformative property of the natural world as "the norm that takes priority for the common good of the whole society."[5] Because Confucians recognize the normative priority of the natural world, and because they acknowledge the relationality between human, the natural world, and the cosmos, scholars such as Tucker and Grim follow Tu Weiming and see Confucianism as anthropocosmic rather than anthropocentric.[6] An anthropocosmic stance, the argument goes, situates humans in a larger—actually cosmic—arena, which provides a framework for a more ecologically (and human) friendly environmental ethic. This stance stands in sharp contrast to Economy's claim that Confucian thought is deeply and problematically anthropocentric.

Can we move beyond the impasse created by these two scholarly camps? I think we can by shifting our focus to some of the earliest Confucian texts and, in the process, find richer intellectual resources to help address the numerous environmental issues that China faces today. First, it is worth noting that the Confucianism and ecology movement tends to focus on Neo-Confucian thinkers. While this focus is not inherently problematic, it is important to remember that while Neo-Confucian thinkers drew extensively from early Confucian texts, their philosophy is certainly not identical to the philosophy of their forbearers. In fact, the early Confucians have received scant attention in this conversation, and yet their texts contain valuable resources for rethinking a Confucian environmental ethic. Here, I focus on the *Mengzi*, a text from the Warring States Period (*c*. 403–221 B.C.E.) of Chinese history and one of the most important and influential Confucian texts next to Confucius's *Analects*. Mengzi's (*c*. 391–308 B.C.E.) thoughts are recorded in a text identified by his name, the *Mengzi*. Any attempt to retrieve an early Confucian account of the human-nature relationship and to

---

4. John Grim and Mary Evelyn Tucker, *Religion and Ecology* (Washington, DC: Island Press, 2014), 124.

5. Ibid., 123.

6. Ibid., 113. See also Tu Weiming, *Confucian Thought: Selfhood as Creative Transformation* (Albany: State University of New York, 1985).

develop a more coherent picture of what Confucian thought can contribute to re-envisioning environmental ethics, must wrestle with ideas in the *Mengzi*.[7]

My specific claim is that in order to even begin to articulate a Mengzian environmental ethic, it is essential to situate his discussion of the environment and environmental management within his broader discussion of virtue cultivation. Attending to notions of wisdom, discretion, and respect, for example, concepts traditionally focused on ordering and perfecting human relationships, can also help guide human-nature relationships. Focusing on Mengzi's virtue-oriented understanding of human flourishing can provide a corrective to both Economy's worry about destructive anthropocentrism that she sees plaguing Confucian philosophy and to the overly romantic picture of a cosmically situated self that Tucker and others attribute to Confucianism. The concept of respect, whether it is directed toward humans or the environment, decentralizes the individual. Thus, we might say that a text like the *Mengzi* provides a vision of tempered anthropocentrism rather than a destructive anthropocentrism that encourages focusing on human needs and values to the exclusion of all other interests.

Highlighting concepts within the *Mengzi* that can help to develop a contemporary environmental ethic goes at least some distance in demonstrating that there is a way to talk about an ethos of conservation in early Chinese ethical thought. A failure to take into account the needs and limits of natural cycles (for example, to overhunt animals or overharvest plants to the point where they cannot replenish in sufficient numbers to maintain the species) significantly reduces the chances of people surviving climatic disruptions and other ecologically related hardships. The *Mengzi*, in short, advocates for an ethic of conservation. Recognizing that there are such cultural resources in these early texts may help to bolster contemporary environmental movements and policies designed specifically for China.

I set the stage for this argument by first considering how contemporary scholars engage Confucianism in the discussion of ecology and environmental ethics. Following this coverage, I briefly present aspects of Mengzi's understanding of virtue and moral cultivation, as this background helps us make sense of why Mengzi talks about the environment in the ways that he does. I then consider how the text talks specifically about the environment and I relate these

---

7. When referring to early Confucian texts, I have in mind texts thought to be composed before 221 B.C.E. The received texts that we have today are products that underwent extensive editing and revision, and they often contain the voice of more than one author. A text like the *Mengzi*, for example, is likely a recording of stories, thoughts, and ideas of the historical figure Mengzi, from which the book derives its name, as well as additions from disciples both contemporary and more distant. However, I refer to the text and the ideas of Mengzi as one entity throughout the chapter.

discussions to notions of virtue cultivation discussed in the previous section. I ultimately argue that the way the *Mengzi* envisions the environment and the human-nature relationship provides rich fodder for contemporary thought. My concluding remarks re-emphasize the need to link discussions of virtue cultivation with considerations of material well-being and, furthermore, the significance of this aspect of Mengzi's thought when one is developing a Confucian environmental ethic.

Confucianism and Ecology

In 1967 Lynn White wrote "The Historical Roots of Our Ecological Crisis," in which he essentially blames the Judeo-Christian traditions for encouraging an ecologically hostile mentality. In essence, White's essay issued a challenge to philosophers and theologians to find ways for various traditions to combat destructive anthropocentrism.[8] Following White's charge, environmentally minded philosophers and theologians turned to "non-Western" or, more specifically, non-Abrahamic traditions, including Confucianism, in the hopes of finding less anthropocentric modes of being and engaging with the environment. Scholars turned to these "non-Western" traditions in order to demonstrate the difference a more holistic, less human-focused understanding of the human-nature relationship can make for developing an environmental ethic. Daoism, Buddhism, and indigenous traditions were frequently tapped. Some Confucian scholars have likewise analyzed early texts, such as the *Analects, Mengzi*, and *Xunzi*, for useful concepts and resources that can speak to contemporary environmental concerns. These texts provide a helpful depiction of the human-nature relationship that deemphasizes the individual and situates people within a much larger framework that includes the natural environment.

Scholars interested in the resources Confucian texts have to offer this growing conversation have devoted much of their efforts to detailing how the Confucian conception of a human being is more capacious than its "Western" counterpart. In other words, humans and how they are situated within the grander scheme of things tend to be less anthropocentric and more cosmic. Environmental ethicists, such as Baird Callicott, find this notion of a deemphasized self compelling and quite similar to the ideal notion of personhood put forward by deep ecologists. Deep ecology's primary philosophical maneuver is to wed an individual's interests

---

8. Lynn White Jr., "The Historical Roots of our Ecological Crisis," *Science* 155, no. 3767 (March 1967) 1203–1207.

and flourishing with the flourishing of the entire ecosystem.[9] Deep ecologists hope that an understanding of individual interests as being identical with ecological interests will lead to more environmentally minded individuals.

Grim and Tucker, in their 2014 book *Religion and Ecology* argue that the Confucian conception of personhood is less akin to the picture put forward by deep ecologists and aligns more closely with pragmatic social ecology. The advantage of working within a framework of social ecology is that it takes the need for good and stable human institutions seriously. But in their introduction to the edited volume *Confucianism and Ecology*, Tucker and John Berthrong emphasize what they see as the anthropocosmic position of Confucianism. Agreeing with Tu Weiming, who first coined the term,[10] Tucker and Berthrong remark that an anthropocosmic stance serves as a corrective to anthropocentrism because it "calls for a sense of relational resonance of the human with the cosmos rather than domination or manipulation of nature."[11] Confucianism, the argument runs, is naturalistic and holistic. Rather than attributing creative processes to a God, Confucianism sees the universe as self-generating. Humans are connected to heaven and earth, and this sense of connection results in a resonant rather than dominating stance toward nature.[12]

I am not completely convinced that the term "anthropocosmic" aids in contemporary understandings about the human-nature relationships, or that it can sufficiently motivate people to actively care about the environment. While an anthropocosmic stance might describe some neo-Confucian thought, it is not clear that it adequately describes early Confucian thought, and in particular the thought of Mengzi. It is true, however, that Confucianism generally, and early Confucianism in particular, are predominantly concerned with human flourishing. While the Neo-Confucian tradition may give thorough consideration to the natural world as a source of value, it is not immediately obvious that early Confucians, including Mengzi, do.[13] Yet, despite the fact that Mengzi does not impute intrinsic value to nature, his writing does reflect what today we might

9. Baird Callicott, *Earth's Insights: A Multicultural Survey of Ecological Ethics from the Mediterranean Basin to the Australian Outback* (Berkeley: University of California Press, 1994), 82.

10. Tu Weiming, *Confucian Thought*.

11. Mary Evelyn Tucker and John Berthrong, eds., *Confucianism and Ecology* (Cambridge, MA.: Harvard University Press, 1998); J. Baird Callicott, *Earth's Insights*, xxxvii.

12. Tucker and Berthrong, *Confucianism and Ecology*.

13. Philip Ivanhoe makes this claim as well, but specifically for the *Xunzi*. See "Early Confucianism and Environmental Ethics," in *Confucianism and Ecology*, 71.

call ecological mindedness.[14] Developing this line of his thought is helpful for our contemporary reflections of environmental ethics and policy, as it is more readily translatable into other value systems. The ease with which ecological and social ideas come together within the *Mengzi* provides a working ideal for developing a social and ecological ethic that incorporates conservation ethics, resource management, and discussions about enabling human flourishing beyond mere survival.

Arguing that the early Confucians have conceptual resources to offer contemporary reflections on environmental issues, as I have started to demonstrate, is not a novel claim. Tucker and Berthrong identify the following characteristics of Confucianism as resources worthy of consideration:

> Its dynamic, organismic worldview, its vitalist understanding of *ch'i* (material force), its respect for the vast continuity of life, its sense of compassion for suffering, its desire to establish the grounds for just and sustainable societies, its emphasis on holistic, moral education, and its appreciation for the embeddedness of life in interconnected concentric circles are only some examples of the rich resources of the Confucian tradition in relation to ecological issues.[15]

The religion and ecology movement, spearheaded by Tucker and Grim, made great contributions to our thinking about how the world's religions can and should be involved in helping to engage more people in the dialogue on environmental problems and efforts for creating a sustainable future. The essays that emerged and continue to emerge from the religion and ecology movement in many of the world's religions creatively engage traditional texts, both ancient and modern, thus increasing awareness about the scope and promise of religious responses to environmental issues and advancing the dialogue, in many ways, between religion and science.

While scholars of Confucianism agree that the early Confucians were deeply concerned with human flourishing, one question remains: to what extent does flourishing, according to early Confucianism, involve or require concern for the

---

14. Those who have made similar observations include Ivanhoe, "Early Confucianism and Environmental Ethics"; Rodney L. Taylor, "Companionship with the World: Roots and Branches of Confucian Ecology," in *Confucianism and Ecology*; Robert P. Weller and Peter K. Bol, "From Heaven-and-Earth to Nature: Chinese Concepts of the Environment and Their Influence on Policy Implementation," in *Confucianism and Ecology*; and Tu Weiming, "Continuity of Being: Chinese Visions of Nature," in *Nature in Asian Traditions of Thought*, Baird Callicott and Roger Ames, eds. (Albany: State University of New York Press, 1989).

15. Tucker and Berthrong, *Confucianism and Ecology*, xxxv.

nonhuman world? In the following section I analyze passages and concepts from the *Mengzi* that specifically reference the natural world in order to assess the sort of resources available for developing a picture of early Confucian environmental ethics. In particular, I focus on how the text depicts humans in relation to both wild and cultivated natural spaces, while also focusing on how the text talks about the concepts of wisdom, discretion, and respect. These aspects of Mengzi's thought are particularly useful for interrogating contemporary discussions of human well-being and both ecological and social flourishing.

Mengzi's Time and Philosophy

Mengzi lived during the Warring States Period of Chinese history in the fifth to third centuries before the Common Era. It was a time rife with conflict as the decline of the previously unified Zhou Empire fragmented into multiple smaller states, each with its own ruler. Conflicts abounded and survival was difficult. While clashes between states were frequent, the period also witnessed a flourishing of philosophical creativity. The time of chaos, as thinkers of that period described their own era, also gave rise to a plethora of philosophically sophisticated positions, many of which have since been categorized into schools of thought. Confucianism, Daoism, Moism, and Legalism, to name the major ones, all had their origins in the Warring States.[16] It is fair to say that all of the texts that have ties to this period were responding to the political atmosphere out of which they emerged. In other words, these texts combine political philosophy with moral philosophy in such a way that it is difficult to refer to one without referring to the other. The *Mengzi* is no exception. It is important to keep this in mind as we think about the *Mengzi* and work to draw out philosophical insights pertaining to the environment.

The *Mengzi* itself is a compilation of stories, many of which focus on Mengzi's encounter with rulers of various states. Mengzi, and any other wandering scholar-officials (*shi* ±) of that time, would have traveled to different states to seek an audience with the ruler. If an audience was granted, the scholar-official had the opportunity to share his philosophical acumen and political vision with the ruler. Ideally, the impressed ruler would offer the *shi* a position in his court as a minister (an advisor of sorts). Not only would this position come with a salary, but it

---

16. I use the term school loosely here, as formalized classifications of texts emerged only during the Han Dynasty (207 B.C.E.–22 C.E.). For a good intellectual history of the Warring States period and the proliferation of philosophical texts, see Benjamin I. Schwartz, *The World of Thought in Ancient China* (Cambridge, MA: Belknap Press of Harvard University Press, 1985).

would also place the *shi* in a position of influence from which he might be able to implement his social and political vision.

Perhaps one of the most prominent aspects of Mengzi's philosophy is his focus on moral cultivation. The scholarship on the Mengzian notion of virtue and self-cultivation abounds, and rather than rehashing everything that has already been done well, I look only at a few crucial ideas, namely, the importance of wisdom, the need for using discretion, and respect.[17] Cultivating virtue is crucial to well-being and, as Peimin Ni convincingly demonstrates, one cannot be considered healthy unless one's heart (*xin* 心)[18] is properly cared for.[19] Mengzi is most famous, perhaps, for his declaration that human nature is good and his belief that all humans contain within them the potential for moral goodness. While the moral potential is present, actually becoming good is another issue and one that is difficult to achieve. This difficulty is not because people are unable to develop morally, but simply because they fail to apply themselves—a move that constitutes a grave failure.

Mengzi uses agricultural metaphors to articulate his ideas about the innateness of moral inclinations. Humans, he believes, are endowed with the four sprouts or beginnings (*duan* 端) of morality that need to be nurtured and cultivated into full-fledged virtues. Just as a farmer must lovingly attend to his seedlings, so too must an individual attend to certain feelings that are indicative of one's capacity to be moral. The sprouts of compassion, disdain, respect, and approval and disapproval are natural endowments awaiting diligent attention and cultivation so that they can develop into their respective mature forms of benevolence (*ren* 仁), righteousness (*yi* 義), propriety (*li* 禮), and wisdom (*zhi* 智) (6A6)—the four cardinal virtues of Confucianism.

For Mengzi, the ability to be moral sets humans apart from the rest of the animals. Stemming from this belief is his assertion that one who lacks any of these fledgling moral inclinations is less than human (2A6). Of course, Mengzi thinks that it is extremely rare for someone to lack these inclinations, and the problem,

---

17. See, for example, Ivanhoe, *Ethics in the Confucian Tradition;* a collection of essays edited by Xiusheng Liu and Philip J. Ivanhoe, *Essays on the Moral Philosophy of Mengzi* (Indianapolis, IN: Hackett, 2002): and Bryan Van Norden's essay "The Virtue of Righteousness in Mencius," in *Confucian Ethics: A Comparative Study of Self, Autonomy, and Community,* Kwong-loi Shun and David B. Wang, eds. (New York: Cambridge University Press, 2004).

18. The character translated as "heart-mind" is *xin* 心. Translated literally, it means "heart." However, the early Chinese believed this organ to be the seat of feelings and emotions as well as of thinking and understanding. In other words, they would not be particularly fond of a theory that understands emotion and reason to be opposed, precisely because both affect the 心.

19. Peimin Ni, "Confucian Virtues and Personal Health," in *Confucian Bioethics,* Ruiping Fan, ed. (New York: Kluwer Academic Publishers, 2002), 30.

rather, is a failure to recognize them for what they are—moral inclinations.[20] Cultivating virtue is essential to human flourishing, then, because without it, one is not realizing one's human potential.

Wisdom, as one of the four virtues, is crucial for well-being. The wise individual properly understands his own nature, Heaven (*tian* 天),[21] and fate (*ming* 命). "One who fully comprehends his heart understands his nature; understanding one's nature is to understand Heaven. Preserving one's heart and nurturing one's nature is that which accords with serving Heaven. Not being conflicted as to whether one dies young or lives to an old age, cultivating one's self in order to await it (death), this is taking a stand on fate" (7A1). As Bryan Van Norden aptly notes, this passage ties Mengzi's "moral psychology to his cosmology."[22] Our ability to be moral is encapsulated in the four sprouts/hearts, and these are endowed to us by Heaven. Realizing our given, moral nature is the Way of the human, and when fulfilled it accords with the Way of Heaven. Fate too is determined by Heaven, and the wise person is able to recognize what can and cannot be controlled. For example, while one cannot control the length of one's life, one can avoid situations that lead to its careless shortening (7A2).

Another central dimension of wisdom comes in an individual's ability to use discretion. Broadly speaking, using discretion entails weighing various options to

---

20. One of the most famous examples of this failure is 1A7, in which Mencius attempts to demonstrate to King Xuan that he does not lack the capacity to be king. Mengzi learns that the king took pity on an ox that was being led to the sacrificial alter. Hearing the ox's cry and seeing its sad eyes caused the king to spare it and sacrifice a sheep instead. Mencius reacts to this story by telling the king, "This heart is sufficient to become King. The commoners all thought Your Majesty was being stingy. But I knew that Your Majesty could not bear the suffering of the ox." (Bryan Van Norden, trans., *Mengzi: With Selections from Traditional Commentaries* [Indianapolis, IN: Hackett, 2008], 8). The King, liking Mengzi's interpretation of his actions, agrees. Mencius's point, however, is that the King is more compassionate toward the ox than he is toward the people. He needs to reflect on the reaction he had to the crying ox and understand that this same compassion is desperately needed toward his people. Mengzi has demonstrated to the king that he is indeed capable of compassion. The problem lies in his unwillingness to act upon it in cases that truly matter (for instance, when his people are starving and in need of assistance). For an interesting essay on Mencius's theory of extension, see David B. Wong, "Reasons and Analogical Reasoning in the Mencius," in *Essays on the Moral Philosophy of Mengzi*) 187–220.

21. The term Heaven in early Chinese thought does not have a fixed meaning. Robert Eno has noticed that Mengzi uses the term Heaven to mean three different things, depending on the point he wants to get across. It can be "a single purposive deity; it is functionally the sum of all the spirits; it is the collective will of the people." *The Confucian Creation of Heaven: Philosophy and the Defense of Ritual Mastery* (Albany: State University of New York Press, 1990), 105. An exact definition is not crucial; what is important is that the way of Heaven and the way of humans are one when virtue is completely cultivated.

22. Van Norden, *Mengzi*, 171.

make a considered and often ritually appropriate decision.[23] This capacity is one highly praised by Mengzi, and it is also one that his various conversation partners seem to lack. An episode featuring a person from the state of Ren demonstrates this deficit nicely. He asks, "If in eating in accordance with ritual one starves and dies, but if in not eating in accordance with ritual one can obtain food, must one accord with ritual?" (6B1). We can easily envision Mengzi, upon hearing this story, rolling his eyes. His reply, more or less, is that of course you eat the food without being concerned for ritual! Although ritual is important—and there are stories in which people put their life in jeopardy because of a breach in ritual (5B7)—sometimes it is trumped by other considerations and needs. The wise understand this and know how to properly negotiate complex situations. Additionally, the ability to use discretion enables one to appropriately navigate various relationships. It allows a minister to know when he can remonstrate with a ruler, and when it is best to leave (5A9). Because of the practical benefits it brings to the individual, discretion is something that Mengzi thinks everyone would do well to learn. Discretion does not necessarily require full-fledged wisdom and therefore is a more realistic goal for individuals to attain. Not only is it handy in daily situations, but it is also crucial for flourishing. One who pays attention to circumstances and can discern the proper action in a given situation is not someone who idly exists in the world. This is someone who remonstrates with authorities when they are in the wrong, and someone who knows when to move out of harm's way. Discretion, then, is something that all should be allowed to learn to develop.

The final concept within the sphere of cultivating virtue that I would like to highlight is respect. Respect is arguably one of the most important concepts discussed in the *Mengzi*—it is, after all, one of the innate moral feelings, and when properly cultivated it becomes the full-fledged virtue of ritual propriety (6A6). All of the relationships require respect, and it generally appears to be a sentiment that moves upward, that is, from one in an inferior position to his superior. However, Mengzi also asserts that those who respect others will be respected by others (4B28). Cultivating the feeling of respect and then being properly respectful does require discretion—the ability to discern who deserves what type of respect in various situations.

It is important to realize that the emphasis is not on *receiving* respect, but rather on *being* respectful. A child is respectful to her parents by upholding their

---

23. For a more detailed analysis of the notion of discretion in early China see Griet Vankeerberghen, "Choosing Balance: Weighing (*Quan* 權) as a Metaphor for Action in Early Chinese Texts," *Early China* 30 (2005): 47–89, and Michael Ing, *The Dysfunction of Ritual in Early Confucianism* (Oxford: Oxford University Press, 2012).

ways even after their death; a minister shows respect to the ruler by remonstrating with him and being demanding of him. It is all about the respect that I owe others and not about the respect I can expect to receive. The emphasis on giving rather than receiving respect stands in contrast to the more traditional understanding of the concept, in which one should expect to receive respect. Contemporary scholars, following Stephen Darwall, often distinguish between two types of respect: appraisal and recognition respect. Appraisal respect is given to those whose accomplishments we deem to be worthy. Recognition respect is owed to all human beings simply because one is human.[24] In much of the justice literature, respect is discussed as something either individuals or groups should receive; it is identified as a right. On Mengzian terms, in contrast, respect is a duty.

The above discussion of virtue cultivation according to Mengzi, while quite brief, helpfully provides a broader context for the following more specific discussion environmental themes in the text. Moreover, I suggest that we extend these virtues to include consideration of the environment—in other words, to understand these virtues as environmental virtues.

Mengzi and Environmental Philosophy

With all of this in mind, I turn to this question: how does the *Mengzi* address the environment, and more specifically, the human-nature relationship? It would be erroneous to claim that the *Mengzi* has a fully developed environmental philosophy.[25] Worrying about the impact of humans on the natural world was not the heightened concern that it is today. However, while not fully fleshed out, there are substantial passages that provide a basis upon which to expound a more robust Confucian environmental ethic. To begin, consider passage 3B9. In this passage, Mengzi is responding to a question posed to him by a disciple, and he tells a story that references the great sage kings of the past, Yao, Shun, and Yu. Mengzi elaborates upon a common theme in early Confucian texts, namely, that as time has progressed, the world has experienced a decline in virtue. Whereas once virtuous rulers ensured peace and sufficient livelihoods for the people, present times are chaotic and basic survival is difficult. Recalling the time of Yao when massive flooding was common and wild animals roamed everywhere, Mengzi comments on what we might call Yao's environmental policy. In response to catastrophic

24. Stephen Darwall, "Two Kinds of Respect," *Ethics* 88, no. 1 (Oct. 1977): 36–49.

25. Philip Ivanhoe also makes this observation in "Early Confucianism and Environmental Ethics," 59.

floods, Yu, a minister at the time, was asked to bring order to the rivers. Mengzi narrates thus:

> He (Yu) dredged the earth from the rivers and guided the water to the sea. He drove the snakes and dragons away and banished them to the marshes. The water flowed between the channels, making the Yangtze, Huai, Yellow, and Han rivers. When the flooding had receded, and attacks by animals had been eliminated, only then did the people live on the plains. But after Yao and Shun passed away, the Way of the sages decayed. Cruel rulers arose one after another, destroying homes to make ponds, so that people had nowhere they could rest. They made people abandon the fields so that they could be made into parks, so that the people could not get clothes and food.... As parks, ponds, marshes, and swamps became more numerous, the animals returned. By the time of Tyrant Zhou, the world was again in complete chaos (3B9).[26]

In a very real sense, nature is the enemy in this passage. It inhibits humans from settling, threatens personal security, and prevents the tillage of fields that would yield crops and other forms of sustenance. The tyrants failed to ensure that people were safe and able to provide for themselves, allowing wild animals to wreak havoc on settlements and allowing rivers to flood and destroy fertile land. What distinguished the sage kings from the tyrants was an environmental policy that also included human beings. The idea is not that animals and different ecosystems are eradicated, but rather to create and maintain a clear distinction between wilderness and cultivated areas. The tyrant, in contrast, lets nature run wild and fails to create a space for humans. This sort of policy, according to Mengzi, has devastating human consequences.

In contrast, sage rulers, or even good rulers, according to Mengzi, practice benevolent government. Being a benevolent ruler entails that one act as a father and mother to the people, ensure that they have means to a proper and sufficient livelihood (3A3, 7A22, 7A23), that taxes are light and appropriate (1A5, 2A5, 7B27), and that the people have access to education (1A7 and 3A5). Mengzi identifies several basic needs of every human that the ruler should make accessible. This access is not accomplished by the ruler giving hand-outs to the people, but by his use of discretion when taking from the people. In short, the ruler must be mindful of circumstances. Consider 7A23:

---

26. I follow Van Norden's translation of the text, unless otherwise noted. See *Mengzi: With Selections from Traditional Commentaries* (Indianapolis: Hackett, 2008).

Mengzi said: "If you make the management of their fields easy and their taxes light, the people can be made wealthy. If you keep them fed and only employ them in accordance with propriety, there will be more than enough material resources. The people will not live without water and fire. But if you can knock on people's doors in the evening, asking for some water or hot embers, and not be refused, then there is enough. Similarly, when sages rule the world, they make grain as plentiful as water and fire. When the people have as much grain as they have water and fire, how can they fail to be benevolent?"

Ensuring that granaries are full and reserves are maintained for times of famine requires the appropriate taxing of the people. When harvests are good, a normal tax can and ought to be collected; when times are hard, the ruler ought to reduce the tax appropriately. What is more, the ruler must then distribute the goods back to the people. A failure to do all this is a serious moral flaw and one that reflects the selfishness that Mengzi sees as plaguing all rulers and functionaries in his time (1B12).

These two passages help establish a foundation for thinking about how we might incorporate developments in ecological sciences into a discussion about Confucian environmental ethics. While managing a large population size and extensive pollution were not concerns of Mengzi's, what was a concern was ensuring people had access to what they needed in order to survive and flourish in times of famine and of plenty. During Mengzi's time this concern entailed making sure river flooding was minimized, that fields were irrigated, and that people had access to good land. Without these things, survival was difficult and any hope of people cultivating virtue was dismal.

Recognizing the importance of conserving natural resources is one of many environmental themes that run through the *Mengzi*; it is a theme that is inextricably linked to governing the people. In 1A3 Mengzi explicitly links good governing to resource conservation:

If one does not disrupt the farming seasons with building projects, but only waits until after the crops have been harvested, the grain will be inexhaustible. If overly fine nets are not used in the ponds, so that sufficient fish and turtles are left to reproduce, they will be inexhaustible. If people bring their axes into the mountain forests only in the proper season, the wood will be inexhaustible. When grain, fish, turtles, and wood are inexhaustible, this will make the people have no regrets about caring for the living and mourning the dead. When the people have no regrets about caring for the living or mourning the dead, it is the beginning of the Kingly Way.

A wise ruler would be mindful of natural cycles as well as the devastating impact of resource overconsumption. The *Mengzi* consistently reminds its audience that human flourishing depends on carefully regulating the land and its resources.

But resource management is not the sole realm in which nature impinges on human virtue in Mengzi's thought. The *Mengzi*, more than any other early Confucian text, makes use of agricultural or nature analogies. The discussion of Ox Mountain in 6A8 ultimately serves as a metaphor detailing both how moral inclinations can be harmed and, furthermore, how appearances—in this case the appearance of a barren mountain—may not reveal the true nature of something. The anecdote runs as follows:

> Mengzi said, "The trees of Ox Mountain were once beautiful. But because it bordered on a large state, hatchets and axes besieged it. Could it re-main verdant? Due to the respite it got during the day or night, and the moisture of rain and dew, there were sprouts and shoots growing there. But oxen and sheep came and grazed on them. Hence, it was as if it were barren. Seeing it barren, people believed that there had never been any timber there. But could this be the nature of the mountain?" (6A8)

Mengzi continues and expands, likening people's neglect of their moral inclinations and their exposure to bad influence to hatchets and axes that fell trees. It is ultimately an argument meant to demonstrate that despite the presence of imperfectly moral people, all people have inborn and natural moral tendencies.

In order for this metaphor to be effective, one must recognize what the nat-ural state of the mountain is (i.e., forested). Furthermore, the metaphor hinges on the recognition that the natural state of the mountain can be damaged. Mengzi not only recognizes that specific harms can be done to the mountain (deforesta-tion, for example), he further suggests that the present and observable state of the mountain cannot possibly be its natural state. In this case the natural state—not the apparent state—is the desirable one.

These passages give us a nice sense of how the *Mengzi* utilizes natural metaphors to reveal crucial aspects of human nature; more importantly, the passages demonstrate an awareness both that humans have the power to control certain aspects of the natural world and that natural cycles and ecosystem dy-namics ought to be respected. The *Mengzi's* environmental philosophy, in short, aims at ensuring human survival and flourishing, but the text situates this aim within a broader awareness of the need for sustainable practices and general re-spect for the power of nature.

Mengzi's environmental ethic is an ethic of conservation rather than of preser-vation. A conservation ethic recognizes that humans need nature to survive, and that significantly disrupting natural cycles or ecosystem stability by over-utilizing nature, is counterproductive and harmful for human flourishing. Mengzi does not attribute something like intrinsic value to nature—in fact, the text conceives of nature in somewhat utilitarian terms. Nature's value, on this account, is determined by its usefulness to humans. Nature, according to Mengzi, is useful to humans in two senses. First, and most straightforwardly, it is useful when it can provide real goods necessary for human survival. Second, and less obviously, it is useful when it can maintain balance and sufficient diversity so that it can sustain human communities. Nature, in short, is useful when it is stable and sufficiently diverse.

The above discussion demonstrates that the *Mengzi* is primarily concerned with human well-being and little concerned with preserving nature as such. While nature, or the environment, plays a supporting role in Mengzi's thought, it is human welfare that dominates his concern for both governing and individual virtue cultivation. While many might see the above discussion as indicative of a lack of concern with the environment, it is worth pausing momentarily to remind ourselves that we are working within a different framework. For Confucians generally, and Mengzi is no exception, humans were seen as possessing the ability to improve nature. Dredging rivers so they were no longer prone to severe flooding improves the river; creating distinct areas for wild animals and domestic settlement improves the area; and as Xunzi (*c.* 340–245 B.C.E.) observes, humans can drastically improve upon natural colors—indigo, for example, the human enhancement of blue—is superior to naturally occurring blue.[27] These are, of course, improvements according to human standards and values, and as such demonstrate an anthropocentric orientation toward nature. However, when paired with the previously discussed concerns surrounding resource management, what emerges is a more tempered anthropocentrism. Improving upon the environment's natural endowments is permissible only insofar as one does not undermine the integrity of the system.

Stated differently, interfering with the environment, as many would describe it today, is not an activity to be avoided. In fact, running interference was necessary for human survival and flourishing. However, as we have already seen, humans must interfere carefully and selectively; interfering haphazardly or with only thought of short-term gains is destructive for all, humans and the environment alike. One might argue that meddling with the environment in any way lessens its ability to flourish; however, Mengzi, and the early Confucians generally, were

---

27. Eric L. Hutton, trans., 荀子 *Xunzi: The Complete Text* (Princeton, NJ: Princeton University Press, 2014), 1.

under no illusion that humans could function, let alone flourish, without some form of land management in place. And while it is true that Mengzi does not speak directly about environmental flourishing, his philosophy does seem to contain a sense of respect for natural cycles and for the ability of the land to give vital sustenance.

Many of the environmental episodes the above section highlighted in the *Mengzi* focus on the role of the wise and discerning ruler. An ability not only to understand what humans need for basic survival and more sophisticated flourishing, but also to discern how use of the environment factors into this flourishing distinguishes a good ruler from a tyrant. Wisdom and discretion, then, can apply to navigating the natural world just as they apply to navigating human relationships. Extending the virtues of wisdom and discretion to include the ability to appropriately interact with the environment seems obvious enough, but what about the respect?

One of the interesting features of the Mengzian conception of respect is that it is conceptualized in terms of duty rather than in terms of desert. I owe someone respect because she exhibits characteristics of a moral individual. In this sense, Mengzian respect is somewhat akin to appraisal respect. The focus, however, is on my cultivation of respect for those worthy of it. Even when we shift our focus from appraisal respect to a more general form of respect, it is still helpful to think of it as a duty, and ironically, perhaps, also as a virtue to be cultivated. To truly respect someone or something, I would argue, involves the recognition of the other as a distinct entity with equally distinct interests and needs. Thus, one who respects another understands the other in all her complexity and in her entirety. In this description, respect involves both wisdom and discretion. Respect requires understanding how things are and how they function, and in turn respect encourages restraint. Applying this outlook to the wise rulers who accurately understood ecological cycles, we could say that he respects the environment by enabling these systems to continue functioning despite human interference. In other words, the rulers who knew not to overhunt or overfish understand and respect the ecosystem. Stated differently, respecting humans entails at least some respect for the environment and its ability to function and produce without serious disruption. While the environment is in a very real sense managed, it is managed so that it can both flourish and allow for humans to flourish.

Some Concluding Remarks

Let us reconsider the Huai River in light of the preceding discussion about Mengzi's environmental philosophy. There are, I contend, parallels between the state of the Huai River and the various kings' (sage and tyrant) land policy in the *Mengzi*. Mengzi praised sage king Yu because he worked with the river and contours of the land to control an unruly river, dredging the river so that it reached into dry areas, thus creating farmable land that made settlement and agriculture possible. Maximizing the use of land and water, ensuring the safety and survival of the people, and distinguishing separate spaces for "wild" nature to exist, Yu, Yao, and Shun enabled the coexistence of what today we might call wild or natural spaces and human settlement. In today's terms, the sage kings' actions were conservation savvy.

The stories about how Yu dredged the rivers have a mythic quality to them. Perhaps it is an origin story of sorts for China's rivers.[28] The life-giving water sources were created by attending to the physical geography of the place and directing the water appropriately. While Yu was clearly manipulating the direction of the water, he recognized that controlling such a massive natural force could happen most effectively if he worked with nature, not against it. This form of manipulation stands in sharp contrast to the way many rivers are controlled, or more precisely contained, today. Damming a river is a different method of controlling a river than dredging, and one that is significantly more destructive of river, and other, ecosystems. While damming does have some benefits (power production, for example), the potential for disasters is multiplied. Pollutants pool and become trapped in the man-made lakes, the variety of fish in the river alter, potentially devastating the native fish population, and when the sluice gates are opened, pollutants damage the river's downstream ecosystems and hurt the ones abutting them. While attempts to control the river via damming can arguably be said to be an attempt to make the land better (more productive) and thus increase human well-being, insufficient regulation of other modes of production have undermined any benefit gained. Instead, mass suffering results when dams collapse or when sluice gates are frequently opened. Thus, instead of aiding in resource production, current damming policies and building hinder many forms of resource production.

What the story in the *Mengzi* suggests, and what ecological science helps bolster, is that there are better and worse ways to control the environment. In the *Mengzi*, then, we have an early example of ecosystems-thinking that is at the service of human well-being. Respecting natural patterns of various systems is then a form of environmental virtue. If I am correct to discuss environmental ethics in the *Mengzi* in terms of virtue, then he contributes to contemporary discussions on

---

28. Thanks to Will Smith for this insight.

environmental virtue.[29] Louke van Wensveen, for example, argues that ecosystem sustainability is essential for virtue cultivation, meaning that conversations about cultivating virtue cannot even begin if humans are unable to secure basic material goods. Van Wensveen, like Mengzi, argues that basic material goods are a necessary but not sufficient condition of virtue.[30] Mengzi develops a robust concept of flourishing that includes both role-based virtue cultivation *and* attention to larger ecological cycles. Thus, in contrast to a more narrowly defined and destructive notion of anthropocentrism that places humans in a superior position to nature, the early Confucians, and Mengzi in particular, provide a tempered anthropocentrism—one that simultaneously places human interests above other interests but also acknowledges the fact that humans must respect and at times acquiesce to the forces of nature.[31]

By attending to an early Confucian text such as the *Mengzi*, we encounter a picture of humans interacting with the natural world that is not overly romantic, but is instead practical. Rather than having humans imagine themselves as situated within the cosmos, Mengzi asks us to reflect on what good and bad environmental management entails. While much of the responsibility for environmental maintenance falls to those in positions of power, Mengzi carves out a space for individual action by reminding us of the importance of cultivating wisdom, discretion, and respect, virtues that everyone can and ought to cultivate.

Finally, acknowledging the intimate connection between ecosystem stability and diversity and human flourishing will go a long way in refocusing environmental policy. What Mengzi helps us recognize is that one can have a human-centered stance toward the world, a stance that is, perhaps ironically, simultaneously centered on ecosystem stability. Preventing ecosystems from regenerating through

---

29. Environmental virtue ethics is a relatively recent approach to environmental ethics, which was developed as a response to what was perceived as overly rigid approaches to environmental ethics. Scholars developing environmental virtue ethics sought to address the issue of motivation. In other words, they asked the following question: if a drastic change in how humans relate to the environment is in order, how do we motivate people to make that switch? Examples of such work includes Louke van Wensveen, *Dirty Virtues: The Emergence of Environmental Virtue Ethics* (New York: Humanity Books, 2000); Phil Cafaro and Ronald Sandler, eds., *Environmental Virtue Ethics* (Oxford: Rowman and Littlefield, 2005); Ronald Sandler, *Character and Environment: A Virtue-Oriented Approach to Environmental Ethics* (New York: Columbia University Press, 2009).

30. Louke van Wensveen, "Ecosystem Sustainability as a Criterion for Genuine Virtue," *Environmental Ethics* 23, no. 3 (2001): 227–241.

31. Philip Ivanhoe distinguishes between three forms of anthropocentrism in his essay "Early Confucianism and Environmental Ethics," in *Confucianism and Ecology*. Epistemological anthropocentrism is the view that we see things from the human perspective, metaphysical anthropocentrism is the idea that humans are the masters of the world, and ethical anthropocentrism is the idea humans decide what does and does not have value (65–66).

excessive use, pollution, or general destruction, Mengzi reminds us, serves only to also prevent human flourishing, at least in the long run. Of course, Mengzi is not the only thinker we can invoke to come to this conclusion; those in the environmental virtue camp make this argument as well. But attending to the *Mengzi* does provide a specifically Chinese rationale for orienting policy around ecosystems in order to enable social and individual flourishing. [32]

32. I would like to thank Susan Blake, Diane Fruchtman Hannah, Michael Hannis, Laura Hartman, Michael Ing, Rich Miller, William Smith, Aaron Stalnaker, and Sian Sullivan for offering feedback at various stages of this project.

17 RELATIONALITY, RECIPROCITY, AND FLOURISHING IN AN AFRICAN LANDSCAPE

Michael Hannis and Sian Sullivan

Introduction

Human flourishing does not happen in isolation. It is dependent on, and in large part constituted by, relationships—with specific others, with multiple communities, and with the world(s) in which one lives. At the interhuman level this theme of relationality has been explored under many labels, including capabilities approaches and relational autonomy.[1] More recently the same insight has informed environmental virtue ethics, which extends the idea of identity-constituting community beyond the human, asking what it is to flourish as part of such a community.[2] What is the relationship between the flourishing of human beings (individually and/or collectively) and the flourishing of the nonhuman world? What kinds of relationships with "others-beyond-the-human" characterize a flourishing human life—and what are the virtues of character that build and nurture such relationships? Such questions break down the false dichotomy between anthropocentrism and ecocentrism, freeing environmental ethics to make

---

1. Martha Nussbaum, *Creating Capabilities* (Cambridge, MA: Belknap Press of Harvard University Press, 2011); Amartya Sen, *Development as Freedom* (Oxford: Oxford University Press, 1999); Catriona Mackenzie and Natalie Stoljar, eds., *Relational Autonomy* (Oxford: Oxford University Press, 2000).

2. Ronald Sandler and Philip Cafaro, eds., *Environmental Virtue Ethics* (Lanham, MD: Rowman and Littlefield, 2005); Ronald Sandler, *Character and Environment* (New York: Columbia University Press, 2007); Rosalind Hursthouse, "Environmental Virtue Ethics," in *Working Virtue: Virtue Ethics and Contemporary Moral Problems*, Rebecca Walker and Philip Ivanhoe, eds. (Oxford: Clarendon, 2007: 155–172); Brian Treanor, *Emplotting Virtue: A Narrative Approach to Environmental Virtue Ethics* (Albany, NY: State University of New York Press, 2014).

meaningful contributions to broader debates rather than staying bogged down in meta-ethical speculation.[3]

A fully flourishing human life requires connection and relationship not only with humans but also with the rest of the world. This kind of relationship cannot be built with homogenized categories such as "nature" or "biodiversity."[4] It requires approaching and understanding animals, plants, forests, rivers, and mountains *as themselves*, rather than *as a class of things* defined only by their shared "nonhuman-ness." Recognizing "otherness" is important in this process, as is recognizing commonality.[5] But both are beginnings, preliminaries to the development of a mature reflective relationship with the "nonhuman." Connection and relationship are still less likely to emerge from thinking about "natural capital" or "ecosystem services." Here the enforcement of commensurability works to *remove* distinctiveness and difference, as more and more domains of the world become abstracted into numbers, absorbed into spreadsheets, and offset in frequently marketized exchanges. Trees become carbon, carbon becomes dollars, and "the world" becomes subsumed into "the economy," rather than the other way round.[6]

One way to resist this culturally hegemonic urge to abstraction is to reflect on direct experience. It seems impossible to directly *experience* "biodiversity" or "natural capital." By contrast, both firsthand and scholarly evidence confirm the transformative potential of real experiences of entities beyond the human, and indeed of the damage caused by the lack of such experience.[7] Another is

---

3. Michael Hannis, *Freedom and Environment: Autonomy, Human Flourishing, and the Political Philosophy of Sustainability* (New York: Routledge, 2015); John Dryzek, "Political and Ecological Communication," in *Debating the Earth (Second edition)*, John Dryzek and David Schlosberg, eds. (Oxford: Oxford University Press, 2005: 633–646); Kerry Whiteside, *Divided Natures: French Contributions to Political Ecology* (Cambridge, MA: MIT Press, 2002).

4. Kate Soper, *What Is Nature? Culture, Politics and the Non-Human* (Oxford: Blackwell, 1995); Donald S. Maier, *What's So Good About Biodiversity?* (New York: Springer, 2012).

5. Simon Hailwood, *How to Be a Green Liberal* (Montreal: McGill-Queens University Press, 2004); Robert E. Goodin, *Green Political Theory* (Cambridge: Polity, 1992); Adrian Martin, Shawn McGuire, and Sian Sullivan, "Global Environmental Justice and Biodiversity Conservation," *Geographical Journal* 179, no. 2 (2013): 122–131.

6. Sian Sullivan and Michael Hannis, "Nets and Frames, Losses and Gains: Value Struggles in Engagements with Biodiversity Offsetting Policy in England," *Ecosystem Services* 15 (2015): 162–173; John O'Neill, *Ecology, Policy and Politics* (London: Routledge, 1993); Karl Polanyi, *The Great Transformation* (Boston: Beacon Press, 1957).

7. David Abram, *The Spell of the Sensuous* (New York: Random House, 1996); Richard Louv, *Last Child in the Woods: Saving Our Children from Nature-Deficit Disorder* (Chapel Hill, NC: Algonquin, 2005); Glenn Albrecht, "'Solastalgia': A New Concept in Health and Identity," *Philosophy, Activism, Nature* 3 (2005): 41–55.

to learn from the experience of others: for example, through close attention to different cultures. Anthropologists have described many understandings of the relationships between humans and the nonhuman world, and these frequently include ideas about nonhuman agency, personhood, and moral status, which can seem challenging to a "Western" mindset. This chapter presents some preliminary reflections from the "ecocultural ethics" component of a research project called *Future Pasts*, supported by the United Kingdom's Arts and Humanities Research Council.[8] In this project we seek to bring ethnographic detail and perspectives from the "anthropology of sustainability" (Sullivan) into dialogue with environmental philosophy and ethics (Hannis).

Ontology, Particularity, and Ethnography

From an anthropological as well as postcolonial perspective, the Western hierarchies of value associated with other-than-human natures, while universalizing, are understood to in fact be highly *particular*, embedded in, and made possible by particular cultural and historical contexts.[9] Importantly for human relationships with natures beyond the human, they restrict the attribution of agency, intentionality, and communication to human actors (and often only some human actors), while backgrounding the possibility that other entities might also enjoy such capacities. This restriction, so characteristic of "the West," is strongly associated with the Enlightenment period and the ushering in of modernity but, as emphasized by Matthew Hall, is rooted in hierarchies of value

8. We gratefully acknowledge support from the Arts and Humanities Research Council (ref. AH/K005871/2), as well as fieldwork support from the National Museum of Namibia and Save the Rhino Trust, Namibia (See http://www.futurepasts.net). The ethnographic material presented here derives from multiple interactions, discussions, and observations. We are indebted to the following individuals for material used from key recorded and transcribed interviews: Welhemina Suro Ganuses (WSG), Ruben Saunaeib Sanib (RSS), Sophia Obi |Awises (SO|A), Nathan ≠Ûina Taurob (N≠ÛT), Christophine Dâumu Tauros (CDT), Michael |Amigu Ganaseb (M|AG), Emma Ganuses (EG), the late Salmon Ganuseb (SG), Max Haraseb (MH), !Nosa Ganases, Martin !U-e So-Oabeb (M!UO). Invaluable translation and logistical support was provided by Welhemina Suro Ganuses, Filemon |Nuab, Ezegiel |Awarab, Elfriede Gaeses, Andrew Botelle, Eugène Marais, and Jeff Muntifering, for which, many thanks.

9. Cf. Dipesh Chakrabarty, *Provincialising Europe: Postcolonial Thought and Historical Difference* (Princeton, NJ: Princeton University Press, 2000); Eduardo Viveiros de Castro, "Exchanging Perspectives: The Transformation of Objects into Subjects in Amerindian Ontologies," *Common Knowledge* 10, no. 3 (2004): 463–484; Phillipe Descola and Janet Lloyd, *Beyond Nature and Culture* (Chicago: University of Chicago Press, 2013); Eduardo Kohn, *How Forests Think: Towards an Anthropology of Nature beyond the Human* (Berkeley: University of California Press, 2013); Sian Sullivan, "Nature on the Move III: (Re)countenancing an Animate Nature," *New Proposals: Journal of Marxism and Interdisciplinary Enquiry* 6, nos. 1–2 (2013): 50–71.

asserted in classical antiquity.[10] This universalizing framework involves fundamental assumptions about the "known" nature of reality. It prescribes what entities can exist, into what categories such entities can be sorted, and by what practices they can be known.

From a cross-cultural perspective, cultural and historical differences generate *plural ontologies*. This plurality, combined with power/knowledge relations infusing historically and culturally situated "regimes of truth"[11] has significant implications for who and what might be meant when the term "we" is invoked, as well as for what entities might socially be brought within the realm of moral considerability by this "we"[12] and thus for what constitutes appropriate ethical practice in relation to these entities.[13] In particular, while the modern ontology of "the West" may be *universalizing*, it frequently does not translate well across different cultural contexts. It is itself particular, rather than universal.[14]

Ethnography, the attempt to understand in detail the makings of social reality in different cultural contexts, without necessary recourse to "the West" as the measure of all things, can add detail, complexity, and nuance to the understanding of different ontological ideas about relationships between humans and other-than-human entities. It seems, however, to have been relatively underutilized in environmental philosophy, apart from quite broad brushstrokes such as Baird Callicott's *Earth's Insights*.[15] From a Foucauldian perspective, ethnography can also enhance possibilities for the destabilization of knowledge categories and practices that seem problematic for the flourishing of diversity, through assisting

---

10. Matthew Hall, *Plants as Persons: A Philosophical Botany* (Albany, NY: State University of New York Press, 2011), 19–26, after Val Plumwood, *Feminism and the Mastery of Nature* (London: Routledge, 2006); see also Michael Marder, *Plant-Thinking: A Philosophy of Vegetal Life* (New York: Columbia University Press, 2013), and further discussion in Sian Sullivan, "(Re-) Embodying Which Body? Philosophical, Cross-Cultural and Personal Reflections on Corporeality," in *Law, Philosophy and Ecology: Exploring Re-Embodiments*, Ruth Thomas-Pellicer, Vito de Lucia, and Sian Sullivan, eds., Routledge Law, Justice and Ecology Series (London: GlassHouse, 2016).

11. Michel Foucault, *Discipline and Punish: The Birth of the Prison*, Alan Sheridan, trans. (London: Penguin, 1991 [1975]); Judith Butler, "Performative Acts and Gender Constitution: An Essay in Phenomenology and Feminist Theory," *Theatre Journal* 40, no. 4 (1988): 519–531.

12. Cf. Kevin Gary Behrens, "An African Relational Environmentalism and Moral Considerability," *Environmental Ethics* 36, no. 1 (2014): 63–82.

13. As noted in Workineh Kelbessa, "Can an African Environmental Ethics Contribute to Environmental Policy in Africa?" *Environmental Ethics* 36, no. 1 (2014): 46.

14. Chakrabarty, *Provincialising Europe*.

15. J. Baird Callicott, *Earth's Insights: A Survey of Ecological Ethics from the Mediterranean Basin to the Australian Outback* (Berkeley: University of California Press, 1994).

with diagnosis of their objects of knowledge, the subjugation of knowledges with which these objects are associated, and the "regimes of truth" that naturalize certain ontologies and associated ethical possibilities over others.[16]

Many indigenous communities globally—by which we mean cultures that have retained some degree of long-term, continuous ancestral connection with land areas—seem to conceive of an expanded zone of moral considerability and reciprocity that includes entities beyond the human[17], as they are embedded and constituted in specific and shifting relational settings[18]. These cultural contexts are frequently also associated with localities now celebrated as "biodiversity hotspots,"[19] where ecosystems characterized by high diversity and the incidence of endemism and rarity remain, within the broader context of a global anthropogenic extinction event. Human cultural arrangements in these contexts have clearly been associated with the maintenance of relationships with diverse natures beyond the human, despite immense modern pressures to transform such cultural landscapes in the interests of economic growth. As Gorenflo et al. state, "the tendency for both [biological and linguistic diversity] to be high in particular regions suggests that certain cultural systems and practices, represented by speakers of particular indigenous and nonmigrant languages, tend to be compatible with high biodiversity."[20] Understanding the ontologies that have made it possible for human cultures in these contexts to maintain particular relational sustainabilities thus seems relevant for learning how to live in more accommodating ethical relationships with many kinds of selves, only some of whom are human.[21] Of particular relevance, as emphasized by Eduardo Kohn, are the ethical perspectives and practices that may arise when people live as if other kinds of being could see "us," and thus act as if the way(s) that "they" saw "us" mattered. As Kohn writes,

---

16. See, e.g., Michel Foucault, "The Subject and Power," *Critical Enquiry* 8, no. 4 (1982): 777–795.

17. Sian Sullivan, "Folk and Formal, Local and National: Damara Cultural Knowledge and Community-Based Conservation in Southern Kunene, Namibia," *Cimbebasia* 15 (1999): 1–28; Kohn, *How Forests Think*; Behrens, "An African Relational Environmentalism"; Kelbessa, "Can an African Environmental Ethics?".

18. Cf. Sarah Whatmore, *Hybrid Geographies: Natures Cultures Spaces* (London: SAGE, 2002); Noel Castree, "A Post-environmental Ethics?" *Ethics, Place and Environment* 6, no. 1 (2003): 3–12.

19. As reviewed in L.J. Gorenflo, Suzanne Romaine, Russell A. Mittermeier, and Kristen Walker-Painemilla, "Co-occurrence of Linguistic and Biological Diversity in Biodiversity Hotspots and High Biodiversity Wilderness Areas," *Proceedings of the National Academy of Sciences* 109, no. 21 (2012): 8032–8037.

20. Ibid., 8037.

21. Kohn, *How Forests Think*; Sullivan, "Nature on the Move III."

[h]ow other kinds of beings see us matters. That other kinds of beings see us changes things. If jaguars also represent us—in ways that can matter vitally to us—then anthropology cannot limit itself just to exploring how people from different societies might happen to represent them as doing so. Such encounters with other kinds of being force us to recognize the fact that seeing, representing, and perhaps knowing, even thinking, are not exclusively human affairs.[22]

Here we seek to illustrate such reflections with detail from one very specific ethnographic context, in which one of us (Sullivan) has worked intermittently since 1992. This is a landscape in west Namibia, known locally as Hurubes, especially by elders from Khoe land-associated lineages (!haoti) known as ||Khao-a Dama, ||Ubun, and !Narenin, who are part of the spectrum of Khoe and San peoples spread throughout southern Africa who speak languages characterized by click consonants.[23] ||Khao-a Dama, in particular, trace their histories over at least a number of generations to Hurubes, although their dwelling practices have been significantly constrained by a series of evictions that (perhaps ironically) have often sought to clear the area of local people in the interests of the conservation of indigenous fauna.[24]

In what follows, and based on field research conducted primarily in 2014–2015, we offer brief descriptions of several knowledge and value practices through which ||Khao-a Dama (and other Khoe and San peoples) have conceived of agency and intentionality as located in entities beyond the human. Through this information we seek to contribute to broader explorations of moral obligations and nonhuman agency in a relational environmental ethics that refracts the oft-posited anthropocentric/ecocentric dichotomy.[25] Key recorded interviews and discussions are referenced here by using a coding system that includes the initials of the interviewee(s) and the place and date of the discussion; interviewee names are listed in footnote 8. The inclusion of full interviewee names is preferred by

---

22. Kohn, *How Forests Think*, 1.

23. See Wilfrid Heinrich Gerhard Haacke, "Linguistic Hypotheses on the Origin of Namibian Khoekhoe Speakers," *Southern African Humanities* 20 (2008): 163–177.

24. For a historiography of land clearances in this area see Giorgio Meischer, *Namibia's Red Line: The History of a Veterinary and Settlement Border* (New York: Palgrave Macmillan, 2012).

25. See also Paul Cloke and Owain Jones, "Grounding Ethical Mindfulness for/in Nature: Trees in their Places," *Ethics, Place and Environment* 6 (2003): 195–214; Robert Melchior Figueroa and Gordon Waitt, "Cracks in the Mirror: (Un)covering the Moral Terrains of Environmental Justice at Uluru-Kata Tjuta National Park," *Ethics, Place and Environment* 11, no. 3 (2008): 327–349.

interviewees and respects the value placed on "being known to know," given multiple layers of knowledge suppression and displacement—from colonialism through apartheid to market-oriented restructuring—that have shaped people's experience in west Namibia. We are not making a comment here on what is becoming known as "African relational environmental ethics" more broadly[26], although the knowledge and value practices we describe might indeed intersect with this approach. We touch on practices relating to ancestors, to different kinds of animals, to a particular class of plants imbued with the power to act to intervene in human fortune and misfortune, and to rain, which under certain contexts is personified as what might be thought of as a supernatural or spirit being called |nanus.

Relating with . . .

The Agency of Ancestors

For elderly ||Khao-a Dama people with associations with Hurubes, moving through the landscape involves greeting and offering practices that connect people alive today with people now physically dead, who were previously associated in some way with these landscapes. While often attenuated through displacement, acculturation, and the variously disruptive effects of modernity, such practices remain current and significant.

Ancestors are communicated with through a practice called *tsē-khom*, understood as "speaking with the ancestors in the day-time,"[27] (thus distinguished from a different practice of communicating with one's ancestors during nighttime healing events in order to understand the causes of sickness)[28]. *Tsē-khom* usually involves the offering and smoking of tobacco, through which ancestors, or *kai khoen*—i.e., big or old people—in the realm of the spirits of the dead are also able to enjoy this smoking. Through *tsē-khom*, ancestral agencies are requested to act in the present to open the road so that travelers can see the best way to go. They are asked for guidance regarding the most appropriate ways to do things,

---

26. See, for example, Behrens "An African Relational Environmentalism"; Kelbessa, "Can an African Environmental Ethics?"

27. N≠UT, CDT, M|G, |Giribes, May95; WSG, Mai, 030314, CDT, M|AG, Hoanib, 070414; RSS, Hurubes/Palmwag, multiple dates 2014–2015 including RSS, Khow, 171114, RSS, Barab, 201114, RSS, Barab, 211114, RSS, SO|A, Kai-as, 221114, RSS, SO|A, Uru, 231114; Khamdesca-Hobatere, 031114; WSG,!N-D, 121114.

28. Translated literally as *tsē* = "to separate" and *khom* = "to keep holy" in Sigrid Schmidt, "Spirits: Some Thoughts on Ancient Damara Folk Belief," *Journal of the Namibian Scientific Society* 62 (2014): 144 (after Krönlein, *Wortschatz der Khoi-khoin [Namaqua-Hottentotten]* [Berlin: Deutsche Kolonialgesellschaft, 1889], 325).

and their support is evidenced through the intuitions people receive in response to queries that may arise as they are traveling. The ancestors are also asked to mediate the activities of potentially dangerous animals such as lions, who are understood very much as other ensouled beings who assert their own agencies and intentionality (see below). Ancestors thus greeted include recent family members whose graves are located in places traveled to and through; unidentified dead (or what Schmidt refers to as "the invisible representations of anonymous dead')[29]; and sometimes a more broadly referenced ancestor-hero known as Haiseb. The latter is considered to have been a real person who was associated with the doing of wonderful and clever things[30], who lived in the distant past and with whom large cairns found throughout the dryland environment from the Cape to the Kunene River are associated.[31]

Ontologically, the ancestors are spirits or souls (i.e., *gagas*[32]) that have left humans whose bodies have died. As spirit beings they have ontological reality in the present: they are not simply people who lived in the past, nor are they entities that require worship. They are understood more as specific types of entities that, through pragmatic relationship practices, are called upon to intervene—to assert agency—in the present, so as to influence outcomes. Sometimes this influence includes intervention in the agency of other nonhuman agents, such as lions, a species with which humans here continue to live in close contact, as they have done throughout the remembered past.

... Animal Agencies

Lions are a key and formidable predator, encounters with whom may result in the loss of human life, or the life of herded livestock. Nonetheless, people in the past sought them out, in order to scavenge meat from their kills,[33] and lions figure in people's realities as animals imbued with agency and intentionality. Just as Kohn

29. Ibid., 135.

30. RSS, Barab, 211114; RSS, SO|A, Kai-as, 221114; RSS, SO|A, Uru, 231114; EG, WSG, !N-D, 191014; WSG, multiple conversations.

31. See also Sigrid Schmidt, *Hai||om and !Xû Stories from North Namibia: Collected and Translated by Terttu Heikkinen (1934–1988)* (Cologne: Rüdiger Köppe Verlag, 2011); Schmidt, "Spirits"; Sigrid Schmidt, "Some Notes on the So-Called Heitsi-Eibeb Graves in Namibia: Ancient Heaps of Stones at the Roadside" *BAB Working Paper* 3 (2014). https://baslerafrika.ch/wp-content/uploads/2017/04/WP-2014-3-Schmidt.pdf.

32. Cf. Adi Inskeep, *Heinrich Vedder's "The Bergdama": An Annotated Translation of the German Original with Additional Ethnographic Material* (Cologne: Rüdiger Köppe Verlag, 2003), 329.

33. RSS, SO|A, ≠Habaka, 141114.

describes for Runa interactions with jaguars,[34] lions are conceived as being able to see, recognize, and represent the people they encounter and interact with. The proximity of lions to humans is indicated by calling to lions as "big brother," "big head," or as a "big dog" (since dogs are seen as also socially close to humans)—names that denote respect and proximity. In non-ordinary states of consciousness associated with healing, Khoe and San reality also embraces the perceptual possibility of shapeshifting between lions and humans.[35] This perception is potentially evidenced by rock art inscriptions of therianthropes—chimerical figures that are part human and part animal—including a famous rock engraving of a lion with a human hand emerging from its tail, found at the World Heritage Site of Twyfelfontein in west Namibia (as shown in Figure 17.1).

Animals generally, though, are considered to be cognate with humans not so much because of their biological and morphological similarities, as in natural history and evolutionary perspectives (although these are important), but because like humans they are animated by a soul that passes from them when they die, with this animation conferring to individuals a sense of self. It is this soul—or *gagas* (as above)—that gives humans and animals their unique "wind" or "breath," confers their abilities to move as well as to assert agency and intentionality, and also informs the qualities of action and behavior from which humans learn how to act appropriately[36]. In the West, by contrast, the conceptual removal of "soul" from animals was notoriously achieved by Descartes's affirmation that they were merely "soulless automata," an ontological strategy that has arguably sanctioned ruthless instrumentalization of animals by justifying moral indifference.[37] In the ||Khao-a Dama context, asking whether or not animals have a soul is responded to as a derisory question.

---

34. Kohn, *How Forests Think*.

35. For discussion of conceptual and material mutability in KhoeSan thought, see Mathias Guenther, *Tricksters and Trancers: Bushman Religion and Society* (Bloomington: Indiana University Press, 1999); Sian Sullivan and Chris Low, "Shades of the Rainbow Serpent? A KhoeSān Animal between Myth and Landscape in Southern Africa: Ethnographic Contextualisations of Rock Art Representations," *Arts* 3, no. 2 (2014), 215–244.

36. RSS, Barab, 211114.

37. Rene Descartes, *Discourse on Method* (London: Penguin, 1968 [1637]), 75–76. See discussion in Alf Hornborg, "Animism, Fetishism, and Objectivism as Strategies for Knowing (or Not Knowing) the World," *Ethnos* 71, no. 1 (2006): 21–32, 24 (after Neil Evernden, *The Natural Alien: Humankind and Environment* [Toronto: University of Toronto Press, 1985], 16–17); Peter Harrison, "Descartes on Animals," *Philosophical Quarterly* 42, no. 169 (1992): 219–227; J. Baird Callicott, "Ecology and Moral Ontology," in *The Structural Links between Ecology, Evolution and Ethics: The Virtuous Epistemic Circle*, Donato Bergandi, ed., Boston Studies in the Philosophy of Science, 296 (Dordecht: Springer 2013), 112; Sullivan, "(Re-) Embodying Which Body?"

FIGURE 17.1 Petroglyph therianthrope consisting of a lion with a human hand emerging from its tail, at the Twyfelfontein UNESCO World Heritage Site, southern Kunene, west Namibia.

Sian Sullivan personal archive, March 21, 2014.

For ||Khao-a Dama elders, soul animates animals at the top of the food chain, such as lions, but it also confers vitality and agency to much smaller creatures such as insects. Social insects such as harvester ants who harvest seeds subsequently gathered by people, and bees from whom people harvest honey, are valued extremely highly. These creatures are so valued not only for how hard they work to gather important foods that are then shared with humans, but also for the *egalitarianism* with which they share both this work and the resulting foods. Great care is taken by people when gathering seeds or honey from harvester ants' nests and beehives respectively, so as to ensure productivity in future years. Human action thus supports the harvesting work done by harvester ants, and neither seeds from harvester ants' nests (seen as the "home"—*oms*—of the ants in a manner that is parallel to the homes, or "*omti*," of humans) nor honey harvested from beehives should be gathered in such a way as to leave nothing for the future sustenance of these social insects.[38]

---

38. Sullivan, "Folk and Formal."

These practices might be interpreted as simply examples of "resource taboos," which in a utilitarian manner act to safeguard human sustenance from one year to the next.[39] But this interpretation does not mesh well with the ontological reality informing such practices. This is because although humans are of course seeking to eat from the multiple kinds of selves with which they live, since these selves are conceived as variously able to also see, represent, and act, an expanded sense of reciprocity and relationality arguably informs these contexts.[40] As Viveiros de Castro writes for Amerindian contexts, the assumed shared hypostasis of soul as animating embodied existence acts to attenuate the emergence of objectification and instrumentalization practices.[41] Associated human behaviors, which (may) consciously realize and sustain the flourishing and abundance of socioecological assemblages rather than of individuals only, arguably recall Arne Naess's concept of self-realization, meaning realization of the ecologically connected relational Self (with a capital S).[42]

... Plants as Agents

Plants, in contrast, are not necessarily considered to be animated by soul in the same way as humans and other animals, mostly because they do not move as animals do. Nonetheless, they are definitely considered to be alive, and to die, just as humans do[43]. Some plants, however, are conferred with special properties of agency: a suite of plants considered to be "*soxa*," i.e., as particularly potent. A cluster of these plants are considered to act in a protective manner, especially against "bad thoughts" or envy ("*surib*"[44]) seen as a cause of sickness when directed toward someone, especially a person who is vulnerable, such as a child, or someone who is already ill or elderly. Importantly, a key aspect of such plants is that they will not work—indeed, they will not stay with the human person seeking their protection—unless something small—a five-cent piece, a piece of a person's clothing—is given to them in exchange. This direct material exchange between human person and potent/*soxa* plant binds the matter and healing

---

39. See, for example, William Forbes, Kwame Badu Antwi-Boasiako, and Ben Dixon, "Some Fundamentals of Conservation in South and West Africa," *Environmental Ethics* 36, no. 1 (2014): 5–30, 10–14.

40. Cf. Kohn, *How Forests Think*.

41. Viveiros de Castro, "Exchanging Perspectives."

42. Arne Naess, "Self-Realization: An Ecological Approach to Being in the World," *Trumpeter, Journal of Ecosophy* 4, no. 3 (1987): 35–42

43. MH, Kham, 021114; RSS, Barab, 211114.

44. Schmidt, "Spirits," 142

action of the plant to a person[45]. Through this material exchange, the agency of particular plants matters in their ability to act in relation to a human self.

... The Personified Agency of Rain

Our last example extends agency and intentionality further still, to include the actions of biophysical entities. For ||Khao-Dama and other related Khoe and San peoples, it is the personified, supernatural force behind the phenomena of rain—known here as |nanus—that asserts agency in selecting those humans who become healers[46]. Healers are thus known as |nanu-aob or |nanu-aos—meaning literally man or woman of the rain. When individuals are called by |nanus they experience a psychological transformation precipitated by a loss of a sense of self. They go into the field and wander around, lost to the normal world of everyday waking ego consciousness. On realizing that they have disappeared, people of their community go looking for them, singing the songs of healing dances called *arus*. It is when nascent |nanu-aob/s hear the threads of the familiar songs of the *arus* that they are able to re-enter the social world, having been "opened" by |nanus so that they can see sicknesses of the people. Through virtue of their selection by |nanus, combined with ritualized practices of consumption of particular rain- and healing-associated substances—such as the *soxa* plant *tuhorabeb* ("*tu*" = rain[47]) which assists with being able to see[48]—healers are conferred certain powers of perception that permit them to see and cure sickness. These powers are independent of other forms of leadership so are not necessarily consistent with any sort of political authority.[49]

This final example takes us toward what "we" might conceive as the "ontological edges" of modernity, to extend a currently lively seam of work in the humanities that explores and opens up some of these ontological edges. This exploration includes work encouraging recognition of the biologically grounded ontologies of being of nonhuman species toward more sensitive attunements with other-than-human presence,[50] as well as work that takes seriously the

---

45. WSG, Mai, 030314.

46. M!UO, Outjo, 061114; CDT, !Nosa, Ses 251114.

47. Cf. Schmidt, "Spirits," 147.

48. N≠UT 1995–1996; !Nosa, Ses 251114. The identity of this plant is known but protected for intellectual property reasons.

49. Cf. Pierre Clastres and Robert Hurley, *Society against the State: Essays in Political Anthropology* (Cambridge, MA: MIT Press, 1988).

50. See, for example, Donna Haraway, *When Species Meet* (Minneapolis: University of Minnesota Press, 2008); Vilém Flusser and Louis Bec, *Vampyroteuthis infernalis* (New York: Atropos, 2011 [1987]); Marder, *Plant-Thinking*.

socioecological and ethical demands of materiality.[51] But for anthropologists and others working in variously "non-modern" cultural contexts there is a whole *other* ontological edge that demands to be taken seriously, as gestured toward in the example above of the personified agency of rain. This is the diverse world of both ancestors and spirits, which in many cultural contexts are known and encountered as agency-enacting entities with ontological reality.[52] As Kohn writes, "spirits are their own kind of real" emerging "from a specifically human way of engaging with and relating to a living world that lies in part beyond the human."[53] Since the spirit realm has its own future-making logics and habits, Kohn remarks additionally that how this reality is treated "is as important as recognizing it as such."[54] In other words, there may be further vistas to explore in an expanded relational and reciprocal ontology, with implications for future flourishings.

Flourishings

We have been able here only to skate over the surface of the above ethnographic examples. In doing so, however, we suggest that the knowledge practices we describe illustrate an expanded sphere of moral agency and considerability, associated with relations of reciprocity with other-than-human entities, relations that may be fruitful for engendering multi-species abundance. A *milieu* of relationality and reciprocity such as that described above, with an ontological assumption of distributed agency accompanied by keen awareness that "difference makes a difference,"[55] might thus act to discourage excessive interference with, and instrumentalization of, other-than-human natures, and conversely to support the flourishing of both human and other-than-human diversities. What ethnography and environmental anthropology can offer to a relational environmental ethics, then, is a deeper understanding of how people might live in specific relational contexts with different kinds of agency-asserting entities, only some of

51. See, for example, Bruno Latour, *Politics of Nature: How to Bring the Sciences into Democracy* (Cambridge, MA: Harvard University Press, 2004); Jane Bennett, *Vibrant Matter: A Political Ecology of Things* (Durham, NC: Duke University Press, 2010); Gabrielle Hecht, *Being Nuclear: Africans and the Global Uranium Trade* (Cambridge, MA: MIT Press, 2012); Mark Jackson, "Plastic Islands and Processual Grounds: Ethics, Ontology, and the Matter of Decay," *Cultural Geographies* 20, no. 2 (2013): 205–224.

52. Cf. Chakrabarty, *Provincialising Europe*; Kohn, *How Forests Think*.

53. Kohn, *How Forests Think*, 217, 216.

54. Ibid., 208, 216.

55. Kohn, *How Forests Think*, after Gregory Bateson, *Steps to an Ecology of Mind* (Chicago: University of Chicago Press, 2000 [1972]).

whom are human.[56] A hope is that through such cross-disciplinary and cross-cultural engagements, pluralistic perspective and dialogue might inform a shift in *trans*cultural solidarities and shared values that responds to the contemporary global "wicked problems" associated with multiple environmental crises and accompanying cultural displacements.[57]

Knowledge, Value, and Symbiosis

In particular, the kinds of practices and associated narratives we gesture toward above indicate that something has been lost in the "disenchanted" modern reality most readers of this collection probably inhabit.[58] This loss makes it harder to work out what it is to really act on the basis of relationship with the non-human. Of course there have been "gains," too: modern humans know a great deal about subjects like evolution, genetics, mathematical ecology, and molecular biology. But this knowledge arguably brings "us" no closer to understanding our own relationships to the rest of the world. It has in fact become commonplace to remark on the danger that scientific prowess can *increase* human separation from the world.

This line of thought can easily run into the quicksand of the old debate between "reductionism and holism."[59] Some varieties of environmentalism have been keen to pin the blame for present ecological problems on modern Cartesian reductionism, in the process downplaying the importance of detailed empirical and experimental methods of environmental observation in non-modern contexts.[60] But this is not the whole story, as evidenced by nuanced debates in environmental aesthetics about the potential role of ecological knowledge in

---

56. Cf. Figueroa and Waitt, "Cracks in the Mirror"; J. Baird Callicott, "Ecology and Moral Ontology."

57. Cf. Patricia Mazzarella, "Introduction," in *Transcultural Dimensions in Medical Ethics,* Edmund Pellegrino, Patricia Mazzarella, and Pietro Corsi, eds. (Frederick, MD: University Publishing Group, 1992), 1–12; Edmund Pellegrino, "Prologue: Intersections of Western Biomedical Ethics and World Culture," in Pellegrino, Mazzarella and Corsi, eds. *Transcultural Dimensions,* 13–19; Valerie A. Brown, John A. Harris, and Jacqueline Y. Russell, eds., *Tackling Wicked Problems: Through the Transdisciplinary Imagination* (London: Earthscan, 2010).

58. Max Weber, *The Sociology of Religion* (Boston: Beacon, 1993 [1963]); Patrick Curry, "From Enlightenment to Enchantment: Changing the Question," in *Law, Philosophy and Ecology: Exploring Re-Embodiments,* Ruth Thomas-Pellicer, Vito de Lucia, and Sian Sullivan, eds., Routledge Law, Justice and Ecology Series (London: GlassHouse, 2016).

59. As discussed in, e.g., Donato Bergandi and Patrick Blandin, "Holism vs. Reductionism: Do Ecosystem Ecology and Landscape Ecology Clarify the Debate?" *Acta Biotheoretica* 46, no. 3 (1998): 185–206.

60. Paul Richards, *Indigenous Agricultural Revolution* (London: HarperCollins, 1985).

properly appreciating and valuing "nature."[61] Does a scientific understanding of exactly what is going on in a forest, for example, just distract attention onto mechanistic details, or does it in fact facilitate a deeper appreciation of the complex interconnected whole? There is no right answer—both may potentially be true. In any case, perceiving and appreciating *relationship* requires properly apprehending both the details *and* the whole. It might be argued that such apprehension cannot be done with the "rational" mind alone. Alternatively, it might be observed that, as has often been noted, there can be many rationalities.[62] From this latter perspective, perhaps scientific ecological knowledge is just one of the rationalities that can potentially help develop the skill—the virtue—of perceiving and experiencing coherence and interconnectedness, of seeing both the wood and the trees. After all, as an anthropology of nature suggests, scientific ecology derives from one of a number of possible ontologies.[63]

This is not, however, to say that environmentalists are necessarily wrong to mistrust "reductionist" scientific paradigms. The existence of multiple anthropogenic ecological crises does strongly suggest a significantly reduced capacity for *symbiosis* between modern humans and our nonhuman companions. (Re) building this capacity for symbiosis is perhaps the most urgent challenge facing humanity. John Barry describes ecological virtue as "a mean between a timid ecocentrism and an arrogant anthropocentrism," centered on "modes of character and acting in the world which encourage social-environmental relations which are symbiotic rather than parasitic."[64] The *absence* of such virtue leads to the destructive modes of social organization we see today, which arguably position humanity as a parasite rather than a symbiont. As Barry's more recent work argues, change requires excavation of the political, ethical, and ontological underpinnings of this destructive modern story of the human/nonhuman relationship.[65] Having other stories to compare it with, particularly ones in which symbiosis is more clearly valued (as, perhaps, in those recounted above), can help with this project.

---

61. See, e.g., Holmes Rolston III, "Does Aesthetic Appreciation of Landscapes Need to Be Science-Based?," *British Journal of Aesthetics* 35 (1995): 374–386, and discussion in Emily Brady, *Aesthetics of the Natural Environment* (Tuscaloosa: University of Alabama Press, 2003), chapter 4.

62. John S. Dryzek, *Rational Ecology: Environment and Political Economy* (Oxford: Blackwell, 1987); Alasdair MacIntyre, *Whose Justice? Which Rationality?* (London: Duckworth, 1988).

63. Cf. Descola and Lloyd, *Beyond Nature and Culture.*

64. John Barry, *Rethinking Green Politics* (London: SAGE, 1999), 33–35.

65. John Barry, *The Politics of Actually Existing Unsustainability* (Oxford: Oxford University Press, 2012).

Egalitarianism and Reciprocity

Valuing symbiosis entails a very different understanding of how egalitarianism, obligation, and reciprocity may work to sustain community. Maintaining a calculative balance sheet of entitlements and obligations between individual "economic actors" does not nurture community. Anthropologist David Graeber argues that it is a modern innovation to interpret mutual obligations in terms of an ethical imperative to "pay one's debts."[66] Non-capitalist cultures, Graeber suggests, would see people who attempted never to be "in debt" as effectively placing themselves outside the community by rejecting the social fabric of reciprocally obligated relationships, thereby choosing instead to define their identity atomistically, and to deal with others as strangers.

To reject such atomism, and to instead celebrate the webs of mutual obligation as importantly constitutive of community, is to embrace a more complex, multidimensional understanding of reciprocity. Possession and exercise of what Alasdair MacIntyre calls *virtues of acknowledged dependence* can allow individuals to understand and discharge their own responsibilities as members of a community, a "network of giving and receiving."[67] These networks form a kind of organic scaffolding supporting community: the exercise and transmission of relevant virtues thus maintains the coherence and integrity of such networks, of the social arrangements within which individual flourishing lives can unfold. Such networks are also essential for individuals' understanding of their own autonomy—as MacIntyre argues, "acknowledgement of dependence is the key to independence."[68]

Expanding this idea to consider virtues of acknowledged *ecological* dependence we suggest supports an "ecological eudaimonism" in which dispositions of character that tend to maintain the integrity of the nonhuman world are explicitly recognized to also be beneficial for the human individuals who exhibit them. These dispositions are beneficial not only because such integrity is itself important for human flourishing, but also because recognition and acknowledgement of our dependence upon nonhuman worlds contribute to our understanding of ourselves.[69] Ecological virtues include traits and dispositions related to aesthetic, emotional, and spiritual perceptions of the natural world, as well as those related to the "rational" perspectives of environmental science. Moreover, what Rosalind

---

66. David Graeber, *Debt: The First 5000 Years* (New York: Melville House, 2011).

67. Alasdair MacIntyre, *Dependent Rational Animals* (London: Duckworth, 1999) 9, 99.

68. Ibid., 85.

69. Michael Hannis, "The Virtues of Acknowledged Ecological Dependence," *Environmental Values* 24 (2015): 145–164.

Hursthouse calls "right orientation to nature" includes respect not only for living things but also for inanimate natural features and phenomena and for the integrity of whole natural systems themselves.[70] This "right orientation" is considered to be a virtue not because it entails respect for the *telos* of living things, but rather on the eudaimonist basis that a human life characterized by a right orientation to nature will be a more flourishing one.[71] Such an orientation would not of course see *all* human impact as ethically problematic, but *would* involve a reflective and respectful approach to the human use and consumption of "nature."

So what is it to flourish as part of a broader community conceived in this way? How is individual flourishing related to the flourishing of the broader community of humans, nonhumans, and "land" (as Aldo Leopold would have it)?[72] How might seven billion or more human beings live in this kind of dynamic reciprocity with the nonhuman world? However this last question is to be answered, it will surely require a very different trajectory from that suggested by recent calls for humanity to embrace its role as "the God species."[73] Acknowledging and assuming nonhuman agency may be a key part of telling a new story that avoids such hubris. For these purposes, nonhuman agency need not necessarily be taken as literally or objectively "true as scientific fact." A heuristic interpretation may still do the job of opening up the required extra reciprocal dimensions, of stretching the imaginative muscles required to really perceive the complex webs of interconnections between living (and nonliving) things.

This is not, however, to suggest that in describing the realities of people mentioned in this text we are merely sharing metaphors or analogies. Theirs are sophisticated practices and narratives that embody accumulated cultural knowledge of "how to live a good life," and as Brian Treanor notes, ecological virtue is in large part developed by and through narratives.[74] Here, and in ideal terms, a life characterized by appropriate relationships with animals, plants, ancestors, and spirits is understood as a better life, a more flourishing life, than one characterized by inappropriate relationships with these agencies. It is also a life perhaps more likely to bring about the flourishing of others, human and nonhuman alike.

---

70. Hursthouse, "Environmental Virtue Ethics." 165–166

71. Hannis, *Freedom and Environment*; Hursthouse, "Environmental Virtue Ethics" 165–166; Allen Thompson, "Natural Goodness and Abandoning the Economy of Value: Ron Sandler's Character and Environment," *Ethics, Place and Environment* 11, no. 2 (2008): 218–226.

72. Aldo Leopold, *A Sand County Almanac* (Oxford: Oxford University Press, 1968 [1949]).

73. Mark Lynas, *The God Species: How Humans Really Can Save the Planet* (London: Fourth Estate, 2012); discussed in Michael Hannis, "Another God Delusion?" *The Land* 11(2012), 10, http://www.thelandmagazine.org.uk/articles/another-god-delusion.

74. Treanor, *Emplotting Virtue*.

A eudaimonist ecological virtue ethics may be well equipped to understand the ethical implications of the deep relationality that seems to be involved in worldviews such as these. Cultivating ecological virtue, on a eudaimonist model, can help bring about a good life for oneself, but without entailing individualism or indeed anthropocentrism. This is because, as with the case material shared here for Khoe peoples in west Namibia, the focus is on relationship with diverse others, interconnection, symbiosis, and the sustenance of abundance into the future.

18 DIALOGUE

Cheryl Cottine, Michael Hannis, and Sian Sullivan

At first glance, it may appear that Namibian ||Khao-a Dama and early Confucian environmental ethics have little in common. Or perhaps the thought might be that they have a lot in common, as representatives of "non-Western" cultures that tend toward animism, incorporate spiritual as opposed to simply materialistic dimensions of relationships with beyond-human natures, and are more in touch generally with the natural cycles of the world. The latter sentiment is perhaps the more problematic, as it risks conflating diversely rich traditions into a homogenous and romanticized ideal. But neither is accurate. Our reflections reveal both important differences between Mengzian and ||Khao-a Dama environmental ethics, and some interesting similarities.

One striking similarity between what might be termed idealistically as "a Mengzian" and "a ||Khao-a Dama" environmental ethic is that both challenge the simplistic assumption that it is necessary to move beyond the human to have a functioning and acceptable ethic. Each, in its own way, breaks down and refracts the sharp distinction often drawn between anthropocentric and ecocentric approaches.[1] In its place we may glimpse elements of what might be termed a relational anthropocentrism, an ethical standpoint that recognizes both the central importance for human flourishing of healthy relationships with agential entities comprising the wider environment, and that respect for nonhuman "others" is required so as to care for both "them" and "us."[2] In particular, both our chapters here point to the false dichotomy

---

1. See, for example, Helen Kopnina, "Wild Animals and Justice: The Case of the Dead Elephant in the Room," *Journal of International Wildlife Law and Policy* 19, no. 3 (2016): 219–235; Helen Kopnina, "Nobody Likes Dichotomies (But Sometimes You Need Them)," *Anthropological Forum* 26, no. 4 (Nov. 2016): 415–429.

2. Graham Harvey, *Animism: Respecting the Living World* (London: Hurst, 2005); Sian Sullivan, "Nature on the Move III: (Re)countenancing an Animate Nature,"

of "anthropocentrism versus ecocentrism" that has so obsessed Anglophone environmental ethics. The chapters illuminate this dichotomy as a very culturally specific intellectual artifact, rooted in precisely the post-Enlightenment binary thinking often (plausibly) claimed by ecocentrists to characterize unreflective anthropocentrism. Anthropology and history are thus both key to building a more nuanced perspective, drawing on the many traditions that have conceptualized humans as *part of the world* rather than somehow apart from it and transcendent over it.

Both our cases also bring out the importance of attending to the very human issues of politics and power that are inextricably intertwined with environmental ethics. For instance, Mengzi makes clear that the tyrants' land management strategies were socially disastrous and, perhaps, environmentally damaging. Irrigation practices, it is implied, became problematic when they ceased to focus on maintaining sustainable local livelihoods. Tellingly, the strategies of cruel rulers appear to have included the exclusion of local people to create depopulated "parks," where nature runs wild. This set-aside "wildness" is associated with both poverty and chaos, signaling poor governance under which both social and ecological dimensions are damaged. There seems a clear parallel here with the modern phenomenon of "displacement for conservation" (famously exemplified in the United States by the forced clearance of Yosemite) that has been so devastating for many people in Africa, including Damara / ≠Nūkhoen in west Namibia.

Indeed, an environmental ethic that seeks to remove people from valued landscapes, rather than working to integrate sensitive human activity *with* beyond-human others,[3] seems often to exacerbate environmental (as well as social) problems, rather than solving them. Rather than addressing problematic relationships between humans and the rest of the world, it displaces them, often causing both human suffering and environmental degradation elsewhere. Ultimately, it builds a world polarized between "denatured" human habitat and an artificially empty and wild "nature" that can be consumptively (and profitably) appreciated by those with sufficient social and financial power.[4]

New Proposals: Journal of Marxism and Interdisciplinary Enquiry 6, nos. 1–2 (2013): 50–71; Esther Turnhout, Claire Waterton, Katia Neves, and Marleen Buizer, "Rethinking Biodiversity: From Goods and Services to 'Living With,'" *Conservation Letters* 6 (2013): 154–161; Michael Hannis, "The Virtues of Acknowledged Ecological Dependence," *Environmental Values* 24 (2015): 145–164.

3. Turnhout et al., "Rethinking Biodiversity."

4. Sullivan, "The Elephant in the Room? Problematizing 'new' (neoliberal) biodiversity conservation. *Forum for Development Studies* 33(1): 105–135; Sian Sullivan, "Conservation Is

To justify such an approach as "ecocentric" is to conjure an *oikos* without humans, a mythical wilderness that can truly exist only in the imagination. It is also to entrench the fatalistic belief that human flourishing is necessarily destructive of nonhuman flourishing. This very modern belief underpins both Promethean narratives of progress and "eco-modernization"[5] and their misanthropic shadows. To challenge an approach that polarizes "wild" and "domesticated" natures is not to endorse "human chauvinism."[6] It is to begin the urgent task of recuperating the kinds of healthy relationships and value practices that might allow all to flourish, and it is to create openness to "non-Western" environmental ethics, such as those gestured toward in our chapters, that may more fruitfully generate socioecological relationships that sustain rather than diminish diversity. Indeed, echoing Cottine's suggestion of an ancient Chinese Mengzian socioecological ethics, anthropologist Philippe Descola asserts that although major contrasts existed for ancient Chinese thought,[7] no strict dichotomy was established between "wild" and "domesticated" that could be mapped easily onto these Western polarities.

Respect is a key component of such relationships. But as Elizabeth Hursthouse argues, what Paul Taylor terms "respect for nature" is not simply an attitude that can be adopted at will.[8] Hursthouse carefully reconfigures it as a virtue that requires cultivation and tending. Following Aristotle (interestingly, a contemporary of Mengzi), she argues that that the cultivation and practice of what she calls "right orientation to nature" requires both appropriate education and life-long cultural reinforcement, as well as individual dedication. In this context she laments the lack of present-day *phronimoi*, i.e., exemplars of this key ecological virtue. Yet, these exemplars are not entirely absent. Again, historical accounts and

Sexy! What Makes This So, and What Does This Make? An Engagement with *Celebrity and the Environment*," *Conservation and Society* 9, no. 4 (2011): 334–345.

5. John Asafu-Adjaye, Linus Blomqvist, Stewart Brand, Barry Brook, et al., *An Ecomodernist Manifesto*, 2015, http://www.ecomodernism.org/manifesto-english; Dieter Helm, *Natural Capital: Valuing the Planet* (New Haven, CT: Yale University Press, 2015).

6. Richard Routley (later Richard Sylvan) and Val Routley (later Val Plumwood), "Against the Inevitability of Human Chauvinism," in *Ethics and Problems of the 21st Century*, Kenneth Goodpaster and Kenneth Sayre, eds. (Notre Dame, IN: University of Notre Dame Press, 1979).

7. As, for example, between "town" and "mountain," where the latter were spaces of asceticism and exile as well as, in the Daoist tradition, the dwelling places of elusive, immortal beings. Philippe Descola, *Beyond Nature and Culture* (Chicago: Chicago University Press, 2013), 45.

8. Rosalind Hursthouse, "Environmental Virtue Ethics," in *Working Virtue: Virtue Ethics and Contemporary Moral Problems*, Rebecca Walker and Philip Ivanhoe, eds. (Oxford: Clarendon Press, 2007); Paul W. Taylor, *Respect for Nature* (Princeton, NJ: Princeton University Press, 2011 [1986]).

ethnographic reports from surviving amodern cultures are invaluable complementary resources here, as our two chapters have indicated.[9]

Of course, it is both difficult and perhaps misleading to affirm correspondences
between two such different case materials. Cottine's chapter analyses a text from
more than 2,000 years ago, to draw particular attention to a pragmatic "ethic of
conservation" through which good governance arises to the extent that respect
for social and ecological realms engenders their simultaneous flourishing, as
well as to establish a reading of the text in which destructive anthropocentrism
is replaced with tempered anthropocentrism. Hannis and Sullivan draw on contemporary ethnographic consultations with extant peoples to affirm perceptions
and practices that entwine humans with variously agential beyond-human entities
in ways that curtail overuse and thereby sustain diversity. Moreover, our chapters
document many ways in which Mengzi and the ‖Khao-a Dama conceptualize differently what environmental respect, relationality, and reciprocity might entail.
For example, Mengzi's focus on the behavior appropriate to an enlightened ruler
of a large and organized territory is quite different from the more decentralized
and personal perspectives shared here of ‖Khao-a Dama "consultants." Yet, we
maintain that in both contexts a pragmatic approach to environmental ethics is
evidenced, arguably one that is congruent with virtue-based ethical frameworks
such as those of Hursthouse or MacIntyre. Both see the flourishing of humans
and of beyond-human agencies as complementary, mutually reinforcing, and
best achieved through the cultivation of awareness and of practices that might be
described today as respectful, as well as ecologically sustainable.

---

9. Hursthouse, "Environmental Virtue Ethics"; Michael Hannis, *Freedom and
Environment: Autonomy, Human Flourishing, and the Political Philosophy of Sustainability*
(New York: Routledge, 2015).

CONCLUSION

Laura M. Hartman

We hope that readers will come to "think of comparative religious ethics as an adventure rather than a settled business or a professional enterprise."[1]

Welcome to the end of the "adventure." I hope that the variety contained herein has not induced methodological whiplash in too many readers. Rather, I expect that this diverse collection has sparked interest and inspiration, prompting readers to find more resources and investigate further details about the ideas collected here. In recognition of the fact that this collection may have raised more questions than it has given answers, I attempt to answer a few questions below.

What Can We Now Say about Flourishing?

Readers may, of course, draw their own conclusions from the collection gathered here. But I wish to note three predominant emphases that seem to emerge from this group of authors: mysticism and the nature of reality (Sciberras, Reveley, Klassen, Cooper); politics, power, and inclusion (Miller, Bell, Baugh, Cottine, Epstein-Levi, and Phillips); and relational or responsive human agency (Cottine, Phillips, Cooper, Reveley, Robinson-Bertoni, Hannis/Sullivan). Each chapter engages these themes in unique and particular ways, but nevertheless these emphases create bridges of commonality as authors explore the topic of flourishing. It may be said, at least, that flourishing as a topic raises questions related to the nature of reality, to power and politics, and to human agency. And within such a statement lie manifold insights and approaches to these questions, as evidenced in the pages above. Readers interested in effecting environmental reforms that aim for human and nonhuman flourishing may benefit from exploring these themes as they interact with beliefs or lifeways of individuals or communities of faith.

---

1. Charles Mathewes, Matthew Puffer, and Mark Storslee, *Comparative Religious Ethics: Critical Concepts in Religious Studies*, vol. 1 (London: Routledge, 2016), 2. Quoting Lee Yearley.

Why Those Particular Pairs?

One of the hardest parts of putting this book together was choosing how to construct the dialogue pairs. Some readers may have wondered, for example, why not pair Phillips and Klassen for their mutual emphasis on technology, or Cooper and Cottine for their shared geographic grounding in China?

I chose the pairs for a variety of reasons; some were methodological pairs, others were based on topic, and still others ended up paired because of practical constraints beyond my control (and I crossed my fingers in hopes the dialogues would bear fruit!). It is quite possible that different pairs would have yielded better dialogues; certainly they would have yielded different ones. I invite readers to imagine their own pairs. Instructors using this text for a class may find it fruitful to ask students to write essays comparing and contrasting the following (in addition to the suggestions in the paragraph above): Sciberras and Phillips on science and religion; Robinson-Bertoni and Phillips on the orderliness of creation; Phillips, Hannis and Sullivan, Cooper, and Robinson-Bertoni on animals; and Reveley, Bell, Robinson-Bertoni, Epstein-Levi, and Baugh on agriculture. There are surely other possibilities in this group as well.

Did the Dialogues Turn Out as Expected?

Not really. There were a few things that I had asked for that didn't materialize in the dialogues, probably for various reasons (not least of which may be the length limit I imposed on the dialogue output). I encouraged authors to get personal with one another—talk about what this tradition means to you as an individual, whether you study your own tradition or are simply drawn to an "other" tradition. If this personal connection happened in the conversations between authors, it did not manifest in the written dialogues, perhaps because as scholars we are trained to maintain a certain "academic objectivity" in our work, or perhaps because the authors preferred some privacy about their personal views.

I also encouraged the authors to envision interreligious collaboration in actual shared environmental projects (e.g., could a Buddhist and a Christian do an ecological restoration project together if it involved killing invasive species?) but that showed up in only a few of the dialogues. Many of the dialogues, in fact, remained rather theoretical more than applied in nature. Perhaps this result further reflects the academic training that many of us receive, with more emphasis on the theoretical than the practical. Instructors using this book for a class should note that students might benefit from attempting to apply insights from the dialogues to applied projects (e.g., given what Cottine, Hannis, and Sullivan write in their chapters, what agricultural practices would be most acceptable in the traditions they study, and why?).

Some dialogues also turned out more interesting and exciting than I expected. Authors found creative comparisons and contrasts that I never would have conceived on my own. Sciberras and Reveley's deep dive into metaphysics, or Cooper and Robinson-Bertoni's conclusion about stewardship surprised me. So did the gentle but persistent challenging that occurred between Phillips and Epstein-Levi, and the fascinating example from Australia that emerged in conversation between Miller and Bell. Klassen and Baugh's frank appraisal of the limits of dialogue and Hannis, Sullivan, and Cottine's pointed takedown of a worldview that separates humans and nature both startled me into more focused attention. All of these examples demonstrate the fruitfulness of dialogue!

Mathewes et al., reflecting on the interplay of method and content in dialogue, envision the possibilities:

> Were scholars to attempt to engage in methodological discussions with others working on a common subject matter but with different approaches—or with others studying a different religious traditions or phenomenon using a similar method—or with others studying an analogous problem in a different tradition, but with a different method—we think that the scholarly benefits would be considerable.[2]

This book has not fully realized their vision, but it is certainly an interesting start. To more fully enter this vision would require a greater depth of dialogical encounter—in person, over time, and with a significant commitment to intellectual challenge and growth.

Why Were the Dialogues So Pleasant?

Readers may have been expecting more disagreement. After all, in practice these traditions vehemently disagree with one another on important elements of doctrine or worldview. There are a few reasons that these dialogues were basically free from acrimony. First, the parties engaging in the dialogues were scholars, not necessarily adherents of the religions, so any doctrinal friction may have been minimized because of a more scholarly approach to the topic. Secondly, there is one worldview-defining element that the parties do have in common: a concern for environmental issues. The urgency and (to some extent) universality of these

---

2. Mathewes et al., 12.

types of problems can lead to a pragmatic desire to set aside differences and seek common ground. Finally, I believe that the setup for the book as "comparative" led authors to seek points of commonality over points of difference. Generally, in the academy we are trained to be critical of texts, but when we interact with another human being we are also socialized to be kind and to seek agreement. I set up personal dialogues, not anonymous critiques, so perhaps it is no wonder there was little substantive disagreement and no real acrimony.

What's Next?

The field of comparative religious environmental ethics is, to date, surprisingly sparse. This book is only a beginning. Collections addressing more specific topics, such as water, land use, and climate change, would be most helpful to this field. Better still, face-to-face dialogues and conversations on these topics could bear significant fruit as we seek flourishing for humans—all humans—in this beautiful, fragile world. May the conversations continue!

INDEX

technology (*cont.*)
  economy and, 219–220
  environmental crisis and, 214, 254
  ethical evaluation of, 179–181
  feminism and, 219
  media and, 161–162, 255
  Pagan views of, 234–237, 254
  precautionary principle and, 194
  slaughter and, 108
  technocratic paradigm and, 210–213,
    221–222
  theological purpose of, 222
telos, 55, 200–202, 205, 222, 295
  evolution, 27–28, 37
  external and internal, 22–25, 26 n. 25
  nirvana and, 40–41
terrorism, 127 n. 4, 247–249
The Case of the Animals vs Man,
  104–105
Tlili, Sarra, 101, 106 n. 57, 116
Torah, 180, 182, 185, 187–188, 190, 196
traditional ecological knowledge, 176,
  280, 282–284, 299–300. *See also*
  indigenous people
Treanor, Brian, 295
Tucker, Mary Evelyn, 97 n. 24, 259–261,
  263–264

Unitarian Universalism, 16, 239, 241–244,
  254, 256
Universal Destination of Goods,
  203–205, 220
Universal Final Good. *See* Final Good

van Wensveen, Louke, 236, 276
veganism. *See* plant-based diet
vegetarianism. *See* plant-based diet
virtue ethics, 4, 87, 236, 276 n. 29, 279, 296

water. *See also* dams; drought; fishing;
  floods; Ganges river; hydropower;
  irrigation; rain; rivers
  access to, 203, 271
  demand for, 147
  economic value of, 154 n. 99
  gardening and, 241
  ground supply, 148–149, 152, 161, 164
  health and, 2–3, 93, 152
  Islam and, 98–99, 166, 247–248
  management of, 112, 145–152, 175,
    274–275
  metaphorical use of, 81, 84, 118
  Mosque use of, 239, 246–247
  pollution, 2–3, 98–100, 110, 112
  sacred, 125, 131, 153, 275
  scarcity, 157, 159, 163–164
  value of, 72–73
Wicca, 228–229, 235–236, 244
Wirzba, Norman, 50, 57 n. 25, 58, 63
Witchcraft, 228–229, 233

yoga, 39 n. 73, 127, 152–153, 175
  biopower and, 131, 134–142,
    150–151, 154
  climate change and, 128–129, 151
  health benefits of, 139–140, 142, 150
  history of, 132–134